...er Communism,
Keynes: The Return of the Master and (with Edward Skidelsky), *How Much is Enough*. He was made a life peer in 1991, is a member of the House of Lords Select Committee on Economic Affairs, and was elected Fellow of the British Academy in 1994.

ROBERT SKIDELSKY

Britain Since 1900

A Success Story?

VINTAGE BOOKS

London

First published in Great Britain in 2014 by
Vintage
Random House, 20 Vauxhall Bridge Road,
London SW1V 2SA

www.vintage-books.co.uk

Addresses for companies within The Random House Group Limited
can be found at: www.randomhouse.co.uk/offices.htm

The Random House Group Limited Reg. No. 954009

A CIP catalogue record for this book
is available from the British Library

ISBN 9780099572398

The Random House Group Limited supports the Forest Stewardship
Council® (FSC®), the leading international forest-certification
organisation. Our books carrying the FSC label are printed on
FSC®-certified paper. FSC is the only forest-certification scheme supported
by the leading environmental organisations, including Greenpeace.
Our paper procurement policy can be found at:
www.randomhouse.co.uk/environment

Printed and bound in Great Britain by Clays Ltd, St Ives plc

To Michael Holroyd

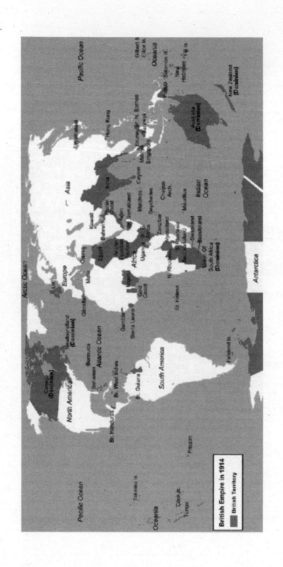

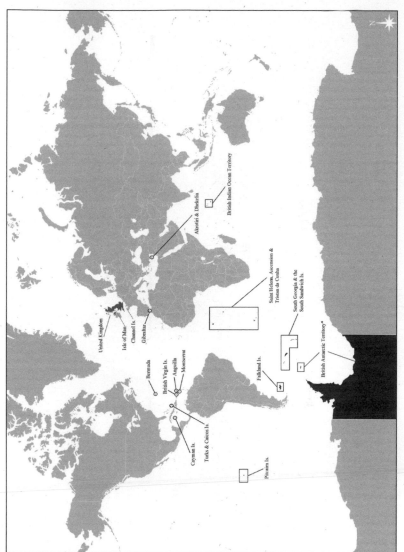

British Overseas Territories in 2014

Contents

Preface

A much briefer version of this book was published as an essay in the multi-authored volume *A World By Itself: A History of the British Isles* (2010), edited by Jonathan Clark. For this stand-alone version I have more than doubled the length, added a chapter on the Blair–Brown years, and rethought my treatments of culture and Thatcherism.

This is a work of analytic history. It is silly to believe that facts tell their own story. They are useless unless arranged and used to answer questions. This involves judgements about what is and is not important, and therefore opinions. Readers may well find my history opinionated. But my aim is to provoke thought, not 'tell it as it was'.

There is a peculiar difficulty about writing contemporary history, which led traditional historians to eschew it entirely. We have not reached the last chapters of many of the stories we tell about ourselves; we may be nearer the start of most of them. That is to say, contemporary history is as much a matter of speculation as of knowledge. We know that the British Empire has ended for good. But what about religion? Or the welfare state? Or marriage? Or culture? In such matters, and many others, our current beliefs have caused us to embark on ways of life which would have been considered most strange by our precedessors, and of whose continuation we can have no assurance. It is always possible to interpret failure according to the old standard as success according to some new hitherto unforeseen standard. But a contemporary historian is not thereby absolved from making judgements about the contemporary world in the light of what he has learnt about the past. In fact the past is his only guide.

Contrary to much current fashion, this book is mainly history from above, because history is generally made from above. I see the British people as (somewhat rebellious) beneficiaries and victims of the actions and behaviour of the governing class. The best examples are the decisions for war in 1914 and 1939. These wars had more effect on twentieth-century British history than anything else. Neither was forced from below: both were a free choice of the ruling class, as was the much more recent war against Iraq. The most that can be claimed was acquiescence, buoyed by popular enthusiasm (in the case of the First World War) and determination (in the case of the Second) once the war had actually started. The welfare state is more complicated. On the intellectual side it was largely the brainchild of William Beveridge; but Beveridge was partly responding to a popular mood.

No hammer-and-anvil view of history can be unqualified. A governing class must always be responsive to the instincts and feelings of the governed, especially in a democracy. Nevertheless, even in a democracy, the ruling class has a great deal of latitude. Divisions within it are also a point of entry for popular politics and mass culture. These exhibit a separate character, and require the attention of the historian in their own right. There have also been examples of people making their own history. The rise of the Labour Party and of the trade unions is a genuine example of history from below; as has been the popular resistance, at different times, of Irish Catholics and Protestants to Westminster blueprints for the future of Ireland. The pop music and fashions of the 1950s, 60s and 70s had a radical working-class edge before they were commercially packaged for mass consumption. Today the masses are tranquillised by shopping.

My history is divided into two parts. 'The Stage of Action' offers an account of the resources – material, moral, cultural, political – which the British brought to their twentieth-century history. The second part – 'The Action' – tells, in chronological order, how these resources were brought into play on the field of action. Readers who want to get to the Action as soon as possible can skip the first part, though they may want to refer back to it if they are left puzzled by the story being told, or the author's judgements of events.

A historian of contemporary Britain is writing about a living, not dead reality. So he should, perhaps, try to sum up his attitude towards the people he is writing about. My own feelings are not straightforward. I was born in China, of Russian, though naturalised British, parents, but was brought up in Britain, and have lived here almost all my life. I have an English wife and three children who would not describe themselves as anything but English. I would not dream of giving my allegiance to any other country. But I cannot avoid something of an outsider's view, and this has no doubt affected the way I write about the British. I am not solidly rooted here, or anywhere.

So what do I see from outside the room looking in? I see one of the greatest constructive people in history, resembling in this respect the Romans, with whom our nineteenth-century rulers came to feel a close affinity. Like the Romans, their genius is essentially practical, but unlike the Romans, who inherited their culture from the Greeks, they have bequeathed the world outstanding achievements in thought, literature, and art. Ordinary people have displayed exceptional fortitude and steadiness in a variety of adverse circumstances. They are prejudiced (like all of us) and more ignorant and philistine than they should be, but they are cheerful, loyal, tolerant, kind and not given to extreme opinions or actions. Their politics are banal, but safe. Britain's weather is dismal, though it makes the countryside beautiful, and until recently at least its food has been execrable.

I feel a lack of intimacy in the soil of the culture, and have lived in this country for too long for it not to have rubbed off on me. I feel myself more British than I would like to be.

I would like to thank David Ashton, Jonathan Clark, Nigel Lawson, David Owen, Frederic Raphael, Kenneth Morgan, Anthony Seldon, Larry Siedentop, and Edward and William Skidelsky for their incisive critiques of sections of earlier drafts; Pavel Erochkine, Louis Mosley, and Pete Mills, who did much of the heavy lifting, as well as contributing many ideas; and my superb editor, David Milner. The responsibility for the final product is mine alone.

List of Illustrations

Leaders of the People

ASQUITH, Herbert Henry (1852–1928), Liberal Prime Minister 1908–16.

ATTLEE, Clement (1883–1967), Labour Prime Minister 1940–51.

BALDWIN, Stanley (1867–1947), Conservative Prime Minister 1923, 1924–9, 1935–7.

BALFOUR, Arthur (1848–1930), Conservative Prime Minister 1903–5, plus long subsequent ministerial career.

BEATLES – John Lennon (1940–80), Paul McCartney (b.1942), George Harrison (1943–2001), Ringo Starr (b.1940), first and most famous British rock group. Dominated the charts in the 1960s.

BEAVERBROOK, Lord, Maxwell Aitken (1879–1964), Canadian-born newspaper proprietor.

BERLIN, Isaiah (1909–97), Russian-born British social and political philosopher.

BENN, Tony (1925–2014), populist left-wing Labour party leader. Last pipe smoker in British public life.

BEVERIDGE, William (1879–1963), author of the Beveridge Report on Social Security.

BEVIN, Ernest (1881–1951), General Secretary of the Transport and Workers Union 1921–40, Minister for Labour 1940–5, Foreign Secretary 1945–50.

BLAIR, Tony (b.1953), Labour Prime Minister 1997–2007. Took Britain into the Iraq War.

BROWN, Gordon (b.1951), Labour Prime Minister 2007–10.

BUTLER, Richard Austen ('Rab') (1902–82), almost leader of the Conservative Party, almost Prime Minister.

CHAMBERLAIN, Joseph ('Jo') (1836–1914), Liberal/Liberal Unionist politician. Colonial Secretary 1905–3. Led Tariff Reform Campaign 1903–6. Split two main parties. 'Made the weather' without becoming Prime Minister.

CHAMBERLAIN, Austen (1863–1937), son of Jo. Beaverbrook said 'He always played the game and he always lost it'.

CHAMBERLAIN, Neville (1869–1940), son of Jo, half-brother of Austen. Prime Minister 1937–40. Architect of appeasement policy.

CHURCHILL, Winston Spencer (1874–1965). Britain's second 'war leader'. Coalition Prime Minister 1940–5, Conservative Prime Minister 1951–5.

COWARD, Noel (1899–1973), English playwright, 'a combination of cheek and chic, pose and poise'.

CRIPPS, Stafford (1880–1952), Labour Chancellor of the Exchequer 1947–50. Symbolised post-war austerity.

EDEN, Anthony (1897–1977), Conservative Prime Minister 1955–7. Led Britain into the Suez fiasco.

ELIOT, T. S. (1888–1965), American-born, major British poet.

FOOT, Michael (1913–2010), left-wing leader of the Labour Party 1980–3.

FREUD, Lucian (1922–2011), German-born British painter.

GAITSKELL, Hugh (1906–63), leader of the Labour Party 1955–63. Tried to repeal Clause IV in 1959.

HAIG, Douglas (1861–1928), British field-marshall, nicknamed 'butcher of the Somme'.

HAGUE, William (b.1961), leader of the Conservative party 1997–2001.

HEALEY, Denis (b.1917), Labour Chancellor of the Exchequer 1974–7. Almost leader of the Labour Party, almost Prime Minister.

HOCKNEY, David (b.1937), English painter.

JENKINS, Roy (1920–2003), reforming Labour Home Secretary 1964–8. Almost leader of the Labour Party, almost Prime Minister.

KEYNES, John Maynard (1883–1946), economist, statesman, author of *The General Theory of Employment, Interest and Money* (1936).

KINNOCK, Neil (b.1942) leader of the Labour Party 1983–92.

LAW, Andrew Bonar (1858–1923), Conservative Prime Minister 1922–3.

LAWSON, Nigel (b.1932), Conservative chancellor of the exchequer 1983–9.

LLOYD GEORGE, David (1863–1945), Liberal politician, Coalition Prime Minister 1916–22. Britain's first twentieth-century 'war leader'.

MACDONALD, James Ramsay (1866–1937), Labour Prime Minister 1924, 1929–31, National Government Prime Minister 1931–5. His oratory was inspirational, but woolly.

McKENNA, Reginald (1863–1943), Liberal Chancellor of the Exchequer 1915–16, whose McKenna Duties ended seventy years of free trade.

MACMILLAN, Harold (1894–1986), Conservative Prime Minister 1957–63. Accused Margaret Thatcher of 'selling off the family silver'.

MONTGOMERY, Bernard (1887–1976), British field-marshall. Victor of El Alamein 1942.

MOSLEY, Sir Oswald Ernald (1896–1980), leader of the British Union of Fascists 1932–40.

NEVINSON, C. R. W. (1889–1946), First World War painter.

NORMAN, Montagu (1871–1950), powerful governor of the Bank of England 1920–42.

ORWELL, George (1903–50), English writer, chronicler of English life, best-known for his dystopian novel, *1984*.

OSBORNE, John (1929–94), English playwright. *Look Back in Anger* was first performed in 1956.

OWEN, David (b.1938), Labour Foreign Secretary 1977–9. Leader of the Social Democratic Party 1983–7.

POWELL, Enoch (1912–88), Conservative Cabinet minister, but best-known for his 'Rivers of Blood' speech in 1968.

RATTIGAN, Terence (1911–77), English playwright of *The Winslow Boy* and *Separate Tables*.

RUSSELL, Bertrand (1872–1970), philosopher, leading British intellectual of the twentieth century.

SHAW, George Bernard (1856–1950), Irish-born playwright and wit, leading British intellectual gadfly of the twentieth century.

SMITH, John (1938–94), leader of the Labour Party 1992–4.

SNOWDEN, Philip (1864–1937), Labour Chancellor of the Exchequer 1929–31, whose policy of fiscal austerity Gordon Brown vowed not to emulate.

SPENCER, Stanley (1891–1959), English painter.

THATCHER, Margaret (1925–2013), Conservative Prime Minister 1979–90. The third 'war leader', but apart from the Falklands, Britain was her battleground.

TAWNEY, R. H. (1880-1962), economic historian, social theorist, main intellectual influence on the Labour Party.

WAUGH, Evelyn (1903–66), major English comic novelist, chronicler of the 'Bright Young Things', e.g. *Vile Bodies*, *Brideshead Revisited*.

WEBB, Beatrice, neé Potter (1858–1943), founder and leader of the Fabian Society. Aimed to permeate the Establishment with socialism.

WELLS, Herbert George (1856–1946), best-selling author, Socialist propagandist and futurist.

WILLIAMS, Shirley (b.1930), Labour politician and academic. Too nice to be Prime Minister.

WITTGENSTEIN, Ludwig (1889–1951), Austro-British philosopher. His *Tractatus Logico-Philosophicus* (1921) was the most influential book of philosophy published in the twentieth century.

WOOD, Kingsley (1883–1943), Conservative Chancellor of the Exchequer 1940–3. Introduced the first 'Keynesian' budget in 1941.

WOOLF, Virginia (1882–1941), major British writer, Bloomsbury Group.

Introduction

The question with which I started was: how successful has Britain been in the twentieth century? This is a reasonable question for historians to ask. They are used to talking about the rise and fall of nations and empires. True enough, such judgements require distance to give them an air of finality, and contemporary history doesn't give us distance. 'We can judge past governments by their results. The merits and failings of contemporary regimes elude us', wrote Guglielmo Ferrero.[1] However, except for events of the very recent past, enough distance has elapsed to venture some conclusions. The fall of the British Empire is hardly likely to be reversed; nor is universal suffrage.

Which of these counts as success or failure is another matter. Over the last century standards in such things have changed. Historians used to judge a nation's performance by its success in maintaining or increasing its power. Today success is much more likely to be judged by such matters as economic and social welfare, the quality of life, and political and moral values, irrespective of what is happening to the nation's power. There is a very good reason for this shift. We live in a more peaceful world than our ancestors and therefore do not need 'hard' power as much as they did – or the 'martial virtues' required for its successful exercise.

Nevertheless, no historian of twentieth-century Britain can avoid highlighting the collapse of Britain's 'hard' power and the reasons for it. Even those who regard it as inevitable and, on the whole, of beneficial consequence, will find it hard to count it as a success for British policy, for it was not actively sought or deliberately brought about.

In terms of the more recent 'welfare' standard of judgement, there are mixed elements of success and failure to record. Certainly the British people are much more prosperous than they were a hundred years ago but not as prosperous as they feel they should have been, given their starting point, and the overall material progress of the western world in that period. In other words, the British economy has been stuttering for much of the time, and the fruits of prosperity have also been inequitably and unequally distributed, by class and by region. The unbroken preservation of our constitution of liberty can be counted as an unequivocal success, though the decline of the politics which made it possible raises a disquieting question mark over the future. This still leaves a judgement to be made about the quality of British civilisation in the twentieth century, for which quantitative measures are much less useful. Have we become as 'dumbed down' as the critics allege? Or have standards here changed as well?

The decline of British power

The main transformation in twentieth-century British history has been the 'end of empire'; one of the most important jobs of the twentieth-century historian is to explain how and why this happened. In the nineteenth century, the empire's heroic age was past, but the empire was still 'rising'. It was still alive and kicking (if feebly) fifty years ago; today it is as dead as the dodo; and has been all but airbrushed out of the standard school histories of the recent past. Britain started the century as Rome and ended it as Italy.

Despite the rhetoric of graceful 'withdrawal from empire', the British Empire was not liquidated voluntarily. Britain fought to maintain its world position – and lost. Perhaps it did not fight hard enough; perhaps it fought the wrong wars; perhaps the British people had already come to value other things more. The empire was destroyed by war as surely as any of the great empires of the past: not by military defeat – though defeat by the Japanese in 1942 was a decisive moment in the demise of Britain's South Asian empire – but by the sapping, over two world wars (especially the second), of the resources, confidence and will necessary to sustain it. As Norman Davies put it, Britain paid for success in the Second World War 'by losing its grip on the empire, by accepting a position of political, economic, and military dependence on the USA, and by colluding in the rise of the USSR'.[2]

The conventional view is that Britain's rulers chose freedom over empire. This was not apparent to any who took the decisions at the time. The collapse of the British Empire was not intended by those who decided on war in 1939: they thought they were fighting to preserve liberty and empire together, just as their ancestors did when they fought Napoleon. But the results were different. In the first case, liberty was preserved and the empire expanded. In the second, liberty was preserved and the empire lost.

The empire was the bedrock of British power, but not the

whole of it. Historians have talked of Britain's 'informal empire', the wider British nexus linked by trade, finance, colonisation and the British navy. There was also the global reach of its ideas, its habits and its culture, nowadays called 'soft power'. All went down, so that in 2013 a visit by Britain's prime minister David Cameron to India aroused less local interest than a concurrent story of a minor scandal.

Could Britain, by better leadership, have continued – at least for a time – to enjoy the best of both worlds: global power *and* liberty? The answer almost certainly is yes, but it would have required a much clearer long-term vision and resolution of purpose than democratic politics normally allows. Running through the story of the destruction of empire is the failure to evolve a successful European policy. Stated baldly, Britain failed either to conciliate its main challenger, Germany, or resist its ambitions *in time*. Conciliation of Germany was difficult enough before 1914, for Germany was a revisionist power. It became impossible with Hitler, who was not only hubristic but barbaric. But if Plan A was unattainable, there was always a Plan B, which required no more than the cold and resolute pursuit of the traditional precept of British foreign policy: to maintain the balance of power in Europe. In the end, it was the infirmity of Britain's commitment to the balance of power which landed it in two empire-destroying world wars. Was this then a failure of democracy? Many have thought it so.

The mishandling of relations with Europe continued after the Second World War. 'Missing the European bus' has become a historical cliché, but Britain did more than just miss the European bus: it did its best to prevent it from starting on its journey, and, having failed to wreck it at the outset, repeatedly put roadblocks in its way. Having failed to play the balance-of-power game properly when it mattered, it tried to do so when it had become irrelevant, sabotaging the benign attempt to unite Europe after 1945. The failure to go with Europe weakened the European Union and made Britain a vassal of the United States.

Historical amnesia has also been applied to the evaluation of empire. The prevalent view is that the British Empire was a bad thing, since it necessarily involved exploiting the ruled for the benefit of the rulers, as well as crippling democracy in Britain itself. If we apply an elementary counterfactual – what would have happened to the colonial peoples had they not been 'conquered' – it is reasonable to claim that the British Empire at least made them actually and potentially better off economically, by giving them access to the capital, technology and legal system of the imperial power.[3] We could also take pride in having bequeathed large parts of the world democratic institutions. The charge that empire inhibited democracy in Britain itself, because it required a hierarchical society and a repressive code of morals at home, carries weight, but only if we view these things as bad.

The history of empire has affected our post-imperial history in three ways. First, the imperial overhang left Britain's rulers with an abiding sense of responsibility for world affairs, which, in their view, was best discharged as the 'junior partner' of the United States, Britain's successor as global hegemon. Secondly, the imperial shadow crucially affected what happened to the British economy. Britain's rulers – and most of its top businessmen and bankers – continued to view it as an 'imperial economy' long after empire was gone. This attitude, manifested in many ways – from the defence of an 'imperial' currency and financial system, to reliance on 'captive' markets for British exports, to the maintenance of an outsize military establishment – shackled the development of a modern economy able to earn its way in a post-imperial world. The flame of empire still flickered under New Labour in Kosovo, Iraq and Afghanistan, until economic exhaustion finally gutted it. Thirdly, the end of empire liberated British culture from its functional role in maintaining empire: it led, that is, to the permissive society of the 1960s and thereafter.

The increase in economic welfare

In terms of economic welfare, there has been a great improvement from the conditions which existed at the century's start. Put simply, the British people are both richer and healthier than they were at the start of the last century. The fact that this improvement was achieved by almost all European countries does not mean it should be excluded from the list of British successes.

The economic condition of the people started to cause concern at the end of the nineteenth century, mainly in the context of military efficiency. With the onset of political democracy, the people started to shape the welfare discussion – improving the material conditions of the masses became the chief purpose of policy; success in doing so the chief test of electoral viability. The people's rejection of Churchill, the triumphant war leader, in 1945, signified the emergence of the new standard of judgement, captured in A. J. P. Taylor's famous conclusion to his *English History 1914–1945*: 'The British Empire declined; the condition of the people improved. Few now sang "Land of Hope and Glory". Few even sang "England Arise". England had risen all the same.'[4]

A key theme in the narrative of improvement was the establishment of the welfare state, from its origins at the century's start to its full flowering in the 1970s. The welfare state is at the heart of the welfare story: Britain's distinctive social achievement, with the National Health Service as the jewel in the crown. Its growth was financed by a very large rise in taxation, initially war-related. *How* successful the welfare state has been is a matter of continuing debate between left and right. For the left it provided, for the first time, a secure habitat for the whole population, thus enlarging the possibilities of human flourishing. For the right, it created a dependency culture which spelt the end of the Victorian virtues of self-reliance, thrift, enterprise – the qualities which had 'made Britain great'. It is now becoming clearer that, however successful the welfare state has been in its own terms, it may be impossible to support a welfare state whose financing depends on continuing economic dynamism. A future historian is likely to detect another 'rise and fall' here, with an incremental process of dismantling welfare entitlements. Instead of providing an alternative to empire, the welfare state may be destined to follow in its retreating footsteps.

Almost all identifiable groups, occupations and regions in Britain benefited from the general improvement in welfare. But these gains were unevenly distributed: some groups gained more than others, if not necessarily at their expense. Women gained more than men, both materially and in terms of respect. Margaret Bondfield was the first woman Cabinet minister in 1929 and since then women have risen to the top of all professions. Over the century, class income divides narrowed and then expanded again. The subordinate nations – Scotland, Wales and Northern Ireland – lost relatively to England for much of the century, though Scotland has recently regained ground. By 2050 an enlarged British population of 78.7 million is expected to include 20 per cent ethnic minorities.[5] As a group, immigrants gained relative to their positions in their native lands; they also brought the economic and cultural benefits which a more cosmopolitan population always confers. However, some native Britons lost jobs and job opportunities; and there was the loss of a secure sense of identity, with largely incalculable knock-on effects.

The relative decline of the British economy

At the start of the twentieth century Britain was an industrial giant. Today it is an industrial pygmy. Manufacturing was industry's bedrock. In 1952 it produced a third of national output, employed 40 per cent of the workforce, and made up a quarter of world manufacturing exports. Today manufacturing is just 12 per cent of GDP, employs only 8 per cent of the workforce, and sells 2 per cent of the world's manufacturing exports. The iconic names of industrial Britain are history: in their place is the service economy and supermarkets selling mainly imported goods.

The relative decline of the British economy seems bound up with the decline of British industry, though the link between the two is complicated. Ever since Joseph Chamberlain started his campaign for tariff reform in 1903, industrial decline was the spectre which haunted British politics, not least because it brought with it the problem of imperial overstretch. The causes of this sickness and what to do about it dominated politics from the late 1950s to the 1970s. As the civil servant Chris Benjamin notes, debates about industrial policy only petered out in the 1970s, 'along with the industries themselves'.[6] The Thatcher 'revolution' of 1979 and its New Labour continuation accepted the replacement of industry by services, especially financial services. According to current orthodoxy there is no a priori ground for saying that industry is 'superior' to services: it all depends on the productivity potential of the two sectors. Further, the need to safeguard 'essential' industries for defence in war has disappeared with the disappearance of war itself as a major contingency. This economistic argument ignores the fact that 'making things' may be an important source of personal and national pride. The decline of British manufacturing also made the UK particularly vulnerable to the global banking crisis which erupted in 2008, and explains its exceptional slowness in recovering from it. It was also a major cause of the growth of inequality.

The preservation of liberty

The largely unsung success story of the twentieth century is the success of Britain's political system in preventing political extremism in the face of quite cataclysmic events, which brought to an end liberty and democracy for long periods in large parts of continental Europe. This is the main justification for the two world wars which brought empire to an end. In the last analysis, the British cared more for their liberties than for world power. Despite some fraying at the edges, Britain remains one of the most civilised and tolerant political societies in the world.

Britain undoubtedly became more *democratic* over the twentieth century, formally and substantively. Universal suffrage was finally achieved in 1928. The working class was incorporated into the political nation largely (though not exclusively) through the Labour Party and trade union movement. However, reformers' hopes for a properly *social* democracy were obstinately blocked by the persistence of the class system (notably in education); by the persistence of poverty and inequality; by certain traditional quirks of the British constitution (for example, the continued non-election of the members of House of Lords); and latterly by the shrinking of politics itself. As a result, the transfer of power to 'the people' was aborted. The people were allowed into the conversation, but the topics were chosen by the elites, old and new. Perhaps this is always bound to be the case.

Britain had its fringes of Communists and fascists, but they never impaired the working of the 'ancient constitution'. Twentieth-century British politics produced three world-class prime ministers – Lloyd George, Winston Churchill and Margaret Thatcher; some top second-raters – Baldwin, Attlee, Macmillan, Wilson and Blair; and a number of outsize 'characters' like Oswald Mosley, Enoch Powell, Tony Benn and David Owen whose quiddities prevented them playing a role commensurate with their abilities.

Their exclusion may be counted a success for the British version of democracy. Among the secrets of this success were the notably pragmatic, utilitarian character of British public life (reflecting in this the unintellectual character of the people), an ingrained tolerance, the efficiency of the parliamentary system in absorbing and accommodating dissent, and a deep-seated attachment to that collection of legal documents, conventions, fictions, case law and historical memory that made up the British constitution. How durable this achievement will be in face of the decay of parliamentary and local politics, the change in the composition of the population, the rise of the 'security state', and the transfer of powers to un-elected European bureaucracies remains to be seen. A historian fifty years hence will either continue to marvel at the resilience of the British system of liberty or lament its demise.

Culture

In any commercial society, the spread of prosperity is bound to produce a 'democratisation of culture' as the masses start competing with the elites for cultural goods. Contemporary British culture is not working-class culture. It is popular culture as shaped by technology, the media and the market. Historians talk of a cultural watershed between the late 1950s and early 1970s, when a traditional culture marked by hierarchy and restraint gave way to an egalitarian, aggressive consumerism. Whether this culture is better or worse than its Victorian ancestor is a matter of judgement. Traditionalists argue that there has been a 'race to the bottom'. Our contemporary culture is degraded and unwholesome. Progressives count as a clear gain the liberation of behaviour from old taboos and taste from the straitjacket of stuffy middle-class convention. Britannia is 'cool'. It may be, though, that less has changed than the optimists and pessimists believe. With culture we are in the land of unfinished business. We face at least the possibility that further advances in digital computers, microbiology and neuroscience will reshape not just culture, but re-engineer the subject of culture – the human being.

Part I
The Stage of Action

Chapter 1

The Material Stage

'The style of life of a species must be consonant with its way of getting a living.'

Joan Robinson, *Freedom and Necessity* (1970)

The most striking material fact in twentieth-century British history is the huge advance in material prosperity. This was a civilisational achievement of a small group of white countries, which starting ahead of the rest of the world in 1900 maintained its advantage throughout the ensuing century. It testifies to the sustaining power of inherited scientific and technological leadership. There were nevertheless unique features of the British experience which will be noticed in the account which follows. The first was the establishment of a welfare state which had a unique structure. The second was the persistent worry that Britain was 'falling behind' in the global economic race, which produced a swing in political economy in the 1980s more extreme than that experienced in any of the group of leaders. Looking at century-wide changes inevitably has a flattening effect. Nevertheless, taking the long view has the advantage of pointing to the persistent historical trends which transformed not just Britain but the whole developed world in the twentieth century, and have started to transform the developing world too.

Population

The most salient facts about Britain's population in the twentieth century are the slowdown in its rate of increase, its ageing, and the change in its composition. This demographic narrative has been common to all developed countries. The population of the UK grew by just over 50 per cent between 1900 and 2000 (from 38 million to just under 60 million) as compared to a growth of 166 per cent in the nineteenth century. Over two centuries it has shown the typical transition from the pre-industrial system with relatively high fertility and mortality to a modern system with relatively low fertility and mortality; and from net emigration to net immigration. In the last twenty years there has been a pick-up in population growth, but only as a result of net inflow, and the higher fertility of immigrants.

In the eighteenth and early nineteenth centuries, improvements in agricultural productivity enabled rapid population growth (people could afford to marry earlier and to have more children). The twentieth century was an era of falling birth rates, interrupted by the 'baby booms' which came after both world wars, and again in the 1960s. The fertility rate fell from 5.5 children per woman in 1871, to 2.4 in 1921, to 1.6 in 2001. There were two main causes for the decline in fertility. The first was the fall in infant mortality – infant deaths fell from 110 per 1,000 births in 1910–11 to 24.5 per 1,000 in 1956 and 5.4 per 1,000 in 2001 – which reduced parents' incentives to have large families, only partly compensated by family allowances for second and third children introduced in 1945. The second cause was the increased participation of women in the labour market as more 'women's jobs' became available, the Second World War in particular being a forcing house for female employment.

Women's labour market participation rate went up from 35 per cent in 1911 to 54 per cent in 1998, and women now account for 80 per cent of all part-time workers. Today women constitute 46 per cent of the labour force as against 29 per cent in 1911. Men work less; women work more (outside the home); and in higher-paid and more prestigious jobs.

These long-term trends were reinforced by the spread of modern birth-control methods. Although some families used birth-control – 'generally crude, unreliable, expensive and difficult to obtain'[1] in the first half of the twentieth century – family planning became effective with the introduction of the contraceptive pill in the 1960s, which greatly reduced the number of unwanted babies.

Secular population trends have obscured considerable fluctuations which repeatedly confounded demographic projections. Malthus was right: good years produce more babies. For example, in the 'you've never had it so good' period of the late 1950s and early 1960s, births per woman shot up to 2.95, with a million new births recorded in 1964 alone. Conversely, the birth rate collapsed during the depressed interwar years and again in the rising unemployment years of the 1970s and early 1980s. Simple extrapolation is not, therefore, an accurate guide to the demographic future.

Life expectancy has also increased – from forty-seven in 1901 to seventy-eight in 2001. This means that the proportion of old people in the population is going up. About 5 per cent of the population was sixty-five or older in 1900, a proportion relatively unchanged for centuries. This increased to 11 per cent in 1951, to 16 per cent in 1995, and is expected to reach 25 per cent by 2031. This increase is largely due to the fall in infant mortality. The lower proportion of infants who die, the higher the average life expectancy, and vice versa.

But people who survived birth are also living longer. Epidemics, which in previous centuries had cut swathes through the living, almost disappeared with improvements in medicine, housing and sanitation.* More recently there has been a reduction in the incidence of the leading causes of premature old age death – coronary heart disease, strokes, cancer and respiratory diseases – mainly as a result of medical improvements, greater coverage of health care (the National Health Service Act of 1948 was a milestone), and healthier lifestyles – better diet, less drinking, and a decline in smoking. At the century's start, a typical working-class diet was heavy on pork, lard, bacon and bread, had no vegetables except potatoes and onions, and no fruit.[2] Today fruit and vegetables from all over the world are cheaply available from any supermarket. Despite frequent complaints about drunkenness, the British are more sober than they were a century ago. In 1949, an estimated 22 million Britons smoked – 13.5 million men and 7.5 million women – that is, 81 per cent of men and 39 per cent of women over fifteen, with 11 per cent of the average household budget being spent on cigarettes. Children were locked in by 'cigarette cards' which came with cigarette packets, runs of pictures and facts about almost everything, but with a heavy concentration on the empire. The fall in proportion of smokers, from 50 to 25 per cent of the adult population since 1970, has contributed to increased longevity.

The averages mask significant regional and class variations. Over the century, Scotland, Ireland and Wales lost population; England, and especially southern England, gained it. This reflected the industrial decline of these 'peripheries'.

---

*Exceptions: the influenza epidemic of 1919 killed 250,000; the AIDS epidemic has killed 20,000 since the 1980s.

The pull of England would in due course stimulate Scottish and Welsh nationalism. In 1900, 46 per cent of the UK population lived in the north (including Scotland) and 54 per cent in the south; by 2000 the figures were 38 per cent in the north and 62 per cent in the south. Britain's population over the century increased by 50 per cent, Scotland's by 14 per cent. In 2010 Scotland's population was only 750,000 more than in 1901, reflecting a large-scale exodus between 1970 and 2000: the emigres included Tony Blair and Gordon Brown. Urban areas of the west central belt which suffered industrial decline saw their populations move back to the Highlands and into the border region and south-west Scotland, with Glasgow losing 10 per cent of its population in the 1980s. Some reverse immigration in the early twenty-first century of Poles and English suggests a population in equilibrium at last.

Also, most immigrants have settled in the south: in 2001, 45 per cent of the ethnic minority population in the UK lived in the London region. The net shift to the south has slowed down since the 1980s, and was reversed in the first years of the twenty-first century. Life expectancy is higher in the south than in the north and among the middle class than among the working class. Birth rates are higher among post-war immigrants than native Britons; infant mortality is higher among single mothers and ethnic minorities, and in Northern Ireland, than in the rest of the UK. Most of contemporary Britain's social and medical problems are concentrated in the poorest, least educated section of the population: they smoke more, drink more, eat worse, take less exercise. As a result they are more prone to cancer, diabetes and cardiovascular disease, dying, on average, seven years earlier than the better off. The British people are taller, but also wider, than they were in 1900. The waddle has supplemented the walk in many British streets.

Migration has affected both the size and composition of the population. The transition from net emigration to net immigration is common to developed countries, though the sources of immigrants and policies towards migration vary from country to country. The nineteenth-century pattern was one of net emigration, continuing well into the twentieth. The UK's population would have grown faster in the early twentieth century had not so many migrants left for the United States, Canada, Australia and New Zealand. In the 1930s net outflows were replaced by net inflows. In the middle years of the century inflows and outflows more or less balanced: Britain lost whites, and gained ethnic minorities. Since the 1990s net migration to the UK has trebled from under 100,000 per year to a peak of over 300,000 in 2006. As a result, immigration, not natural growth, has become the main driver of British population growth.* Since 2001, the population of the UK has grown from 59.1 million to 63.2 million, an increase of almost 7 per cent in ten years. Up to two thirds of recent population growth can be attributed, directly or indirectly (through impact on fertility rates), to immigration. Britain started the century exporting people to the empire; it ended with the former empire exporting people to Britain.

In the 2011 census in England and Wales, 86 per cent of the population were classified as white, and 14 per cent as Asian, black or 'other ethnic group', an increase of 6 percentage points on 2001. The largest ethnic minority group is by origin Indian (2.5 per cent of the total population but 18 per

---

*In 2010, family reunion made up 17 per cent of all migration of non-EU nations to the UK, a decrease since its peak in 2006. Despite increasing from 35,000 a year in the 1990s to 56,000 a year in 2010, family reunion represents a smaller proportion of non-EU net migration than it did twenty years ago.

cent of the ethnic minority population); the second largest is Pakistani. New Commonwealth immigration transformed major cities into racially mixed populations unimaginable in 1900. Prior to the 1950s, immigration was mainly 'white' (Irish, Jewish). The Irish, in particular, settled in England and Scotland in large numbers before 1914, especially in London, Liverpool, Manchester and Glasgow, sucked in by the demand for cheap factory labour. Irish immigration continued in the 1940s and 50s into new centres of manufacturing like Luton and Coventry, and to jobs in transport and the building trade. Irish doctors and nurses were recruited into the National Health Service. As Irish immigration dried up, these jobs were taken by ethnic minority immigrants. The 1950s and 1960s were periods of mass immigration from the New Commonwealth countries, in particular the Caribbean, India and Pakistan. Migrants from Bangladesh, Hong Kong and Africa followed. The 1980s onwards witnessed a dramatic increase in the number of asylum seekers – refugees from dictatorships or conflicts round the world.[3] Since the 1990s net inward migration from all sources has averaged about 150,000 a year, with increasing numbers from eastern Europe, particularly Poland. Britain's population is projected to grow to 73.2 million by 2035, and two thirds of this increase will be the result of immigration (47 per cent because of immigration itself, 21 per cent because of migrants' children being born in Britain).

More immediately than the birth rate, migration responds to fluctuations in the labour market. Periods of heavy unemployment in the first half of the twentieth century saw a net exodus from the UK, as well as widespread internal migration from the depressed to prosperous regions. New Commonwealth immigrants were sucked into the UK in the 1950s and 60s by

the demand for labour. But policies towards entry and settlement have modified the simple economics of migration.

With a laissez-faire tradition, the need for an immigration
policy was only slowly accepted. Immigration from the
Commonwealth was not subject to control till 1962. In the 1950s
and 60s migration for settlement was the rule, with spouses
and other dependants let in. Following the Immigration Act of
1967, a 'guest worker model' was adopted: immigrants were
allowed in to do specific jobs for limited periods, with no expectation of settlement. After 1997, limited settlement rights were
conceded.

Population is a rich field for narratives of rise and decline,
as it touches on perceptions of genetic, military and cultural
survival. The slowdown in population growth was alarming
to an imperial power faced with powerful rivals. In Edwardian
times fears of a declining population were linked to fears of
its declining quality. They were revived in the interwar years,
when there was talk of 'race suicide'.

The Italian economist Vilfredo Pareto thought it was
better for the poor to have many children, and the rich to
have few, since most of the poor's children die, leaving only
the healthiest from which future elites would be recruited.
However, the huge reduction in infant mortality put paid to
this argument: the new problem was the survival of the unfit.
The eugenic movement of the 1900s aimed to improve the
quality of the population by restricting births of the 'dysgenic'
(code for lower classes). The birth-control movement
sponsored by Marie Stopes, who founded Europe's first birth-
control clinic in 1921, was dedicated to spreading knowledge
of contraception among those classes felt to be in greatest
need of it. Despite the spread in contraceptive practice, the
class gap in fertility persisted; this was later reinforced by

What defines Britishness today?
2. English Defence League marchers (l); 3. Attending the Queen's Golden Jubilee (r)

the ethnic gap. Eugenic concerns continued to surface from time to time until it became too politically incorrect to voice them. (Keith Joseph's 1974 speech at Edgbaston, which argued that excess lower-class fertility was lowering the quality of the British population, probably cost him the leadership of the Conservative Party.)

Immigration has produced repeated panics about being 'swamped'. Hostility to ethnic minority immigration climaxed with Enoch Powell's 'rivers of blood' speech in Birmingham in 1968. Governments responded by restricting entry, and outlawing discrimination and incitement to race (and later) religious hatred. Supporters of immigration point out that not only is it good for immigrants, it has also helped economic growth by restraining wage inflation as well as providing Britain with a variety of cultural and economic services

beyond the wit of the home population. Anti-immigrant feeling has been driven by fear of job losses, and also by racism.
Many object to Britain being turned into a multicultural society. Earlier panics have recently been reinforced by terrorist
outbreaks and the fear of 'Islamisation'.

Urbanisation

Urbanisation has been a trend common to all developed countries, only offset to a small degree by a reverse movement of
'second homes'. More and more people live in towns, and
have urban jobs. This is the result of the long decline in agriculture and rural industry. But the patterns of urbanisation
reflect population shifts from declining to expanding regions,
from older administrative to new commercial and industrial
centres, preferences in styles of urban living, and family structure. The growth in the size of cities (particularly urban
sprawl) also reflected the growing ease of moving about: railways, bicycles, motor cars.

By 1840 Britain was already the most urbanised society in
Europe, with almost 50 per cent of the population living in
towns of over 1,000 people. Urban population then grew much
faster than total population; by 1901 it had risen to 77 per
cent of the total and by 1991 was 90 per cent. There was widespread internal migration in line with economic restructuring.
Already in the nineteenth century population was tending to
cluster in new areas of dominant industries: steel trades in
Sheffield, cotton in Manchester, shipbuilding on the Clyde.
From the interwar years onwards, people left the declining
industrial regions to seek jobs in the south and Midlands, seat
of the 'new economy': 500,000 Scots went south in the 1920s.
London became increasingly dominant administratively,

financially and culturally, though its population declined relative to the total.

The most striking feature of twentieth-century urbanisation was the colonisation of the countryside by the town. Lord Salisbury promoted 'villa Conservatism' for 'office boys'; Conservative governments in the interwar years pushed owner-occupation as a bulwark against Bolshevism. Towns expanded outwards, not upwards. The growing middle classes wanted houses and gardens, not flats, and the working class were entitled to no less. According to specifications laid down in 1918, working-class houses built with government money were to have a density of no more than twelve houses per acre. New estates conforming to these specifications were built on the outskirts of London and other cities. Even by the 1990s, flats were only one fifth of the housing stock.

The British, when given the chance, have instinctively gravitated to that mixture of town and country known as suburbia, contrary to the wishes of the planners, who sought to house them in self-contained functional cities. Existing towns spilled over into conurbations and commuter belts. Today 'rural', over much of England, signifies simply lower densities than in towns, rather than a particular way of life centred on farming. Towns like London, Manchester and Birmingham swelled by day and shrank by night, as commuters travelled to and from their jobs along clogged roads and in packed rush-hour trains: only 42 per cent of those who worked in Newcastle in 1971 lived in the city. Economic clusters or nodes with spokes of up to fifty miles were created at the expense of continuous congestion. Traffic jams in London had become chronic by the 1920s. Outward expansion went hand in hand with the depopulation of inner cities. London's population fell from a peak of 8.3 million in 1951 to just over 7 million in

2001. Post-1945 dispersal brought about urban decay, as the middle classes fled, old factory jobs disappeared, and inner-city populations were relocated. In the 1950s and 60s streets of two-up, two-down inner-city terraces, where everyone know each other, were demolished and replaced by large council housing estates – most visibly tower blocks. Though they often represented an improvement on existing housing, cost-cutting meant many estates were poorly constructed and lacked amenities. By breaking up previously mixed areas, they sharpened class divides; by cutting the threads of community they produced alienation, vandalism, neglect and high crime levels, which accelerated as short-term tenants replaced long-term residents. Council estates concentrated the most deprived sections of society. The biggest problem was not the brutalist architecture – some estates, like London's Barbican and Lillington Gardens, are now held in high regard – but the failure to address the underlying social problems.

Under New Labour in the early 2000s many council estates were sold off or demolished in programmes of regeneration. In practice, this meant that old tower blocks were replaced with new ones, or tarted up with colourful cladding, with smaller flats marketed as 'luxury accommodation' and priced out of the reach of former council-estate residents. Regeneration was most successful when the middle classes did it, buying up decaying Georgian, Victorian and Edwardian terraces on the cheap and renovating them, in a process called 'gentrification'. Both outward and return movement were governed by changes in the relative price of property, as economists would have predicted. In 1914 only an estimated 10 per cent of the population owned their own homes; by the end of the twentieth century Britain had become a 'property-owning democracy', with 70 per cent of the population (or the banks and building societies from whom they had borrowed) owning their own homes, and most of the rest renting from private or 'social' landlords. (The pattern in Scotland, Wales and Northern Ireland is little different.) For the first time since the Industrial Revolution the majority owned an asset other than their labour power. Conservative and Labour competition over housing policy started in the 1920s. Rent controls, dating from the First World War, promoted by Labour, and only intermittently reversed by the Conservatives, made private letting unprofitable. (The assured shorthold tenancy, introduced in 1996, revived the private rented sector by making it profitable to 'buy to let'.) In its place, governments subsidised both private ownership and social housing: the former through mortgage interest tax relief (from 1963 to 2000), the latter through Exchequer subsidies for local-authority house building, started in the 1920s. German bombing in the Second World War provided a stimulus for ambitious rehousing schemes. The post-war Labour government used the New Towns Act of 1946 and the Town and Country Planning Act of 1947 to build new towns on greenfield sites in order to disperse both people and jobs from inner parts of cities subject to 'overcrowding' and industrial decay, while designating areas of the countryside 'green belts' on which no development was allowed. The battle of council-house building was joined in the 1950s, with the Conservatives promising to build more houses than Labour. The countryside became an endangered habitat which, like its wildlife, had to be protected by special legislation from the encroachment of human predators.

Urban areas had to accommodate the rising demand for household units as families grew smaller. The average size of households fell from 4.6 in 1901 to 2.4 by the century's end: the outcome of declining fertility, the virtual extinction of residential domestic servants and lodgers, and the increase in single-person households of the young and the old. Although the population was not growing by much, there was always an excess of 'families' over 'housing units'.

The economy

Britain grew immensely richer in the twentieth century. Its real gross domestic product (the amount of output measured in constant prices) increased sixfold. This growth was caused by population and productivity growth. Unlike in earlier centuries, population growth slowed down, while productivity went up, allowing a four and a half times average increase in real income per head. Also, unlike in earlier centuries, economic conditions became more equal across the whole of the United Kingdom, leaving relatively minor variations by comparison with former times. Contemporary British civilisation is built on a base of massively increased purchasing power. This is mainly spent on buying consumption goods and services, which have significantly increased in quantity and variety. The fact that the British people are so much 'better off' than they were in 1900 does not mean that they are happier or better or better-adjusted. They just have more money to spend.

Britain's average real income per head went up over the century from £4,300 in 1900 to £20,120 in 2000 (measured in 2008 pounds), a growth of 1.6 per cent a year. By 2008 average real income per head was £27,000. Despite this performance, Britain fell steadily down the league table of top countries in terms of income per head – from fourth in 1913 to twelfth in 2000.

While real GDP went up six times, nominal GNP increased

more than 50 times. The difference between them reflects the impact of inflation. In the nineteenth century there was no prolonged movement of prices in either direction: the price level was about the same in 1900 as it was at the end of the Napoleonic wars. The twentieth century was an inflationary one, though the extent of inflation is exaggerated, partly because it took place in short bursts. Price increases over the century averaged 4.25 per cent per year, hardly catastrophic. Cumulated over the century it looks worse: it would take £64.30 in 2000 to buy what £1 did in 1900. However, general price indices understate the rise in the cost of living for rich people. For example, prices of personal services have risen much more than the general price level. People on modest incomes could afford more servants in 1900 than they can today.

Over nine decades from 1910 to 2000, prices rose in eight of them: the 1920s was the only exception. Some attribute inflation to democracy; others to trade unions. More plausibly price cycles reflect changes in the structure of the economy. At the end of the century the reduction of inflation was widely credited to 'inflation targeting' by an operationally independent Bank of England. Its task was made much easier by cheap imports and an avalanche of cost-reducing inventions.

Unemployment averaged 5 per cent a year between 1910 and 2000, fluctuating around this rate from 7 to 15 per cent between the wars, and between 1 and 3 per cent from the 1950s to the 70s. A post-war peak of 11.3 per cent was reached in 1986. Average unemployment in the last decade of the twentieth century, at 5.6 per cent, was very close to that of the first decade and indeed to the forty years before 1914 (though there are acute difficulties of measurement). These figures suggest a 'normal' British unemployment rate of about 5 per cent, which was widely assumed, even by Keynes, to be equivalent to full employment in British conditions.

Averages tell you nothing about distribution. All indicators of living standards went up in the twentieth century but this was accompanied by changes in the distribution of wealth and incomes. The economist A. B. Atkinson summarises the century's experience as follows: 'Britain's distributional history of the twentieth century appears to have been one of equalisation over the first decades, and between 1938 and 1949, followed by more hesitant redistribution in the post-war period . . . These moves towards reduced income inequality were dramatically reversed in the 1980s with a sharp rise in inequality, a rise which was large by historical standards.'[4] Pre-tax incomes at the very top rose much faster than others, with the differential between top and average pay soaring to over 100 per cent. The Gini coefficient, which measures inequality (1 is complete equality) rose from 0.24 in 1977 to 0.34 in 2000. The index of GDP rose from 100 in 1997 to 135 in 2007, but median household income only from 100 to 115.

The 1970s was the high tide of redistribution. Today the inequality of wealth and incomes is back to what it was before the Second World War.[5] In 1899 the social reformer Seebohm Rowntree found that nearly 30 per cent of the population lived in poverty, defined as around 50 per cent to 60 per cent of median incomes.* Using a comparable yardstick, the economist Brian Abel-Smith and sociologist Peter Townsend found 10 per cent in poverty in the 1960s, with pensioner poverty

---

* Despite the arguments about absolute and relative definitions of poverty, in relative terms calculations of the poverty line have remained remarkably constant since Rowntree's study: between 50 and 60 per cent of median income.

particularly acute. There was a reduction in the late 1970s, but by 2010 17 per cent were living in poverty (before housing costs). The data are consistent with a long-term fall in poverty (albeit with the 1930s breaking the trend) until the 1960s and 70s, followed by a sharp rise under Major and Thatcher, and a modest fall under New Labour since 1997. It is hard to say how much of the recent rise in inequality and poverty has been due to reduced taxation or increase in pre-tax wage dispersal.

Averages also hide important regional variations. Real wages in the peripheral nations rose more slowly than in England, where they increased faster in the south than in the north. Unemployment, too, was higher in the peripheries. For much of the twentieth century the northern and western parts of the UK stagnated, while the southern and south-eastern parts boomed. This was in contrast to the nineteenth century, and the pattern persisted despite regional policies.

Britain's economic experience in the twentieth century resembles that of other European economies. National income, as already noted, expanded faster than population; the structure of the economy shifted from industry to services; the state's role in the economy increased; taxes went up to pay for it. Europe as a whole (that is, including Britain) would have been a lot wealthier but for the two world wars. Britain's victory in the second war caused it, if anything, to grow more slowly than non-Communist Europe.

Over a hundred-year period what emerges is the long-run stability of Britain's economic performance. Whatever the policies adopted for its improvement, the 'trend' rate of growth of the British economy could not be dislodged from about 2 per cent a year, higher than in the nineteenth century, as one would expect from a more fully industrialised economy. There was a somewhat higher inflation rate than in the nineteenth century, and about the same rate of unemployment. For those experiencing it, it was the instability, rather than steadiness, of the performance which impressed.

It was not, of course, an unchanging economy. Britain began the twentieth century with industrialisation already well advanced, services being the second pillar. In 1870 extractive and manufacturing industry accounted for 42 per cent of the workforce and services 35 per cent; by 1913 each represented 44 per cent of employment, with the residual labour absorbed by agriculture. In 2001, industry accounted for 22 per cent of employment and services for 78 per cent. (By 2010, the former had fallen a further 3 per cent.) The trend to services is common to all developed countries; in Britain it has gone further than in most.

Britain started the period with a smaller share of agricultural employment than any other industrial nation, and this may have reduced its growth potential in the twentieth century. Over the course of the twentieth century, employment in agriculture, forestry and fishing declined from 13 per cent to 1.6 per cent. Land, however, can be used for many purposes other than growing or grazing, so many owners of large estates retained their wealth. This was the basis of continuing aristocratic control of government in the nineteenth century, which did not survive the break-up of landed estates in the twentieth. The countryside faded as a political issue, despite Lloyd George's 'Land Tax' proposal in his 1909 budget. Today, despite (or because of) the fall in agricultural employment, debates over the use of the countryside have revived.

Manufacturing remained steady for the first seven decades, making up around a third of employment. After the Second World War miners, dockers, car workers, and steel workers comprised the bulk of the industrial workforce. Then there were three culls: the early 1980s, the early 1990s and the recession which started in 2008. Between 1979 and 2007, manufacturing halved from 25 per cent to 12 per cent as a proportion of the economy. In 1979, there were 7 million working in manufacturing, today 2.5 million.

The biggest areas of growth were in the public sector (administration, education and health), the wholesale and retail trades, and financial and other services. Together these three sectors make up almost three quarters of today's employment.

Within these sectors, we can track changes in occupational groups. Between 1921 and 2003, the strongest growth was in managerial, professional and technical jobs, whose share rose sixfold from 6.2 per cent to 40.1 per cent. The only other growth area was in clerical jobs, whose share almost doubled from 7.3 per cent to 13 per cent. Manual labour went into a decline in the 1970s, falling from 61 per cent to 31 per cent in 2003, a lower proportion than any other major European economy. Surprisingly, given the expansion of the service sector, sales and customer service jobs declined from 9.1 per cent in 1921 to 7.9 per cent in 2001, the result of automation and disappearance of the 'corner shop'.

The British economy was restructured in three stages. Before the First World War it was 'fabric and mineral-intensive'. The staple industries, for both home sales and exports, were textiles, coal mining, iron and steel, and shipbuilding. Employment and production in all these sectors declined between the wars, as British costs rose relative to those of competitors. Most interwar unemployment was concentrated in them; and their locations – Lancashire, South Wales, the north-east coast, and the Clyde – came to be known as the 'special areas'. The service sector also changed:

domestic service fell, new professionals rose – teachers, nurses, accountants. Employment in government also expanded.

From the 1930s a new economy grew up, based on houses and housing appliances, cars, chemicals, metals, cheap consumer goods and retail distribution. It was built on greenfield sites in the south-east and Midlands. Its origins lie in the conjuncture which pulled Britain out of the Great Depression: plentiful, cheap, non-unionised labour; a fall in food and raw-material prices which created a growing margin for consumption and investment; cheap money which fuelled a private housing boom and with it a market for construction materials and household appliances; suburbanisation which demanded roads, cars, buses and garages to connect the new households to jobs and shops. The new economy catered predominantly to domestic demand; it was assisted by protection, or in the case of electrical industries by government monopoly (the National Grid, established in 1933); it was much more highly concentrated than the old. The motor vehicle industry was dominated by six large companies: Austin, Ford, Morris, Standard, Vauxhall and Rootes. Between them they made 330,000 cars a year. Surging home-market demand not only compensated for the decline of older industries like coal and steel, but, with government support and the stimulus of the war economy, pulled them out of depression so that prosperity spread, though unevenly, through the country.

It was the new economy, based on mass production and mass consumption, which laid the basis of the new British civilisation. The share of manufacturing in both employment and GDP stayed steady, but its composition changed: motor cars went up, textiles went down. But by the 1970s many of the manufacturing firms created in the 1930s and strengthened by the war had become 'lame ducks' and could only be kept going by government support. This was due largely to managerial complacency (the imperial overhang), poor industrial relations and unsteadiness of investment. When Thatcher ended protection and subsidies in the early 1980s, Britain's manufacturing went into precipitate decline, which steepened under New Labour in the 2000s. Aerospace, ship-building, motorcycles, electrical engineering, domestic vehicles, the giants of yesteryear shrank or disappeared out-side the field where government was providing finance or soft orders. The decline and fall of the British car industry, which in the 1950s had developed a world-beating small car, the Mini, is the saddest of many sad stories in the saga of industrial decay. Today all of Britain's car industry, except for manufacturers of London taxis and a few specialist produc-ers, is foreign-owned. Nor were the fading smokestack industries compensated by cutting-edge innovations. Chris Benjamin notes 'the virtual absence' today of 'a significant [British] presence' in industrial applications of micro-miniaturisation and nanotechnology.[6]

What industry lost, to the accompaniment of massive unemployment, went into a 'post-industrial' economy based on services – retail, real estate, financial and business, legal, health and social work, educational and leisure (transport remained constant). Mines and industrial plants closed; shop-ping malls and offices rose in their place; under Blair and Brown the 'creative', financial and retail services dominated the private sector; health, education and welfare services the public sector. The last time Britain ran a balance of trade sur-plus in manufacturing was in 1982. Islands of industry, notably in pharmaceuticals, food processing and telecommunications exist in a sea of services. This is in sharp contrast to continental countries like Germany, which maintained their manufacturing base. Some of Britain's bankrupt plant was bought by foreigners, who achieved results beyond the wit or capacity of their British owners. Marketing replaced production; people started to work not in industry but in public relations.

One particular element of the service industry, domestic service, has long fascinated connoisseurs of class. In 1911, 14 per cent of the labour force and just under 40 per cent of the female labour force in England and Wales worked in domestic service.[7] Though immediately after the First World War the number of servants declined, in 1931, after a revival, it still employed around 24 per cent of women and about 8 per cent of the entire workforce. After the Second World War, there was a long-term decline in domestic service, though the profession did not disappear. In the 1980s, domestic service saw a resurgence as manufacturing declined. By 1997 £4 billion a year was being spent on cooks, cleaners, gardeners and child-carers.[8]

Was the post-industrial economy a forced or a natural growth? The switch to services was similar in all developed countries. It reflects the fact that at higher income levels the demand for health, education and recreation grows faster than the demand for food, clothing and so on. What was exceptional in Britain was the absolute decline in manufacturing, its speed, the indifference with which it was greeted, the failure to build up a new generation of manufacturing capacity, and the sharp increase in inequality which resulted. These were all consequences of the Thatcher revolution.

In the nineteenth century, Britain was the world's leading trading nation. In 1910–13, 30 per cent of British GDP was traded, and Britain still had 25 per cent of world trade, down from 40 per cent in 1870. There was always an import surplus, covered by 'invisible' earnings from financial, insurance, and shipping services. Britain owned 43 per cent of the total stock of overseas investments and £200 million a year was being invested abroad. By the end of the twentieth century Britain's foreign trade was still just under 30 per cent of GDP and London was still the world's busiest financial capital. Britain's relative position, however, had declined. Its share of world trade was now only 7 per cent, and the role of the City of London had changed.

Changes in the composition of British exports have mirrored changes in the structure of its economy. Before the First World War, 65 per cent of British exports were made up of textiles, coal, iron and steel, shipbuilding, machinery, cutlery, tools and hardware. Industries producing these made up to 50 per cent of British industrial production, and employed 25 per cent of the workforce. It was the decline in the export demand for these goods which led to high unemployment in the 1920s. Because of depressed world conditions, recovery in the 1930s was mainly a home market recovery; by 1938 exports had shrunk to 11 per cent, and imports to 18 per cent, of GDP. The post-war years were dominated by the Labour government's 'export drive'. Machinery, electrical goods and motor cars led the way. By 1950 exports stood at 22 per cent of GDP. Today, Britain imports food, semi-manufactured and manufactured goods, and fuels; of its exports, 35 per cent are services, 65 per cent goods, mainly machinery (cars, transport), chemicals and fuels. The share of goods (as opposed to services) in exports has declined by 13 per cent since 1950. The negative balance in trade in goods has remained, except in 1980–4 when recession led to a massive fall in imports and the UK became a large net exporter of oil. Since the 1950s this negative goods trade balance has been partly offset by the export of services ('invisibles'), with financial services and net income from foreign investment being a major element in recent years. A flexible currency helped exports, but with the shrinkage of manufacturing the capacity to take advantage of a cheaper currency has fallen.[9]

One striking continuity was the persisting dominance of the City of London in the economy and in world finance, at no time no more flamboyantly displayed than at the century's end, despite intermittent attempts by reforming governments to make 'Finance less proud and Industry more content'. The City of London's position was never uncontroversial. In 1914, its direct economic significance was that it served as the balancer of Britain's external payments, its earnings covering deficits in the visible trade balance going back to the start of the nineteenth century. This role remained throughout the century. Its indirect significance was twofold. First, London was the pivot of a system of international investment which created new markets for British goods in 'developing countries'. Secondly, it was the manager of the gold standard which facilitated trade by providing the world with fixed exchange rates. Both roles were taken over by the United States after the Second World War, at least till the 1970s. In the 1930s, the importance of the City in the British economy declined with the collapse in world trade and the restriction on capital exports. Its revival dates from the 1950s with the liberalisation of exchange controls and the establishment in London of the 'offshore' Eurobond market. Its position as the world's largest financial centre was secured by the 'Big Bang' of 27 October 1986, which allowed in foreign firms and abolished the distinction between stockbrokers and traders, though its role changed from channelling British savings abroad to channelling foreign savings into Britain and everywhere.

There were three main charges against the City of London. The first was that it diverted British savings abroad. Second, it was said to have drained the provinces of people and talent. The third charge was that it maintained an overvalued exchange rate to serve its own interests. This 'strong pound' bias has survived into the era of floating exchange rates, with the further development of the City's role as a magnet for foreign capital. Since 2008 two further charges have been added: firstly that the British economy's dependence on financial services has made it particularly vulnerable to economic collapses, which usually originate in the banking sector. The second concerns the disproportionate rewards claimed by bankers for services, many of which have been described by financial regulator Adair Turner as 'social waste'.[10] The City of London has become Britain's 'oil curse', keeping the pound too high in international markets, and constituting a vested interest which far outguns every other sector. Despite the economic collapse of 2008, the City's dominance is set to last.

In 1914 Britain was not just at the centre of world commerce and finance, but also at the centre of an imperial system of formal and informal dependencies and clients. There was a direct connection between finance, trade, empire. Sterling loans were tied to orders for British exports from the colonies (chiefly to build infrastructure) and also to food and resource extraction from empire primary producers (which assured British consumers cheap food and British industry a cheap flow of primary products). The provision of capital was often accompanied by insistence on control and management of the foreign enterprise. Imperial economics became a conscious system in the 1930s as Britain's world position slipped, with

the Ottawa Agreements and sterling area regarded as interlocking parts of the same defensive system. Labour's post-war
planning presupposed its continuation; Britain's application
to join the EEC (subsequently the European Union) acknowl-
edged its demise. The fast-growing markets were elsewhere.
The share of Britain's exports to its Dominions and colonies,
having risen from 34 per cent in 1913 to 47 per cent in 1938,
had fallen below 25 per cent by the 1970s, while the share of
Britain's exports to European countries rose from around 20
per cent to 58 per cent over the same period. The last vestiges
of imperial preference and the sterling area disappeared when
Britain joined the EEC. That was the end of imperial economics, but not of imperial blinkers.

Technology

Twentieth-century British lives were transformed by the mass-
production methods which resulted from technological
progress. Mass production produced huge economies of scale
which, by bringing down the average price of many goods and
services, put them in reach of average incomes. The consumer-
ist society of today is built on mass production. Technology is
an aspect of the material framework, because it determines the
standard of living, the distribution and availability of jobs, and
division of time between work and leisure. But it also pene-
trates deeply into politics and culture. It has transformed the
method of politics and created a 'democracy of consumerism'.

The most significant technological innovations are not
always the most recent or the flashiest. The economist
Ha-Joon Chang points out that labour-saving devices in the
home – the washing machine, the vacuum cleaner, the
microwave – have been far more significant for the way we

live than the Internet. These humble household appliances freed up women to enter the labour market and accelerated the decline of domestic service.[11] Plastics revolutionised building materials, packing and clothes.

In the nineteenth century, clothes, generally handmade, were bought to last; in the twentieth century machine-made clothes were bought to throw away. The Bonsack machine, capable of mass-producing cigarettes, spread smoking from the elite to the masses. The rotary printing press, which raised printing speed from 5,000 papers to 30,000 an hour, made possible mass circulation newspapers.

From being a society where few people moved much, or often, from their jobs and localities, twentieth-century Britain became a nation on the move – at home and abroad. Motor cars and lorries gradually replaced railways and canals as means of moving people and goods. The railway age peaked in 1920 with 2 billion passengers and over 20,000 miles of rail

4. 'The Tube Train' by Cyril Edward Power.

track. Trains allowed the late Victorian managerial class to move out to the suburbs. In the twentieth century motor cars gave all classes unprecedented freedom of movement. In 1913 there were 34,000 cars; this rose to over 1 million in 1929, almost 5 million by 1960, and 25 million today, with more than 70 per cent of households owning at least one car. Motor cars created the supermarket and destroyed the neighbourhood shop. The railways could not compete. The then chairman of British Railways, Richard Beeching, cut the railway network of 20,000 miles by a quarter during the mid-1960s, and today it is half what it was at the century's start, with fewer passengers travelling. (An exception to this decline was the city 'metro', a Victorian innovation.)

The Conservative statesman Arthur Balfour came up with the thought that 'the motor car will help solve the congestion of traffic'.[12] The government responded to growing car ownership by building more roads, though from the motorist's standpoint, never enough. The number of trunk roads (including 2,000 miles of motorway, started in 1958) has doubled in the last sixty years, but road space remains scarcer in the UK than elsewhere in Europe – eleven miles per 1,000 cars as opposed to the European average of fifteen.

The gain in mobility carried large external costs. As the historian Arthur Marwick wrote, 'The guts were torn out of such cities as Newcastle, Glasgow and Birmingham and replaced with an ugly jungle of urban motorways and highrise buildings.'[13] The M1 and M25 became nightmares almost as soon as they were opened and no official was ever held accountable for the gross miscalculation of traffic volume. To offset congestion and pollution, many towns have adopted pedestrianisation policies; a congestion charge was introduced in London in 2001. The motor car increased the crime rate. Not only did it offer a new object of theft and vandalism, but it spawned a rash of motoring regulations, and with them, motoring offences. Already by 1938, these accounted for 60 per cent of all convictions. 'With their new motor cars, the middle classes for the first time found themselves systematically on the wrong side of the law.'[14]

It was the aeroplane which put 'abroad' within reach of the average British family. Air travel, for business or vacation, remained an elite activity till well after the Second World War. Passenger liners still plied the oceans; British families took their chilly summer holidays in Blackpool or Bournemouth. Imperial Airways had linked the empire together by the 1930s; jet passenger services came with the Comet in 1952. Mass air travel only took off with a huge fall in the cost of air transport and the development of the 'package holiday' in the 1960s. In the 1980s, thousands of so-called football 'fans' travelled round European stadia, greatly increasing Britain's reputation for loutishness. The number of passengers recorded at Britain's airports rose from 2 million in 1950 to 150 million by the end of the century. By this time 17 million Britons a year bought foreign package holidays. They flocked to the French and Spanish rivieras in Ryanair and EasyJet planes.

The revolution in communications accelerated mightily in the twentieth century, with a profound impact on the patterns of consumption and recreation. The cinema was not remarkable technologically. 'Motion pictures' or 'films' were simply speeded-up sequences of photographs. 'Talkies' came in after 1927, colour in the 1930s. Going 'to the pictures' was the dominant form of entertainment in the forty years between the rise of radio in the 1920s and rise of television in the 1960s. The interwar years were the great cinema-building age. In place of church construction, splendid 'picture palaces', sometimes of neo-Gothic splendour, rose in their place. The number of cinemas fell from a peak of 4,901 in 1939 to 495 in 1996, with annual ticket sales dropping from 1.64 billion in 1946 to 60 million in 1984. The decline of the cinema did not mean the death of the film, only the collective watching of films. In 1976 the video home system (VHS) was launched, in 1997, the digital video disc (DVD), and in 2006 the Blu-ray disc.

The emancipation of film-watching from cinemas was the result of a huge development in the use of electricity. Its use for residential and industrial purposes started in the late nineteenth century with the invention of light bulbs, and extended as the century went on to heating, refrigeration and air-conditioning systems. Its greatest social impact, though, has been on communications. Electrical cables had been laid under the Atlantic in 1867. Telegrams peaked in 1920 when 101 million were sent. But the telephone – invented by Alexander Bell in 1876 – would be the twentieth century's favourite means of communicating. Some 850 million telephone calls were recorded in Britain in 1920; this had risen to 20 billion by the end of the century. In 1965, the first commercial telecommunications satellite was launched, and the first cordless telephone went on sale two years later. Today there are 55 million mobile telephone subscribers in Britain. By the end of the century, language had become the last barrier to virtually instant verbal communication over distance between the world's people.

'Wireless' was a way of transmitting voice messages and other sounds without a cable. The words 'London calling' first crackled out of crystal sets in 1922, via the 2LO transmitter operated by what would become the British Broadcasting Corporation. The BBC's monopoly, and with it the notion of 'shared experiences', was broken when commercial radio was legalised in 1973. Today there are nearly 700 radio broadcast stations. Radio's heyday was in the 1940s. It was given a new lease of life in the 1960s, when the BBC launched Radio 1, offering a non-stop supply of pop music, as a response to the proliferation of pirate radio stations.

Technology changed the way British people listened to music. At the beginning of the twentieth century, music was performed live or sold as a score. The onset of radio began the shift from performed to recorded music. Yet it was only in the 1960s that sales of individual vinyl records replaced sales of sheet music as the measure of a band's success. Pop music was rarely transcribed or published, and many successful pop musicians never learned to read music. By the 1980s, advances in digital recording meant that the virtuoso performance was no longer necessary; post-production became just as important as the musical raw material.

Television, which extended the 'wireless' concept to images, would replace the radio as the main source of non-print information and home entertainment. BBC TV was launched in 1936 with a variety show featuring a horse named Pogo and a song 'Here's Looking at You'. In June 1937 the Wimbledon Tennis Championships were first broadcast, and a year later the FA Cup Final. But not till 1956 did ownership of domestic TV sets become sufficiently widespread for their sales to feature in the retail price index. Up to 1964, when BBC 2 started, the BBC offered a single channel, with six hours watching a day, and no advertisements. Colour television spread gradually in the early 1960s. The BBC's monopoly over viewing ended with the licensing of commercial television in 1955. Sky TV started in 1989. By the end of the century, 97 per cent of British households had one or more TV sets; today they have a choice of 450 channels; television can be watched twenty-four hours a day; most programmes are financed – and interrupted – by advertising.

The Football League resisted the routine televising of league matches for decades, in the belief that it would cannibalise ticket sales. Football fans were only allowed highlights on the BBC's *Match of the Day*. Eventually the top football teams decided they wanted the television revenue for themselves, breaking off to form the Premier League in 1992 and selling the rights to Sky. The fear of falling ticket sales proved unfounded; attendance at games increased steadily to levels not seen since football's post-war heyday – by 2008 35,000 fans would fill the stands for top league matches. The influx of television cash turned English football into big business, which attracted a huge worldwide audience.

Television took its toll on the print media. The peak of newspaper circulation was reached in 1950 with a total of almost 21 million daily, and 31 million Sunday newspapers sold. Thereafter a decline set in as first television and then the Internet took over their main news functions. In 2010, despite a larger market, both dailies and Sundays sold under 10 million copies.

Today electronic communication has become the dominant form of transmitting messages. In 1976 Queen Elizabeth II became the first monarch to send an email. The use of the Internet became general in the 1980s, and more and more people started to surf the net. By the 1990s, fibre-optic cables were offering faster transmission and more connections. Schools started using the Internet as an electronic library. By 2010, 19.2 million UK households had broadband connections. Television is being crowded out by the informational and interactive possibilities opened up by broadband. Those aged between sixteen and twenty-four spend seven hours less a week watching television than their elders.

Chapter 2

The Cultural Stage

Iggy Pop, Lou Reed and Patti Smith are our very own
Goethe, Gide and Gertrude Stein.

Morrissey, *Autobiography* (2013)

*What is culture?**

The term itself invites imprecision. It can be used to describe
the 'way of life' underlying any activity, as in football culture
or business culture; or it can be used about artistic expression
or taste; or, following its root in 'cultivation', it can refer to a
stock improved from its original or wild state, or the means of
so improving it. This chapter is about the cultural resources
the British brought to their twentieth-century history, as distinct from their material ones described in the last chapter. It
excludes political resources, which are the subject of the next
chapter. (Political resources are partly cultural, partly material, but one cannot write about everything at once.) But it is
broader than 'tastes and manners' because it includes moral

---

* I have been influenced by T. S. Eliot's *Notes Towards a Definition of Culture*. Eliot
distinguishes between the culture of the individual, the group, and the whole society. He
writes: 'It is part of my thesis that the culture of the individual is dependent upon the
culture of a group or class, and that the culture of the group or class is dependent upon
the culture of the whole society to which that group or class belongs. Therefore it is the
culture of the society that is fundamental.'

ideas and behaviour. And it draws on the idea of cultivation to ask whether British culture was better or worse at the end of the twentieth century than it was at the start. We are dealing, that is, with a phenomenon of interconnected parts, which includes judgements of value.

Deliberately excluded from what follows are science and technology.* Material things and technology have shaped our culture but are not of it. The spread of prosperity has made culture democratic; the revolution in communications has influenced its content. In the past, culture was mainly, though not exclusively, transmitted through books; today it is through cinema, television and the internet. These are the products of a technology unknown in previous times. This makes a difference. The written word allows continuous engagement with ideas. Dispersed images and sounds make for dispersed minds. They have made the British even less receptive to ideas than they used to be.

Have morals in Britain got better or worse over the last hundred years? Has taste been improved or 'dumbed down'? These questions are impossible to answer conclusively. But the

---

* The distinction here is between culture and civilisation. Civilisation refers to the total way of life of a group of countries, as in 'Western civilisation', which includes its material and scientific conditions. Culture is particular to a people, whereas science and technology are, in principle, universal languages. The English remain distinctly English and the French French even though they have roughly the same standard of living and share the same science and technology. This is because the English speak English and the French speak French, and these different languages express and reflect different customs, tastes, ways of thinking. The mid-twentieth-century debate on the 'two cultures' – literary and scientific – between C. P. Snow and F. R. Leavis was therefore misnamed. Leavis was talking about culture; Snow about science, Leavis about the particular language of the English, Snow about the universal language of science. They were talking at cross-purposes. See C. P. Snow, *The Two Cultures* (Part I 1959, Part II added 1964) and F. R. Leavis, *Two Cultures? The Significance of C. P. Snow* (1962 lecture, first published 2013). Stefan Collini discusses Leavis's response in 'Leavis versus Snow', *Guardian*, 16 August 2013.

idea of 'cultivation', with its corollary idea of the setting of bounds, limitation, gives a basis for judgement. A nation's culture is rooted in its historical sense. Over the century, the British lost the strong sense of who they were: they suffered an identity crisis. Inherited moral rules were loosened; inherited artistic canons emasculated. This left individual choice as the one acceptable measure of value. My thesis is that contemporary liberalism, by defining culture in purely individualistic terms, has misunderstood the relationship between culture and society. How much difference this has made to the lived culture of the British is a matter of dispute. Specifically, the nature and effect of the so-called 'cultural watershed' of the 1950s and 60s is debated between historians. When all the dust has settled it may well be found that less has changed, for better or worse, than the apostles or critics of those decades supposed. Nations are not easy to shift from their historical moorings.

In the Victorian scheme, the church regulated morals, the upper class regulated taste and manners, and the idea of 'Britishness' wrapped them up in a national identity, which bound together the classes as well as the nations of the British Isles in a 'British' character – John Bull, never defined, instantly recognisable. The Victorian ideal of the 'Christian gentleman' neatly combined moral, societal and national values. Morals were not a matter of 'taste'; taste was a matter of morals; and morality was connected to what it meant to be British. As in all societies, there was a place for bohemianism, where the rules did not apply. But there was a common thread given by history.

By the end of the twentieth century, morals had become secularised, taste was a matter of opinion, 'gentleman' a condescending obituary description, and the national identity – forged over centuries of warfare and imperial exertion – had become ironic: the Union Jack stuck on a pair of pants rather than on the masthead. For many of the older generation, Britain became unrecognisable.

The forces of change

How did this change come about? Stefan Collini argues that affluence, commerce and technology deprived the elites of their power to 'police' the tastes of the masses.[1] This neat summary contains much truth. Prosperity meant that the common people had access to many more cultural goods than before; commerce made the individual sovereign over their choices; technology increased the supply and changed the nature of what was offered. Technical changes – particularly the invention of the pill – cut the link between sex and procreation. By the late twentieth century Britain had become a *business* society and business knows only the consumer. But Collini's summary omits the role of the elites, especially the 'thinking' classes, in changing popular consciousness. It was the elites who led the retreat from Victorianism. On the one hand, unlike the French elites, they abandoned to the market their claim to police the tastes of the masses. On the other hand, they actively promoted a moral and legislative programme which aimed to displace the common people's view on such things as religion, empire, race, immigration, gender, sexual orientation, crime and punishment. What was sauce for the goose became sauce for the gander. Also, by championing an alienating modernism in architecture, abstraction in painting, and atonality in music, the cultural elite lost its authority to shape mass taste.

The decline of religion

The main driver of moral change in twentieth-century Britain was the decline of religion. Religion, like the empire, has become embarrassing to the late twentieth-century mind, belief in God being regarded as a sign of mental incompetence. Therefore there is a tendency to write it out of twentieth-century British history. But this is bad history. The Christian religion remained a force, albeit a declining one, in personal and public affairs for the first half of the century. Although they did not go to church except for baptism, marriage and funerals, most people knew the Bible and sent their children to Sunday school. This connection to religion disappeared in the second half of the last century. It is what is meant by secularisation: the decline of religion as a source of moral thinking and artistic inspiration. Nineteenth-century Britain was a religious society, with expanding secular bridgeheads; twentieth-century Britain was a secular society with shrinking religious fragments. There were some signs of a religious revival at the century's end, as secular creeds lost their lustre.

The decline of religion is partly captured in figures. Measured by worship, the British were not particularly religious in the nineteenth century and became less so as the twentieth century wore on. The numbers record the drop in church membership and church attendance, most striking in inner cities and council estates, less in the countryside, suburbs and small towns; more among the unskilled working class than among the middle class, less among women than among men. There is a gradual fall on all these measures until 1960, and then a collapse. All of a sudden Britain stopped being a religious society. Catholicism bucked the trend but only because its congregations were swelled by working-class Irish immigrants. The figures also register, late in the twentieth century, the arrival of new Pentecostal religions in the wake of immigration from the Caribbean and Africa. They also record the feminisation of Christianity – by 1994, 13 per cent of ordinands and 57 per cent of missionaries were women. Whether this reflects a shortage of male supply or an increase in female demand is hard to say. Occasional church attendance – at Christmas and Easter and for baptisms and weddings – is still quite common; 50 per cent of the British are classified as 'notional' or 'implicit' Christians, but the majority have no regular connection with the institutions of religion, Christian or otherwise. Churches, deprived of their congregations, have been turned into cafes. Religion has become a leisure choice.[2]

What brought about the decline of religion? The standard explanation is urbanisation. Nineteenth-century Britain was already the most urban society in Europe, and experienced the largest recorded growth in the size of cities. Christianity, mainly in the form of Methodism, was inculcated in the northern towns early in the nineteenth century as social and factory discipline. But despite Victorian efforts, church-building, and therefore churchgoing, never kept pace with the growth of the urban population. By 1900, a large fraction of the population was already 'unchurched'. In the twentieth century, the number of church buildings declined from 13.8 per 10,000 people to 8.2. This was faster than the decline in congregations per church, from 155 to 122 (41 per cent as against 21 per cent), suggesting that the British would have been more churchgoing had facilities been provided for them to worship.[3] The result was to create a state of 'believing without belonging'.[4] Religion, in effect, became privatised, its unfocused spirituality – not to mention credulity – no longer restrained by the discipline of regular worship, or linked to prescription of behaviour. The Nonconformist sects, being less of a 'church' than the Church of England, suffered most from the privatisation of belief, the Methodists and Congregationalists being the chief losers of both buildings and congregations.

But sociological explanations of religion's decline cannot explain the loss of belief itself. Religious beliefs are not just socially useful habits which fall away when they are no longer required. The decline of religion was elite-driven, with the conversion of an influential fraction of the intellectual class to atheism. Whereas the Victorians had promoted Christianity as a civilising force, at home and abroad, influential twentieth-century thinkers like Bertrand Russell, H. G. Wells and Bernard Shaw attacked religion as 'superstition', and the churches as the main obstacle to the rational treatment of social–moral questions such as birth control, divorce, homosexuality, the role of women and so on; a line of attack going back to the Philosophical Radicals of the nineteenth century. Twentieth-century analytic philosophy was aggressively atheist, with religious belief denounced as a species of 'nonsense'. Thus the repudiation of religion was part of the intellectual demand for the reconstruction of society on 'rational' lines. The result was a cascade of 'permissive' legislation in the 1950s and 60s. In the second half of the twentieth century, state education was secularised with the abolition of collective acts of Christian worship. As a result the door to the rich cultural heritage of Protestant Christianity – the Bible, prayer book, order of service and Wesleyan hymnary – became closed to most schoolchildren. The expulsion of religion from education was actively promoted by the Department of

Education. What 'unchurching' and atheism did jointly was to undermine the authority of religion. Lives were no longer lived in the shadow of God; religious experience (or inspiration) ceased to shape the moral and artistic life of the country. The Christian frame of reference dissolved.

However, science only partly inherited the space left vacant by religion. Science weakened the function of religion as 'solace' for earthly suffering as medicine pushed mortality ever further into the future; machines have helped to abolish the misery associated with extreme poverty. But science lost its status as a comprehensive replacement for religion. Communism was the most prominent of the several pseudo-scientific gods that failed.

What the older generation saw as liberation from religious mumbo-jumbo turned into new forms of credulity. Most people remain superstitious; most still believe in ghosts. Statistics encounter widespread scepticism. Christianity may be, as Frederic Raphael says, 'too demanding for the English', who have become 'so accustomed to mouthing what they please that harder tack would break their teeth'.[5] Anthropologist Roger Sandall calls the 'New Age' religions which sprouted at the end of the twentieth century 'Stone Age beliefs with a digital upgrade'.[6]

The heat also went out of religious politics. British politics was never divided along church–state lines because Anglicanism was the state religion. Nineteenth-century political parties were divided between church and chapel, with the Tories representing Anglicanism, and the Liberals the Nonconformist and Dissenting sects. Political language was heavily flavoured with biblical quotations, and God was often the clinching argument in political debate. Once the denominations, including Catholics and Jews, had been freed from their civil disabilities, a process completed by the third quarter of the nineteenth century, British politics became secular. Class replaced religion as the denominator of political allegiance and generator of political programmes. The decline of Nonconformity and the Liberal Party went together, with Labour taking over much of the Nonconformist vote. The political parties of the twentieth century inherited religious memberships but not religious causes. It became bad form to refer to God in public.

This did not happen all at once. In the first half of the twentieth century religion prospered. As A. N. Wilson says, there were far more interesting scholars, administrators, bishops and priests than in the Victorian age – people such as 'G. K. Chesterton, T. S. Eliot, Graham Greene, Evelyn Waugh, John Betjeman, C. S. Lewis. Many of the most popular writers, such as crime writers, were Christian. Church music flourished, and Church architecture.'[7] The Archbishop of Canterbury in 1936, Cosmo Lang, claimed to speak for the nation in his famous broadcast condemning Edward VIII for his desire to marry the American divorcee Wallis Simpson. Britain is still not allowed a Catholic monarch.

Religious allegiance proved most resilient where it expressed national or group identity. Northern Ireland remained politically divided along sectarian lines, and this was true in some parts of Britain, notably Merseyside and Clydeside, where the Protestant working class – 'Angels in Marble' Disraeli had called them – voted Conservative, and Irish workers, mostly Catholic, voted Labour. In Liverpool, the cry of 'No popery' resonated till the 1950s, ensuring the Conservatives local dominance. Nonconformity defined Welsh national identity, as did Judaism that of the 120,000 Jewish immigrants who fled the Russian pogroms to settle in

Britain in the early 1900s. With the large recent Muslim immigration into Britain, religion may again become one of the flags under which nationalist politics sails.

The Salman Rushdie affair in 1989 signalled the revival of sectarian politics, as the multicultural model of settlement favoured in Britain, unlike the assimilationist one of France, encouraged a mosque culture which connected British Muslims to their co-religionists abroad. The issue of state support for 'faith' schools, which last disturbed politics in the 1900s, returned in the 1990s. However, religion is unlikely to revive as a commanding public philosophy. In the past it provided spiritual cement for a quasi-military, hierarchical society. It has little appeal for a society of spectators and consumers, each with his or her tastes.

A great deal of Christian ethics survived in secular form. It could hardly be otherwise: Britain was no longer Christian, but it was a Christianised country. If Britain has become, as many claim, a more humane society, this reflects the influence of Christianity, though it has been more the forgiving, 'love thy neighbour' Christianity of Jesus than the judgemental Christianity of the Old Testament. The Anglican Church – the nation's dominant religious affiliation – was transformed from being the 'Tory Party at prayer' into an engine of social reform, in the course of it shedding much of its theology. Protestantism fed the secular creeds. The idea of duty was strongly ingrained in the Balliol-educated leaders of the ruling class, under the long-lingering Platonist influence of that college's master, Benjamin Jowett. The habit of thrift was considered an important support for the market economy until it became a victim of the welfare state, Keynesian economics, and instant credit. Labour famously owed more to Methodism than to Marxism: the socialist vision of secular salvation was simply the transposition of millennial longings on to a secular plane. The long history of Protestant–Catholic wars provided the British with a ready-made anti-popery narrative into which to place its twentieth-century conflicts with Germany. The conviction that the Brussels bureaucracy is a papacy in secular disguise waxes strong in politicians and publicists devoid of obvious religious belief. Moral interventionism in Kosovo and Iraq is secularised missionary zeal.

Although the atheistic twentieth-century Bloomsbury group renounced the sexual morals of its ancestor Clapham Sect – including the Victorian horror of homosexuality – it fully retained its Puritan iconoclasm. These atheists held atheistic convictions with all the passion of true believers, and saw it as a moral duty to blaspheme as frequently as possible. The secular state is full of vicars and evangelists, preaching secular virtue at home and abroad.

The collapse of deference

Victorian society was hierarchical; at the top of the hierarchy of deference stood the aristocracy. It was a patriarchal society, with women being subordinate to men at all levels, and children being subordinate to their parents. Like religious culture, aristocratic culture was both high and low. Aristocracy was an ideal of learning, manners and leisure which was, at the same time, closely connected with the common life and feeling of the countryside. It was about having good taste in books, painting, music, furniture, clothes. It involved knowing about the classics and not knowing about science; it involved country pursuits like riding, hunting, shooting and fishing. It was not elevated, but it was genuine, because it was organically connected with the life of the countryside.

The real, but limited, openness of the rural social system also gave 'bettering oneself' a cultural, not just an economic, meaning. It was not only a matter of getting richer, but of adopting the manners and tastes of the class above. At the top of the ladder of aspiration was that of the 'gentleman', and the public-school system was designed to turn out 'Christian gentlemen'. Culture was a badge of material success. So social hierarchy readily translated into cultural hierarchy.

This cultural transmission belt collapsed in the course of the twentieth century together with the political authority of the landed class. Material improvement raced ahead of cultural enrichment. This is the basis of the charge of 'dumbing down'. Indeed, there was something of a reversal as the well born found it convenient to adopt plebeian camouflage.

Alasdair MacIntyre argues that cultural authority can exist only in a community in which there is an agreed way of doing things; it presupposes prior acceptance of common standards. It is embodied in the leaders of the society, but they are followed because they are in important aspects of feeling and experience at one with the people. This shared way of life was already eroded in the nineteenth century; it disappeared in the twentieth, with the countryside reduced to minor dimensions, and with the society of ranks giving way to the society of classes. Where standards of value are in flux, the only unifying force is money.[8] The capture of culture by the market was made possible by the disappearance of ways of life and habits of thought which had sustained traditional culture. Culture became a market brand dreamt up by entrepreneurs, advertisers and satirists.

Deference survived in specialised institutions such as the armed forces and in mixed-class spectator sports like cricket and tennis with their division into amateurs ('Gentlemen') who played for fun and professionals ('Players') who played for money. National Service, which ran from the Second World War to 1960, epitomised the view of society as a hierarchical structure, with its ranks of officers, non-commissioned officers and squaddies. Sergeants were the backbone of the British Army, just as butlers were the backbone of great houses. Both were often cynical about their masters, but devoted to the institutions which they served. In cricket, retired professionals were first allowed into the MCC as 'honorary members' in 1949; the annual Gentlemen versus Players match was not abolished till 1962, with the ending of amateur status. It was a sign of changing times when Yorkshire's Len Hutton became the first 'player' to captain England in 1953 (though when he first entered the Members' enclosure at Lords he was greeted in total silence). Football went through the same passage. In the first half of the twentieth century, it was working-class players from the north and Scotland who were usually professional, while in the south, middle-class amateurs were still common. Professional football was one of the few jobs which carried a maximum wage, which was only removed in 1961 by the threat of a strike by the Professional Footballers' Association. The distinction between professional and amateur footballers was finally dropped in 1976 as amateurism withered. Now professional football is one of the highest paid of all professions, its stars commanding stellar salaries.

Attempts to find replacements for vanished forms of cultural authority foundered on the absence of a political and social stratum in which the culture of the nation could plausibly be said to be embodied. 'Tory democracy' was an urban version of the rural myth. When Lord Randolph Churchill talked about 'the aristocracy and working class united in the

indissoluble bonds of a common immorality', he was expressing the relaxed Tory attitude to the pleasures of the people;
Tories were the party of the pub as well as the church. Lord
Hailsham said of them: 'The simplest of them prefer fox-hunting, the wisest religion.'[9] In more sober vein, Tory democracy
emphasised a common patriotism uniting rulers and ruled,
with a corollary duty of the rulers to care for the people. As a
political myth, 'Tory democracy' continued to resonate till
mid-century. It sustained the Conservative position in
Scotland and northern England; it eased Conservative acceptance of the welfare state and Keynesian economics; Harold
Macmillan was its last (almost) authentic spokesman.
Thatcher's 'popular capitalism' of the 1980s tapped working-
class acquisitiveness but had little in common with the older
Tory democracy, except in its prejudices.

Early in the last century, writers of the left hoped that
working-class culture would become the national culture of a
true democracy. If the British owed their 'ancient liberties' to
the aristocracy and middle class, they owed their democracy
to the working class, especially to the nineteenth-century
Chartists and the early Labour Party. Writers such as Richard
Hoggart, Raymond Williams and R. H. Tawney believed that
in a socialist Britain the communal traditions of the working
class could provide an egalitarian alternative to the paternalism of the aristocracy and the individualism of the middle
class. Hoggart railed against the Americanisation (i.e. commercialisation) of culture as cutting off young working-class
males from their roots. He hated the Teddy boys of the 1950s
flocking to dance halls and milk-bars, and lounging around
jukeboxes. He objected to the trivia of the newspapers not
because it prevented people being highbrow, but from becoming 'wise in their own way'. Working-class experience,

suggested Raymond Williams, could offer 'ways of living that could be extended to the whole society'.[10] The Christian socialist R. H. Tawney saw in working-class fellowship the kernel of an egalitarian social order. What these and other writers saw as praiseworthy about working-class culture was its stress on solidarity, its stubborness, its earthiness, its passion for education.

The idealistic expectations for a working-class culture took little heed of the reality of working-class existence and the changes in it wrought by affluence. Solidarity – in any case fractured among competing crafts – was largely a product of poverty, and escape from poverty was what workers wanted. Education and collective self-help might be a means to this. But with improved real wages following the Second World War, workers rejected the Austerity Britain projected by Labour. Thirteen years of Conservative rule, following the defeat of Labour in 1951, inaugurated the consumer society. Workers now travelled to work in cars and shopped in supermarkets. Bingo halls replaced trade-union libraries. The sociability of pubs, working men's clubs, mechanics' institutes, of two-up two-down terraced houses in industrial towns where everyone knew each other and children played in the streets, gave way to a privatised world of concrete housing estates with improved mod cons and TV-centred home entertainment. Guaranteed full employment after 1945 dampened working-class enthusiasm for education, with youngsters anxious to leave school as quickly as possible.[11] All the working-class institutions devoted to sociability and self-improvement went into terminal decline.[12] The last stand of working-class culture ended with the defeat of the coal miners in 1985: the Durham Miners' Galas continue, minus the mines. What had been the working class became avid consumers of commercial entertainment.

This left the upper middle class as the sole potential social embodiment of a national culture. At the end of the nineteenth century, liberals expected deference to aristocrats to be replaced by deference to Oxbridge-educated professionals. Middle-class elites saw themselves as 'disinterested', subservient neither to aristocracy nor democracy, but bringing the light of reason and evidence to bear on social and economic problems. This seemed a plausible, and progressive, evolution and in one sense has come to pass. The Keynesian welfare state was built by middle-class professionals, claiming authority by virtue of superior education and special knowledge. Most of the economic, constitutional and political reforms of the last century have been initiated by this intellectual class. They governed Britain better than the old aristocracy did, but never established a comparable cultural authority. Their most serious attempt to do so, Reith's BBC, foundered on the decay of middle-class confidence in its own values. The middle class never really believed in its right to cultural rule.

Perry Anderson has attributed this to the fact that Britain never had a 'bourgeois' revolution, as in eighteenth-century France. The aristocracy continued to command the heights of social and cultural esteem. Thus British intellectuals never saw themselves as a meritocratic elite, but rather as a part of the 'Establishment', whose natural habitat was the colleges of Oxford and Cambridge.[13] This picture can be overdrawn. There *was* a thriving bourgeois culture in the nineteenth century, based on a radical criticism of privilege. Noel Annan called it the 'intellectual aristocracy'. But it failed to reproduce itself. The real aristocracy tore the guts out of bourgeois radicalism with the lure of gentlemanly status.

The fact that the middle class never became the top class is important. Its haunted place in the middle of the social system

bred continuous status anxiety. Torn between its social aspirations and fear of being reduced to the ranks, the middle class
set out to make itself as culturally different as possible from
the classes below, in accent, education, taste and lifestyle. As
John Carey has noted, 'fear of the masses' permeated literary
culture from the end of the nineteenth century. No doubt he
exaggerates when he claims that the elites deliberately set out
to make reading 'too difficult for the masses to understand'.[14]
Nevertheless, culture, as historian Ross McKibbin writes,
became the acceptable, apolitical battleground for the class
war.[15] It was better to have an exclusive culture than a shared
culture. The passing of the Edwardian music hall, that
'intriguing mix of high and popular culture', where opera and
ballet would mingle with animal acts and 'nigger minstrels',
marked the growing separation of culture into class compart-
ments.[16] High culture was for the educated; low culture for
the proles. Middlebrow taste expanded with the growth of the
middle class, but it was swamped by the products of
the TV-dominated entertainment industry.

If the middle-class intelligentsia had a cultural ideal it was
that of Bloomsbury's world of beauty, learning, friendship.
But without roots in the countryside, the military, or the
sports of the field, Bloomsbury culture was much too esoteric
to serve as the foundation of a democratic culture. Its connection was to bohemianism not to ordinary life.

In quantitative terms, the British are not only more prosperous but much better educated than they were a hundred
years ago. At the turn of the last century most pupils left
school at eleven: today compulsory education goes up to sixteen (about to become seventeen) and most teenagers continue
in education till eighteen. In the 1960s, only 5 per cent of
eighteen-year-olds went on to university: today it is 40 per

cent. The proportion of girls in higher education has also risen steadily. State-financed expansion of education – including higher education – was justified on utilitarian grounds: improved educational opportunity was needed to unlock the human resources Britain required to compete in the modern world. Some hopes of the reformers have been realised. The spread of education has made Britain more culturally egalitarian; it has also enlarged access to elite positions. What has suffered is the traditional concept of education itself. This is what the writer Kingsley Amis had in mind when, in response to the plan to expand higher education, he remarked in 1963 'More means worse.' Taken literally this is nonsense: it cannot make matters worse to supply educational opportunities which had never existed. But the traditional purpose of university education was to elevate the mind and spirit. The redefinition of the university's mission as being to invest in the 'human capital' needed by the economy was never going to create the cultural ladder anticipated by reformers.

School education became the decisive encounter in the cultural class war. The chance to use state education to create an autonomous middle-class culture was lost when Robert Morant, author of the Education Act of 1902, decreed that 'the future pattern of English culture must not come from Leeds and West Ham but from Eton and Winchester'.[17] Instead of building up the grammar schools as an independent cultural institution, successive governments were content for them to be appendages of the Victorian fee-paying public schools (themselves set up to ape aristocratic culture), educating office clerks. This led aspiring middle-class parents to prefer even bad private schools, which had higher social status and turned out pupils with the 'right' accent. The end of empire in the 1960s gave a chance to rid the grammar schools of their aristocratic trappings. Instead, most of them were abolished and absorbed into all-ability comprehensives, which, with few exceptions, inherited the low cultural aspirations for their pupils of the working-class secondary-modern schools.

The failure of any class to define a national cultural ideal made it easy to whip up resentment against 'elite' culture. At the start of the twenty-first century, the Conservative leader, David Cameron, a rare Old Etonian at the top of British politics, was driven to asking plaintively why a privileged background should 'disqualify you from talking about issues'.[18] This pinpoints the cultural distance Britain had travelled in the twentieth century.

The decline of Britishness

It was Protestantism that forged Britain into a recognisable nation during the eighteenth century. Recent historians have familiarised us with the notion that the 'British nation' was a myth, born of the long struggle between Protestant England and Catholic Europe, a myth which was associated with the expansion of the English Crown throughout the British Isles and also overseas. In extreme form this thesis has it that the three 'nations' of Ireland, Scotland and Wales were colonies of England, and 'Britishness' was a colonial myth invented to disguise the reality of their subordination. One implication of this perspective is that Britain has long been a culturally diverse society – in 1989 Professor Hugh Kearney identified eight cultures – held together by a national project. Once this project dissolved there might be nothing to hold 'Britain' together.

Unlike other European countries which struggled to establish national frontiers, the twentieth-century British never had to define a specifically 'British' identity against others.

The identity came with the job: what the British had was patriotism, not nationalism. Britain was England; and England was the centre of a world empire. The smaller nations of 'Britain' partook of the radiance of England, which submerged memories of their separate nationalities. With empire gone, the European Union offering wider links, and 'Britain' no longer a unique success story, union no longer seemed to offer the same advantages. From the late 1960s, the submerged national cultures started to assert themselves in Northern Ireland, Scotland and Wales. But there was no specifically 'English' nation to assert, and patriotism was at a discount.

The end of empire is thus a particularly significant event in the dissolution of 'British' culture. Victorian moral standards were closely linked to the maintenance of Britain's position as a world power. Empire required an imperial ruling class, born into and bred for the job of ruling, and the production (and reproduction) of such a class was the chief aim of the Victorian public school. The code of the officer and gentleman, with its high sense of duty and its repression of personal feeling, was the morality of the ruler. Although few Britons worked in or visited the empire, elite values serving the vocation of imperial rule had a disproportionate influence on the life of the nation. With the liquidation of empire in the aftermath of the Second World War this moral code lost its hold on the ruling class. Just as the elites had upheld traditional morals, so their repudiation of these spread down the social scale. 'Letting it all hang out' replaced the stiff upper lip.

By displacing British power from the centre of the story, imperial demise required the discovery of new ways of being British. The endless discussion about what it means to be 'British' or 'English' testifies to the loss of the old securities: no one bothered to talk about this in the first half of the century, because everyone knew what being British meant. Popular culture was one expression of the search for a new measuring rod, the 'soft power' of football and pop music, compensating for the waning of Britain's 'hard power'. Another expression of lost identity was the attempt to create an enlarged British identity – a 'Londonistan', so to speak – from the mingling of races and religions created by mass immigration from the 'New Commonwealth', most obviously in music, food, fashion and drugs. A third expression of Britain's identity crisis was the anguished debate about its relationship to Europe and the United States. In one sense, Britain 'joined' Europe, but its political, popular and business culture became increasingly Americanised, especially after Thatcher.

The collapse of 'old' Britishness was not unresisted. Britain was linked to its empire by extensive British settlements in the 'white dominions', most of working-class origin. Among all social groups there were 'diehards' who resisted the dissolution of empire in the name of Britishness, not imperialism. Others who upheld some earlier version of 'what it means to be British' were coal miners with their patriotic socialism, and the football hooligans of Thatcherism, whose drunkenness and violence were a pathetic attempt to display the virile qualities which had supposedly made Britain great. Other losers included the white Rhodesian settlers, the Northern Irish Protestants, and the dockers and Smithfield meat porters who in 1968 marched in support of Enoch Powell to resist ethnic-minority immigration. They were deemed obsolete and retrograde. What they shared was a reminiscence of a Britishness which had existed in the mind but had never had to be defined.

The secular replacement – individualism

The decline of hierarchy led to the triumph of individualism. Deviant tastes in sexuality and fashion, hitherto tolerated in bohemian circles or as marks of aristocratic eccentricity, were championed as liberating possibilities for all. Large areas of the moral and artistic life, hitherto bound by custom and rules, became matters of personal preference. The individual was put at the centre of a picture without a frame.

Individualism came in three different guises: utilitarianism, self-expression and human rights. Utilitarianism was the main influence on legislation; Jeremy Bentham was its nineteenth-century philosopher. It was a doctrine of consequences, with God removed from his position as final judge. Social policy must be judged by results, expressed as a quantitative balance of the happiness and pain they produced. Bentham's twentieth-century heirs set themselves the task of tearing up society's organic connections and replacing them with mechanical joints.

There is a tension in utilitarianism between laissez-faire and regulation. Nineteenth-century utilitarian arguments favoured laissez-faire policy because utilitarians believed that individuals were the best judges of their own interests, and social and political controls were in the hands of the privileged and prejudiced. This bias towards laissez-faire reflected the influence of economics. Economic activity, argued the economists, should be left to self-interested individuals disciplined by the market. Self-interest without access to credit could be an austere doctrine. It dictated frugality, or postponement of immediate satisfaction, for the sake of long-run benefits – an interesting survival of theology. Nevertheless, by setting up the market, and therefore money, as the sole standard of value, economics pushed individualism towards consumerism.

At the same time, utilitarians recognised that self-interested behaviour by individuals could, through selfishness, short-sightedness or ignorance, produce bad consequences or 'harms' for third parties. Under the inspiration of the great Victorian reformer Edwin Chadwick, public-health boards were set up to clean sewers to prevent epidemics; the first food-adulteration Act dates from 1860. 'We will not be bullied into health' thundered The Times, to no avail. Economists developed the doctrine of 'externalities' or 'spillover' effects to justify subsidising 'goods' like education and taxing 'bads' like alcohol consumption. The doctrine of the declining marginal utility of money (a rich person gets less satisfaction from an extra pound or dollar than a poor person) formed the intellectual basis of redistributive taxation. However, where individual action or taste did not produce measurable harms to third parties – unmeasurable harms were ruled out – individual preferences should decide outcomes.

This non-interference argument lay behind the legalisation of suicide, of homosexual acts between consenting adults, of divorce by mutual consent. On the other hand, the harm criterion gave the late twentieth-century British state the warrant to outlaw sexually, religiously, or racially abusive language and behaviour on the ground that it might conduce to violence. It abolished fox-hunting with dogs, ostensibly on the basis of cruelty to the fox (though a stronger motive may have been puritan hostility to the pleasure the sport gave to the rural toffs who supposedly did the hunting). Legislative curbs on 'antisocial (though not necessarily illegal) behaviour' proliferated under Tony Blair's New Labour. Capital punishment was defended till the 1950s on the ground that it deterred murder. When evidence seemed to show that it had no such deterrent effect, it was abolished.

A second replacement for hierarchy was self-expression. The offshoot of the nineteenth-century Romantic movement, expressive individualism became the main influence on life-styles. It originated in the view that every nation and epoch has its own genius. The twentieth century transferred the Romantic ideal of the community to the individual.

Expressive individualism was a revolt against the artificiality of rules, conventions, manners. If self-expression and authenticity are good, it is wrong to repress any parts of them for the sake of hollow social convention. Expressive individualism stood for freedom of personal taste – I don't know about art, but I know what I like; freedom of personal behaviour – I have a right to express my personality; freedom from expert tutelage – my opinions are as valid as anyone else's; and, in the arts, the privileging of 'creativity' and 'inspiration' over rules and skills.

Expressive individualism was the credo of the permissive society of the 1960s. In a fine book, the political philosopher David Marquand has traced its effects on public life. They were summed up in the feminist slogan 'the personal is the political'. Marquand wrote: 'Increasingly we demand of our rulers not just that they be competent at ruling but that they be authentic human beings as well: that they appear before us unmasked.'[19] In the older culture, hypocrisy, which ran through all classes, was a defence of privacy: the revolt against the artificial amounted to abolition of privacy. Everything must be allowed to 'hang out'. Marquand also points out that the liberated individual of the 1960s was first cousin to the Thatcherite consumer of the 1980s, with authenticity branded in clothes and music.

Straddling the two domains, and overlapping with older moralities, was the doctrine of human rights. The philosophy of natural rights – rights which adhere inalienably to individuals by virtue of their being human – originated in the natural-law discussions of the medieval schoolmen. John Locke's right to life, liberty and property was the secular expression of this discussion. These are rights which cannot be alienated by government or society. From the 1960s onwards, individual rights started mutating into human rights. Human rights are claims of groups for legal protection and advancement: the right to national self-determination is the chief example. In such cases, the claim to group rights – such as the claim to equal respect – can be seen as a translated claim to individual rights, on the ground that respect for the group is a necessary condition of respect for its individual members. In twentieth-century Britain the claims for gender, racial and sexual equality were increasingly couched in the language of human rights.

The distinction between utilitarianism and expressive individualism is chiefly a matter of domain. Utilitarianism can accommodate expressive individualism on the assumption – made by Mill, though not by Bentham – that individuals are the best judges of their own interests. So to maximise liberty (within the harm constraint) is to maximise general happiness. This, in a nutshell, is the argument of Mill's hugely influential treatise *On Liberty*, and the principle behind the social reforms of the 1960s.

The point about these replacement philosophies was that they undermined existing cultural authority without replacing it with anything. This amounted to surrendering culture to money. This capitulation went further in Britain than in other rich countries because of the relative weakness of the British state and private philanthropy as supports for culture, in contrast to continental Europe and the United States respectively.

Never before in human history has the care of culture

been entrusted so wholly to individual preferences and market forces. The experiment is not over; its final fruits have not been harvested. The most that a historian, with the past as his guide, can surmise is that the experiment is unlikely to end well. Individualism is bound to undermine itself because it destroys the social basis of individuality. It therefore leads inexorably to the regulated (and over-regulated) state. What starts off as an attack on irrational restraints on individual freedom – those dictated by religion, privilege and prejudice – ends up as a gilded cage of consumption policed by utility.

By their fruits: the three views

There are three views about what has happened to British culture in the twentieth century. These are, roughly, that the changes in British culture have been for the better, that they have been for the worse, and that much less has changed than both optimists and pessimists believe.

Moral panics

A typical expression of the first view is contained in a 2014 edition of the *Big Issue*. Its editor John Bird looks back on the 'bad old times' of the 1950s and 60s, when disabled people were called 'spastics', when women and girls were simply regarded as sex fodder, when foreigners were despised, when children could be beaten on public transport. 'I remember all these times, and the racism and classism – the anti-humanity of it all – and thank the Lord that we got out of it.' Two things changed it. First, 'the liberals took over the running of the madhouse. They started to allow more things than the oppressive Toryism that ruled . . . And then middle-class film-makers and TV writers and directors started to make films and documentaries about us just as we changed.' Second 'was our embrace of consumerism . . . We became customers, and suddenly coppers, teachers, magistrates, shopkeepers and politicians seemed to realise our evocative power – our money.' The good old days, he concludes, 'were not that good, and I am so glad we are where we are. But we've still got a shit lot to do to make this society more just and free.'[20]

The argument here is that a combination of liberal agenda and money has made British society non-judgemental, to the great benefit of all except bigots.

The counter-argument is that non-judgementalism is precisely what is wrong with our culture. Its critics make a crucial distinction between non-judgementalism and tolerance. A civilised society should be tolerant of deviance, without believing that all tastes and lifestyles are equally good. Non-judgementalism, the argument goes, undermines the moral frameworks necessary for individual flourishing.

Critics of 'our way of life' fasten on the decay of marriage. The indicators of the fall of marriage are legion: fewer marriages, more divorces, more fleeting liaisons, more children born out of wedlock; as, supposedly, are their fruits: more sexual promiscuity, more child abuse, more crime, more violence, more hooliganism, more drunkenness, more drug-taking.

After a big increase in the marriage rate in mid-century, the number getting married fell from 426,200 in 1972 to 276,960 in 2000.[21] The mean age of marriage has also risen, married women under twenty-five being rare. Unlike in former times, delayed marriage is preceded, or replaced entirely, by cohabitation. The proportion between twenty-five and thirty-four cohabiting in the late 1990s exceeded the number of those married. There has been a startling increase in the number of divorces: the average per year in England and Wales rose from 812 in 1901–5 to 141,140 in 2000, with the biggest jump following the Marriage Act of 1969 which introduced the principle of no-fault divorce. Since 1993 there has been a decline in numbers of divorces, but this has been because fewer people have been getting married.

Surveys of sexual activity (obviously an imperfect measure) show it is now higher than ever. In 1974–5, 42 per cent of single girls aged sixteen to nineteen claimed to have had sexual experience (but only 17 per cent in Scotland). The figure was well over 60 per cent at the end of the century.

In recent years, moral panic has focused on the increase in births to single, generally teenage, mothers. Having stayed broadly the same – at about 5 per cent – from Elizabeth I to the start of Elizabeth II, the percentage of children born out of wedlock rose to 9 per cent in 1976 and to 40 per cent by 2001 – higher in Wales and Scotland than in England, lower in Northern Ireland. Eighty-eight per cent of teenagers who give birth do so outside marriage, but many older women also do this (20 per cent of women over thirty). In absolute numbers 238,100 of the 594,600 births registered in the UK in 2001 were outside marriage. In the past, extramarital conceptions usually led to marriages; by the 1980s most ended up either in abortion or illegitimate birth and the same is true today.

The facts are not in dispute; what is disputed by optimists and pessimists, or progressives and conservatives, is the evaluation of the facts. Is the breakdown of the traditional family a social disaster, or an evolution towards a more spacious, humane interpretation of family life? Two views have held the field. On the one hand, it is claimed that family breakdown is the effect of changed economic and technological conditions: the greater participation of women in the labour market has made the traditional two-member family, with man as breadwinner, obsolete; women's commitment to careers has lessened their disposition to have children; contraception enables them to control the number of partners and rate at which they have children, and there are more social services to look after such children as couples, cohabiting or not, do have. In short, men and women have less need, and therefore less desire, than they did before to construct a monogamous married life together, so why should they? On the other hand, the declinists argue that the effect of the decline in traditional families on parenting has been disastrous; and that much of the decline could have been prevented by more generous tax treatment for married couples. They would also claim that technical fixes, like the pill, cannot healthily compensate for the decay of commitment.

The support of Britons for the institution of marriage is stronger than their behaviour would indicate. 70 per cent believe that it is better for parents to be married, and 57 per cent are even happy for governments to encourage marriage as the 'normal' state. This is markedly different from the 'non-judgemental' public discourse on the subject, which claims that marriage is only one of a number of family choices. This suggests that some part of moral behaviour is conditioned by the law, and would be different if the law were different.

Conservatives attribute the rise in the crime rate to the breakdown in family life: children are not 'nurtured' properly. In Edwardian Britain it was widely believed that crime in the twentieth century would yield to material and moral progress. In fact, the number of indictable offences per 1,000 people grew 37.5 times, from 2.4 in 1900 to 90 by the end of the century, with the biggest rise occurring in the last third of that century. Reported crime rates reached their peak in 1992 when 110 indictable offences per 1,000 of people were recorded. Violent crimes remained a small proportion of total crimes in the twentieth century, but their proportion more than doubled from 2.4 per 1,000 in 1900 to 5.5 in 2001. Sex offences increased in absolute numbers from 1,582 in 1900 to 35,000 – far more than the increase in population – at the end of the century, but fell as a proportion of all crimes.

There was a similar trend in homicides. In 1900 there were 9.6 homicides* per million people in England and Wales. The number of homicides went down to its lowest level of 6.2 in 1960 and then started to grow. Between the early 1960s and 2001 the number more than doubled to 14.5. This increase started with the abolition of capital punishment in 1965. Prison numbers show the same disproportionate increase. The average prison population in 1900–1 was 16,000. By the end of the century the figure rose to over 65,000, three times the increase in population. There was a significant downward trend only between 1900 and 1915 and in the interwar years. Women prisoners were a falling percentage of the prison population until the 1990s (16 per cent in 1900–1, 2.5 per cent in 1968, 6.1 per cent in 2002).

Police numbers have increased by 300 per cent over the century (as against a 50 per cent growth in population). The rise in police numbers was especially rapid in the 1950s and 60s when the crime rates picked up. Again, it is hard to separate the crime numbers from changing elite attitude to crime and punishment, as reflected in legislation. The public is consistently more punitive than the legislators. Contrary to popular opinion, drunkenness and consumption of alcohol per head decreased slightly over the twentieth century, after

---

* Includes murder, manslaughter and infanticide.

rising sharply in the mid-century years. However, the decline in alcohol consumption was offset by the increase in binge drinking (in 2000, one in four adults, and 42 per cent among 16–24-year-olds, were binge drinkers) and drug-taking. Recreational drug use – a cant phrase suggesting that drug-taking is a leisure choice like ping-pong – increased, partly because more drugs have become available. It is very difficult to measure trends in the production, trafficking and consumption of illicit drugs. Such evidence as exists suggests that drug use increased substantially in the 1970s and 80s, remained comparatively stable in the 1990s and started to decline at the end of the century. The UK followed the US pattern, with the use of cannabis and MDMA increasing in both countries in the 1990s. Cocaine became the drug of choice for the elites in the finance and entertainment industries.

Although there are problems with all the data, the trend seems clear. From the 1960s onwards there were signs of social breakdown, which coincide with liberalising argument and legislation.* By comparison with the century's first fifty years, Britain became a violent and unruly country, and anthropologist Geoffrey Gorer's picture of 'football crowds . . . as orderly as church meetings', and George Orwell's description of 'a gentle-mannered, undemonstrative, law-abiding' people, faded into memory.[22] Conservatives like James Bartholomew blamed the breakdown of morals on the welfare state and its culture of 'entitlements', contrasting the 'sense of honour or duty' portrayed in the film *Brief Encounter*

---

* A correlation tells us nothing about causation. The causative role of changes in legislation on behaviour and social attitudes can reasonably be disputed. The causation may run the other way. Or both permissive legislation and the erosion of moral rules may be related to more general economic and social changes. We are dealing here with a case of multiple causation, which makes cultural history particularly difficult.

(1962) with the adulterous sexual liberation of *Shirley Valentine* (1999). Theodore Dalrymple adds to the indictment the non-judgementalism of the elites.[23]

Moral panic focused increasingly on the Problem of Youth. Young people between the ages of fifteen and twenty-five were overwhelmingly responsible for bad behaviour. The older generation never accepted the emancipation of the young from parental control. 'As many as 84 per cent of us now agree that young people have too much freedom and need more discipline. Similarly, when you ask the British what educational issues concern them most, pupil behaviour and discipline comes out far ahead of attainment, exams, class sizes or anything else'[24] – that is, far ahead of what legislators think important. The tabloids pictured whole neighbourhoods as surrendered to gangs of feral youths who vandalised housing estates and terrified little old ladies.

But then something important happened. The Blair government which took office in 1997 caught the contemporary mood that 'something needed to be done'. It aimed to 'kick-start a new *Gemeinschaft* society' as one writer put it,[25] by cleaning up the worst of the slums and introducing a series of legislative curbs on bad behaviour. These measures may have contributed to a cyclical recovery in law and order. It may also be that the feminisation of culture – the influence of women and gays over time on the tone and content of personal behaviour and public life – helped produce a softening of manners.

Whatever the cause, although the British may no longer be quite so gentle or undemonstrative as depicted by George Orwell, they are more tolerant and law-abiding today than they were twenty or thirty years ago. Young people are more sexually, and variously, active than they used to be in the 'bad old days' (itself an affront to the older generation), but have latterly

become less rebellious and less criminal. They have been educated and cajoled to be empathetic and polite. The thin morality
of decency and respect has replaced the thick morality of the
Victorians. Tamed by the *douceur* of consumption, the legalisation of hitherto forbidden practices, and renewed job insecurity,
the young have become almost too anxious to please.

Dumbing down?

The 'dumbing down' discourse partly reflects the pathos of disappointed hopes. Increased prosperity was expected to lead to
the 'elevation' of mass taste. This was very reasonable: as more
and more people became middle class, middle-class tastes would
spread. Up to a point this has happened: more people than ever
read books, and take up sports and hobbies; technology and
travel have given them access to hitherto elite cultural goods.
But conservative critics take scant pleasure in these improvements. They believe that popular culture has been so degraded
by pop music, television and advertising that the median level of
culture has fallen even if the average level has risen.

The conservative critics (mainly writers) deplore the fact
that reading and writing no longer set the cultural tone.
Britain has become a watching and listening rather than a
reading society. By the 1990s, the book trade was well on the
way to becoming a branch of the television industry, with
most best-sellers originating as ideas for television programmes. The titles which sell best are, with a few notable
exceptions, about diets, hobbies ('special interests'), lifestyle
revelations ('misery memoirs'), or are overwhelmingly pulp
fiction, as ephemeral as most other consumption goods, to be
read and thrown away on train journeys or holidays, when
television or the Internet is less available. It is the evanescent

quality of most contemporary reading matter, rather than any decline in the number of published titles, which has led literary figures to assert that our culture has been dumbed down.

The decline in reading habits is not the only thing which concerns them. More alarming is commercialisation. This, in their view, has infected the whole culture, dragging it down to a lower level. Business values have displaced any intrinsic standards of judgement; what is best is simply what sells best. However, this may be to get the story the wrong way round. The surrender of culture to commerce was not inevitable; it was a policy based on the individualist philosophy outlined above, which forbade state interference in matters of personal taste. It would have been possible, by 'arts policy', to have protected, through larger subsidies than those allocated by a niggardly Treasury to bodies like the Arts Council, those bits of the culture which were commercially unviable, but which the state considered were worth defending. This has been done in many countries on mainland Europe; it was abandoned in Britain.

The question why the elites abandoned taste to money brings us back to class. The argument of John Carey and George Walden is that the elites either acquiesced in, or actively promoted, a plebeian culture, in order to protect their own 'high culture' from infection by lower values or simply to make money, or both.[26]

No generalisations about culture are safe; but a persistent thread running through our story is the defence of middle-class status through cultural separation. This has taken place at different levels, most obviously through accent and education. But it has also involved, for the arts establishment (including the academic establishment), the creation of an exotic 'high culture', inaccessible except to the few of exceptional wealth, taste or discrimination. Its chief expression was modernism. But, as Gabriel Josipovici has persuasively argued, modernism, which aggressively discarded traditional genres, notably failed to establish accepted canons of taste because of its deliberate alienation of popular feeling.[27] The avant-garde remained resolutely avant. The future will show whether postmodernism 'increasingly populist, streetwise and vernacular' – can re-establish the link between high taste and popular taste, or, to put it differently, between art and commerce.[28]

Commercial culture means newspapers, television and advertising: that is, entertainment and shopping. As early as 1925, the journalist J. A. Spender faced squarely the question of the cultural effects of the mass media:

> The exploiters say that they [the newspapers] provided a vast deal of innocent amusement and instruction for a public starved by their predecessors, and that in giving them what they wanted instead of what solemn Puritans thought they ought to have they relieved the tedium and fatigue of the common life. The critics say that they debased the public taste and filled the minds of their readers with crime, sport, gambling, adultery and every sort of vulgarity. Certainly they seemed to assume that the common mind was incapable of consecutive ideas and inordinately concerned about the doings of actors, athletes, jockeys, prize-fighters and the idle and self-advertising rich. On the other hand they provided a multitude of women, who had been forgotten by the older Press, with a great deal of useful, homely and entertaining reading-matter of a quite innocent kind. I will not attempt to strike the balance.[29]

Spender was making the valid point that, without counter-vailing forces, a competitive mass media would be driven to offer culture in its least demanding form. And this has happened. The press circulation war has dragged down the broadsheets towards the level of the tabloids: with a few exceptions they produce the same truncated viewpoints and adjectivally-challenged prose as the tabloids.

Television viewers are fed a non-stop diet of entertainment. Much of it is enjoyable; some of it is informative; there is a lot of comedy, and the laughter is not all canned. But it is supremely uneffortful. The BBC's landmark television series, *Civilisation* (1969), written and presented by art conoisseur Kenneth Clark, was the epitaph not only for Reith's model of broadcasting, but for the oligarchic civilisation it so lovingly portrayed.

The tabloids are worse, expressing populist resentment against thoughtfulness in a vicious form. In 2014, the writer Hilary Mantel, after being savaged by the *Daily Mail* for a lecture she gave on the royal family, was driven to remark: 'I do think the level of public debate is debased . . . What appals me is that people mistake the constant stream of abuse for some kind of freedom.'[30]

The last third of the twentieth century was the golden age of the performer, exemplified in the proliferation of pop and football 'idols', sometimes called 'icons'. In this world, excellence is equated with professionalism, the ability to do something well, rather than with whether it is worth doing. Wherever skills can be measured – as in sport – they have gone up. Because high levels of achievement require professional discipline, a society which celebrates high achievement is one that retains a place for at least the traditional Puritan virtue of hard work, even though much of that work is directed to making money, and sustained by drugs.

Popular culture has culminated in celebrity culture. Before the First World War, the public depended largely on scandals about aristocrats or gruesome murders for the vicarious enhancement of drab lives. The tabloids, cinema and television changed all that. In the entertainment business, people of ordinary background, looks and tastes can become instant celebrities. All true celebrities have feet of clay, so that the populace can see in them a reflection not only of their dreams but of their own banality.

Banality, sentimentality, cheerfulness, humour, contempt for ideas, with lavish helpings of sex and swearing: these were the hallmarks of British popular culture at the end of the twentieth century. Less had changed than progressives hoped or conservatives feared. This is much how George Orwell described the British in the 1940s.

Appendix:

Judgements of Culture

In her novel *The Radiant Way*, Margaret Drabble wrote of the expectation of her generation that 'everything would get better and better all the time'. However, it is increasingly hard to fit the story of twentieth-century British culture into the narrative of things getting 'better and better all the time'.

Historically, opulence has generally been associated with high civilisation: the great cultural achievements of the past were built on the fruits of wealth. In great opulence, though, were also to be found the seeds of decay: the elites become sybaritic and soft. The masses lose respect for them; both succumb to the standard of money.

Three historically influential ways of thinking about culture centre on the role of the city, of commerce and of democracy. These are all linked, if only contingently. There have been non-commercial cities, non-commercial democracies and commercial autocracies. But in western society urbanisation, commercialisation and democratisation have tended to go together, each reinforcing the effect of the other. All three can be interpreted optimistically or pessimistically.

Traditionally, there have been two views of cities. On the one side, they have been seen as centres of civilisation, an escape from what Karl Marx called 'rural idiocy' – a tradition which goes back at least to Plato. Today's champions of urban life see cities as unleashers of creative energy, centres of cosmopolitanism, and oases of personal freedom. However, for traditionalists, urbanisation was a harbinger of decay. They associate moral health with rural experience and its decay with urban life. The city is a foul swamp which drains its inhabitants of morality and martial virtue. No one gave more graphic expression to this image of the city as the Great Satan than did Oswald Spengler, who in 1917 fused the two facets of cultural and moral decay in a passage of massive pessimism:

> To the world city belongs not a folk but a mass. Its uncomprehending hostility to all the traditions representative of the Culture (nobility, church, privileges, dynasties, conventions in art and limits of knowledge in science), the keen and cold intelligence that confounds the wisdom of the peasant, the new-fashioned naturalism that in relation to all matters of sex and society goes back far beyond Rousseau and Socrates to quite primitive instincts and conditions, the reappearance of *panem et circenses* in the form of wage-doles and football grounds – all these things betoken . . . the opening up of a quite new phase in human existence.

The city is the home of the 'scribblers', the journalists who present reality to the deracinated masses. Of central importance in Spengler's gloomy vision was the collapse of the family. 'Children do not happen, not because children become impossible, but principally because intelligence at the peak of intensity can no longer find any reason for their existence.' City civilisations will be dominated by the sterile male and the unfruitful woman. In Spengler's view, order in this kind of society can be given only by what he calls Caesarism. Power without form is the only thing which can hold together formless mass. Liberal democracy is a 'brief transition' between dynastic rule and 'the age of great individuals in a formless world'.[1] Spengler's *Decline of the West* was an epitaph of the Old Europe of mixed farming and urban communities, destroyed by the First World War.

Closely connected with cultural narratives based on the impact of the city are ones based on the composition of the population. The great city has always been racially and religiously mixed, as contrasted with the countryside with its much more homogeneous population. The optimists praise multiculturalism as liberating settled populations from narrow and parochial views and routines. Older historians were disposed to use the word 'polyglot' to describe mixed populations, and to see the spread of polyglotism as a sign of decay, because it destroyed social cohesion; a polyglot population could only be controlled by despotic means.

The impact of commerce on culture has been a major theme of cultural commentary. By champions of the market economy trade it has been hailed as wholly beneficial. It emancipates people from soul-destroying drudgery, as well as generating, and giving people access to, cultural products unimaginable in former times. Commercial society has also been widely viewed as the upholder of virtues protective of culture. As sociologist Daniel Bell puts it, it joins the economic and cultural realms by a single character structure – that of the Puritan and his calling. Successful performance in commerce is based on self-discipline, delayed gratification and restraint.[2] It is often claimed that the market economy is blind to race, gender and sexual orientation, and works towards removing any political and social discriminations

which limit it. It thus reinforces the aims of political
liberalism.

On balance, pessimistic accounts of the impact of commerce on culture, from both conservative and socialist
thinkers, have tended to drown out these hosannas to the
market. Commerce, the pessimists say, makes money the sole
arbiter of value, destroying any notion of intrinsic worth. For
the sociologist Georg Simmel, money pulls the level of the
highest to that of the lowest, by reducing judgements of quality to judgements of quantity: the better is simply what costs
more.[3] Karl Marx joined ancient and contemporary critics of
commercial society in claiming that capitalism destroys all
forms of cultural authority based on monarchy, church, army,
family and so on. Because its motive force is greed, it cannot
create new authority structures to put in place of those which
it pulverises. 'All fixed, fast-frozen relations, with their train
of ancient and venerable prejudices and opinions are swept
away, all new formed ones become antiquated before they
can ossify. All that is solid melts into air, all that is holy is pro-
faned, and man is at last compelled to face with sober senses,
his real conditions of life, and his relations with his kind.'[4]
This confrontation with reality would lead to the abolition of
capitalism, and the coming of socialism. Marxists have then
been faced with the problem of explaining why this has not
yet happened. Their classic answer is that the masses were
bribed with the profits of imperialism. A more subtle recent
explanation has focused on the lure of consumerism. Both
serve to hide from people their 'real conditions of life'.

Democracy is first and foremost a political principle, which
demands the free choice of rulers in competitive elections,
and promotes the political education of the people through a
process of discussion and debate. It is thus a crucial safeguard

of freedom. However, an important subsidiary justification has been that, in a democracy, cultural values are freely chosen rather than handed down from above. This frees the people from the straitjacket of imposed cultural forms, releasing their creative energies. But again the pessimistic note is louder, partly because it is more ancient, and it too goes all the way back to Plato. In the Platonic scheme the agents of cultural decay are money and democracy. Aristocracy, the rule of the best, is replaced by plutocracy, the rule of money. Plutocracy, lacking a principle of legitimacy, is overthrown by democracy, the rule of the mob. Plato describes the 'democratic city' as a place in which the young no longer respect their parents, elders and teachers; in which adults ape and pander to the young; in which there is no difference between citizens and foreigners; and in which there is complete sexual liberty and equality. Democracy can no more produce a stable structure of authority than plutocracy, and yields to dictatorship or tyranny, which in turn is overthrown by a new aristocracy which restores the ancient virtues.[5] It is a closed circle: all attempts to create justice in fact create a new bondage. The cycle endlessly repeats itself.

The stirrings of the permissive society in the 1960s produced an outpouring of Platonic angst. The political scientist Samuel Huntington noted in 1975 that 'people no longer felt the same compulsion to obey those whom they had previously considered superior to themselves in age, rank, status, expertise, character, or talents'. Sociologist Michel Crozier wrote: 'citizens are learning to reject and discard traditional hierarchical values and social control based on them . . . Traditional institutions like the church, the schools and the army are collapsing . . . Traditional conceptions of rationality . . . are being called into question.'[6] Only in the 'people's democracies' of

Communism could these stirrings be repressed (at least for a time). Yet in these societies, the people did not get the culture they wanted, but the culture their rulers decided was good for them. Clearly at issue are two radically different views of human nature. The closed circle of Plato, with its pessimistic view of human possibilities, was standard till the French Revolution. With Rousseau, a more optimistic view was born, in which the destruction of authority was the prelude to liberation. Beyond Plato's circle stretched Utopia. Today's optimists welcome the destruction of authority systems as liberating individuals from repressive systems. The traditional view that human nature is inherently flawed and needs to be held in check confronted the assertion that it is perfectible and, under free conditions, can be trusted to 'choose the good'.

None of the traditional narratives of cultural progress or decay consider the possibilities of a scientific civilisation. They all take technology as given; the cycle of rise and fall takes place within a static material world. This enables them to treat human nature as roughly constant. The possibility of a thorough-going transformation of human nature by machines is beyond their ken, because it has so far not been part of any historical narrative. As such they are of limited application to a world given its dynamism by science and technology. What can be claimed, though, is that science is no guarantee of the continuation of culture, in the sense most people have understood that term − as the flowering of individuality within a framework of moral rules. Only the general truth is true for scientific purposes. Despite their lack of a scientific dimension, therefore, historical discussions of culture remain useful in that they can introduce some order into what is otherwise a confused trade of opinion as to what has happened to British culture in the twentieth century.

Britain was the most urbanised society in Europe from at least the early eighteenth century, but for a long time it exhibited the paradox of an urbanised society with rural values. This infuriated Marxists who complained that it had not experienced a 'bourgeois revolution'; by conservatives, on the other hand, this 'ruralism' was regarded as a precious repository of virtue, an antidote to revolutionary ferment, and a guarantee of social stability. Britain's rural values, in short, long survived the disappearance of agriculture as a primary mode of living and apprehending the world. But by the second half of the twentieth century rural values were powerless to resist the magnetic pull of city life, and especially the pull of London which became the hub of liberated morals, commercialised culture and cosmopolitan population.

In contrast to the United States, the commercialisation of British society, while already well advanced by the time of the outbreak of the First World War, was retarded by two world wars and the intervening Great Depression. Thus older cultural values and projects still held sway. Mass-consumption power did not become a reality till the 1950s.

The progress of democracy in the twentieth century was retarded by a constitutional settlement which had put power in the hands of a liberal aristocracy. This model of oligarchic democracy was still alive, if not well, in the 1950s, signified by the term 'Establishment'. Together with martial values (the British were always notable warriors) and non-commercial motives it was sustained by an imperial mission which did not finally subside till the Suez fiasco of 1956. Anti-Establishmentarianism only got going when the Establishment was seen to have lost its grip. Worse than the folly of Suez was its failure.

From the late 1950s onwards, all these barriers to progress

or decay, depending on view, broke down with the onset of mass affluence, the spread of effective contraception, the onslaught on the Establishment by the satirists, cynics and the Angries, the revolt of the young against lifestyles left over from the Victorian era, and a raft of liberalising legislation. Suez was a crucial watershed, which showed up the ruling class as a hollow shell. At the same time the Marxist vision of social progress was confounded by deindustrialisation and the disappearance of the male-dominated working-class culture. Virtues once required to keep industrial capitalism and empire going, and for which the moral and cultural education of previous generations had been a training, were no longer needed: why delay gratification; the age of ease and plenty had arrived. As Spengler foresaw, in this respect accurately, we had reached the threshold of a new civilisation.

Chapter 3

The Political Nation

Class war, socialism, fascism were un-English ideas, only suitable, if suitable at all, for foreign countries unlucky enough not to have developed the English gentlemanly habits of conciliation and compromise that would see us through the problems of the twentieth century.

Peregrine Worsthorne, *In Defence of Aristocracy* (2004)

Politics is a separate part of a nation's culture and needs to be treated separately. The uninterrupted survival of the British state is *the* grand narrative of Britain's twentieth-century political history. Reformers railed against its unfitness for the tasks of the modern world and were fertile with plans for rationalising it. They ignored its success in perpetuating itself and with it the liberties which had grown up alongside, and which were protected by its survival. Its system of pragmatic adversarial politics was an unrivalled mechanism for channelling conflict into Westminster and there robbing it of its reactionary or revolutionary sting. This was never shown to better advantage than in the interwar years, when liberal states toppled like ninepins.

Britain was a union state.[*] It never experienced a

---

[*] The distinction between 'union' and 'unitary' is explained by Vernon Bogdanor in his review of Linda Colley's *Acts of Union and Disunion* in the *TLS* of 4 April 2014. A unitary state implies a 'Jacobin state, built around an unambiguous political centre and following policies of administrative standardisation'; a union state 'offered scope for the indigenous institutions of the non-English parts of the United Kingdom to be preserved'.

centralising revolution; and two world wars killed off the nineteenth-century liberal programme of 'devolution all round'. 'Home Rule' was for the empire: the Scots and Welsh as well as the English were governed from Westminster. The one exception, Northern Ireland, allowed its own 'devolved' Parliament in 1920, was more colony than mother country. This situation suited both major parties, especially the Labour Party, which aimed not to reform the state, but capture it for socialist projects. The banner of regionalism, localism and voting reform was carried by the Liberal Party, but for most of the century the Liberals were minor players.

The British constitution[1] was simple: 'The voters voted, the government governed, and the voters then decided whether they wanted the government to continue to govern. Civil servants served the government of the day and nobody else. Parliament was more passive than active. The courts held the ring and made sure that everybody obeyed the law. And that was about it. Almost everything else was embellishment and detail.'[2]

As the twentieth century ended, there was a feeling that the 'ancient constitution' had run its course. It was paternalist, centralist and based on manners and conventions that were disappearing. It was not suited to an era of identity, regional, and multicultural politics, and it discouraged active citizenship. Its informal system of checks and balances had atrophied. Reformers want it to be replaced with a written constitution that provides for a formal bill of rights, a proper federal structure and a separation of powers. Much of the reformers' criticism was based on the idea that the existing constitution offered no barrier to 'elective dictatorship' – the spectre raised by Lord Hailsham in 1976. There was much talk of the need for 'democratic renewal'. It was time for subjects to become citizens.

The political realm, the elements which render a state effective, is much wider than the constitution itself. Beyond the constitution, there is the political nation in which it is embedded, as constituted by the party system, the social structure and the media.

The Crown in Parliament

The British constitution is not a contract between the state and its citizens, drawn up at a single moment of time, but a codified accumulation of rules and conventions. Over three centuries it evolved seamlessly from a monarchical oligarchy to a bourgeois democracy. The trappings of the former remain, but power is exercised by the latter. No doctrine of popular sovereignty intruded to confer legitimacy on these arrangements.

The historian J. M. Roberts has written that 'the institutional core of the story which runs from Anglo-Saxon times to our own is the story of a state structure built round the English monarchy and its effective successor, the Crown in Parliament'.[3] The Commons replaced the closet and preceded the ballot. This has given the British state its 'ancient' character. Formally this structure has hardly changed since Edwardian times. But beneath the facade little has stayed the same, and the pace of change speeded up under New Labour.

Britain is thought to have a parliamentary system, but formally it is a royal system which works through Parliament – a parliamentary monarchy. The state undertook the monarch's functions in the monarch's name. This has always given the executive a dominating position. There is no division of powers, just a division of labour between the governors and the governed.[4] The monarchy lost its executive role in the eighteenth century, but the royal prerogative remains intact, to the annoyance of constitutional reformers. For nearly two centuries the crown has been in the capable hands of the House of Windsor, its sense of duty combined with modest qualities being ideal for the purposes of constitutional rule. As a result Queen Elizabeth II retains all the formal powers of Queen Victoria.

The 'Crown in Parliament' is still sovereign, and can enact and repeal any law it wants. In theory, Parliament's sovereignty is no more restricted by membership of the European Union than it is by any treaty obligation: Britain retains the legal right to leave the European Union, though the costs of doing so would no doubt be very high. Similarly Westminster retains sovereignty over the devolved governments in Belfast and Edinburgh – as it showed when it imposed direct rule on Northern Ireland in 1972. At what point powers unused cease, for all practical purposes, to exist, becoming, in Bagehot's words, merely 'dignified', is a topic much debated among constitutional lawyers and political analysts. The constitution is not static, it is written in action.

Over the century, the prime minister has become much more important. Britain is still commonly described as having Cabinet government, but except in periods of crisis Cabinet government has become prime ministerial government, or perhaps 'coterie government'. This change was foreshadowed by Lloyd George with his 'garden suburb', advanced by Harold Wilson with his 'kitchen Cabinet' and was consummated by Tony Blair, who surrounded himself with cronies, and treated both Cabinet and Parliament with ill-concealed contempt. The institutional foundation of prime ministerial power lies in the fact that the prime minister is the party's (not the monarch's) choice, and the source of all preferment. The prime minister's ministerial colleagues serve at his pleasure. Weekly Cabinet meetings still continue, but their main function is to rubber-stamp pre-agreed policies hammered out in informal groups or subordinate committees, usually chaired by the prime minister.

A prime minister in control of his party undoubtedly wields enormous power. Thatcher showed this in pushing through her 'revolution'. Buttressing party discipline is the prime minister's control of patronage. Depending on the size of the majority up to half of government MPs can be on the ministerial payroll, and others take unpaid political jobs like parliamentary private secretaries in hope of preferment. The majority party can dethrone prime ministers (as the fall of Margaret Thatcher showed), but such assertions of independence are notable for their rarity. On the other hand, rebellions against the party 'whips' have become more frequent. In the 2001–5 parliament, Labour MPs rebelled against the whip in 20.8 per cent of all votes, the highest proportion since 1945. Large majorities encourage rebellions, which is why prime ministers are ambivalent about them. In 2003, 139 Labour MPs voted against Blair's decision for war against Iraq, the largest party rebellion since the Corn Laws. He carried the policy only with the support of the Conservatives.

Parliament still has two 'houses', Commons and Lords. The House of Commons is (2012) elected from 650 constituencies, each returning a single member on a simple plurality of votes.* It has hardly changed, though great parliamentary occasions

---

* For the first decades of the twentieth century, the number of MPs was 670, fixed by the Third Reform Act 1884. For the 1918–22 parliament, the Commons was at its largest ever, with 707 MPs. Since then, the number has fluctuated between 615 and 659. Multi-member constituencies and university constituencies (whose voters were graduates) were abolished in 1950. The (2010) proposed cut of fifty MPs will take the Commons to its smallest since 1800.

are rarer, and it now has public bill and select committees to scrutinise the actions of the executive. The House of Lords remains outwardly the same, but some new wine has been poured into this very old bottle. The Parliament Act of 1911 restricted its power to veto bills passed by the Commons to two years; this was reduced to one year in 1949. In 2000, 660 hereditary peers were 'culled' from the Lords, with ninety-three remaining temporarily. There are now 765 lords.

Parliament evolved as a check on 'royal' government, and despite its emasculation, it still retains this role. Prime ministers are vulnerable to loss of personal popularity and mounting irritation on the back benches, from ministers sacked or those not preferred. Back-bench rebellions in the Commons rarely destroy governments but they can force changes in proposed legislation. The Lords, too, is a far from toothless tiger. Somnolent for most of the century, it returned to life with the Life Peerages Act of 1958 which created a new category of appointed 'life peers' whose titles expire with them. Under New Labour governments from 1997 to 2010, 40 per cent of government defeats in the Lords brought about changes in bills. A rebellion of government backbenchers in the Commons, especially if supported by the Opposition, can trigger off a Lords rejection of proposed legislation, which the government is then reluctant to overturn. Lords' opposition stopped New Labour's attempt to increase the period of detention without trial to ninety days. Reformers argue that an elected House of Lords would be more 'legitimate' and therefore able to be a stronger curb on prime ministerial government. But this would not be so if it becomes a second-class House of Commons.

Civil Service

In Bagehot's classic account of the British constitution, civil servants are treated as 'clerks'. The theory was that ministers make policy and are answerable to Parliament for it. Civil servants are just that – servants. Their job is to carry out their ministers' wishes and administer the state. They no more run the government than the kitchen runs a great house. But this theory was never an accurate description of reality. Officials advise ministers and to that extent share responsibility for their policies and actions. The lack of explicit responsibility fed exaggerated stories of their power. In the many inquests on 'the decline of Britain' which ran from the 1960s to the 1980s, civil servants emerge as the villains of the piece, ruining the country through their incompetence and bad advice. Businessmen attacked them for their lack of practical knowledge; left-wing critics for suborning the 'democratic' will; Thatcherites for upholding the interventionist state. The ease with which they could thwart the political intentions of their masters was satirised in the television series *Yes, Minister*. Latterly, political scientists of the 'public choice' school have analysed their propensity to empire-building.[5]

Vernon Bogdanor writes that the 'Civil Service was subject to more change in its structure and organisation between 1979 and the end of [the twentieth] century than at any time in the preceding 125 years'.[6] Thatcher and Major displayed their anti-bureaucratic zeal in downsizing the number of permanent officials from 750,000 to 480,000, mainly through privatisations and outsourcing. New Labour continued in the same vein, having been imbued with the same ideological tendency. In the words of the political scientist Anthony King, 'Labour's language sounded like a dialect of Thatcherism, its vocabulary rich in words and phrases like competition, best value, internal markets, public–private partnerships, purchase–provider splits, the private finance initiative and reform of the public service.'[7] A new animal, the 'special adviser', was introduced by Harold Wilson in the 1960s to guard ministers against the wiles (and alleged Conservative leanings) of the Civil Service.

Amidst these vicissitudes, the Treasury retained its position as the pre-eminent department of state. The Foreign Office shrivelled with the shrivelling of British power, its splendid quarters on King Charles Street full of the ghosts of past glories. The Treasury, more modestly housed on Horse Guards Road, as befitted an institution devoted to frugality, owes its continuing power to its historic role as controller of the public purse. It has thus served as a bulwark against what Keynes called 'the wicked Chancellor'. It lost power in the two world wars, but always bounced back. However much governments, especially Labour governments, sought to subordinate it to their spending programmes and industrial policies, it stuck to its economising principles, and waited for the (predictable) failure of these policies to regain control. When Chancellors like Austen Chamberlain, Snowden, Neville Chamberlain, Selwyn Lloyd, Geoffrey Howe and George Osborne tried, from time to time, to rein in government 'extravagance', they always found in the Treasury an enthusiastic ally. Attempts to set up rivals, like George Brown's Department of Economic Affairs (1964–7) invariably foundered.

Local government

The formal doctrine of parliamentary sovereignty excludes any independent lawmaking powers; indeed it excludes any

notion of the 'separation of powers' as in the American constitution. Local government provides for a dispersion, but not a
separation, of powers. Until recently, local authorities could
do only what the Westminster Parliament authorised them to
do; the Localism Act of 2011 gave them a 'general power of
competence' allowing them to do anything they were not
specifically prohibited from doing. It is too early to say what
advantage councils will take of this.

The basic trend in local government has been towards its
emasculation, and with that the disappearance of its role of
checking centralisation. Until the 1950s there was little
change in the structure inherited from the nineteenth
century, with its complicated and often illogical and
inefficient array of county councils, borough councils, district
councils, rural councils and parish councils, amounting in all
to several thousand 'local authorities'; to which was added a
London County Council established in 1889 for the government of London, with its own subordinate tier of twenty-eight
borough councils. For long this ramshackle structure was
complacently regarded as a splendid stage for local democracy.
There then started successive and continuous upheavals
which resulted in a 'cumulative loss of autonomy, [a]
cumulative loss of freedom and [a] cumulative loss of power'.[8]
Central government repeatedly redrew local government
boundaries and reshuffled its tiers; deprived local authorities
of their main functions; reorganised their internal government structures; reduced their workforces; imposed caps on
what they could spend and told them what they could spend
it on. It replaced the London County Council with a Greater
London Council (1963), abolished it (1985), and reconstituted
it as a Greater London Authority with a directly elected
mayor (1998). Central government could do all these things

because it faced no constitutional impediment. Direct election was the foundation of the power of the mayors of London, its extra legitimacy attracting such outsize political personalities such as Ken Livingston and Boris Johnson.

Progressives had always hoped that local government would be the laboratory of democracy, trying social experiments on a small scale. This hope was dashed as the control of central government tightened. No twentieth-century civic government can compare with Joseph Chamberlain's rule in nineteenth-century Birmingham. The reason is clear: local authorities lost control of many services and local revenues were insufficient to finance what remained. Neville Chamberlain, Joe Chamberlain's son, tried – in the Local Government Act 1929 – to strengthen local government by giving it new franchises and revenues, but it was a losing battle. In the 1940s, central government took over the public utilities and hospitals, hitherto municipal enterprises. They refused to allow local authorities a revenue base sufficient to pay for the expanded spending required for schools and council housing, which, as a result, had to be financed by the centre. In the 1950s, more than two thirds of local-government spending was paid for by local rates, taxes and fees. Following the abolition of the poll tax it fell to 30 per cent; by 2010 this had risen to around 40 per cent. He who pays the piper calls the tune. Local authorities have become little more than agents of central government.

As Anthony King well puts it, the notion of government requires a sphere of activity in which the authority is free to act; that the sphere should be large and varied; and that it should be supported by an independent revenue base. Lacking these prerequisites, the label 'local government' has become a misnomer.[9] By contrast, the devolved authorities of

Northern Ireland, dating from 1920, and Scotland and Wales, created in 1998, are genuine governments, though subordinate ones.

The law

For most of the century the judges' view of their role was simple. Parliament made the law; the judges' duty was to declare, interpret and apply it. They could not declare Acts of Parliament illegal, only actions by ministers which, in their view, showed them to have 'taken leave of their senses'.[10] Conservative and Labour governments were equally keen to stop the judges from tampering with 'their' laws. Thus the protection of British liberties given by the 'rule of law' was less extensive than is commonly supposed. Preservation of liberty depended on the self-restraint of government. Legal interventionism declined in the first half of twentieth century as the paternalist, social democratic view of the state gained ground. In the 1960s, the judges, like the House of Lords, started to wake up. In 1966, Lord Denning argued that their function was to make law, not just apply it. This inaugurated the era of 'judicial activism'. Judicial activism was the result of a decline in deference to Parliament, the growth of regulation, and UK membership of the European Union, which provided an external source of law. These changes meant that the 'rule of law' became an increasingly central part of the British constitution. From the 1960s, the control of behaviour through moral rules gave way to control through legal rules, and this enhanced the position of the judiciary.

In successive rulings, the scope of 'judicial review' of ministerial actions was enlarged; 'interpretation' was widened to include the intention of the legislation as well as its text. In

1998 the Human Rights Act, which incorporated the European Convention of Human Rights into British law, greatly extended the scope of judicial review. Formally it left the sovereignty of Parliament untouched – Parliament remained free to repeal the Act or pass laws inconsistent with it – but it included provisions which made it very difficult for it to do the latter. In 2005, Blair casually transferred the appellate functions of the Law Lords to a new Supreme Court. Promoted as a step towards a formal division of powers, what it in fact achieved was to deprive Parliament of judicial input into the making of laws. In 2012, the first non-lawyer, Chris Grayling, became Lord Chancellor, a wonderful case of pouring new wine into an old bottle.

The tendency, and sometimes the intention, of these changes was to ensure that legislation and administration conformed to 'the rule of law' without challenging the formal doctrine of parliamentary sovereignty. As a result, they set up conflicts between the government and courts which increased noticeably under the Major and Blair governments. The Blair government restricted the right to trial by jury, and attenuated legal aid, the latter on cost-cutting grounds.

The party system

Britain is a representative democracy. People do not make laws directly, but through their elected representatives. Successive extensions of the franchise – to women in 1918 and 1928, and to eighteen-year-olds in 1969 – have made Parliament more 'representative' of the population, but has not made MPs more representative of their constituents: working-class MPs were more common in 1914 than today. Since mass meetings expired after the First World War, and active membership of political parties shrank to near zero after the Second, the connection between politicians and 'the people' has grown ever weaker, despite attempts to strengthen it by devices such as referendums. Some analysts have suggested that mass apathy portends the death of democracy: it may simply denote mass alienation from the language of contemporary politics.

It was the enlarged electorate established in 1884–5 which created the modern party system; and the voting system which determined its shape. This voting system, – known as 'first past the post' – remains intact for national and local elections. (Proportional Representation has been introduced for European, Scottish, Welsh and London mayoralty elections.) It has given Britain a two-party system, with one party normally winning a majority of seats in the House of Commons. This system might have been tailor-made to ensure the executive's ability to act royally, by guaranteeing it, in normal times, a parliamentary majority. One flaw in the system, from the democratic point of view, was that there was little connection between parliamentary strength and proportion of votes cast in general elections. In 1951, for example, the Labour Party won more votes than the Conservatives, who nevertheless returned to power with a parliamentary majority of twenty-six. For most of the century parties with a minority of votes controlled a majority of parliamentary seats. The declining Liberal Party was the main victim of this democratic deficit, Labour replacing it in 1922 as the alternative to the Conservatives. For this reason the Liberals have for long been advocates of proportional representation. The two main parties were quite happy with the existing voting system, which enabled them to alternate in power on a regular basis.

In shorthand description the two main parties have been divided into progressive and conservative. The Liberals, later

Labour, were the accelerator, the Conservatives applied the brake. Others have put it differently: the Conservatives stood for monarch and empire, Labour for democracy and reform. Like all political clichés, this contains some truth, but not much. The Conservatives could also be reformers; Labour's core support was a morally conservative working class. From Thatcher onwards, the neat dichotomy dissolved. Both parties have had to reinvent themselves: Labour as pro-business, the Conservatives as 'caring'. The leaderships and policies of the two main parties have come to seem interchangeable.

Although in the twentieth century the Conservative Party was more in government than was Labour, both parties had problems in maintaining their electoral support. It was the middle class – business and the professions – which provided the Conservatives with their core voters. But for most of the century the middle class formed a minority of the electorate. The Conservative Party therefore had to extend its appeal to at least sections of the working class. This it managed to do quite successfully, though at the expense of embracing policies of economic intervention and welfare provision anathema to its active members. In the latter part of the twentieth century, the Conservatives had to adapt to the 'liberal' social agenda which made defence of traditional values seem antediluvian. Margaret Thatcher did this successfully by replacing Tory paternalism with an individualism which promised economic benefits for all classes. The price, though, was to leave her successors with a party dubbed 'nasty' and 'uncaring'. The Labour Party had the support of most of the working class. But its electoral prospects were dimmed by its commitment to public ownership (which the workers did not want), by the growing unpopularity (after the 1970s) of the trade unions, and by the gradual 'embourgeoisement' of the working class itself through affluence. It was only at the end of the century under Tony Blair that it shed these handicaps, mostly by embracing Thatcherite policies and 'middle England' sentiments. Blair was the first Labour leader with a wide cross-class appeal.

Coalition government never flourished outside war: not only was the electoral system against it, but so were the chequered reputations of the Lloyd George coalition of 1918–22 and the National Government of 1931–5. Periods of coalition for great emergencies were always followed by an eagerness to resume 'party warfare' and return to a 'politics of principle'. With the decline in support for the two main parties and the partial revival of the Liberals, the day of coalition government, common in the rest of Europe, may have dawned.

The peak of the two-party duopoly was in 1951, when the Conservatives and Labour together took 96.8 per cent of the vote, on a turnout of 82 per cent. Since then the percentages voting for both parties, and indeed turnouts at general elections themselves, have declined. Even though Labour had large parliamentary majorities from 1997 to 2010 its share of the popular vote declined to little over 30 per cent. Its further weakening in 2010 produced not a Conservative government but a Conservative–Liberal Democrat coalition. Constitutional reformers hoped to bring about coalition politics through proportional representation. As it is, the shrinking appeal of the two main parties promises to achieve the same effect without a change in the voting system. It is unlikely though that the two-party system will violently fracture. The main parties have become empty vessels, ready to be filled with whatever liquids are being brewed beyond Westminster.

Breakaways from the main parties flourished briefly, then disappeared, killed off by their inability to establish positions in Parliament commensurate with the votes cast for them. The nearest to success was the 'SDP–Liberal' Alliance, which came close to replacing Labour in 1983. The most successful of the small parties were those with regional concentration. The Liberals almost disappeared in the early 1950s because their votes were too evenly spread. Then came a slow revival, spreading out from the 'Celtic fringe'. Renamed Liberal Democrats to incorporate Labour's breakaway Social Democratic Party (SDP), they have regained the parliamentary strength in the Commons they had in 1929, with fifty-two seats out of 641 in the 2001 elections, sixty-two in 2005, and fifty-seven in 2010. The Unionist parties of Northern Ireland have returned an average of twelve seats between them since 1974, when they broke from the Conservatives. Minor parties have occasionally played a pivotal part: for example, Scottish Nationalists and Ulster Unionists toppled the minority Labour government in 1979. The Communist Party never got more than two seats in Parliament (in 1945). It finally expired in 1991. The far left's strength lay in the labour movement, infiltrating small cadres of militants into key positions in local Labour parties and trade unions. 'Red Robbo', Derek Robinson, a radical folk hero, almost brought the car industry to a standstill in the 1970s. The century's end brought a proliferation of small parties – Greens, BNP, UKIP – only the first of which has gained a UK parliamentary seat, but which all have some influence within larger parties.

Popular politics have subsided in the twentieth century. Ironically, they were at their peak in the nineteenth century when most adults lacked the vote: there have been no mass movements to rival the Chartists. The main traditional indicators of political participation – membership of political parties, identification with political tendencies, attendance at political meetings, voting – have been in steep decline. Since the 1970s, the parties have lost two thirds of their members.

Political oratory is a shadow of its former glory, with mass meetings replaced by sound bites on television and radio. Rhetoric was always a key part of persuasion, but as the century wore on the politics of gesture and 'spin' increasingly replaced the politics of choice. For all his addiction to coterie politics Blair was an exception: genuinely eloquent, with rhetorical and forensic gifts of a high order.

Issues and interests, the bread and butter of the old politics, have lost their force. Political parties no longer 'educate' democracy – that task is left to the media and think tanks. Politicians no longer interest the public, except when they are subjects of scandal. Even in the 1940s George Orwell was drawing attention to the decline of political language.[11] Euphemism had replaced plain statement, as politicians found it increasingly necessary to disguise the true nature of reality. The political need to use language unclearly has grown apace with multiculturalism and political correctness, reinforced by the actual deterioration in the written and spoken word. From not wanting people to understand what they are saying, public persons have ceased to understand what they are saying themselves. It is little wonder that the voters turn off.

One consequence of the decay of political parties has been that they have come to rely increasingly for their funding on rich private donors, individual and corporate, in search of peerages and other preferments. Thatcher dismantled the local base of the Conservative Party; Blair tried to dismantle the TU base of the Labour Party. As a result, British political parties have become top-down electoral machines, rather than bottom-up shapers of political opinion. They no longer exist to mobilise support for policies but to mobilise votes behind leaders competitive only in their struggle for power. In the nineteenth century democracy arose as a check on oligarchy.

Today it may well be giving way to plutocracy. Consumer choice has not only largely replaced political choice; but political choice has been redefined as a subset of consumer choice, with politicians seen as 'entrepreneurs' offering electors a choice between different brands of the same good. In this, as in other ways, Britain has become more Americanised than Europeanised. However, such choice is limited to the 'politically correct', leaving a large swathe of popular feeling on public issues like capital punishment outside the ambit of politics. But perhaps it has always been thus: the 'ancient constitution' was inherently oligarchic, and it has remained so.

Class and power

There is always a power elite, in the sense that in every society there is a small group who make the most important decisions affecting people's lives. But this group need not be drawn from a single class. It may be more or less 'open'. And its power is not, at least in democracies, absolute: it is subject to all kinds of institutional checks, which force it to take account of interests and feelings other than its own.

In the nineteenth century there was a very close connection between the power elite and the aristocracy, at all levels of government. With the decline of the landed interest, this group lost its power (though not its sense of social superiority) to the upper middle class, made up of top managers, professionals and civil servants. In the new dispensation, power followed wealth – that is, it remained concentrated. According to the Registrar General the top managers, professionals and administrators comprised 2 per cent of the population in 1931; by 1961 it was 3.6 per cent. In 2001, the equivalent figure was 9 per cent. On another measure, it was estimated that in 2012, only 300,000 taxpayers, or 1 per cent of the total, had annual incomes of £150,000 or over.

In the twentieth century the points of entry to the power elite gradually opened up to the rest of the population – through the Labour Party, the trade unions and the grammar schools – and, not least, through enlarged career opportunities for women. However, the entry was limited. Not only did the Conservative Party hold power for most of the century, but many of the leaders of the Labour Party were drawn from the middle or upper middle classes. Individual trade union leaders like Ernest Bevin, who became a powerful government minister, entered the power elite. But generally speaking the unions saw their role as oppositional: to check the bosses, not to become bosses themselves. Brains have always been valued in a rather condescending way. Yet the grammar schools (entirely 'free' after 1944) provided a real ladder for bright working-class children to enter the power elite, usually administrative, via Oxford and Cambridge. However, this channel dried up with the abolition of most grammar schools in the 1960s and 70s. Nor must it be assumed that brains are a credible obstacle to the claims of birth and wealth. Persons of high intellect, but small fortunes, often speak the words birth and wealth want to hear but cannot formulate themselves. This gift is modestly, sometimes extravagantly, rewarded, but there remains a whiff of 'flunkeydom'. By the early twenty-first century, both birth and brains had been engulfed by money. Oligarchic power had been largely replaced by plutocratic power. The rich openly ruled.

For most of the century class was the central, though not exclusive, determinant of political allegiance. It was more central to British politics than in other European countries, because of the relative absence of criss-crossing allegiances. Class politics dominated in the long period between the decline of religion at the century's start, and the 'rise of the nations' towards its end.

The two main parties weren't exclusively single-class parties. Conservatives captured a share, sometimes called 'deferential', of the working-class vote; Labour a share, sometimes called 'thinking', of the middle class. Both drew on older religious allegiances: the Tories on Protestantism, Labour on Catholicism. Marxists expected class politics to lead to class war. This did not happen, because of the unique accommodative properties of the political system and the pragmatic character of the British people.

In the last quarter of the twentieth century class politics was dissolved by two forces: the decay of manufacturing which dismembered the old working class; and the end of empire which led to the resurgence of Scottish and Welsh nationalism. Over half the population still think of themselves as working class (middle class means being educated), but there is no identifiable class interest. The end of empire undermined the idea of a single political nation, violently in Ireland, peacefully in Scotland and Wales. Conservative, Labour and Liberal Democrats are increasingly regional parties. The effect of regionalisation on the mandate to govern is partly encapsulated in the 'West Lothian' question, which asks why Scottish MPs should have the right to vote at Westminster on English matters when English MPs have lost the power to influence the affairs of twenty-first-century devolved Scotland. In the referendum of 2014, Scotland voted to remain part of the UK, on the promise of increased powers for the devolved government. It is unlikely, though, that this will start a move to a full-blown federal structure. England is simply too big relative to the others.

The Fourth Estate

In the nineteenth century, no one doubted that journalism was the 'inferior branch of the political profession'.[13] The politician made the news, newspapers circulated it, commented on it, and checked the abuse of power. They were predominantly political and owed steady allegiance to one or other of the two great parties: they were servants of the political class not its masters. Entertainment and lifestyle reportage were developed by the tabloids. But over the century newspapers have come to dislodge the politicians from their place in the power structure. Now the media creates the news and abuses the power of transmission – to sell papers, but also to satisfy the power lust of their proprietors, editors, journalists. Their entertainment role has developed into promiscuous intrusion into private lives. Appearance can take the place of reality, but also engineer the reality, so the distinction disappears. Politicians have been reduced to 'managing' news they no longer create, in order to get their voices heard. This was to culminate in the 'spin doctor' regime of New Labour.

The media was left as the main conduit between the politicians and the public, with the control of the conduit the prize for politicians and proprietors. Monopoly, or oligopoly, was the consequence of the circulation war. In the 1880s, there were eight London evening papers; today there is one, the *Evening Standard*. (It is free, so depends mainly on advertising revenue.) Alfred Harmsworth, later Lord Northcliffe, was the prototype of the modern press baron: the outsider from modest Anglo-Irish stock who bought his way to the pinnacle of political influence via the circulation and strategic importance of his titles. Max Aitken and Conrad Black (both Canadian) and Rupert Murdoch (Australian) have followed in his footsteps. Having started the *Daily Mail* as a popular news-paper in 1896, Harmsworth acquired *The Times* in 1908, then the semi-official organ of the government of the day. In addition to *The Times* and the *Daily Mail*, the Harmsworth family came to own the *Sunday Times*, *Observer* (sold to the Astor family in 1911), *Daily Mirror*, *Daily Record*, *Sunday Dispatch* and *Sunday Pictorial*, the last two long gone, a portfolio that Murdoch would envy. The terms of the corrupt bargain – access in return for support – were sealed long before New Labour carried it to a higher level.

Early twentieth-century Britain possessed a three-layered newspaper structure. At the top were the 'heavies' or qualities like *The Times* (3p) which had a circulation of 35,000 in 1904 out of a total *voting* population of about 5 million. Three middle-level newspapers, priced at a halfpenny, started up at the turn of the century to cater to an expanded readership and electorate: the *Daily Mail* (1896–), *Daily Express* (1900–), and *Daily Herald* (1912–64), the first two maverick Conservative, the third Labour (it became the TUC's official paper in 1922). In addition to news, the middle-level papers carried gossip, sports, women's features, 'human interest' stories, serials and prizes. By 1930 their circulation was between five and ten times higher that of the 'qualities'. Tabloids like the *Daily Mirror* (1904–) and *Daily Sketch* (1909–71)catered to the working class. Their further adaptation to popular taste took the form of photos on the front page and a vigorous display of national prejudice. Sunday newspapers were slower to catch on, but by 1930 the scandal sheet *News of the World* was well ahead of the field, clocking up an astounding 8 million readers by 1951. (It was closed down in 2011, after a series of 'hacking' scandals.) The three levels, and their circulations, neatly mirrored the occupational structure. Both 'quality' and 'popular' press have gone downmarket in the last forty years, but the gap between them has widened: the qualities are worse and the tabloids are much worse.

The daily newspaper used to perform two functions: to supply the public with news and views and businessmen with advertising space. It still does both. But reporting and comment are bound to be poisoned at source if they are not independent. In practice, both have been increasingly subordinated to the demands of commerce. This requires not only the slanting but the trivialisation of news and opinion.

The media have passed from being transmitters to creators of news. As Marshall McLuhan famously proclaimed in the 1960s, 'The medium is the message'. Even more than newspapers, television filters, mediates and manipulates 'the news', making it increasingly hard to distinguish between manufactured crises and real crises; or more accurately, the media event has become the real event. Ministers are forced to resign if their private lives are exposed by the media, even though they may be perfectly capable of doing their job. The media have become the senior branch of the political profession, with politicians as their puppets.

Chapter 4

The Irresistible Rise of the State?

'Every additional state interference creates the increasing need for administrative compulsion and restraints, which results from the unforeseen evils and shortcomings of preceding compulsions and restraints.'

Walter Lippmann, *The Good Society* (1943)

The state loomed much larger in the twentieth century than in the nineteenth. This was because the scale of private economic activities was larger, the social problems more visible, the effect of economic fluctuations more severe, and the demand for state intervention much greater following the extension of the franchise to the propertyless classes. The individualist, small-scale, decentralised character of economic and social life gave way to the world of blocs: business became more concentrated; factories became larger; voters were mobilised into national parties; populations flocked into cities; communications became national. The growth of the Victorian social conscience allied to revelations of widespread 'poverty in the midst of plenty' eroded the laissez-faire philosophy that had dominated the nineteenth century. The role of the state as owner, stabiliser, administrator/regulator and social-service provider grew enormously in the first three quarters of the twentieth century. Then came the feeling that the state had become 'too large', and from Margaret Thatcher onwards determined, and partially successful, efforts were made to prune the leviathan. But it remains a giant compared to its puny nineteenth-century ancestor – which, we should remember, governed a vast empire.

Before 1914, the ordinary person barely noticed the existence of the state except in war. In 1910, the government owned only the post office and a few ordnance factories, employed 2 per cent of the population, and spent 12 per cent of the national income. The First World War pushed it into a commanding role, as servant of the people, but also their master. At its peak in 1976, the state owned 20 per cent of the economy, employed 25 per cent of the workforce and spent or transferred 47 per cent of the national income.

Over the twentieth century, public spending grew at 3 per cent a year, faster than population, which grew by 0.4 per cent a year, and GDP (at constant prices) which grew by 1.9 per cent a year. This is one important measure of the growth in state size. By far the greatest increase in public spending as a proportion of national income was accounted for by welfare payments to individuals and families, free or partly free services, notably education, medical care and housing, and (till the 1980s) subsidies to the nationalised industries.

The growth of the state was caused both by the expansion of existing functions and the addition of new ones. The nineteenth-century state grew through municipalisation, the twentieth-century state through centralisation. Municipal gas, water and electricity supplies date from the 1880s. In the twentieth century, central government took over the main transport networks – railways, roads, ports and waterways – and all (or most) gas, water and electricity undertakings; while the original post office monopoly was successfully extended to cover the main fields of electronic communication.

A second example of expansion is regulation. By the end of

the nineteenth century, economic activities were already hedged round with 'manifold and minute regulations and restrictions – factory acts, railway safety and mercantile and marine acts, licences and restrictions on the manufacture and sale of intoxicants, penalties against adulteration, and many statutes'.[1] In the twentieth century an increasing range of private activities were brought under the law, or administrative control, on the two broad grounds of the state's obligation to prevent harm to third parties, and an obligation to provide protection for disadvantaged groups. Noise and pollution control are examples of the first, protection for tenants and ethnic minorities of the second.

Finally, there was welfare. In the nineteenth century, most of what we call welfare was the province of municipal and private philanthropy. In the twentieth century the local authorities' role in providing welfare was transferred to central government and its scope vastly increased as the welfare state was set up in the 1940s.

In the twentieth century, the state assumed two distinctively new functions – as owner/planner and economic manager. A whole slew of private, non-utility businesses were nationalised, coal, steel, aerospace and the motor car industries being key. The state started to subsidise or protect agriculture, textiles and shipbuilding. It financed mergers, rationalisation and research. At various times, with more or less conviction, it ventured upon central planning, regional planning, population planning, land-use planning and planning of incomes. It built thirty new towns. With Margaret Thatcher, state ownership and planning went out of fashion, the government 'privatising' almost all the industries which previous governments had nationalised. As a result the state's (central and local government) share in total investment fell from 50 per cent to 25 per cent by the end of the century, and its ownership of the commanding heights of the economy receded to a rump, the biggest part of which was the Royal Mail, which the monarch had owned since 1516. The government also gave up most of its extensive planning functions.

The nineteenth-century state took no responsibility for the level of economic activity. In 1944, the government accepted a duty to maintain full employment, and by the 1960s, to achieve a satisfactory rate of economic growth. These functions decayed following the Thatcher revolution of the 1980s.

To pay for the state's increased activities, taxes had to rise sharply from their nineteenth-century level, though for most of the century they rose less than public spending. This left governments with deficits for much of the period. These did not lead to a continuous increase in the national debt, because GDP, especially after the Second World War, grew faster than the deficits. Taxes started to go up at the start of the twentieth century to finance rearmament (Dreadnoughts), old-age pensions and National Insurance. Income tax was 4 per cent in 1909, and people on incomes below £100 – that is the working class – were exempt, paying only indirect taxes, mainly on drink. In his 'people's budget' of 1909, Lloyd George raised income tax to 6 per cent, introduced a 'super-tax' of 13 per cent on incomes over £5,000 a year (the start of the graduated income tax), and increased death duties in two steps. In the 1914–18 war, the standard or basic rate of income tax went up to 29 per cent and super-tax to 58 per cent. In the interwar years the basic rate ranged between 20 and 25 per cent, with a top rate of 50 per cent, but then went up again to 27.5 per cent in 1939. In his 1941 budget, Kingsley Wood raised the basic rate to 50 per cent with a top marginal rate of

97.5 per cent. By lowering the tax threshold, Kingsley Wood created 3.5 million new taxpayers, who paid by compulsory deduction from wages at source. In 1939 fewer than 4 million paid income tax; in 1979 nearly 26 million did. This was a revolution in the relationship between workers and the state. The standard rate came down under the Conservatives from 47.5 per cent in 1951 to 38.75 per cent in 1959, but went up again under Labour in the 1960s and 70s. Since the Thatcher period there has been a noticeable decline in the burden and 'progressivity' of direct taxes, with revenue losses partly off-set by increases in indirect taxes like VAT. Top rates on unearned and earned income fell from 98 and 83 per cent respectively to 40 per cent in 1988–9, with the basic rate cut from 33 per cent to 25 per cent; there were also big reductions in corporation taxes and death duties. Income tax (standard and top rate) was lower in 1989 than in 1938, but many more people paid it.

To administer its hugely expanded estate, the government employed a growing army of non-industrial civil servants (in popular language, the bureaucrats). Their numbers increased from 50,000 in 1902 to 746,000 in 1977, though it fell back to 516,000 by 2000. In addition, there has been a luxuriant growth of non-governmental organisations (NGOs), set up to carry out specific functions. Whenever the government took on a new responsibility it spawned a board, authority, commission, council or committee. There were boards for the nationalised industries, regulatory authorities governing commercial activities, agencies for spending public money, and bodies which combined social goals with quasi-judicial functions, like the Equality and Human Rights Commission.

Reasons for the growth
of the state

Why did the state grow so large? Until the 1970s most studies of the growth of twentieth-century government assumed that it was an ineluctable response to changes in the structure of the economy and society; an aspect of modernisation, like the decline of religion. The growing density of population, the growing size of business units, the increasing complexity of communications and legal systems, the growing demand for health, education and welfare seemed to mandate a larger investment, regulatory and social service role for the state. However, simple determinism will not do. It is true that as societies get richer, an increasing share of their spending will go on health, education and provision for old age. But how much of this is private and how much public (i.e. tax-financed) will depend on politics, ruling ideas and events. As with religion, there is a supply and demand problem. One might think of politics providing the demand for a larger state and ideas the supply, with the two world wars shifting the trend towards statism.

On the demand side democratic politics was the crucial driver. The key change from the nineteenth century was the enlargement of the electorate without a corresponding enlargement of the obligation to pay direct taxes. As two economists put it, somewhat decorously, 'the widening of the franchise increased the political importance of the group most likely to believe that public expenditures should be increased for their benefit, but that the necessary revenues should be raised from the . . . richer by such means as progressive taxation'.[2]

The historical facts are clear enough. The proportion of adult males having the vote rose from one in five after 1832 to one in three after 1867 to three in five after 1884. After 1928 all men and women over 21 could vote in national elections. The effect of these successive extensions of the franchise was to destroy the links between voting, property owning and paying direct taxes. Traditionally, there was no theory of voting apart from tax-paying, which was in turn linked to property. In the mid-nineteenth century John Stuart Mill argued that voting should be tied to an obligation to pay taxes, and these taxes should be highly visible – direct, rather than indirect. 'Those who pay no taxes,' he wrote, 'disposing by their votes of other people's money, have every motive to be lavish, and none to economise.' If every voter were taxed, the poorest would identify their interest with 'a low scale of public expenditure'. Those in receipt of state benefits would be disqualified from voting.[3]

In the twentieth century, the view that voting should be linked to paying direct taxes went by the board. In the mid-nineteenth century, numbers of voters and taxpayers were almost identical at 500,000. For the first half of the twentieth century income tax was paid by only a small proportion of the enlarged electorate. In 1905, the majority of adult males had the vote, but the standard rate of income tax, applying to incomes of over £600, excluded 90 per cent of the working population. By 1919–20, some 5 million persons had become assessable for tax, but more than half of these were relieved from income tax through allowances: the vast majority of the working class paid no income tax at all. Even in 1938–9, fewer than 4 million assessments for income tax were made, from an employed population of over 20 million. It was only in the Second World War that income tax became a mass tax for the first time with 12 million taxpayers. By 1960 the vast majority of the working class was liable to pay income tax.[4] But because, by mid-century, income tax had become sharply progressive and redistributive, most voters could still feel they were getting more than they paid for.[5]

In local government, Mill's principle of no representation without taxation survived in attenuated form. Voting in municipal elections was confined to ratepayers, and local services were provided from the rates. The link between local voting and local taxes broke down, as an increasing share of local-authority spending started to be paid for by national taxation, and an increasing proportion of local voters had their rates subsidised. Margaret Thatcher's attempt in 1989 to restore a strong link between the right to vote in local elections and paying local taxes (the community charge or poll tax) was defeated by riots.

The intellectual tradition of the nineteenth century was generally hostile to state activity. This hostility arose from the importance attached to individual liberty, and the preoccupation with creating wealth, particularly in the light of population pressure. A minimal state was advocated for both reasons. The goal of Victorian financial policy has been summarised by G. K. Fry: 'Ideally central government in particular was to be kept small in relation to the economy. The budget was to be balanced. Taxation was to be kept low, and with it the level of public expenditure. The reduction of the debt was a priority.'[6]

At the end of the nineteenth century came the 'revolt against laissez-faire', spearheaded by the growth of a middle-class social conscience, a growing concern with 'national efficiency', the revival of socialist thinking under the impact of the economic fluctuations of the 1880s and 90s, and the ascendancy of Hegelian philosophy in the intellectual elite. These currents came together in New Liberalism – the dominant intellectual movement of the first part of the twentieth century. New Liberalism offered a theory of rights, a theory of positive freedom and a theory of property. The classical liberal notion of rights *against* society was dismissed as nonsense, since it was society which conferred rights. Rights must be judged by social utility. Freedom was redefined as power – the power of an individual to realise his moral potential. Property ownership had to be justified by social utility – a bridge to the Fabian theory of 'rent' which pointed to progressive taxation of the 'unearned increment' and even further to public ownership. New Liberals were convinced that the tendency of social evolution was to replace individual by collective action, that 'advancing civilisation brings with it more and more interference with the liberty of individuals'.[7] Almost no one active in public life in the first half of the twentieth century was wholly immune from these influences – politicians like Asquith and Churchill, administrators like Beveridge, and leaders of the rising Labour Party.

A second, later, intellectual influence of great importance was the Keynesian revolution in economics. In the nineteenth century it was widely believed that state expenditure was a subtraction from wealth creation. This view was based on the assumption that markets automatically produced a reasonable level of employment. (And if they did not, emigration to the empire and elsewhere provided a 'vent' for redundant population.) In the conditions of mass unemployment between the wars, and with opportunities for emigration drying up, Keynes showed that it was possible for state spending to create wealth by generating a higher level of economic activity. Keynesian theory provided advocates of particular spending programmes with an indispensable general argument for increasing state spending. In the 1960s Keynesianism provided a rationale for government planning of demand to overcome the problem of slow growth.

These specific intellectual influences needed to be considered in the context of the growth of the social sciences and with it the belief in the power of deliberate social action to alter for the better an existing state of affairs. Friedrich Hayek complained of the 'uncritical transfer to the problems of society . . . of the habits of thought of the natural scientist and engineer'[8] while the economic historian Max Hartwell commented that 'given desirable ends, the social scientists said, it was possible to direct society towards these ends . . . by conscious planning and bureaucratic manipulation . . . Thus, all social problems . . . could . . . be solved by government intervention'.[9] The social sciences gave to utopianism, for the first time, a power of action. Distant ideals, as well as age-old problems, entered the sphere of practical politics. Professional and expert lobbies arose to press on government policies for remedying disease, poverty, ignorance, crime, discrimination, and so forth. And government was able to tap the results of social research on these problems for the purposes of policy. The idea that intellectuals stood above politics and ideology, providing disinterested solutions to social problems, disarmed suspicions formerly attaching to government intervention.

The crucial *events* tilting public life towards statism were the two world wars, which demonstrated the power and efficacy of state action. In 1914–18 and again in 1939–45 the extent and activities of the British state expanded enormously but failed to contract once the war was over. Government in 1939 was bigger than it had been in 1914, and became still bigger after 1945.

The importance of war for the role of the state has long been recognised by historians. War brings state and people closer together. As the military historian Michael Howard put it: 'Military activity led to growing demands on communal resource of money and, sometimes, manpower. The demands of the Prince led to counter-pressures from the representatives of the people for participation.'[10] It is the bonding, in war, of rulers and ruled, state and society, which makes possible the expansion of government by consent. After the war, the consent diminishes before the state contracts.

The 'minimal' state of the nineteenth century was plainly associated with the absence of major wars, and more importantly the expectation that war would be a diminishing factor in international life. The abolition of income tax – 'the war tax' of the Napoleonic Wars – in 1816 began the process of dismantling the war state. The gradual conversion to free trade was a sign of confidence not just in Britain's manufacturing supremacy, but in peace.

The twentieth century reversed both fact and expectation. Not only were there two great wars but peace was a time of 'cold war', leading the economic historian Alan Milward to remark that 'the legal status of peace is far more "costly" than most former wars'.[11] One clear effect of living in an age of war has been the rise in military spending. In Britain defence spending rose from 2–3 per cent of GDP in the nineteenth century to 8 per cent in 1950. War and cold war also create the idea of strategic industries which have to be fostered and maintained by the state, thus giving a specific impetus to protection, public ownership and regulation.

However, the increased share of GDP taken by military spending was one of the least important legacies of the wars. By 2000 the 'peace dividend' had reduced defence spending back to 2.5 per cent of GDP. Much more important was the inspection process to which the wars subjected existing social arrangements. Government attempts to mobilise society and economy for war generated, as a by-product, increased knowledge about social inefficiencies – in education, health, nutrition and housing: a learning process boosted in the Second World War, by the bombing of houses, hospitals and schools.

However, the wars also loosened the 'bonds of revenue'. In 1961 two economists Alan Peacock and Jack Wiseman argued that major disturbances like wars increase people's tolerance for high tax levels. Increased taxes, accepted for war purposes, do not come down to pre-war levels when the war ends. Therefore, after each war, the 'size' of the government has gone up. In short, the welfare state rose with the warfare state.[12] The ratchet effect of the wars fits the data tolerably well between 1914 and 1961. The trend, however, might well have been upwards in any case: in Sweden, which was neutral in the two wars, taxes and spending rose even higher than in Britain. Spending increases in the 1960s and 70s seem to have been driven by 'the explosion in entitlements', which resulted in millions of new benefit claimants.

Most of the stimulants to a bigger state faded in the last third of the twentieth century, without being replenished. An increasingly affluent electorate started to prefer lower taxes to higher social spending, thus tightening the 'bonds of revenue' loosened in the wars. Disappointment with the results of Keynesian economics, the welfare state, the nationalised industries, as well as the failure of indicative central planning to improve Britain's slow rate of growth, shifted the intellectual climate to the view that government was the problem, private enterprise and markets the solution. This created the indispensable background of ideas to Thatcherite policy. And, luckily, there has been no repetition of the great wars which helped create the leviathan state. It will be more convenient, however, to consider the events and policies which brought about a partial retreat of the state in the political narrative of Part II.

Chapter 5

Edwardian Britain: Stirrings of the Twentieth Century

Most of the worst convolutions of history have occurred during the intervals of transition when the seat of empire, having abandoned one abode, had not yet fixed upon another.

Brooks Adams, *America's Economic Supremacy* (1900)

These two great peoples [the British and the Germans] have nothing to fight about, have no prize to fight for, and have no place to fight in.

Winston Churchill, speech to the Swansea miners, 1908

High noon of empire

In 1900, Britain was the greatest power in the world. The British Empire was at the heart of its world position, but not the whole of it. Britain's world power extended beyond that quarter of the global map painted red. Much of Latin America, notably Argentina, was part of its 'informal empire', the policies of whose governments were largely subservient to British interests. Apart from this, Britain was superior to comparator countries in five respects. The British navy was the world's most powerful. The City of London dominated world finance. Britain was the world's largest trading nation. Britain had colonised more of the world with its settlers, both inside and outside the empire, than any other European country. And there was widespread admiration for British institutions. It was the only world power of that age, but not a superpower. Britain's writ did not run in the United States. And it was not a hegemon in Europe, but part of 'the balance of power'. It owed its greatness to its people, its system of government, its commerce and finance, its navy, and its ideas. A little over sixty years later its empire was gone, and with it most of its previous world position. It is one of the tasks of this book to explain why.

The empire was both a source of strength and weakness. It conferred a double benefit by helping Britain maintain the European balance of power and managing the world economic system.

Both the settled and conquered parts of the empire propped up British power. The white colonies were additional population, available – though not in predictable form – for the defence of the 'mother country'. India and Egypt checked Russian expansion in the Near East and Central Asia, and Indian troops were also available for this purpose. These benefits were cheap at the price. The colonies of settlement took responsibility for their local defence; and Britain was able to defray the costs of ruling and garrisoning India through 'home charges'. In the semi-peaceful nineteenth century British defence expenditure amounted to only 3 per cent of GDP.

The empire provided sheltered markets for British manufactures and important sources for foodstuffs and raw materials. India proved useful in another way. It ran balance-of-trade surpluses with the United States and Europe. Britain could use these surpluses, held as sterling reserves in London, to offset the deficits in its own trade with North America and Europe. Here were the roots of the later 'sterling area'. Also, colonial governments borrowed in London to finance railways and port facilities built by British firms, thus providing Britain with a double business benefit. This was one of the ways British exports were kept going after the 1880s. In other words, empire was an essential part of the machinery of the liberal capitalist world order. And the British were tough-minded about the advantages which empire brought.

However, there were sources of weakness. The empire's resources could not simply be commandeered by an imperial tax. It was too dispersed to be unified militarily. It sprawled across five continents like a gigantic jellyfish, lacking a central nervous system, its extensions invitingly available to any determined regional predator.

By the end of the nineteenth century, the Victorian strain of anti-imperialism had died down, partly because the empire was cheap to run, partly because Europe as a whole had become imperialistic. The empire had supplanted Protestantism as the chief source of national identity. Many Britons took pride in it; the Scots and Irish in particular made a living from it. There was a genuine imperial patriotism. Empire was part of Britain's social and moral system. Rule abroad reinforced hierarchy and discipline at home. It helped shape the ethos of Britain's administrative elite, public school and Oxbridge-educated. Empire served as a vent for social conflict, offering 'outdoor relief' for the more bullying members of the upper classes and emigration outlets for surplus agricultural labourers. In 1895 Cecil Rhodes called empire a 'bread and butter question. If you want to avoid civil war, you must become imperialists.'[1] The word 'empire' gave an exaggerated impression of British power, but it conferred prestige, and prestige is an undoubted element of power. Lord Curzon's dictum reigned, that when Britain ceased to rule India it would sink to the rank of a third-class power. Nevertheless, the benefits of empire, psychological and material, depended crucially on a lack of challengers. By the early twentieth century this could no longer be taken for granted, and the costs of defence were rising. Premonitions of decline were in the air. The only question was: would it be peaceful or violent?

The empire was most vulnerable at its heart, because Britain itself was vulnerable to invasion. Hence imperial supremacy depended on naval supremacy – not just to protect the sea lanes to the empire, but to command the approaches to Britain itself: the Channel, the North Sea, the eastern Atlantic. This was the lesson of the Armada and Trafalgar. If naval supremacy was the first requirement, a pacific Europe was the second. Despite repeated efforts to shrug Europe off, Britain could not ignore it. The British method for achieving a Europe which posed no security threat to it was to maintain a European balance of power. No single power must be allowed to dominate the continent of Europe, and particularly to establish itself in the Low Countries, Belgium and Holland. Ever since Protestant Britain took on Catholic Spain in the sixteenth century, Britain had emerged as the 'indispensable nation' in the European balance, ready to throw its weight against any power which threatened it. Churchill would later describe this as the 'wonderful unconscious tradition of British foreign policy'. This required that it stay free of 'entangling alliances', ready to jump as the situation required.

The flaw in Britain's strategy was that the nineteenth-century revolution in transport and communications had started to unite Europe, both economically and militarily. Armies could be moved around much more quickly than in 1815. Geopoliticians like Halford Mackinder argued that the improvement of internal communications was shifting power from seaborne to land-based empires, and that the future lay with continental-sized states. In the absence of an actual British Army on the Continent, a country like Germany with interior lines of railways could hope to defeat France and Russia before British intervention became effective. The British remembered Waterloo; the Germans remembered Sedan.

British power in 1900 was not what it had been in 1815. In 1815 it had 50 per cent of world military capability. By the start of twentieth century this was down to 25 per cent – equal to the United States, and with Germany and Japan catching up.[2] The relative decline in British military power mirrored the relative decline in its industrial power: by 1900 the USA was producing more coal and iron than Britain, and the USA and Germany more steel. This was partly because they had larger populations. But, in addition, Britain entered the twentieth century lacking a large slice of modern war-making capacity – combustion-engine manufacture, machine tools, fine measuring, optical and scientific instruments, chemicals, products of the so-called 'second industrial revolution'. The ruthless analyst of British decline Correlli Barnett is scathing: 'British industry . . . was in many ways a working museum of industrial archaeology.'[3] The 'workshop of the world' was 'well on the way to becoming a technological colony of the United States and Germany'.[4] Barnett's view is retrospective. Britain's economy had not been built up as a war machine, because the nineteenth century did not require it. It presupposed a generally pacific world.

By 1900, Britain's strength rested not on its industrial base, but on trade and finance, and both depended on the British navy. The British economy could not support a navy invincible against any combination of powers, and by 1907 the British had to be content with a 'two-power standard': the British navy would be twice as large as the next one. However, a two-power standard British navy could not hope to rule the Atlantic, the Mediterranean, *and* the Pacific. 'Glorious isolation' was no longer possible: 'only diplomacy', Michael Howard writes, 'could solve the strategists' dilemma'.[5]

The most cost-effective agreement would have been with Germany. The problem of how to deal with Germany dogged British foreign policy from the start of the century; Britain's twentieth-century history was determined by its failure to solve it. Joseph Chamberlain, the Colonial Secretary from Birmingham, argued in 1899 that 'the natural alliance is between ourselves and the great German Empire'. By 'ourselves' Chamberlain meant the British Empire: a union of related races under a single crown. Chamberlain was the most creative British statesman of the Edwardian age. With a flash of intuition he realised that Britain's imperial future depended on making a *partner* of Europe's strongest nation, not on trying to maintain the European balance of power. This first approach to an Anglo-German axis foundered on Germany's support for Krueger in the Boer War and Germany's challenge to Britain's naval superiority, in Norman Stone's view 'the greatest mistake of the twentieth century'.[6] There would be a second approach in 1912, equally fruitless. The alternative was to neutralise potential challengers outside Europe. By submitting its territorial claims in the Venezuelan boundary dispute to an American arbitration commission in 1899, Britain conceded US supremacy in Latin America. In 1902 came the Anglo-Japanese alliance which, on renewal in 1905, committed Japan to support the British position in India against Russia. Britain resolved its African and other colonial disputes with France in an 'entente cordiale' signed in 1904; an entente with Russia, Britain's challenger in Persia and Afghanistan, followed in 1907. The accommodations with France and Russia amounted to a diplomatic revolution. However, they resulted in 'ententes', not military alliances. As Churchill pointed out, Britain incurred the responsibilities of an alliance, without its benefits.

The economy

Britain's reverses in the Boer War (where it had taken 300,000 British troops to defeat 70,000 Dutch farmers) led to a rare outbreak of national self-questioning, Rudyard Kipling excoriating 'the flannelled fools at the wicket or the muddied oafs at the goals' who had fought so ineptly. The 'audit' on the Boer War concentrated on two issues: Britain's relative economic decline and the 'social problem'.

Contemporary opinion sensed what was later quantified, that the British economy was losing ground, especially to the United States and Germany, and that if this trend continued it would start slipping down the political ranking of nations. As the historian Paul Kennedy has remarked 'Power rests, ultimately, upon the relative wealth and strength of the country possessing it.'[7] Contemporaries assumed an automatic connection between wealth and power. Wealth rested on trade, and the security of trade depended on the British navy. It followed that anything which weakened British power would damage its trade and thus it economy.[8]

In its period of rude health the British economy had struck foreign observers as being built for success. Voltaire in the

eighteenth century found admirable the English combination
of liberty and commercial enterprise. He particularly noted
the openness of the aristocracy to trade: 'A peer's brother does
not think trade beneath him', which he contrasted with the
exclusiveness of the French aristocracy.[9] The American Ralph
Waldo Emerson, visiting England in the 1830s, found the
secret of English success in their genius for practical logic and
detail. 'Everything in England', he wrote, 'is at a quick pace.'[10]
By 1900, the American Brooks Adams was telling a very different story. Contractors complained that English firms were
dilatory, and that the English seldom left their sport or dinner
for business. Shops opened late and closed early; workers
turned up late on Monday after a weekend of boozing; the
railway system was obsolete, and so on.[11]

Britain, it started to be argued, suffered from the handicap
of an 'early start'. In its institutions and habits, especially in
the dominance of small firms and craft unions and of the
political economy of laissez-faire, British industry was rooted,
as Thorstein Veblen put it, in an 'obsolete state of the industrial arts'.[12] Veblen's most telling insight was sociological: a
society which first breaks through to a high living standard
will be the first to decline, because it will be the first to
develop playful and decorative habits at the expense of useful
social practices. Much contemporary reporting was in this
vein. 'The once enterprising manufacturer has grown slack,
he has let the business take care of itself, while he is shooting
grouse or yachting in the Mediterranean', wrote one com-
mentator in 1909. Veblen added a typical observation: energies
which in German businessmen and workers were devoted to
their business were in England squandered on hunting, shooting and football. Contemporaries picked out 'mental inertia'
as the feature of the English character most damaging to

Britain's future. Having settled their principles and practices, the English had given up trying to understand the changing world beyond their shores. Everything in Britain was best and for the best.[13]

The mind of Joseph Chamberlain was far from inert. He saw the chance to link the theme of empire unity to a plan for Britain's industrial regeneration. At Birmingham Town Hall on 15 May 1903, he launched his campaign for tariff reform. Chamberlain rightly pointed out that 'it is not a question of whether we are richer now than we were fifty years ago . . . It is a question of which of us in the race for existence . . . is progressing more rapidly.' Imperial sentiment, revealed by the Boer War, justified aiming for a full political union of the empire, with an imperial government. This would enable the united resources of the empire to count for one in a world balance of power. But like the founding fathers of the European Union, Chamberlain recognised that such a goal could only be approached by practical economic bargains. As a first step, he wanted Britain to abandon its free-trade policy (which he called the 'convenient cant of selfish wealth') as its main competitors already had, impose a tariff on foreign manufactures, and construct an economic system based on 'imperial preference'. In return for preferential entry for British manufactures into colonial markets, Britain would impose import duties on non-empire corn and meat. Thus he hoped to galvanise British industry, safeguard domestic employment, and pave the way for 'that closer federal union I believe to be the real destiny of the British race'.

Chamberlain was the spokesman of industrial as opposed to financial capitalism. He wanted Britain to give up its City-centred imperialism and convert its empire into a Greater Britain, made up of 'our people'. Only thus would it hold its own in a new world of super-states. The main intellectual weakness of his tariff reform programme was that it artificially conflated two problems: the problem of imperial unity and the problem of British industry. Manufacturers wanted protection against German competition; they were not interested in preferential entry into tiny colonial markets. But the decisive objection was political. Chamberlain admitted that his scheme of taxing foreign foodstuffs would raise the domestic cost of living. This proved fatal to his policy. The working class rebelled against the threat of 'stomach taxes', returning the free trade Liberal Party to power in the 1906 general election with a large majority.* But imperial economics did not die. Indeed, with the establishment of imperial preference in 1932, the empire became, for a time, a key part of Britain's economic system.

Chamberlain's programme ran up against the free-trade vision of a liberal world trading system for which Britain would continue to provide capital and financial management. Replying to Chamberlain, the future Liberal prime minister Henry Herbert Asquith argued that the 'real enemies of British trade' were 'defective knowledge, inferior processes, lack of flexibility or versatility, a stubborn industrial conservatism'. Why was British industry becoming less competitive? Chamberlain said: 'We are losing our foreign markets, because whenever we begin to do a trade the door is slammed in our face with a whacking tariff.' For Asquith, inefficient industrial practices 'have done us infinitely more harm than all the tariffs and all dumping syndicates ever created'.[14]

---

* General Election, 12 January–7 February 1906: Conservatives 2,451,454 (157 MPs, 43.4 per cent of the vote), Liberal 2,757,883 (400 MPs, 49.4 per cent), Labour 329,748 (thirty MPs, 4.8 per cent), Irish Nationalists 35,031 (eighty-three MPs, 0.6 per cent).

Left-wing critics like J. A. Hobson, whose anti-Boer War polemic, *Imperialism*, was published in 1902, rejected both imperial and free-trade policies. A more equal distribution of national income, Hobson claimed, would eliminate British 'over-saving' in relation to domestic investment, and thus the need to export capital and jobs. Hobson's 'under-consumptionist' theory can claim the distinction of having anticipated both Lenin and Keynes.

The tariff reform controversy intersected with the debate on social reform. The extension of the franchise to the male working class in 1884–5 had brought the 'labour question' into politics; Charles Booth's studies of the London working class revealed the shocking fact that up to one third of the labouring poor in the world's richest capital were living 'at all times more or less in want'. But the crucial catalyst of reform was the audit of the Boer War which demonstrated the deplorable physical condition of British Army recruits. An unhealthy, stunted and ill-educated working class would be incapable of sustaining Britain's world position. The state tentatively started to address social problems in the name of 'national efficiency'. An early fruit of the new concern was the Conservative Education Act of 1902 which provided state support for secondary education. The Liberal government set up a Poor Law Commission in 1909. Its majority report oscillated between encouragement of voluntary institutions like the Charity Organisation Society, and recognition of the need for state action; its minority report, inspired by Beatrice Webb, was a bold administrative blueprint for the abolition of destitution through an 'enforced minimum'. The Liberal government introduced tax-financed old-age pensions in 1908; and a National Insurance Act in 1911 which provided a minority of workers protection against unemployment and sickness. Chamberlain wanted to finance social reform from the yield of his food taxes; the Liberals from taxes on the rich. The defeat of Tariff Reform in 1906 led inescapably to Lloyd George's populist budget of 1909, designed to raise revenue to build more Dreadnoughts *and* pay for social reform. The welfare state was born as a by-product of the warfare state.[15]

These early twentieth-century exchanges staked out future positions in the economic and social debate. Chamberlain offered social imperialism, Asquith liberal imperialism, and Hobson economic nationalism. Both Chamberlain and Hobson identified the structural dominance of the City of London as the cause of Britain's industrial decline. Chamberlain's defeat by the free-traders was a decisive moment. Not for the last time, Britain decided to stand on its ancient ways. The defeat of protectionism ensured that laissez-faire economics, represented by the City and its associated networks, would continue to dominate British economic policy. It also tended to confirm the inherited structure of the British economy. Britain concentrated on exporting its traditional staples in which it had long had a comparative advantage. This biased the debate on education against technical training. There was a geopolitical aspect to the debate. Later analysis suggests that Victorian businessmen were not falling down on their job, but behaving and investing rationally, given their situation. This does not alter the fact that what was rational for individual businessmen was contributing to the weakening of British power on which the British economy depended.

Politics – the Dangerfield thesis

In his melodramatic book *The Strange Death of Liberal England*, published in 1935, George Dangerfield portrays a pre-war Britain threatened by social revolution and territorial break-up, from which it was only rescued by the First World War. The malign conjuncture he discerns was the threat of a general strike coinciding with civil war over Ulster; this coming on top of the constitutional crisis following Lloyd George's 'people's budget' of 1909, and the urban violence unleashed by the suffragettes.

Dangerfield's was a salutary counterblast to the Edwardian nostalgia industry, itself a reaction to the horrors of the First World War. There is no doubt that the five years leading up to 1914 were an angry period. Nevertheless, to talk about the crisis of the British state is vastly overdrawn. There had been no external national failure – the usual precipitant of revolution. The constitutional crisis had been resolved by abolishing the Lords veto in 1911; women would have got the vote sooner rather than later. Dangerfield grossly overestimates the power of the 'new world coming to life' and underestimates the strength of the 'old world that was dying'.[16] The death which he thought had already happened was, in fact, brought about by later events.

Historians like Ross McKibbin have argued that liberal England was doomed because class was replacing rank and religion as determinants of political allegiance. But this was a slow process, and it was never complete. The Nonconformist vote continued to sustain the Liberal Party long after class analysis had consigned it to history's rubbish bin; and it is impossible to explain the huge success of twentieth-century conservatism without reference to its Protestant, anti-Catholic support from the working classes of Lancashire and western Scotland.

It is true that the trade union movement was growing, sections were becoming more militant, and that, as a consequence, the economy was becoming less flexible.* But only 20 per cent of the workforce was unionised at the time of Edward VII's death in 1910, and only a tiny fraction of this was socialist or syndicalist. Trade unions were defensive not revolutionary. The industrial unrest which peaked in 1911–12 was mainly a cost-of-living question: real wages fell as prices rose by 9 per cent between 1909 and 1913, provoking a spate of strikes by miners, railwaymen and transport workers, who formed a Triple Alliance in 1914. A single industry, coal mining, which had the most obstinate set of owners and workers in the country, was at the centre of the industrial storm, as it was to be till the 1980s. Most of the days lost through strikes in 1912 – the peak year of industrial unrest – were in coal mining. Dangerfield's suggestion that but for the war there would have been a general strike of 'extraordinary violence' in September 1914 is unconvincing.

It is true that the Liberal Party never held power independently again after the First World War. But the evidence does not suggest that the Liberals in 1914 were already doomed as a governing party. The new Labour Party, which had forty-two seats in the Commons in 1910, was still a trade union appendage of the Liberal Party, which had partly stolen its clothes. The radical intelligentsia was liberal, not socialist. The predominant political fact between 1906 and 1914 was not the advance of Labour but the recovery of the Conservatives. By 1914, the Labour Party leaders were

---

* The legal position of the trade unions was strengthened by the repeal, in 1906, of the Taff Vale judgement of 1901, which had allowed unions to be sued for damages by their members, and by an Act of 1913 which lifted the ban on use of union funds for political purposes. Until the Thatcherite legislation of the 1980s unions enjoyed 'immunity from tort'.

bidding for places in a Liberal government. But for the war, a situation in which, for a long time, a trade-union-led Labour Party remained a junior partner of a reformist Liberal Party is perfectly imaginable. It was the war which made Labour the dominant party on the left.

Economic growth, however uneven, was starting to elevate the material condition of the people. Even before the state intervened massively in these respects, manual workers were becoming healthier, better educated, better housed and more secure, as their incomes rose and through efforts of collective self-help and philanthropy. During the so-called depression of 1873 to 1896 real wages had gone up as prices of necessaries fell. Workers' consumption rose and leisure increased. The nine-hour working day and the fifty-four-hour working week had become standard; Saturday half-days were becoming common, a prerequisite for the spread of organised sport. The average football league match attendance rose from 6,000 in the 1888–9 season to 11,200 in 1902. By 1914, the country had between 3,500 and 4,500 cinemas, with an average of twenty-two cinemas for every town with a population over 100,000. The number of visitors to Blackpool in season rose from 1 million in 1883 to 4 million in 1914. Economic growth increased the demand for clerical and professional jobs, promising educated women an independent income and status. From Edwardian Britain we can already project forward the 'affluent society' which only arrived in the 1950s.

The 'ancient British state' had proved remarkably successful at accommodating middle-class aspirations within a quasi-medieval formal structure. Conflicts of interest were contained in a structure of hierarchy and deference. Britain maintained a liberal aristocratic civilisation, to which the middle class aspired. The public schools continued their Victorian task of producing a bourgeois version of a ruling class fit to govern the empire. Workers still knew their place in the social order, and most of them – Irish immigrants being a notable exception – lived and died in the same place, socially and geographically.

Before 1914 territorial disintegration seemed a greater menace than did social revolution. The chief threat came from Irish unrest; and late nineteenth-century British statesmen devised various formulae to placate Irish griev-ances while keeping Ireland attached to the Crown. The most famous was Gladstone's 'Home Rule'; but there was also the attempt to head off Home Rule, by proposing a lesser 'devolution all round' for the four 'nations' of Ireland, Wales, Scotland and England. In fact, Ireland was *sui gen-eris*, and the devolutionary agenda was soon abandoned. There was an 'Irish problem', not a 'British' problem.

Though constitutionally represented at Westminster by around 100 Irish MPs, Ireland had never accepted full inte-gration into the Protestant British state. Irish nationalism crystallised in the demand for Home Rule offered by Gladstone in two bills of 1886 and 1892, which failed to pass the Lords. The Conservative mixture of repression and land reform killed off Fenian, or rural violence, but not the demand for Home Rule.[*] The inconclusive general elections of 1910, which left the Liberal government dependent on the eighty Irish Nationalist MPs led by John Redmond, forced the prime minister, Asquith, to return to the Gladstonian

---

[*] Ireland was the only place in Britain where the enclosure movement of the sixteenth and eighteenth centuries was reversed, with the Wyndham Act of 1902 subsidising Irish tenants to buy out their landlords.

Home Rule agenda.* In 1912 he introduced a third Home
Rule Bill.

This set the scene for a two-year struggle. The Liberals
would not accept the exclusion of Protestant Ulster from
Home Rule because Redmond could not concede it; the
Conservatives rejected Home Rule altogether. What made
Ulster's future central to the struggle was the abolition of the
House of Lords veto in 1911.† This removed any constitutional
obstacle to Home Rule, leaving only violent opposition from
Ulster itself. The Ulster Volunteers, headed by Sir Edward
Carson, leader of the Irish Unionists, prepared for resistance
to 'rule from Dublin'; Balfour's successor as Tory leader,
Andrew Bonar Law, the Canadian-born son of a Scottish clergy-
man of Ulster descent, encouraged them with inflammatory
speeches; in response, the Irish Nationalists formed their own
volunteer force. In their efforts to accommodate Catholic
nationalism, the liberal imperialists of Whitehall under-
estimated the force of Protestant nationalism – a mistake they
were to repeat in the 1970s. By 1914 both sides were arming.
In Dangerfield's view, but for the war there would have been
a civil war in Ireland spilling over into England and Scotland.
The alternative, and more plausible, hypothesis is that but for
the war, Home Rule would have gone through in 1914 with

---

* General election, 14 January–8 February 1910: Conservative (Unionist) 3,127,887 votes
(273 MPs, 46.8 of the total vote); Liberal 2,880,581 (275 MPs, 43.5 per cent); Labour
505,657 (forty MPs, 7.0 per cent); Irish 124,586 (eighty-two MPs, 1.9 per cent).
General election, 2–19 December 1910: Conservative (Unionist) 2,420,566 (272 MPs, 43.6
per cent), Liberal 2,295,888 (272 MPs, 44.2 per cent), Labour 371,772 (forty-two MPs, 6.4
per cent), Irish 131,375 (eighty-four MPs, 2.5 per cent)

† The House of Lords was left with a two-year suspensory veto. This meant that the
Home Rule Bill would automatically become law on the third occasion of its passage
through the House of Commons.

the six counties of Ulster temporarily, and eventually permanently, excluded.* With Home Rule in place, a growing net
flow of revenue from the British Exchequer to Ireland would
have made it much harder for Ireland subsequently to break
free. *Pace* Dangerfield, it was the war, not the pre-war troubles,
which killed Home Rule for Catholic Ireland.

Bloomsberries and Fabians

H. G. Wells likened Queen Victoria to a 'great paper-weight
that for half a century sat upon men's minds, and when she
was removed their ideas began to blow about all over the
place haphazardly'.[17] The Bloomsbury Group were the first
iconoclasts of the twentieth century. Their attacks on the
empire, Victorian morals and Victorian taste set in motion
the intellectual dismantling of the Victorian moral and social
order. In rejecting the symbols of Victorian authority they
taught a generation to doubt authority as such. From
Bloomsbury, wrote Noel Annan, 'came our distaste for the
Establishment'.[18]

A paper read by the Cambridge undergraduate Desmond
McCarthy to the Apostles – a secret 'conversation' society
– in December 1900, could serve as Bloomsbury's manifesto
for the twentieth century. The key difference from their
predecessors, McCarthy says, was that his generation took
'everything more *personally*' than they did. This was due to
'all institutions, the family, the state, laws of honour, etc

---

* Following the 'Curragh Mutiny' in March 1914, when it seemed that British troops
would refuse to 'coerce' the Protestant counties of Ulster into a united Ireland, Redmond
had accepted the principle of temporary exclusion. An all-party conference at Buckingham
Palace in July 1914 accepted it in principle, but foundered on the question of how big the
excluded area should be. The Protestants wanted and eventually (in 1921) got six counties.

which have a claim on the individual . . . having failed to produce convincing proofs of their authority'.[19] Expressive individualism emerged from its Victorian chrysalis.

Edwardian Bloomsbury championed not just iconoclasm in art but freedom in sex. The Bloomsbury 'moment' in 1907 when Lytton Strachey, pointing an elongated finger to a stain on Vanessa Bell's dress, enquired 'Semen?' controverts Philip Larkin's conceit that 'Sexual intercourse began in nineteen sixty-three'. But the turning inward demanded by McCarthy was possible only to an intellectual and artistic elite possessed of some private income.

Edwardian Bloomsbury did not see itself in the vanguard of popular enlightenment, but rather as educators of the aristocracy. Their cultural tastes were avant-garde, distinctly highbrow, what would later be called modernist. They tried to discover objective value in art and literature to replace the conventional storytelling of the Victorians. For example, the Bloomsbury art critic Roger Fry developed a purely 'internal' way of judging a work of art, expounded in his doctrine of 'significant form'. He wrote: 'The aesthetic emotion is an emotion about form. In certain people, purely formal relations of certain kinds arouse peculiarly profound emotions.'[20] Just as the moral intuitionism of Cambridge philosopher and Bloomsbury guru G. E. Moore was an attempt to rescue morals from religious dogmatism and conventional opinion, so Fry's aesthetic intuitionism was an attempt to protect art from bad taste. T. S. Eliot had the same idea when he wrote: 'Poets, in our age, must be difficult.' Ezra Pound would not have disagreed, and he certainly succeeded.

In the history of philosophy, the doctrine of intuitions in morals and art is little more than a stepping stone to subjectivism; for Bloomsberries it marked out an objective standard superior to convention. But its temper was esoteric, not proselytising. It sought to repel the masses, not embrace them. There can be no authority without contact, and it was contamination by lower-order values that Bloomsbury feared most. Bloomsberries were not 'leaders of the people' in the biblical sense, and often not 'wise and eloquent in their instructions'.

The Fabians, another fraction of the dissident Edwardian intelligentsia, aimed to imbue the ruling class with a 'sane collectivism'. They hated Bloomsbury because of their lack of concern with public causes and what Beatrice Webb called their 'anarchic ways in sexual questions'.[21] Sidney Webb deplored the goal of self-realisation. 'We have no right,' he said, 'to live our own lives. What shall it profit a man to save his own soul, even if thereby one jot less good is done to the world?'[22] He knew what he was talking about: his wife Beatrice told him she was marrying 'the head only'. Although the Fabians were the first generation of British socialists, they were the last generation of pre-democratic reformers – the last who could ignore and despise the masses who were supposed to benefit from their plans. They saw themselves as the 'scientific' managers of a socialist state, a role which has often appealed to intellectuals of modest birth and wealth. Their support for local government – 'gas and water socialism' – was bureaucratic rather than popular.

Uniting Bloomsbury and the Fabians was a common fear of the mob. Bloomsbury pulled towards expressive individualism, the Fabians towards utilitarian collectivism. Neither, before 1914, pulled very far. Despite their atheism and socialism, both kept up respectable middle-class appearances.

Part II
The Action

Chapter 6

The Age of Lloyd George
1914–1922

Throughout the countries which had participated in the war there is a still a tendency among many bereaved ones to assuage themselves by the thought that their dead had fallen for something noble and worthwhile . . . Mischievous delusion. Their dead are victims – neither more nor less – of the folly of adults who having blundered the world into a ludicrous war, now build memorials – to square it all up.

William Gerhardie, The Polyglots (1925)

Slaughter

The First World War of 1914–18 is history's supreme example of an unnecessary war. It is made so both by the triviality of the reasons for it, and the scale of its destructiveness. It accelerated the decline of Europe, discredited the old ruling class, and unleashed demons which commanded much of the twentieth century. Most of the progress which is said to have resulted from it would have come about any way through normal social and economic development; and some effects deemed progressive at the time can now be seen as highly retrogressive. That it still has its defenders stems from the tribute comfort pays to adversity, cowardice to heroism, and the identification of virtue with death.

In her book *Alfred and Emily* (2008), Doris Lessing imagines what would have happened to her parents' lives but for the First World War. (Her conceit is not just that Britain stayed out, but that it would not have happened.) In his review of the work, Paul Binding wrote:

> The war-free England that gives Alfred his harmonious, productive life has conserved its Edwardian/ Georgian self with remarkable purity. Its dominant culture is bucolic; sport, practical and neighbourly charity, and a cheerfully carnal uxoriousness are its outstanding features. Prosperity has continued, though poverty, mostly urban, does exist, and is fought by individual dedication and private resourcefulness. [The 'people's budget' of 1909 clearly had no real consequences.] In the wider world, we learn that Austro-Hungary and Turkey imploded in the earlier 1920s, affecting little in English life except metropolitan fashion. But many . . . do come to feel a lack in their lives which they think only wars can fill. Alfred's sons, though not Alfred himself, will hear the call to battle.[1]

This is a possible, and by no means implausible future. In fact the war happened, and twentieth-century British history is largely its consequence. One need not regard pre-1914 European society as perfect to wish that it had been allowed to develop in peace, or to be intensely curious about *how* it would have developed.

The First World War features in both the narrative of the 'decline and fall of the British Empire' and the narrative of the 'rise of the people'. Despite the horrific slaughter it brought about, left-leaning historians have seen it as an engine of progress: it made the state responsible for the welfare of the people, and pointed to state planning as an alternative to capitalism. But equally plausible is an opposite hypothesis: that victory in the war deluded and exhausted Britain at the same time.

It is not quite true to say that the war came unheralded, out of a clear blue sky. Like the *Titanic* as it sailed full speed ahead in 1912 into the iceberg which sank it, Europe was not short of warning signals. Anglo-German naval and commercial rivalry was a fact. The German Kaiser was prone to bellicose utterances. Spy thrillers by writers like William Le Queux, John Buchan and Arthur Conan Doyle fed the reading public with tales of the evil machinations of foreign governments (though the baddies were as often Russian as German). But overconfidence undermined watchfulness. Small wars were possible; but a great war was unthinkable. As Keynes wrote: 'The projects and politics of militarism and imperialism, of racial and cultural rivalries, of monopolies, resrictions, and exclusion which were to play the serpent to this [pre-war] paradise, were little more than the amusements of [the] daily newspaper, and appeared to exercise almost no influence at all on the ordinary course of social and economic life, the internationalisation of which was nearly complete in practice'.[2]

Britain on its own could not have stopped a European war – certainly not in the last few days of peace. What it could do was to stop Germany and its allies from winning it quickly, or winning at all. This it did in four years of bloody fighting. Its part in preventing Germany establishing a premature, and no doubt Prussianised, European Union was a source of much pride. In fact, it is the only retrospective justification now given for its participation in the conflict. Had the British remained neutral, the Franco-German war might have been as short as 1870, Lenin ended his days as a disgruntled pamphleteer, Hitler eked out his living as a water-colourist.[3]

David Owen has argued persuasively that Britain should have stuck to the tradition of the balance of power – that is, not tied itself to any of the power blocs. This would have enabled it to keep its lines of communication with Germany open. Instead the Foreign Secretary, Sir Edward Grey, a man of upright character, but wooden intellect, allowed the start of military conversations with France in 1905, which, despite his denials, amounted to an 'honourable undertaking' to dispatch an expeditionary force to France if it found itself at war with Germany. Moreover, he neglected to tell the Liberal Cabinet till 1911 about these conversations, even though the Germans knew about them.[4]

There was a radical tradition in British foreign policy, strongly represented in Asquith's Cabinet, which rejected such balance-of-power calculations. The radical thesis was, roughly, that wars benefited rulers and arms manufacturers, not the mass of the people, and that, in any case, Russia was a greater danger to civilisation than was Germany. However, this Cobdenite tradition of non-interventionism was challenged by Gladstone's 'moral interventionism' on behalf of small nations. The radicals needed a moral excuse to go to war. Germany provided it by invading 'neutral' Belgium on their expected way to Paris. This swung the Welsh Chancellor of the Exchequer Lloyd George, an outsize product of a small country, and the bulk of the Liberal non-interventionists to the war side. (Though Lloyd George may have been maneouvring himself as a potential war leader before that). The German blunder of invading Belgium, dictated by the logic of the Schlieffen Plan, provided Asquith's Cabinet with the necessary reconciliation of morality with realpolitik. The most reluctant to go to war, Britain was the quickest to turn it into a moral crusade against Prussian militarism.

Grey told Parliament on 3 August 1914 that, in going in, 'we shall suffer but little more than if we stand aside'. This extraordinary statement rested in part on the widespread expectation of a quick victory. The British grossly over-estimated the strength of finance; the Germans grossly overestimated the power of the offensive. But Grey also hid from Parliament the fact that Britain was bound by a secret treaty with France to fight a continental war. The reforms of Haldane, Asquith's Secretary of State for War from 1906 to 1911, had created the Imperial General Staff, the Territorial Army and the British Expeditionary Force. The 160,000-strong BEF was sent over to France as soon as the war broke out in time to take part in the decisive Battle of the Marne which put paid to the Schlieffen Plan. Most of it was destroyed in the process. By November 1914 a continuous trench line ran from the North Sea to Switzerland, 'resembling', writes John Keegan, 'a layer of scar tissue, picked at and irritated, over the site of an unsuccessful surgical operation'.[5]

The pattern was now set for four years. From the end of 1914 the Germans maintained a defensive line in northern France, and concentrated on achieving victory over Russia in the east. (The exception was the failed attack on Verdun in early 1916 which turned into an epic of French resistance.) The French and British repeatedly tried to break through the German line in big offensives, to recover land and resources lost to the Germans. All failed, at horrendous cost. There was a similar stand-off at sea: the British imposed a naval block-ade, which Tirpitz's fleet was unable to prevent; the Germans responded with submarine warfare which almost brought the British to their knees. For a couple of years it was touch and go as to who would be able to starve out whom sooner. Eventually the British won the Battle of the Atlantic, as they would in the Second World War, since the German strategy of trying to sink all ships bringing supplies to Britain was bound to bring America into the war on Britain's behalf.

The stalemate on the western front opened up a debate between the 'westerners' and the 'easterners'. The 'westerners' wanted to win the war by a frontal attack on the German position. The 'easterners' favoured the strategy of knocking out one of Germany's main allies, the Ottoman Empire. This played to traditional British naval, financial and imperial strengths: others would do the main fighting, while Britain subsidised its allies and harassed the enemy on the flanks as it had done in the Napoleonic Wars.

The disastrous failure of the bungled attack at Dardanelles (April 1915 to January 1916) put paid to the 'eastern' strategy. The triumph of the 'westerners' was symbolised by the appointment of Sir Douglas Haig (of Haig whisky) as commander-in-chief of the British Army in France at the end of 1915. On the first day of the Battle of the Somme, 1 July 1916, 21,000 British troops were killed, 40,000 wounded, the greatest loss of life in British military history on a single day. A gain of seven miles between July and November cost the British 420,000 casualties all told. At Arras, Ypres and Passchendaele the following summer, 70,000 British troops were killed, a further 200,000 wounded. On 21 March 1918, the Germans, victory in the east finally achieved, flung everything into a last assault on the west, but the French and British, now reinforced by the Americans, held firm, turning defence into attack. The Germans had nothing left and surrendered on 11 November 1918.

With the extraordinarily high rate of casualties more and more troops were needed to ensure victory. At first, Britain, alone of the belligerents, raised its armies by voluntary enlistment; conscription only started in 1916. By November 1914 800,000 had volunteered, inspired by Kitchener's famous poster 'Your country needs you'. By the end of 1915, the number of volunteers had risen to 2.5 million The professional and commercial classes, as well as the Scots and the miners, joined up in disproportionate numbers. By 1918 Britain had mobilised over 6 million troops, over a quarter of its male population. The British Empire contributed 2.6 million, almost half of them Indian and, except for the Canadians, mostly deployed in the Middle East. New Zealand sent 20 per cent of its male population. The bravery of the Anzacs in the failed attack at Gallipoli is one of the most glorious and tragic episodes in Britain's imperial history.

How was the slaughter machine kept going? Patriotism and a sense of duty give part of the answer. The perception of Germany as the bully of Europe predates the war. The German attack on France and Belgium simply confirmed it. In that age of deference, people trusted their leaders. The generals were massive authority figures, their failings well hidden from the public. The unity of the two front benches of Parliament in supporting the war was crucial. No front-rank Liberal or Conservative leaders (Lord Lansdowne excepted) emerged to question the principles of the war; criticism was confined to its conduct. Anti-war politicians like Labour's Ramsay MacDonald were howled down. Anti-war feeling spread widely only once the war was over, casting its long shadow over the 1930s.

Rudyard Kipling greeted the war with one of his most bellicose ballads: 'For all we have and are,/For all our children's fate,/Stand up and take the war,/The Hun is at the gate!' After he had lost his only son he wrote: 'If any question why we died,/Tell them, because our fathers lied.' The slaughter machine was kept going by the lying machine. For the war to continue at all, wrote the poet Robert Graves, it was necessary 'to make the English hate the Germans as they had never hated anyone before'. This was the chief aim of wartime propaganda, in which the invention of German atrocities played a part. In 1914 prominent writers were coralled into a War Propaganda Bureau set up by Lloyd George. It published over 1,000 pro-war pamphlets, its earliest being a largely, but not completely, invented account of systematic German atrocities in Belgium. (The torching of the university town Louvain in August 1914 was a real, but isolated, crime.) The media did not have to be commandeered; they enlisted voluntarily in the war effort. The few dissident journals, mainly Irish, were suppressed; censorship was mostly self-censorship. Lord Northcliffe, owner of *The Times* and the *Daily Mail*, was put in charge of propaganda aimed at enemy cities; Lord Beaverbrook, who acquired the *Daily Express* in 1916 together with his peerage, was made minister of information by Lloyd George in February 1918, both press lords neatly combining two disinformation roles in one. Hitler and Goebbels were greatly impressed by their efforts and sought to model Nazi propaganda on them. Lloyd George cynically remarked to C. P. Scott in December 1917, 'If the people really knew, the war would be stopped tomorrow. But of course they don't.' British Military Intelligence (MI5) was set up shortly before the war to counter espionage, sabotage and subversion. It was used not just to flush out German 'spies', but to monitor the activities of Irish nationalists and militant shop stewards.

The churches also gave the war legitimacy. The Anglicans and most Nonconformist churches buried their differences to support the war; only the Vatican took a stand against it, though this was not supported by most Catholic priests. Most padres did their duty of comforting the wounded and dying.

Peer pressure was very important. Men were shamed into volunteering by being given white feathers by their wives or sweethearts if they didn't; many joined because their 'pals' in factories, mines, villages or offices did so. As the war became grimmer, voluntary enlistment fell off. The men went on fighting because they trusted their officers and because they were part of a social system of war in which it was unthinkable not to. Some cracked, but only a tiny fraction were shot for desertion or cowardice. Instead shell shock was diagnosed as a medical condition. Men grumbled about conditions in the trenches; they skived as much as they could; they were comforted by religion, alcohol, fags, football and prostitutes. They relieved their suffering with black humour: early in 1916, the 12th Battalion Sherwood Foresters began publishing the *Wipers Times*. Its brand of surrealist, anti-Establishment satire, the British version of Dada, became a fixture of British comedy. Many in the trenches experienced a growth of spirituality; perhaps they fought for a better life. But in the end, as Niall Ferguson rightly says, 'men kept fighting because they wanted to'.[6]

Lloyd George

David Lloyd George, who took over from Asquith in a palace coup on 6 December 1916, was Wales's chief contribution to twentieth-century British history. Asquith wanted to run the war much as the Liberal government had run the peace, in a hands-off way. He retained a large Cabinet, whose interminable meetings left plenty of time for the prime minister to write gossipy letters to the 'splendid, virginal' Venetia Stanley. With the non-arrival of victory his premiership went into decline, and on 19 May 1915 he was forced to concede a coalition with the Conservatives and to move Lloyd George from the Exchequer to the newly created Ministry of Munitions. The new ministry, galvanised by Lloyd George's drive, became 'the pioneer of state interventionism',[7] ordering weapons on a vast scale, regardless of cost. Some 500,000 new workers entered the munitions industry, half of them women. Mistrusting permanent officials, Lloyd George turned to businessmen to provide the necessary 'push and go'. He toured the country making fiery speeches about the need to expand weapons production and cut alcohol consumption.

Asquith's premiership was doomed by conscription and the failure of the Somme offensive. As A. J. P. Taylor wrote, 'By the autumn of 1916 liberalism was played out. The only logical alternatives were to abandon liberalism or abandon

5. The Welsh Wizard: David Lloyd George

the war.'[8] Lloyd George's success in producing shells made him Asquith's obvious successor, and he became prime minister on 7 December 1916 with the Conservative leader Bonar Law as Chancellor of the Exchequer. His new government was supported by nearly all the Conservatives, over half the Liberals, and by the Irish Nationalists.

Lloyd George is the first of Britain's three great twentieth-century prime ministers, and now the least appreciated. His decisive contribution was not to military strategy, on which he was a tyro, but in organising the home front for victory. His virtuosity in keeping the victory agenda going in face of huge difficulties, domestic and external, and without solid political support, stamps him with greatness. The case against him is that he never contemplated a negotiated peace; in fact, he put it beyond reach by his 'Knockout Blow' interview to an American journalist in September 1916.

For all his loathing of war, Lloyd George preferred the atmosphere of war to that of peace. He stood for a non-socialist radicalism, with its Nonconformist hatred of landlords and financiers, and its vision of tuneful and prosperous male voices ringing across the valleys. He loved singing hymns himself and telling funny stories about Welsh preachers. But socialism, he declared, 'is like the sand of the desert. It gets into your food, your clothes, your machinery, the very air you breathe. They are all gritty with regulations, orders, decrees, rules.' He saw in the 'new patriotism' created by the war a chance to advance a social-reform programme, free from the blockages of party politics. He was a politician of situation, not principle; and war was the situation which gave fullest scope to his executive abilities. He had no time for class: the Lloyd George liberals were upwardly mobile professionals and self-made men. He was the great outsider of

British politics, who forced himself to the centre by sheer vitality. As a politician his great strengths were a strategic vision, his willingness to listen, and his ability to persuade. He was a brilliant negotiator, his mixture of blandishment and threats being crucial in managing the trade unions before and during the war, and the Irish in 1921.

His persuasiveness was based on his great charm. A magnificent head of hair was mounted on a short body, and even shorter legs. He lacked any trace of humbug, was fun to be with, and was brilliantly witty in his judgements of people and events. He and Churchill were responsible for most of our best political one-liners. His sense of humour was basic: he laughed himself almost to death when someone produced a bag of air which burped. Everything had to revolve round him: he gobbled his food and had his guests' plates cleared away as soon as he had finished. Considering his political dependence on the Nonconformist vote, he took immense risks with his sex life – and got away with them, because in those days intrusive newspapers did not exist.

His fatal flaw was an inability to inspire trust. 'We are governed by a crook', wrote Keynes in 1918. This was the Asquithian view, but it went beyond Asquith's supporters. Lloyd George was convinced he was weaker than he actually was. So he shrank from personal confrontations, preferring indirect methods. As a result he got a reputation for deviousness. He often suspected conspiracies when there were none, and was suspected of organising them even when he had not. 'There is no friendship at the top', he used to say. Lloyd George had no friends – only admirers and vassals.

Unlike Asquith, Lloyd George was not a party man. Indeed in 1910 he had proposed a Liberal–Conservative coalition to set aside old issues in order meet the needs of the new century. He disliked the formalities of politics, and soon dispensed with the prime minister's chore of writing a weekly letter to the king, replacing it with bland Cabinet minutes. 'He detested titles,' wrote Taylor. 'This, no doubt, is why he distributed them so lavishly.' His instruments were the platform and the press. He was a brilliant public speaker, in the tradition of Welsh preachers; and courted newspaper editors and proprietors, because he thought of them as a conduit to 'the people'. His friendship with C. P. Scott, owner and editor of the *Manchester Guardian*, kept him his radical base. But he also cultivated self-made press lords, like Alfred and Harold Harmsworth and Max Aitken, ennobling all three. Through the platform and the press, Lloyd George sought to become the *vox populi*, bypassing Cabinet and Parliament. Unrooted in party, his power was personal, not institutional. Like Tony Blair later, he ran a court, not a government. Almost half the Liberal Party remained Asquithian. He alienated Labour by forcing Arthur Henderson out of the War Cabinet in August 1917. The Conservatives did not love him. They remembered his contemptuous assaults on landlords in his Limehouse speech of 1909, and returned the compliment by calling him 'George'. They used him to win the war, just as he used them to win supreme power. It was not a marriage built to last.

The limitations of his personal power soon became apparent. He was the war leader, but prime minister of a government dominated by the Conservatives, and hostage to a jingoistic press. This limited his ability to impose his authority on the military. He set up a Supreme War Council in November 1917 as a way of overruling the generals, but it took him more than a year to send Sir William Robertson, chief of the Imperial General Staff, packing. He had one spectacular success. On 25 April 1917 he went to the Admiralty and insisted, over the objections of the naval chiefs, on imposing the convoy system on British shipping. This soon staunched shipping losses to submarines, on which Germany relied to force Britain quickly out of the war. He could do little, though, to undermine the 'western' strategy, in face of royal, Conservative and press support for the generals, especially as Russia collapsed. The Flanders offensive, ending in the mud of Passchendaele and 270,000 casualties, was the price for his inability to thwart Haig, a consummate court politician. The prime minister was reduced to withholding reinforcements from the western front in order to prevent a repetition of the butchery. This nearly cost him his job in the Maurice Debate of 9 May 1918, when he escaped what was in effect a Liberal censure motion. Ninety-eight Asquithian Liberals voted against the government. This marked the moment at which the Liberal Party split irretrievably. No one realised that Lloyd George's triumph on this occasion was the start of his decline and fall.

Lloyd George's war machine

The planning system for total war was only gradually evolved in response to the war's specific crises by men who had no experience of state planning.

The Munitions of War Act of May 1915 brought the munitions industry under government control. It gave legislative underpinning to a deal with the trade unions, under which they agreed to 'dilution' (allowing unskilled workers to do the jobs of skilled craftsmen), and compulsory arbitration in return for government promises to restrict wartime profiteering and uphold the principle of free collective bargaining. Intervention spread with the Military Service Act of 27 January 1916, which imposed military conscription on all bachelors between eighteen and forty-one; this was extended to all men between these ages in July 1916. Military conscription ended the system of voluntary enlistment and the free market in labour which depleted vital industries haphazardly. It was thus the means to industrial conscription. Failure on the Somme led, by stages, to food rationing and coal, manpower and shipping control. New war ministries – of Labour, Shipping, Food, Health and National Service among them – and over a hundred new boards, were set up to direct the flow of resources to priority sectors, most of them run by businessmen and imported civil servants. Prices, wages, rents and profits were brought under control. Subsidies for food-growing started in 1917, with 4 million acres brought back under plough. This reversed seventy years' free market in foodstuffs.

Friedrich Hayek remarked that 'once the free working of the market is impeded beyond a certain degree, the planner will be forced to extend his controls until they become all-comprehensive'.[9] This is in essence what happened. But Britons did not believe they were on the slippery slope to serfdom, shielded from such reflections by the cheerfully untheoretical bias of the national character. They accepted planning as a necessity of war, which would be abandoned once peace returned. Conscription, in a technical sense, operated only in the military sector, and then only from 1916. Conscientious objectors – 16,000 in all – were allowed to appeal to a tribunal. Compulsion was mostly a reserve power, rarely used.

Despite some fraying at the edges, there was just about enough consent for industrial planning to be carried out by voluntary agreement – 'supervised self-government' in Keith Middlemas's phrase. Owners continued to run the 'national-ised' industries; the TUC acted as the government's recruiting agent in directing the flow of labour and limiting workers' rights for the duration. Both expected to return to their old 'free market' habits after the war. Some looked beyond this to a new era of tripartite partnership between government, business and labour. A few saw a blueprint for socialism.

War spending had to be financed. Again, there was much learning on the job. At first the government covered its spending by heavy short-term borrowing – the accepted device for a short war. This proved inflationary, with purchasing power spilling back into the private economy as the government spent the borrowed money. Most of the doubling of cost of living that occurred in the war came in the first couple of years. The role the budget could play in diverting resources from private to government consumption without inflation was understood by only a few, notably a brilliant young Treasury official, John Maynard Keynes. Even less was the war budget understood as a means of securing a rough equality of sacrifice. At the Board of Trade, Sir George Askwith, the government's chief industrial conciliator, was one of the few to recognise that keeping prices stable – what he called 'the cost-of-living question' – was the key to controlling wages.

The real squeeze on private consumption started with Reginald McKenna's first budget of September 1915, which, in addition to a steep increase in taxes, imposed the 'McKenna Duties' on luxury imports, ending seventy years of free trade. (Lloyd George scribbled to a colleague across the Cabinet table: 'So the old system goes, destroyed by its own advocates.') McKenna also imposed an excess-profits tax of 50 per cent. Raised to 80 per cent by Bonar Law in 1918 it was by then providing the Exchequer with nearly half its revenue. The government had also improved its technique of borrowing, shifting from unfunded to funded debt. There were four war loans in 1914, 1915, 1917 and 1919. By absorbing liquidity, long-dated stock had an anti-inflationary effect. An issue of war bonds, attractively priced, raised £649 million in 1917–18 and £987 million in 1918–19. Of the government's domestic war expenditure, nearly 30 per cent was raised by taxation, and the rest borrowed – worse than Pitt had achieved in the 1790s, but better than the other belligerents. This left the national debt at the end of the war at just over £6 billion, or 135 per cent of national income, up from 25 per cent in 1914. No less than 17 million Britons held some form of government debt, mostly in post office savings certificates. The millions of bondholders created by the war made up the deflationary coalition of the 1920s.

External war spending had to be covered by selling gold and foreign assets and borrowing from the United States. The official history of the Ministry of Munitions states that 'it was only the ability of the Allies to import shell and shell steel from neutral America . . . that averted the decisive victory of the enemy'.[10] This meant that the United States could have brought the war to an end – at least by 1916, when Britain's gold reserves were almost exhausted.

The crisis came at the end of 1916. On 24 October, McKenna minuted: 'If things go on at present . . . by next June or earlier the President of the American Republic will be in a position . . . to dictate his own terms to us.' These words fix the moment when financial hegemony passed irrevocably across the Atlantic. The Allies were only saved from defeat by the lunatic German decision to restart unrestricted submarine warfare on 1 February 1917. On 6 April the United States declared war on Germany. This ended the dollar shortage, allowing Britain to borrow freely in the USA till end of war.

By the end of the war, it had sold £1.25 billion or a quarter of its foreign assets. It had borrowed £2 billion from America (the whole of its pre-war national income). Broadly speaking, Britain had lent its allies the money to buy munitions by selling off its securities and borrowing from the United States. This was the reality behind the determination of the victors to extract large reparations from Germany, and Keynes's much more sensible idea of cancelling all inter-ally war debts.

The First World War was a war run by civilians for generals; a military dictatorship disguised by Lloyd George's charisma. Military demands were never considered in relation to political strategy but as determining it. The purpose of planning was to supply the armies with what the generals wanted, rather than sustain the economy, society, and Britain's post-war position. The result was a labour surplus in the armed forces and shortages everywhere else. Britain was far more profligate with its 'man' power than were the Germans. It was also less successful at conserving its financial resources. Both failures impaired its post-war prospects.

Failure to control the flow of men into the armies put a severe strain on the partnership with labour. Labour played no part in the strategic direction of the war. The government needed the co-operation of the trade unions to make military and industrial conscription work; but there was a limit to how far the TUC would, or could, contribute to military and industrial enlistment without losing control to the radical shop stewards' movement, particularly powerful in the engineering and shipbuilding industries. Despite repeated efforts, the government could not tie workers to their jobs – and thus stop them from bidding up wages in sectors of shortage. Most of the strikes in the war were cost-of-living questions. The government rarely broke up strikes, preferring to settle on the men's terms. Bonar Law remarked prophetically in

January 1918: 'Once the workpeople got the notion that they were dealing with the Treasury, and not with the employers, there could be no end to their demands, and future strikes would be against the government.'[11] Finally, there was no central planning body to impose priorities. The war industry ministries simply grabbed the scarce resources, especially labour, for themselves, at premium prices. Despite Lloyd George's efforts, the machine created for winning the war was palpably defective. The upside of this was that it lessened the attractions of central planning for the purposes of peace. Contrary to conventional wisdom, the superiority of the planned economy was not the lesson most Britons took from the war.

Economic and social consequences of the war

One adverse consequence of the war for Britain is undeniable. It greatly retarded the growth of wealth. At its most basic human and material level it was much more destructive than the 'balance of power' wars of earlier centuries. British casualties were over 10 per cent of the workforce: 723,000 killed, and almost three times that number wounded. (Crippled beggars became familiar on British streets between the wars.) The rest of the empire lost 213,000 killed, with another 427,000 injured. The quality of the population declined. For the aristocracy and officers, the ratio of those killed to those who fought was one in four, twice as high as for ordinary ranks. There is no need to accept the myth that the 'brightest and best' perished in the trenches to believe that the disproportionate toll the voluntary recruiting system took of the aristocracy, middle classes and skilled workers led to a loss of energy and talent. Quite simply, Britain failed to preserve its human capital. It also lost four years of investment in capital equipment, a once-and-for-all loss. Real income per capita in 1926 was lower than it had been in 1913. This may be contrasted with an average rate of growth of real per capita income of just over 1 per cent a year from 1900 to 1913. Had the First World War not happened, or even had it stayed out of it, Britain would have been a much richer country in the 1920s and 30s than it was.

The reason some historians have seen the war as an agent of advancement is that it fits their model of political progress. It advanced democracy and it advanced organised labour. What the suffragettes had been unable to achieve by chaining themselves to railings was granted as a 'reward for war service': women over thirty got the vote for the first time (in 1928 women of twenty-one got the vote also, equalising the genders) and millions of extra men were also enfranchised. This almost trebled the electorate – from 7.7 million in 1910 to 21.4 million in 1918. The Labour Party replaced the war-shattered Liberal Party as the main political opposition to the Conservatives. It emerged from the war with a new constitution pledging it to the 'common ownership of the means of production', and a new political self-confidence. Of more practical importance, Labour's constitutional provision for individual membership opened up the party to middle-class radicals. The trade union movement gained in numbers – up from 4 million to 8 million members – in prestige, and in power. During the war it had bargained with the government almost as a sovereign power; in 1920 the TUC set up a General Council as a 'general staff' for organised labour. The war left 'a mighty leviathan of government'.[12] This was expected to be the basis of an interventionist state. Another consequence of the war was a big rise in taxation, especially of the wealthy, and a consequent compression of incomes. The army of progress, it might seem, had struck its tents, and was on the march to a better world.

But the 'British revolution' obstinately refused to materialise. More women voted Conservative than Labour. True, the war had strengthened the Labour Party; but by so doing, it consolidated the hegemony of the Conservatives, by giving birth to the bogey of socialism. This was not the old reactionary right. The war had shown the Conservative Party that it needed Labour's co-operation to govern. Labour wanted recognition, not revolution. War experience pointed to a conservative-slanted consensus, not revolution or reaction. The war produced a generation of defeated politicians who clung to the frail lifeboat of decency.

The interventionism of the war was not institutionalised in peace. Lloyd George set up a Ministry of Reconstruction in July 1917 under Christopher Addison. The government would provide 'homes fit for heroes'. The Haldane Committee was set up to rationalise the machinery of government; Herbert Fisher at the Board of Education wanted to raise the school-leaving age to fifteen and take in hand technical education; the Bryce Report recommended a partly elected House of Lords. These reconstruction plans fell to harsh economic reality. Most of the wartime ministries and boards were scrapped, the coal, railway and shipping industries returned to private control, plans to nationalise electricity and raise the school-leaving age were shelved. The national minimum wage was abandoned, together with plans for an 'industrial parliament'. Reconstruction and reform expressed a fleeting mood, not a philosophical choice – nor a political reality for a coalition.

The war had seemed to herald a new era in industrial rela-tions. Wartime innovations pointed to a system of corporatism. The Whitley Councils, formed in 1917, were designed to replace collective bargaining with arbitration. But the war failed to forge a new compact between the unions, the employ-ers and the state. Industrial relations remained fissiparous, and mainly adversarial. As a result, the central problem of industrial relations – namely, how organised labour fitted into a capitalist economy – remained unattended.

After the war the British rediscovered the joys of mental inertia. The war confirmed them in their 'sense of underlying insular identity and common fate'.[13] They had to differentiate themselves as much as possible from the Germans. So they stripped themselves of anything that could be construed as Prussianism. Pre-war social reformers who had called for the state to organise 'national efficiency' rediscovered the virtues of muddling through. Hegel was out; character and sound judgement back in fashion. It was the Webbs, with their chilling Prussianism, who now seemed out of date. The monarchy, which had changed its name from Saxe-Coburg-Gotha to Windsor in the war, reinvented itself as a purely British institution. The war gave amateurism a boost: had not make-do, after all, won out against Prussian preparations? With amateurism went sportsmanship. 'The British soldier is fighting for fair play,' declared Lloyd George vacuously. Sport – especially football – could bring social peace. For striking workers to play football with the police in 1926 was considered to be typically, and helpfully, 'British'.

There was a modest advance in social equality. Tax rates were permanently higher, though they came down from their wartime levels. The landed aristocracy lost most of its remaining political clout, partly because, with fixed rents and falling agricultural prices after the war, a quarter of landed estates were sold off and divided up into 'villas'. It had become unthinkable to have a prime minister in the Lords, as the magnificent Marquess of Curzon, Foreign Secretary and ex-viceroy of India, discovered in 1923. After the war, England was more middle class than aristocratic, although it was a middle class permeated with Arcadian longing. Women also chalked up economic and social gains. Having replaced men in factories and on tramways, they were not so ready to go back into the home. But the war gave only a modest boost to women's industrial employment, and the ensuing depression sent them back to domesticity – and domestic service.

Contrary to much received wisdom, the war strengthened rather than weakened social conservatism. Historians like Samuel Hynes and Arthur Marwick have argued that it produced a moral, cultural and aesthetic revolution. The Victorian moral order, they say, died in the trenches. Patriotism, discipline and obedience led to mass slaughter; progress was a soiled creed. Britain entered a spiritual crisis, of which one expression was the cynicism and promiscuity, despair and drunkenness, recounted in the works of Evelyn Waugh, Cyril Connolly, Michael Arlen and Aldous Huxley. The madcap behaviour of the Bright Young Things, the parties, the gambling, was a response to the crisis of values. Freud came into his own; 'we are all psycho-analysts now', wrote the *New Statesman* in 1923. 'The important thing', wrote the now elderly Fabian Sidney Webb to the French historian Elie Halevy in 1926, 'is that people in general, in all classes, seem to have lost practically all their "taboos" in sexual relations . . . .[this] may prove to be more "revolutionary" in its results than any other change of thought'.[14] His wife Beatrice found the cultural scene equally depressing, reverting time and again to the 'mania [of the young] for the sub-human in art, literature, music, manners – Epstein, D. H. Lawrence, Aldous Huxley, Jazz music'. She noted shrewdly that rejection of the super-human was bound to lead to the subhuman.[15]

The post-war behaviour and tastes discerned by the Webbs may have been portents of things to come, but as yet were true only of a tiny metropolitan minority. The continuity with Victorianism was shaken but not broken, despite the so-called moral *caesura* of the war. In fact, just because the war had been so horrible, it produced, in reaction, not a loosening but a tightening of the moral and aesthetic coils which had held Victorian society together. Over the whole landscape of intellectual and cultural life, the war produced exhaustion, not renewal. The great public intellectuals of the twentieth century – Russell, Keynes, Beveridge, Shaw, Wells – were products of Edwardian, not wartime sensibility – or they were foreigners like T. S. Eliot.

What the war did do was to destroy the heroic ideal of war. The pity of war and the suffering of the individual became paramount; the defectiveness of the leaders taken for granted. The old men of 1914 had betrayed the young by send-ing them to the front for no good cause. There they were betrayed by stupid generals – 'the fierce and bald, and short of breath' – and those bloodthirsty padres who perverted sacri-fice to God into killing for country. At home they were betrayed by profiteers, civilians and women who cheered them on with the romantic patriotism of Rupert Brooke. In 1916, Lytton Strachey published *Eminent Victorians*, a work of historical satire, in which he mocked Victorian icons, includ-ing Gordon of Khartoun whom he depicted as a religious crackpot, alcoholic and paedophile. The book entered four editions in six months. Keynes's *Economic Consequences of the*

Peace (1918) adopted Strachey's ironic style in its sardonic depiction of the wartime leaders at the Paris peace conference, mulling over frontiers and territorial changes while Europe starved. His powerful polemic did much to discredit the Versailles peace treaty. By the end of the 1920s, a spate of memoirs had reinforced the unheroic image of war. They shared a sense of what Paul Fussell called 'the irony of hope abridged'.[16]

The literary reaction to the war launched the pacifist mood, which had such an influence in the 1930s. It also explains the wary, sceptical and mocking mood of those who fought in the Second World War: 'the dominant feeling in 1939 among the young', according to Noel Annan, 'was that although the bloody old men had got us into this mess we had to fight – only this time with no bloody heroics'.[17]

In summary, whereas the First World War was a tremendous shock, its main result was not to shock the British out of old habits, but to reinforce them. Pulling back from the excesses of the war occupied most of the energies of the political class, leaving it bereft of new ideas.

Consequences of the war for Britain as a great power

The war weakened Britain as a great power. This was not at first apparent. The British Empire had acquired new limbs – former German colonies in Africa, parts of the Ottoman Empire in Mesopotamia, Transjordan, Palestine. These were all formally held under mandate from the new League of Nations, in deference to the new doctrine of 'trusteeship'. A complicated commitment in the Balfour Declaration was to create a Jewish 'national home' in Palestine, then largely occupied by Arabs. In Europe, three autocracies had collapsed, the independence of the Low Countries had been preserved, and ten new European states created. Except for Russia, where Bolshevism succeeded tsarism, Europe was now formally 'democratic' in all its parts. But the formula of democracy in Europe and trusteeship in Asia and Africa was an unstable basis for the continuation of empire.

Britain was not weakened politically relative to Europe. In fact it emerged stronger than its defeated enemies. The important point was that Europe itself was weakened relative to the rest of the world. It lost its place as a centre of world civilisation and economy, and Britain went down with it. Ideologically, Europe was hit by the twin assaults of Wilsonian national self-determination and Bolshevism. The former was an open challenge to continued imperial rule; the latter to the capitalist system. Both had defined pre-war European civilisation.

The condition of Europe's overseas empires had been European peace. Once the Europeans started fighting each other on a large scale the days of empire were numbered. The war shattered Britain's aura of invincibility. Restless subjects were emboldened to use force against British rule; psychologically the British were less willing to use force to maintain it.

The war also hit Europe economically, none more so than Britain, its leading economic power. It disrupted the global trading and financial system which Britain had orchestrated and on which it depended not just for its living, but to support the empire and its position in Europe. Industrial supremacy had long since gone; but wartime interruption of supply chased British exports from Latin America and Asia. The Indian tariff of 1917, to provide revenue for the government of

India, decimated Lancashire's exports of cotton goods to India. The loss of European markets was crucial. The post-war British economy was too weak to rebuild London's financial supremacy. Britain never enjoyed full employment between 1920 and 1940. A weakening economic base supported undiminished global commitments.

After 1918, there could be no doubt that the United States was the most powerful nation in the world. Henceforth, the British Empire existed by permission of the United States. The rise of both the United States and the Soviet Union to superpower status was delayed, in the first case, by self-imposed isolationism, and in the second by the domestic convulsions accompanying the Bolshevik Revolution. This left Britain the sole world power *faute de mieux*, and nurtured the illusion that the medium-sized European states with their huge external appendages continued to be arbiters of their own fate, and the world's.

The decline and fall of Lloyd George

Lloyd George looked set to dominate post-war politics. The 'man who had won the war' went to the country on 14 December 1918 as head of a coalition of Conservatives and Lloyd George Liberals, promising 'to make Britain a fit country for heroes to live in' – as well as to hang the kaiser and make Germany pay the whole cost of the war. 158 coalition Liberals received his 'coupon': 133 were elected, together with 335 Conservatives, and 10 coalition Labour. The Asquithian Liberals, left outside the Lloyd George umbrella, were decimated.[18] Only twenty-eight survived, with Asquith himself unseated at East Fife. Seventy-three Irish Sinn Fein MPs refused to take their seats. The quasi-presidential regime

Lloyd George established between 1918 and 1922 was the nearest Britain approached to populist dictatorship.

Labour, with sixty-three seats, became the official Opposition to the coalition, a pole position in Parliament. Yet it would have been premature to speak of a decisive Labour breakthrough. The coalition won 45 per cent of the votes cast (though on a turnout of only 10.77 million or 59 per cent of the eligible voters). However, the two 'wings' of the Liberal Party polled 25.6 per cent altogether, more than Labour's 22 per cent, and with 161 MPs to Labour's sixty-three. Even though the 'coupon' Liberals were sheltered from Conservative competition, it is highly likely that had a reunited Liberal Party (especially one under Lloyd George) fought the 1918 election it would have come second to the Tories in both the country and Parliament. Liberals and Labour gained an identical share of the popular vote in the two elections of 1922 and 1923 which followed the collapse of the coalition. But electoral geography had started to turn against the Liberals: it was now taking more Liberal votes to win them a seat than it took Labour. With the destruction of their Irish Nationalist allies by Sinn Fein in 1918, and the establishment of the Irish Free State in 1921, the Liberals were also gravely weakened against the Tories. The dramatic collapse in the Liberal position took place in 1924, the first experience of Labour government producing a huge shift in votes and seats from Liberals to Tories. The division of political Britain into a predominantly Conservative south, a Labour north, a contested Tory–Labour Midlands and a Liberal 'Celtic fringe' was established for the next fifty years.

The historian Maurice Cowling has argued that the key to the confused politics of the period 1920 to 1924 was the attempt to evolve a successful style of resistance to Labour, with the Conservatives winning out over efforts to create a Lloyd George-led 'centre' party. This is certainly an important theme. The Conservatives were torn between resuming political independence and using a man of the left to neutralise the numerical superiority of a mainly working-class electorate. Conservatism's electoral success depended on not fighting the class war – indeed, denying its existence – and the broader its church, the more plausible its classless appeal. However, one should not presume too much on hindsight. For most politicians, it was still the Conservative–Liberal battle that counted. It was not clear that the Liberal Party was doomed. Lloyd George might jump either way. Thus attempts in the early 1920s to reinvigorate the historic Conservative and Liberal battle were just as important as efforts to construct a successful opposition to socialism.

The victorious Lloyd George coalition was immediately confronted with a 'guns versus butter' dilemma. Expanded commitments – in Russia, Europe and the Middle East – had to compete with a big promised social-reform programme. In foreign policy, the story of the coalition is one of retreat from imperial overcommitment; in domestic policy, it is one of retreat from wartime promises. Within three years, the commitments and promises had been scaled down to what Britain could afford, and Lloyd George himself chased from power.

The Versailles Treaty, signed on 7 June 1919, failed to produce a pacific world, in which imperial dominion could be quietly enjoyed. This was because the war failed to solve the German problem. Lloyd George spent the first six months of his peacetime premiership negotiating the treaty with Germany; and much of the rest of his premiership trying to undo its consequences. He managed to get the indemnity demanded of Germany scaled down in 1921, though the

Germans soon defaulted on their monthly payments. But the collapse of the central empires left unstable frontiers, with millions of Germans left in the successor states of Austria, Czechoslovakia and Poland.

The most important act of British scaling down was the jettisoning of the policy of naval supremacy. The Americans were determined to end the anomaly by which the Monroe Doctrine depended in part on British control of the Atlantic. They told the British that unless Britain accepted naval parity with the United States, they were prepared to outbuild the British navy. Before 1914, Britain had taken up the German naval challenge; now it gave way to the United States. It realised that in America it faced a more powerful, but also less hostile, challenger. The Washington Naval Agreement of 1921 fixed the relative strength of the American, British and Japanese navies at 5:5:3. As a result, 'a permanent shift in world power was consummated without a shot being fired'.[19] As a condition of the agreement, the United States insisted that Britain give up the Anglo-Japanese alliance. This proved to be fatal for the survival of the British Empire in Asia, since in the Far East America would be the rival, not the underwriter.

The war weakened the British position in Ireland and India. The Dublin uprising of 24 April 1916 was the first step in the unravelling of the British Empire. Brutally suppressed though it was*, it pointed the way to Indian and later nationalism. It also started the long history of British guilt. If empire had to be maintained by 'frightfulness' it was not worth having. But historians mislead if they also see 1916 as the start of the dissolution of the British state. Ireland was part of the

---

* Fifteen leaders of the rebellion were shot; 1,867 imprisoned. Yeats wrote 'A terrible beauty is born.'

empire, Scotland was not. In terms of Britain's 'ancient constitution' it was a one-off event, Irish conditions not having a parallel in any other part of the British Isles.

Ireland was the thorn, not the jewel, in the imperial crown. More than the uprising, it was the British attempt to introduce conscription in 1918 which killed Home Rule, and united Catholic Ireland behind Sinn Fein, the political wing of the Irish Republican Army. The seventy-three Sinn Fein MPs elected to Westminster in 1918 set up a separate Parliament, appointed their own government, and declared Ireland a republic; Michael Collins, an outstanding guerrilla commander, set about organising the IRA to win independence by force. Learning from the failure of the Easter Rising, he worked out the blueprint for a new kind of 'asymmetric' warfare, whose aim was not to win military victory but to render a continuation of repressive policy politically and psychologically impossible for the occupying power. Collins's tactics worked brilliantly against the shell-shocked British. Lloyd George tried to counter with the Black and Tans and Auxiliary police, who became notorious for the use of 'reprisals' against the civilian population. But Lloyd George was not cut out to be 'Bloody Balfour'.* Besides, he needed American help to pacify Europe. While claiming to have 'murder by the throat', he opened unofficial negotiations with Arthur Griffith, acting president of Sinn Fein. In July 1921 a truce was declared. In November 1921 a treaty was signed which made Catholic Ireland a self-governing Dominion under the Crown, like Canada, Australia, New Zealand and South Africa. Protestant Ulster accepted Home Rule as second best to direct rule from London. Michael

---

* A. J. Balfour had, as Secretary of State for Ireland 1887–91, ruthlessly crushed the Fenian uprising.

Collins, the chief Irish peacemaker, purported to be astonished by the British capitulation: 'You had us dead beat . . . We thought you must have gone mad,' he told Lloyd George. In 1937, the prime minister De Valera would send the king's Governor General packing. In 1949, Ireland formally became a republic, outside the Commonwealth.

Indian nationalism learnt from Ireland's successes – and failures. As a reward for Indian help in the war, the Secretary of State for India Edwin Montagu had, in 1917, promised it 'self-governing institutions'. ('Self-government' has been crossed out on Curzon's insistence.) In 1919, though, Mohandas Karamchand Gandhi (known as Mahatma) started his popular resistance campaign against British rule. But passive resistance turned violent. Europeans were killed and their property plundered. On 13 April 1919 General Dyer ordered his troops to fire on an unarmed crowd of thousands assembled illegally in a square in the middle of the Sikh holy city of Amritsar, killing 1,800 and wounding hundreds of others, in order, as he put it to the official inquiry, to 'produce a sufficient moral effect throughout the Punjab'. The massacre forced Gandhi to call off the Punjab campaign but radicalised the Indian National Congress, hitherto a constitutional pressure group. The new leadership of the Nehrus, father and son, committed it to a programme of *swaraj*, or freedom (code for independence). On their side, the British had little stomach for repression of the 'Prussian' type, and there was no repetition of the Amritsar massacre. For the next twenty years the British alternated between locking up Gandhi, Nehru and other nationalist leaders, and trying to win them for a programme of constitutional progress to modified Dominion status at an undefined future date.

The domestic policy of the Lloyd George coalition was

marked by retreat from reconstruction. The inflationary boom with which peace started seemed to make reconstruction less urgent; the ensuing depression made it unaffordable.

The government had formally unpegged the pound from gold in March 1919, fearing social unrest if demobilisation led straight to the dole queue. The pound depreciated by 35 per cent against the dollar, and low interest rates produced an inflationary boom, running from April 1919 to April 1920. Wages had risen faster than prices in the last two years of the war, but rationing had prevented people from spending their increased incomes. With the 'bonfire of controls', the public went on a spending spree, consumption leading investment. Once the boom got going, prices were pushed ever higher by gambling in commodities, shares, property. Lloyd George wanted 'cheap money' to finance his 'homes for heroes'. So banking and political logic combined to keep money amazingly cheap long after the boom showed signs of getting out of hand. With wages now lagging behind prices, there was a spate of strikes: in an echo of 1911–12, 40 million days a year were lost on average in 1919 and 1920. The Labour Party, spurred on by the Miners Federation, pledged itself to the nationalisation of the coal mines. The majority of the Sankey Commission recommended it in 1919, but the government turned it down.

Gradually the Bank of England and the Treasury regained control of financial policy from the politicians who had usurped it during the war. Lloyd George instinctively mistrusted the advice of Treasury officials. He brushed aside Treasury warnings that 'capital is not unlimited' with the remark that his wartime experiences refuted the Treasury view. He could not, though, resist the argument that inflation had to be liquidated, and even reversed, if sterling were to return to the gold standard at its pre-war parity with the dollar: an objective proclaimed by the Cunliffe Report in August 1918 and accepted by the government in November 1919. Bank Rate was put up to 7 per cent in April 1920. Consumer spending fell first, followed by investment spending. Prices started to tumble in October; unemployment rose sharply in November. Over the next twelve months output fell by 15 per cent and unemployment rose to 22 per cent. The last two years of the coalition were thus dominated by the most ferocious slump of modern times. Small-scale efforts to relieve it were entirely swamped by its impact on the budget.

'Economy' (now called 'austerity') was the orthodox response demanded by the Treasury, and economy meant the scrapping of social reform. The Treasury regained control over public expenditure, and with it came the return of the Treasury view, now more rigorously formulated, that public spending was less productive than private spending. Public spending was slashed; taxes came down (though not to the pre-war levels). Despite an extension of unemployment insurance in 1921 (to cope with the huge number of extra unemployed created by the depression), the embryonic welfare state remained essentially as it had been left in 1914. A major casualty was Christopher Addison's housing programme, which aimed to build 500,000 new houses for working-class heroes, with the help of a subsidy from the government to the local authorities covering most of the capital cost.* From the start the programme was undermined by long delays and escalating costs. Addison's administration of the housing drive was the chief target of a vociferous 'anti-waste'

---

* Technically the capital cost discounted by rents which working-class tenants could afford.

campaign. The programme was soon scaled down: first to 250,000 then to 176,000 houses. Addison was removed from Health, and left the government in July 1921, protesting loudly at the triumph of reaction. In fact, the rate of local authority housing completions was not too bad – 110,000 in 1921–2, which is identical with the Labour government's achievement in 1946. Neville Chamberlain for the Conservatives slanted the subsidy towards private housing in 1923, and John Wheatley for Labour back to municipal housing in 1924. Slum-clearance legislation dates from 1930. It took another war to make house-building a litmus test of political performance.

In July 1921, Lloyd George set up a committee of businessmen headed by Sir Eric Geddes to advise the government on economies. It recommended cuts of £87 million; the government cut £64 million in its 1922 budget, the so-called 'Geddes Axe'.* Capital spending and subsidies proved easier to cut than cash transfers, as all later governments found out. More important than the suggested cuts was the philosophic rejection by the Geddes Committee of the expanded role of the state. The pre-war state, its report implied, was adequate to its tasks. For years, historians treated such an attitude as antediluvian. In the 1980s, the antediluvian sprang back to life.

The political issue dominating the coalition was Lloyd George's future. Was he the problem or the solution? As long as the Conservatives felt they needed him, he had some hope of constructing a new Centre Party to resist Labour. As the coalition's fortunes declined so did Lloyd George's attraction for the Tories. In 108 by-elections between 1918 and 1922 the

---

* In fact, it accepted only £52 million of the Geddes cuts, adding £12 million from other sources.

coalition lost thirty-seven seats, seventeen to independent Conservatives (whose number of MPs increased from forty-eight to sixty-five), thirteen to Labour and seven to the Liberals. The drift back to party politics was unmistakable. The resignation from the government of the Conservative leader Bonar Law, on grounds of ill health, on 17 March 1921, gave the Conservatives a 'leader in waiting'. Fusion also became less attractive to the coalition Liberals as Liberal fortunes improved, with Asquith being returned for Paisley in 1920. The prime minister tried to safeguard his political future. Instead of reforming the House of Lords he sold peerages and other honours to businessmen (a barony cost £50,000 upwards), accumulating a personal fund which reached between £1 million and £2 million, for use by any party which would have him. But his reputation never recovered from the stench of the honours scandal. At the start of 1922, Lloyd George proposed to hold an election to capitalise on his Irish triumph. Bonar Law vetoed it, fearing a break-up of the Conservative Party. Foiled of a dissolution, Lloyd George toyed with resignation, but like most men in power he had come to believe he was indispensable.

It was his overambitious foreign policy which brought him down. Having pacified Ireland, he turned his still formidable energies to the pacification of Europe. He worked out a network of complicated, interconnected deals in which French financial claims against Germany were to be partly traded off against a British guarantee of France's security, and debt settlements were linked to the issue of new loans to Germany and Russia. The flaw in the grand design was that it depended on American money, which was not available. As the historian Kenneth Morgan notes, Lloyd George 'was yoked with a view of world leadership which was rejected equally by a tired, timid public at home, and by inflexibly nationalist antagonists abroad'.[20] The international conference at Genoa in April 1922, intended to seal the interlocking set of bargains, ended in a fiasco, robbing Lloyd George of the foreign-policy triumph on which he relied 'to restore his star to the zenith'.

However, it was his adventurism, not his attempts at appeasement, which brought his rule to an end. In the wake of the Ottoman collapse, British and French troops were stationed in Constantinople and the Straits. As an erstwhile radical Welshman, Lloyd George was enamoured of small nations, which sat uneasily with his newly acquired sense of imperial responsibilities. He loathed the Turks, loved the Greeks, and backed the Greek prime minister Venizelos's mad plan to establish a Greek Empire in Asia Minor which would bring civilisation to the heathen and support for Britain's position in the Middle East. When the Turkish leader Mustapha Kemal drove the Greeks out of Asia Minor in September 1922, British and Turkish armies faced each other at Chanak, on the Asiatic shore of the supposedly demilitarised Dardanelles. Lloyd George called on the empire to support Britain in a war against Turkey. The empire refused. The French deserted him. This time so did the Conservatives. Their leader Bonar Law published a letter in *The Times*, on 7 October, which said that Britain could not be the 'policeman of the world'. It was a rare public acknowledgement of the truism that Britain should tailor its suit to fit its cloth. It also doomed the coalition. A meeting of Conservative MPs at the Carlton Club on the morning of 19 October unhitched the Conservative Party from the Lloyd George chariot. Stanley Baldwin, president of the Board of Trade, said 'a dynamic force is a very terrible thing'. This marked the undynamic

Baldwin as the coming man. The party voted by 187 to 87 to quit the coalition, a vote so momentous that the 1922 Committee of Conservative backbenchers took its name from the date. Lloyd George resigned at four o'clock and the king sent for Bonar Law. Lloyd George never held office again.

The break-up of the coalition in 1922 poured domestic politics into the two-party mould which has lasted, with some aberrations, to this day. Baldwin succeeded the dying Bonar Law as Conservative prime minister in May 1923. He completed what the Carlton Club meeting had started by drawing the coalition Conservatives back into the Tory camp. This ensured that the Conservatives and not a doctrinally naked Centre Party would emerge as Labour's main opponent. His master stroke was to appeal to the country in December 1923 on the old Conservative platform of protectionism. Although disappointing electorally, this was a key move in re-establishing a distinct Conservative identity; that it pre-empted Lloyd George taking up the protectionist cause himself was not a trivial benefit. The general election threw Lloyd George back into the arms of Asquith, and removed the lingering attraction of coalition to Conservative leaders like Austen Chamberlain. In December 1923 Ramsay MacDonald formed the first of his two minority Labour governments. The reformatting of British politics was completed in October 1924 when the Conservatives returned to power with a thumping majority, with Labour still in contention, and the Liberals reduced to a third-party rump. As Keynes put it in 1926, the future task of Liberalism would be to supply the Conservative Party with Cabinets, and the Labour Party with ideas. *Pace* Dangerfield, liberalism lived on, despite the destruction of its political vehicle.

Chapter 7

The Silver Age of British Power 1922–1939

Although about one third of the present century has passed, Great Britain still depends on an economic structure and on methods which often definitely belong to the last century ... in this 'happy valley' time doesn't seem to flow as quickly as elsewhere. England still lives in atmosphere of the past, and this is one of the secrets of her extraordinary charm.

Andre Siegfried, *England's Crisis* (1933)

For four hundred years the foreign policy of England has been to oppose the strongest, most aggressive, most dominating Power on the Continent, and particularly to prevent the Low Countries from falling into the hands of such a Power ... Thus we preserved the liberties of Europe, protected the growth of its vivacious and varied society, and emerged ... with an ever-growing fame and widening Empire ... This is the wonderful unconscious tradition of British Foreign Policy.

Winston Churchill, address to the
Conservative Members Committee
on Foreign Affairs, March 1936

From dynamic centre to soft centre

The age of Lloyd George was succeeded by the age of Baldwin and MacDonald. Hyperactivity gave way to an inactivity more in keeping with Britain's reduced circumstances and post-war fatigue. In 1923, MacDonald claimed that 'there are only two parties in politics today . . . the capitalist party and the Labour and Socialist party'. This set up the rhetorical debate which was to dominate British politics for most of the century. The reality was less dramatic. The socialist advance MacDonald envisaged was of the imperceptible variety. This enabled him to form a close political partnership with Stanley Baldwin, even before they got together in the same government in 1931. Together the two leaders dominated interwar British politics. Each was prime minister for seven years, Baldwin in 1923, 1924–9 and 1935–7, MacDonald in 1924 and 1929–35. MacDonald reined in the left and Baldwin reined in the right. Their partnership was fortified by their common loathing of Lloyd George.

Baldwin was a man for the times. It was the war and its convulsions which jolted him into his pre-eminence. In a war-free Britain, he would have had a career much like his father's – that of a middle-ranking industrialist and politician. He inherited not just the family's ironworks, Baldwins, and his father's directorship of the Great Western Railway, but also his father's constituency of Bewdley in Worcestershire. He got his first political job at the age of fifty, in 1917 when he was appointed as parliamentary private secretary to the Conservative leader Bonar Law. Six years later he was prime minister. Once he reached the top, he took considerable pains to stay there, becoming, in Churchill's words, 'the most formidable politician I have ever known'. He knew what he was talking about,

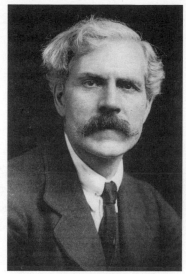

The Soft Centre
6. Stanley Baldwin (l); 7. Ramsay MacDonald (r).

since Baldwin outmanoeuvred Churchill just as successfully as he had outmanoeuvred Lloyd George. Baldwin embodied the revulsion against Lloyd George and his clique. 'We are sick of Welshmen and lawyers,' said the Tory Lord Winterton, 'of the best brains and supermen. We want the old type of English statesman, who is fair-minded, judicious and responsible, rather than the man who is so clever that he thinks ahead of everyone else.' Baldwin satisfied these requirements. He set out to restore decent standards in public life. In a notable swipe at the Lloyd George system, he condemned the press lords Lloyd George had created as an 'insolent plutocracy . . . aiming at power without responsibility – the prerogative of the harlot throughout the ages', a phrase supplied by his cousin Rudyard Kipling.

The challenge facing the Conservative Party in an era of independent working-class politics was how to offset the huge working-class preponderance of voters. The middle class was still very small: in 1938, only 18 per cent of the population were salary earners, and 8 per cent self-employed.[1] Baldwin understood that the only path to electoral success was to refuse to fight the class war; indeed, it was to deny that it existed. He was the first practitioner of what came to be known as consensus politics – government from the moderate centre. He was a Tory paternalist. His paternalism was largely a matter of language. He could express non-political, 'soft' Christian, family and patriotic ideas in moving words. He denounced 'the hard-faced men who looked as though they had done well out of the war' (while privately and anonymously giving £150,000, a third of his fortune, to the Exchequer); he prayed for 'Peace in our time, O Lord'; he evoked a gentlemanly ideal of 'Englishness'. His ruminating oratory gave him a moral authority unique in interwar politics. However, he had no active paternalist programme, and wrung his hands at his inability to prevent the decay of industrial Britain. He also understood that the working class was not synonymous with the trade unions and Labour Party. Women were not unionised; Protestant workers voted Conservative in regions of high Irish Catholic immigration; a section of the working class had a vested interest in capitalist success as a result of their housing and their savings. The Baldwin style brought electoral but not political hegemony. The Conservatives deferred to working-class sensibilities more than the workers deferred to upper-class leadership. They won a large proportion of the working-class vote by not frightening them. The price paid was the party's inability to carry out its preferred policies, or indeed any coherent policy. Accommodation was the order of the day. This constantly threatened breakaway movements to the right.

In foreign policy, Baldwin displayed a similar inactivity, his refusal to fight the class war being matched by a refusal to prepare for any other. An acute critic, John Strachey, saw him as 'a perfect statesman for an empire in decline; he realises instinctively that almost anything anyone does will only make matters worse'. One of his favourite ruminating spots was Aix-les-Bains, where he spent lengthy annual holidays. Holiday time was the time he liked best.

Like Lloyd George, MacDonald was a 'lad o' pairts' denied opportunities by the British class system. He was shut out of the Liberal Party. The Labour movement gave him and other talented working-class leaders the chance to play a part in great affairs. Philosophically, MacDonald was a democratic collectivist Fabian. Like the Fabians he believed in the 'inevitability of gradualness'. 'Socialism', he once wrote, 'comes as the dawn.' This meant one did not have to do too much to bring it about. The First World War dislodged his career violently from its established groove. MacDonald's opposition to the war made him a hero of the left to which he never belonged. The Labour Party overtook the Liberals as the main opponent to the Tories. Once he became leader of the Labour Party in 1922, he was determined that Labour should prove itself 'fit to govern' in its own right, and not as a junior partner of Liberalism.

The strength of MacDonald's party position was that he embodied Labour's split personality, 'torn between practical policy and emotional protest', as Richard Crossman later put it. In the Labour Party, moral tone has always been more important than achievement, and MacDonald provided it in bucketloads. His rhetoric provided the left with a cause within the Labour Party, while he and his astute party manager Arthur Henderson were careful to deprive it of influence. He also enlarged Labour's appeal to the radical intelligentsia, chiefly the anti-war Liberals, the notorious vagueness of his oratory helping in both respects, before it finally descended into incoherence. (His unique ability, Churchill noted, was to 'compress the largest number of words into the smallest amount of thought'.) He was eager to encourage upper-class recruits: his first Cabinet was stuffed with Liberal as well as Tory grandees. Some of these recruits gave him more trouble than he bargained for, none more so than the intellectually brilliant but demagogic young MP Oswald Mosley who joined Labour in 1924. When MacDonald formed his first government in 1924, the rich locked up their silver: a few fled abroad, never to return. After a few months of him, they breathed easier. He made Labour respectable. This was his service to social democracy. His success in politics, helped by his 'classless' Scottish accent, gave him an entry into society, and a flirtatious friendship with Lady Londonderry, the grand Conservative hostess of the 1920s. So he boxed the political compass.

The Baldwin–MacDonald duumvirate helped keep Britain free from the violent social and political convulsions which wrecked democracy over much of Europe between the wars. This was a notable achievement, which we can appreciate better today than could the impatient radicals who lived through it. The cost, though, was stagnation, complacency, loss of energy. These men, and the society they reflected, recoiled from the bloodletting of the First World War. They craved 'peace in our time', but the times were out of joint.

This was not at first apparent. Lloyd George had failed to pacify Europe, but the French army, American money and the passage of time brought about some healing. The French army was the most useful. With Germany completely disarmed by the Versailles Treaty, Britain could afford to freeride on the

French defences. The Ten Year Rule adopted in 1919 assumed that there would be no great war for ten years and that Britain would not need an expeditionary force in that time; the 'rule' allowed defence expenditure to be slashed from £604 million in 1919 to £111 million in 1922, and it was cut even further in the mid-1920s by Churchill at the Treasury. By this time there were grounds for believing that the good times were returning. In 1923, Britain settled its war debt with the United States. In 1924, the Dawes Plan fixed the total amount and annual schedules of German reparations at levels which the Germans said they accepted. The Locarno Treaty of 1925 completed the work of Versailles, with Britain, France, Germany and Italy guaranteeing the Franco-German frontier. These steps led to the return of American private capital to Europe. New 'disarmament' conferences were planned: the first to reduce tariffs, the second to reduce military forces. There were the first tentative moves to European unification. There were hints, in China and the Middle East, that Britain's grasp was weakening. But generally the 1920s was a silver age for British power: like Baldwin, it did not have to do too much work.

The war had showed the worth of empire, but failed to produce an imperial policy. The pre-war effort to unite it economically had failed, as had the wartime effort to unite it politically. The empire lacked a doctrinal basis. In 1917, the South African leader Jan Smuts tried to provide one. The white Dominions were not an empire in the classic sense, but a 'British Commonwealth of Nations'. In a common Anglo-Saxon stock, there existed a popular foundation for commonwealth. Each Dominion would have the British monarch as head of state, but its parliaments would not be subordinate to the imperial Parliament at Westminster. This fine accommodation to reality, sanctified by the Statute of

Westminster in 1931, left the actual legal status of the Dominions ambiguous: independent in fact, they lacked the symbols of nationhood. And what about the colonies? Were they, too, headed for Dominion status in an enlarged 'Commonwealth'? Although British colonial attitudes were permeated by racism, racism never became an official doctrine, as it was to become in Germany or, later, in South Africa. The British government, in establishing representative institutions in the Cape Colony in 1854, had insisted on a 'colour-blind' franchise: all were entitled to vote on a common roll, subject to a property qualification. The far-reaching implication of this measure was that responsible government was the right of all races, and there would be no attempt to keep the coloured empire in subjection against its will. But there was no need to think this through just yet.

In place of imperial doctrine there was imperial sentiment. As the empire became less substantial, its hold on the popular imagination grew, its symbols and rituals serving as a unifying myth and comforting evocation of greatness. Imperial decorations like CBE, OBE and MBE entered the honours lists under George V in 1917. 'Empire Day' was started on 24 May 1902, the date of Queen Victoria's birthday, but only became an official holiday in 1916, when commemoration for the imperial dead started to mingle with imperial festivity. It continued to be called that till 1958. Mostly white schoolchildren throughout the empire saluted the flag, sang patriotic songs, held parades, and listened to speeches intended to be inspirational, before being let out of school – which no doubt contributed to its popularity.

Nor was there any need yet to think about Europe. In 1930, the Foreign Office's official response to the Briand Plan for European unification ran: 'We warmly desire to improve the co-operation of the European countries for the promotion of their common interests and will help bring it about. We cannot, however, help to create any political or economic group which could in any way be regarded as hostile to the American or any other continent, or which would weaken our political co-operation with the other members of the British Commonwealth.'* The fuzzy 'three-circles doctrine', which saw Britain retain its world position through its place in three discrete power blocs, had made its appearance. It was to dominate British foreign policy for most of the rest of the century.

The flagging economy

The flaw in Britain's world position, even in the relatively benign decade of the 1920s, was the malfunctioning of its economy, hitherto the bedrock of its international role; and this was to contribute to the collapse of the world economy in 1929–30. The war brought to an end the liberal era of British-managed globalisation. One clear sign of this was the end of mass migration. When the British economy slumped in the nineteenth century it exported people; in the interwar years they joined the dole queues at home. The war had also made the British economy less flexible, more corporatist. In the interwar years, consolidation, not expansion, was the order of the day, on both sides of industry. This inevitably gave rise to the notion of a negotiated rather than competitive industrial system.

The percentage of insured workers registered as unemployed averaged 10–12 per cent between 1923 and 1929. This

---

* Lord Rosebery is credited with the first use of the word 'commonwealth' to describe the white empire, in a speech in Adelaide in 1884.

was much worse than before the war. Governments of both parties stood aside, reflecting the current belief that the best thing government could do was to do nothing. Economic policy was left to the Treasury and the Bank of England who put their faith in sound money, balanced budgets and international trade.

The most popular explanation of continuing British unemployment was war-related. The war, it was said, had disrupted Britain's established trading networks. Britain's old trades – coal, cotton, shipbuilding and metals – were losing world market share, and Britain was losing its share of that. However, the real problem was Britain's failure to win a leading share in the export of new products. 'In nearly every major industrial category,' writes economic historian Derek Aldcroft, 'whether expanding, declining or stable . . . Britain's share . . . declined, especially between 1913 and 1929.'[2] Britain was finding it harder to compete all round. In 1924 the volume of exports was only 72 per cent of pre-war, with imports at their pre-war level. Relative economic decline, which had started before 1914, was halted, except in relation to the United States, by the fact that Britain's European competitors, especially Germany, were doing even worse, and the Great Depression which hit the whole world in 1929 made such comparisons irrelevant.

It now seems clearer than it did at the time that between 1919 and 1922 the British economy suffered from two major 'shocks'. The first was a 'supply' shock – a once-and-for-all increase in British unit labour costs. Second was a 'demand' shock – the savage deflation of prices to prepare for the return to the gold standard at the pre-war parity – which left the real wage (the purchasing power of the money wage) higher at the end of the depression in 1922 than it had been in the boom of 1920. The results were good for those in work, but they meant there were less of them. Keynes was one of the few who appreciated the impact of the 'demand' shock on Britain's economic performance. Britain's export performance would have been significantly better, and its unemployment less, had his policy of low interest rates and a 'managed' exchange rate been adopted. But this would have removed the essential role of unemployment (or its threat) in disciplining the labour force.

Instead, once the depression of 1921–2 had bottomed out, economic policy was geared to refixing the pound to the gold at its pre-war parity, which entailed deflating the economy by means of high interest rates to restore the pre-war sterling exchange rate of $4.86 to the pound. The restoration was accomplished by Churchill at the Exchequer on 28 April 1925. Churchill soon judged his decision to put sterling back on the gold standard as the worst mistake of his life. A paternalist at heart, he would have preferred 'Finance less proud and Industry more content'. But financial discipline, argued his Treasury advisers, was the only way of restoring 'reality' to wage bargaining. Keynes was scathing: 'The policy [of restoring the pre-war parity] can only attain its end by intensifying unemployment without limit, until the workers are ready to accept the necessary reduction of money wages under the pressure of hard facts.'[3]

Keynes was the most creative mind to apply itself to economics in the interwar years. The Treasury, echoing orthodox economics, blamed excessive unemployment on excessively high real wages. Restoration of full employment required the restoration of wage flexibility. But the right could not contemplate the political cost of carrying out the orthodox remedy of breaking wage resistance by 'intensifying unemployment without limit'. The left had no independent economics to challenge the orthodox argument. Its criticism of capitalism was at heart moral. Its programme of nationalisation and redistribution seemed irrelevant to the problem at hand, and in any case was politically unattainable. Keynes realised that any solution to the unemployment problem along orthodox lines was blocked. So he switched attention from the problem of inefficient supply to the problem of insufficient demand. The economy, he argued, was 'stuck in a rut' from which it needed to be rescued by an 'impulse, a jolt, an acceleration'. Workers could and should not be forced to accept wage reductions by the pressure of starvation. Rather 'we must seek to submerge the rocks in a rising sea' of prosperity. The theoretical demonstration that an 'under-employment equilibrium' was possible had to wait for the publication of Keynes's *General Theory of Employment, Interest, and Money* in 1936, but it was implicit in Keynes's policy advocacy long before. The one politician who grasped the political importance of what Keynes was saying was the rising Labour star Oswald Mosley, a

8. Economics to the Rescue
John Maynard Keynes

convert to socialism from the Tory backwoods. Mosley was one of the most powerful raw intelligences in twentieth-century British politics. He must be credited with the first clear statement of the 'output gap', later a familiar part of the Keynesian toolkit. 'At present, Socialist thought', he wrote in 1925, 'appears to concentrate almost exclusively upon the transfer of present purchasing power by taxation, and neglects the necessity for creating additional demand to evoke our unused capacity which is at present not commanded either by the rich or the poor.'[4] There was a gap between consumption and production which needed to be filled by additional government spending. Consensus could be built on a full employment basis. But the Keynes–Mosley approach involved abandoning two of the three pillars of Britain's successful Victorian economy: adherence to the gold standard and the doctrine of the balanced budget. (A little later both men would also abandon free trade.) This was a step too far for the Baldwin–MacDonald leadership.

Keynes's prediction that the Bank of England would shrink from applying in full rigour the measures that its policy entailed was soon borne out. The return to gold led to the first and only general strike in British history, with coal once more at its heart. Sterling, it turned out, was somewhat overvalued against the dollar, more so against the European currencies. The coal owners demanded a 10 per cent wage reduction to offset the 10 per cent reduction received per ton of coal sold abroad. The Miners Federation refused. The Samuel Commission, set up to resolve the problem, recommended immediate wage cuts to be followed by reorganisation. The miners rejected the cuts, and the owners the reorganisation. On 5 May 1926, the General Council of the TUC called a general strike in support of the miners. Terrified by the thought that this might be a revolutionary act, it called it off a week later. The miners were starved back on the owners' terms in the autumn. Though a purely defensive action, the General Strike was enough to deter employers from any concerted attack on wage levels. So heavy unemployment remained, especially in the export sector, with the overvalued pound maintained by high interest rates and short-term borrowing from abroad.

Mass unemployment was, in fact, the condition of the Baldwin–MacDonald consensus. For one thing it tamed the unions. The twentieth-century pattern is clear: the unions slept when prices were falling, and became alert when they were rising. Given the industrial militancy which accompanied inflation, it is not altogether surprising that policymakers chose deflation. What made heavy unemployment tolerable was the relatively generous amounts, and conditions for the receipt of, unemployment benefit, and the ability of employers, especially in the cotton trade, to manipulate the 'dole' to keep their employees working 'half time'. Industrial stagnation was the price of industrial peace.*

Signs of intellectual rigor mortis were apparent in other spheres. The First World War carried to a further level Bloomsbury's discrediting of the Victorian gentleman among the thinking classes: he became a joke figure, on his way to Colonel Blimp. But whereas Edwardian Bloomsbury was animated by the hope of a new world opening up, the avante-garde

---

* True to his pacifying instincts Baldwin opposed most of the legal controls on union activity demanded by Lord Birkenhead, the Lord Chancellor, in the aftermath of the General Strike. These were similar to those enacted in the 1980s by Mrs Thatcher. Birkenhead proposed ending immunity for trade union funds, secret ballots on strike action, restriction on picketing, and a change in the basis of the political levy from 'contracting out' from to 'contracting in' to membership of the Labour Party. Only the last was adopted: it was repealed in 1945.

of the 1920s was driven by self-hatred and despair. The authentic literary voices of the 1920s were Evelyn Waugh and T. S. Eliot – the 'vile bodies' depicted by the former partying drunkenly on the desolate landscape evoked by the latter. In painting, the iconoclasm of post-Impressionism gave way to the horrors of surrealism, reminiscent of Bosch, Brueghel and Goya. 'The modernist', writes Noel Annan, 'believed art should portray society as disintegrating and decomposing. If society is dehumanised, why depict people as recognisable human beings? They should squint out of paintings like the deformities they had become.'⁵ The 1920s saw an outbreak of anti-war novels and plays: C. E. Montague's *Disenchantment* (1922), R. C. Sheriff's play, *Journey's End* (1928), Richard Aldington's *Death of a Hero* and Robert Graves's *Goodbye To All That*, both from 1929. Alec Waugh's *The Loom of Youth* (1917), the first of many anti-public school novels, showed how badly the public-school system wove it.

The stronger reaction, though, was to fall back on the old virtues. To the extent that the war had cracked the traditional hierarchy, bourgeois morality became more important as a defence of the social order: old legislation was strictly enforced by Baldwin's puritanical Home Secretary Joynson-Hicks. Radclyffe Hall's lesbian novel *The Well of Loneliness* had to be withdrawn by its publisher in 1928, D. H. Lawrence's *Lady Chatterley's Lover* was banned for obscenity in 1929. The erection of Epstein's nude sculpture *Day and Night* (1928) at London Underground's headquarters was only allowed after Epstein agreed to remove a couple of inches from the penis of the smaller figure. John B. Souter's *The Breakdown* (1926) was removed from the Royal Academy's summer show for showing a naked white woman dancing before a seated black saxophonist. Lord Byng, the Metropolitan Police commissioner, almost brought London's nightlife to its knees, with sex clubs and prostitution subject to well-publicised crackdowns.

Moral uplift was given a boost by the BBC, started in 1922. Under its first director general, John Reith, it aimed to elevate public taste and encourage the use of middle-class English. Its first broadcast was the six o'clock news. This was followed by the weather forecast. Serious drama alternated with talks, interviews and discussions (published in the *Listener*) and classical music. The commitment to elevate was reflected even in the scheduling: some regular programmes were broadcast at different times each week, to discourage 'lazy listening'.

Aesthetic conservatism accompanied moral conservatism. Modernism made few converts in art, literature or architecture. As Ford Madox Ford noted, the 'complete absence of art' was as much a 'national characteristic' of the British in 1921 as it had been before the war.[6] In literature, it was the middle-brow which attracted middle-class readers: Arnold Bennett, John Galsworthy and Somerset Maugham, not James Joyce or Virginia Woolf. Public architecture remained neoclassical or neo-Gothic. Baldwin's speeches were suffused with rural nostalgia.

Politicians and the slump

In the 1930s external shocks destroyed the hope that Britain might enjoy its diminished estate in peace. Three portents foretold a much more troubled world: the Great Depression of 1929–33, the growing unrest in India, and the appointment of Adolf Hitler as German Chancellor. These, and especially the last, confronted the pacific duo of Baldwin and MacDonald, with problems which threatened to overwhelm them.

MacDonald formed his second minority Labour government in 1929 just before the Great Depression hit.* The
economic slump raised the numbers of insured unemployed to over 20 per cent between 1930 and 1933. It was
still nearly 12 per cent when war broke out in 1939.† The
world depression can plausibly be regarded as a delayed
effect of the war. The war had disorganised world trading
patterns. It had created large imbalances between the primary producing and manufacturing sectors of the world
economy. The new nations set up by the Versailles Treaty
all had their separate tariff systems, so the average level of
protective tariffs rose. The piecemeal return to the gold
standard had led to a system of misaligned currencies and
rival financial centres – London, New York, Paris – whose
co-operation was at best fitful. On top of this, and partly as
a consequence, Britain had lost the trading and financial
clout to stabilise the system as it had before 1914. Charles
Kindleberger has discussed Britain's leadership of the pre-
war economy in terms of three functions: keeping an open
market for imports, providing the world (via the City of
London) with development capital, and acting as a 'lender
of the last resort' to distressed economies. The war, by
weakening the British economy, had fatally impaired these
functions, so that when depression struck, the old offset-
ting pre-war mechanisms were absent. As Kindleberger
explains, Britain could not and the United States would not

---

* 30 May 1929. Conservative: 8,656,473, 38.2 per cent, 260 seats; Liberal: 5,308,510, 23.4
per cent, fifty-nine seats; Labour: 8,389,512, 37.1 per cent, 288 seats.
† Insured workers were those covered by the National Insurance Act of 1921. They
excluded those employed in agriculture, railways and domestic service. On the basis of
how unemployment is now calculated, the figures would have been a few percentage
points lower.

provide the needed stabilising leadership, and so each nation scrambled to protect itself against the blizzard by measures which made it worse, the United States leading the way with the gigantic Hawley–Smoot tariff of 1930. There was thus no international check to the downward spiral set in train by the collapse of commodity prices and Wall Street in 1929.[7]

Britain escaped relatively lightly from the depression, partly because its economy was already quite depressed. Between 1929 and 1932, industrial output fell by 12 per cent, compared with 41 per cent in Germany. In the 1929 election Lloyd George promised to 'conquer unemployment', as he had conquered the Germans, by spending £100 million on public works. But the electorate no longer trusted him and, despite lavish expenditure from his 'fund', the Liberal recovery was modest. MacDonald's image of the world helplessly engulfed in an 'economic blizzard' was more appealing to a nation wearied of political stunts. In a blizzard a government, like a household, was supposed to batten down the hatches and wait for the storm to pass. Economic battening down took the form of governments reducing their spending as their income from taxes fell. Why this would do anything to promote recovery was no better explained by Philip Snowden, Labour's puritanical Chancellor, than it was to be by George Osborne in 2010. Labour's redistributionary programme was premised on a constantly fattening capitalist goose. It had no nourishment to offer the sickly animal which British capitalism had become.

In MacDonald's government, the Lloyd George spirit was represented by Oswald Mosley, who was made Chancellor of the Duchy of Lancaster. His job was to be a kind of ginger assistant to the Lord Privy Seal, J. H. Thomas, an amiable, corrupt railwayman, and 'more ginger than assistant, I have no doubt', Churchill growled. After nine months vainly suggesting various public works schemes (during which time unemployment went up by 50 per cent), Mosley produced a 'Memorandum'. The nation, he told MacDonald, must be mobilised for a supreme effort. There must be a small War Cabinet, serviced by a think tank headed by Keynes; a protected home market, with government money for modernising the older, and developing newer, industries; a £200 million programme of public works. When Snowden rejected the Mosley proposals, Mosley resigned in May 1930, making a resignation speech so masterful that only his later fall from grace prevents it from being recorded as a parliamentary classic. A few months later he started the 'New Party' in which his associate John Strachey soon detected 'the cloven hoof of Fascism'. MacDonald was not entirely unsympathetic to Mosley's proposals. He appointed Keynes to an advisory council; he mused that 'what we have to do is to pile up and pile up and pile up the income of industry in this way and that way and the other'. But these intellectual doodles had no chance against the 'Treasury view' which held that any money spent by the government was a subtraction from more profitable uses by private industry.

What followed was, in a way, a replay of 1921–2. With unemployment rising, it proved impossible to balance the budget. In February 1931, following the precedent of the Geddes Committee, Snowden appointed an 'economy committee' headed by an accountant, Sir George May, to suggest cuts. The May Report, published on 31 July, projected a budget deficit of £120 million for 1932–3, and proposed to meet £97 million of it by cutting unemployment benefits and the salaries of teachers, military personnel and police. A fortnight earlier the Macmillan Report had revealed that many of London's merchant banks were insolvent. The Conservative Opposition demanded rapid enactment of the May Committee's economies to restore confidence in the pound. On this the Labour government broke. In anguished discussions in mid-August the Cabinet agreed to £56 million of cuts, but nine members baulked at cutting the standard rate of unemployment benefit, which would have raised the total of cuts to about £70 million. The Conservatives and Liberals told MacDonald that £56 million was insufficient.* Instead of resigning, MacDonald, who had personally agreed to cuts of £70 million, accepted King George V's invitation to form a National Government with the Conservatives to 'save the pound'. He was followed into the new government by four members of his Cabinet but supported by only thirteen of his party, the rest, led by Arthur Henderson, going into Opposition.

The pound refused to be saved. Following a 'mutiny' of naval ratings at Invergordon which seemed to portend the end of the empire, the flight from sterling accelerated, and on 21 September the gold standard was suspended, never to be restored. 'No one told us we could do that,' a Labour minister, Thomas Johnson, was reported to have said. It is astonishing how easily the mighty pound collapsed. Loans could still have been obtained. The reality was that the pound was sacrificed to maintain the solvency of the City, and that no political party was willing to demand more sacrifices from the British people for its defence. Urged on by the Conservatives, MacDonald appealed to the country for

---

* Lloyd George was out of action in this period undergoing a prostate operation. The Liberals were represented by Sir Herbert Samuel and Sir Donald Maclean.

a 'Doctor's Mandate' on 27 October 1931. The result was the greatest landslide in British history, the government winning 554 seats to Labour's fifty-two. Of the 554, 473 were Conservatives. MacDonald had been worth 3 million votes to them, and a further four years as prime minister was his reward.*

'What would we think of a Salvation Army that took to its heels on the Day of Judgement?' asked Mosley on his way into fascism. In fact, 1931 was not British capitalism's Day of Judgement; only 'magneto trouble' as Keynes more accurately diagnosed it. The engine started stuttering back into life as soon as Britain left the gold standard. The pound sank, stimulating exports, interest rates fell to 2 per cent producing a private-housing boom, with its associated level of high demand for consumer durables and the growth of building societies to finance home buying; the war debt was refinanced at lower cost; money was provided for the older industries to shed their surplus capacity; the introduction of protection and a favourable shift in the terms of trade left more purchasing power to be spent on home-produced goods. The essence of the 'business conservatism' of the 1930s was that it raised profits relative to wages, through devaluation, protection, cheap money, restriction of capital exports, and encouragement of cartels and collusive behaviour.[8] This stimulated business to invest: extra investment provided extra employment.

This mixture of policy and events enabled the National Government to preside over a substantial market-based recovery which helped the growth of a mass-consumption economy.

---

* On a turnout of 76.3 per cent, the Conservatives won 11,978,745 votes, over 3 million up from 1929, and Labour 6,649,630, down by almost 2 million. The biggest losers were the Liberals, split once more, down from 5,308,510 to 2,212,404 votes.

The big political beneficiary of the recovery was the Conservative Party. Baldwin replaced MacDonald as prime minister in June 1935, a general election in October 1935 confirming what was now a purely Conservative regime with another massive, though reduced, majority. Neville Chamberlain replaced Baldwin in May 1937. Little has been written about the domestic policies of the National Governments, because there was little to write about. It was a period of legislative lull. Budgets were balanced without the aid of Keynesian stimulants; there were no significant innovations in social policy. A miserly £8 million was allocated between 1934 and 1938 to the 'special areas' of heavy unemployment. Baldwin handled the abdication of King Edward VIII with consummate tact and skill.* The National Government fulfilled its economic purpose simply by being there.

Why did the slump of the 1930s fail to shake Britain's social and political order? The question has often been asked. The Webbs argued that MacDonald had succumbed to the 'aristocratic embrace'. The more general thesis of the left, reproduced in dozens of publications down to the 1980s, after which such discussions appeared redundant, was that the British working class had been betrayed, as it would continue to be, by a leadership wedded to parliamentarism, compromise and respectability. The idea, implicit in such accounts, is that of a potentially revolutionary working class. But the premise is false: there was very little evidence of revolutionary fervour. Trade unions were defensive, not revolutionary. More

---

* The king, a troubled, raffish figure, succeeded his father King George V on 20 January 1936. But before he could be crowned, he abdicated because the Establishment would not allow him to marry a divorced American lady, Mrs Wallis Simpson. He was succeeded by his brother George VI who, together with his wife Queen Elizabeth, provided the correct domestic symbols of depleted royal power.

interesting is the failure in the interwar years to develop a middle-class radicalism in opposition to the restored forces of Treasury orthodoxy and City finance. Keynes and Mosley were almost alone. It was in this respect that the collapse of the historic Liberal Party was a great misfortune. The replacement Labour Party was debarred by its socialist commitment from having new ideas about how to make the capitalist system work better. As a Labour Party manifesto of 1934 put it: 'There is no halfway house between a society based on private ownership . . . and a society [based on] public ownership.' The halfway house was, in fact, the work of two Liberals, Keynes and Beveridge, but it took another world war for it to be built.

The device of a national government was a superb political ploy, neutering both right and left, in the classic style of Whig statecraft. Yoked together, MacDonald and Baldwin could now do what they had done separately in the 1920s, which was to crowd out extremism. Labour was irrelevant in the 1930s. In 1932, their leaders Lansbury, Attlee and Cripps called for immediate nationalisation of banks, land, transport, power, coal, iron and steel, insurance, abolition of the Lords, and lawmaking by 'enabling Act'. Huge 'National' majorities guarded against such horrors. There was a mild interest in 'planning': a rising Tory star, Harold Macmillan, saw it as offering a 'middle way' between capitalism and socialism, but outside intellectual circles, the planning movement had no resonance. Political extremism passed Britain by. With spectacularly bad timing, Oswald Mosley turned his New Party into the British Union of Fascists in October 1932, just as recovery started. It maintained a noisy but ineffective presence on the political scene, before being wound up by the government in 1940. Had not temptation come to him when he was too young and high-spirited to resist it, Mosley would have been a huge presence in twentieth-century politics. As it was, within a few years, he had sunk from hero to zero. Likewise, the Communist Party stayed tiny, despite some success at Cambridge University. The unemployed remained fatalistic, making the best of things on what George Orwell called 'a fish-and-chip standard'. The famous Hunger Marches, which the Communist Party organised, never attracted more than a couple of thousand marchers: the Jarrow March became a folk legend because it was the only one which was not Communist-led.

Skilful though Britain's political arrangements were, the main reason for lack of political ferment is that the interwar years were not nearly as bad as folklore made them out. Persistently high unemployment was confined to 'the special areas'. These included Scotland, whose disproportionate industrial decline led to the foundation of the Scottish National Party in 1928. Elsewhere it was balanced by the spread of affluence. Between 1932 and 1937, GDP rose by 23 per cent, or 4 per cent a year – a faster rate of growth than anywhere outside Scandinavia. Business confidence was boosted by the size of the Conservative majorities; Conservatives majorities were boosted by the prosperity spreading in the south and Midlands through ribbons of new housing to new factories built on greenfield sites, as business responded to the opportunities opening up for home consumption.

The planners, inspired by the ideas of Ebenezer Howard, wanted to build self-contained garden cities, towns designed 'for a full range of healthy living and industry of a size that makes possible a full measure of social life but not larger, surrounded by a rural belt; the whole of the land being in public ownership, or held in trust for the community'.[9] Letchworth was started in 1905, Welwyn Garden City followed in 1920. But there were few imitators. The middle and aspiring classes preferred suburbia, scaled-down country houses on the outskirts of cities, decked out in neo-Elizabethan cladding surrounded by gardens, equipped with modern comforts, serviced by new retail outlets, and linked to factories and offices by branch railways lines and motor cars. The mainly right-wing governments of the interwar years encouraged this type of owner occupation as a 'bulwark against bolshevism'. Through a system known as 'the builders' pool', lower middle-class and securely employed working-class buyers were, in effect, able to buy homes on hire purchase.

But the working class benefitted too. Britain remained highly divided by class, but there was enough easement of working-class conditions to blunt an overt class-war appeal. Average wages almost doubled between 1913 and 1938, increasing discretionary spending power. J. B. Priestley saw a new Britain of 'arterial and by-pass roads . . . giant cinemas and dance halls and cafes, bungalows with tiny garages, cocktail bars, Woolworths, motor-coaches, wireless, hiking, and factory girls looking like actresses'.[10] By 1939, 'the British were drinking and brawling less, and reading, smoking and gambling more'. While 15 million could enjoy a week's annual paid holiday by the sea in Butlins camps or Blackpool, 10 million bicycles and new bus routes gave workers unprecedented access to the countryside. Their health improved: by the 1930s a typical sixteen-year-old boy applying for a job with the Post Office was sixteen pounds heavier and one and a half inches taller than his equivalent had been twenty-five years earlier. For the young, the cinema and dance hall competed with boxing and football. Most working-class youngsters now went to the movies once or twice a week, with darkened cinemas providing exciting erotic opportunities. They paid more attention to their grooming, with cheap, off-the-peg suits from Burtons, and brilliantined hair. The older generation complained about the 'effeminisation' of youth, the corruption of Hollywood: yet these were the Tommies of the Second World War.[11]

The success of 'business Conservatism' of the 1930s, in marked contrast to the failure of foreign policy, stimulates an obvious counterfactual question. Suppose there had been no war in 1939. The Conservatives would almost certainly have won comfortably for a third time in a row in 1940. Would the course of politics and economics have been differently set? No doubt the people would have 'risen': but they would have risen in a different way. The mass consumption society of the 1950s would have come sooner, but minus Keynesian demand-management and the Beveridgean welfare state.

MacDonald and Baldwin were also successful in lowering the political temperature in, and on, India. Throughout the interwar years the Indian Raj was slowly slipping from Britain's grasp, but there was no policy available except to postpone the rate of slippage. The MacDonald–Baldwin strategy for keeping India in the empire was to involve the Indian political class in its government. This would avoid the mistakes over Ireland. One problem, as with Ireland, was the Tory Party, the diehard wing of which now found an improbable leader in Winston Churchill, scornful of any 'appeasement' of the 'half-naked fakir' Mahatma Gandhi. 'If we were to wash our hands of all responsibilities', he told Parliament in 1931, 'ferocious civil war would speedily break out between the Muslims and the Hindus.' It must be made plain to the Indians that the British were 'there for ever'. Lord Irwin (later Lord Halifax), the viceroy from 1926–31, took the diametrically opposite view that generous concessions to Indian nationalism were the only way to maintain law and order without extreme repression. Baldwin adroitly managed to confine Churchill's following of MPs to fewer than one hundred. Both sides were deluding themselves: the moderates in their belief that India could be peacefully groomed for Dominion status, Churchill in believing it could be held by force without 'frightfulness'. Churchill failed to derail the Government of India Act of 1935 which created an All-Indian Federation of British-ruled provinces and princely states.* What he derailed was his own career.

The Indian context is important for understanding Britain's slowness in 'facing up' to the dictators. Almost singlehandedly Churchill kept India at the centre of Tory politics during the first two years of Hitler's dictatorship, with most of Baldwin's waning energy devoted to preventing a split in the Tory ranks. 'Appeasement' was Churchill's dirty word for policy to Gandhi, not to Hitler. It was not till August 1935 that Churchill himself started to mend his political fences by pointing to dangers 'larger and nearer than Indian dangers'. By then he was completely discredited with the Baldwin loyalists, who assumed that his new campaign for rearmament was simply a further step in a career devoted largely to self-promotion.

Chamberlain's decade

The 1930s was Neville Chamberlain's decade. Prime minister from 1937 to 1940, he had been Chancellor of the Exchequer

---

* The Act remained a dead letter, because the princely states failed to come into the federation; but it became the basis of the post-imperial constitution.

for the previous five years, and the driving force in Baldwin's government.* Lloyd George called him 'a very good Lord Mayor of Birmingham – in a bad year', a good joke which captured the fact that Chamberlain, like his father, remained a provincial figure, the product of Midlands and British industry, not of London, the City and Foreign Office. He lacked Churchill's majestic brilliance, MacDonald's oratorical gifts, Baldwin's emollient charm. He has been unthinkingly treated as a kind of extra wheel in the MacDonald–Baldwin chariot, but he was made of much more recalcitrant material. He was censorious by nature, did not suffer fools gladly, and treated the Labour Party like dirt – rather as did Margaret Thatcher whom, in some ways, he resembled. But he was not a reactionary: in fact, he was a reforming minister of health under Baldwin in the 1920s, who expressed in deeds the sympathies, including a love of nature, he could not find words for. He made up for his defects with a clear mind, confidence in his own abilities, immense energy, single-minded purpose, skill in party management, mastery of practical detail, and a profound hatred of war. 'In war, whichever side may call itself the victor, there are no winners but all are losers', he said in 1938.[12] What might in other times be counted as a virtuous sentiment in a ruler was to be held against him. Chamberlain was an imperial statesman. The white Dominions were far more important to him than was Europe. He had a clear plan for preserving the empire, which was to develop it as an economic unit and get rid of European complications by reaching accommodations with the dictators. Had events – that is,

---

* Baldwin swapped places with MacDonald just before the 1935 election, and stepped down as prime minister in 1937. Election results: 14 November 1935. Conservative: 10,025,083, 47.8 per cent, 386 seats; Liberal: 1,414,010, 6.7 per cent, twenty-one seats; Labour 7,984,988, 38 per cent, 154 seats.

Hitler – been kinder to him, he would have gone down as one of the greatest British statesmen, the 1930s as one of Britain's most successful decades, the Chamberlain dynasty, father and two sons, as the most remarkable British political family of the century.

With the fall of the pound in 1931, it was time to try Chamberlainite economics. In 1931 the Import Duties Act imposed a tariff on all foreign imports, including food, ending almost a century of free trade. This opened the way to a systematic policy of imperial preference. In a highly complicated set of bargains, acrimoniously negotiated at Ottawa in October 1932, Britain exempted empire foodstuffs from the provisions of the Import Duties Act (though not from some quotas), while the white Dominions plus India agreed to give preference to British exports by raising their tariffs against foreign manufactures. The Ottawa Agreement established the most extensive system of tariff discrimination in the world. It annoyed the United States, and hit the British consumer. Its effect was mixed. It achieved some trade diversion, which was its object, but not enough to compensate for the collapse of Britain's trade with the non-empire world. Its main effect was to accelerate the British trend to national self-sufficiency. By 1938 foreign exports accounted for only 11 per cent, and imports 18 per cent, of British GNP, compared with 28 per cent and 31 per cent respectively in 1913.

The 'sterling area' which emerged in 1931 was the financial counterpart of these preferential trade arrangements. When sterling was devalued against the dollar in 1931 about twenty countries, not all in the empire, devalued their currencies in line with sterling in order to preserve their entry to the British market. Some of them agreed to exchange the gold and dollar surpluses earned from their foreign trade for sterling reserves held in London, in return for privileged access to the British capital market. This recycling mechanism enabled London to preserve some of its traditional business, and Britain to balance its accounts with the non-sterling world and maintain a small reserve of gold and dollars as a war chest. In the 1930s, finance was indeed less proud and industry more content, as Churchill had wanted in 1925. But industrial contentment was secured by protection and cartelisation, which would damage the future competiveness of the already weakened British economy.

Imperial economics pointed to isolation from continental Europe. The diplomatic framework for this had been the Locarno Treaty of 1925, negotiated by Austen Chamberlain, Neville's elder brother and Baldwin's Foreign Secretary. This apparently achieved what had eluded British diplomacy before 1914 – the security of western Europe against German attack. (It did not cover frontiers in eastern Europe.) Yet, despite Locarno, twenty years after the Versailles Treaty Britain found itself once more at war with Germany. Why was this? Many historians question the wisdom of Britain going to war in 1914; hardly any doubt that the war which started in 1939 was a 'good war'.

The consensus is somewhat mysterious, given the fact that Hitler's Germany posed less of a direct threat to Britain than had the Kaiser's. Hitler did not challenge the British navy, or British commerce; he did not covet the British Empire – in fact he admired it – he had no Schlieffen Plan to attack western Europe; he wanted to do a deal with the British. British policy-makers believed rightly that his long-term goals were to the east, and even here they were reasonably acquiescent, Baldwin remarking in 1936 that if there was 'any fighting in Europe to be done', he would like to see 'the Bolshies and the Nazis doing it'. An agreement with Germany would have had the additional bonus of freeing up resources to defend the Asian empire. So why did Britain go to war to stop Hitler from recovering Danzig, a German city in Poland which the Versailles Treaty had detached from Germany against the will of its inhabitants, and which most people in Britain, if they thought of it at all, agreed he could have for the (decent) asking?*

Although the decision for war united the nation in 1939, and has been overwhelmingly endorsed by historians, there was an almost equal consensus for peace before 1939. Churchill, leader of the anti-appeasers, was an isolated figure till after Munich. Accommodation with Hitler, however distasteful, might be a realistic option for a weakened Britain, and this was the object of Neville Chamberlain's appeasement policy. But Britain's leaders lacked the ruthlessness (and probably public support) to pursue it to its bitter end, especially in face of the brutality of the Nazi regime.

The question whether Britain had been wise to go to war in 1939 was answered by the war itself. The judgement of Nuremberg in 1946 gave the moral indictment of Nazism its legal imprimatur, finding the German leaders guilty not only of planning and waging aggressive war, but of unspeakable crimes against humanity. Britain's own performance in the war was exemplary, so much so that to question its value became impious. The war stood for too many things on which the British looked back on with pride, not least of which was a vanished moment of national unity and social

---

* At Versailles, France and America had proposed to give Danzig to Poland; Lloyd George had arranged for it to become a 'free' city under League of Nations administration. It sat astride the 'corridor' created to separate East from West Prussia.

hope. That in the longer perspective, the conflict between Britain and Germany brought about the collapse of European power, including British power, counted for little in the way the British drew up their balance sheet.

The interesting question is whether it would have been more difficult to avoid war in the 1930s than it had been in 1914. Although Hitler did not directly challenge Britain, he did want extra bits of Europe, so an accommodation with him would have involved, as a minimum, tearing up the Versailles Treaty, and quite possibly more than that. In other words, 'talking' to Hitler would have entailed a much more difficult conversation than talking to Bethmann-Hollweg, the pre-1914 German Chancellor, quite apart from the question of Hitler's character and the nature of Nazism.

How might such a conversation have gone? Hitler would have demanded a 'free hand' in eastern Europe. It would have been contrary to the best traditions of British foreign policy to have voluntarily surrendered half of Europe to the mercy of national socialism, even ignoring its effects on the European balance of power. A variant would have involved accepting Mussolini's idea of a Four Power Pact of Germany, Italy, France and Britain to replace the almost defunct League of Nations. But war-avoidance policies of this kind ran up against the barbarity of the Nazi regime.

On the other hand, for most of the 1930s – until at least the Munich Agreement in September 1938 – Britain had no need for this kind of conversation. Britain and France together, could have won a war against Germany – *and Hitler knew it.* This put them in a very strong position either to insist on strict enforcement of the Versailles Treaty (till 1936) or to demand cast-iron military guarantees in return for any territorial concessions. It was a dreadful failure of diplomacy by both powers jointly not to take advantage of this situation. With one exception (see below p. 225) Britain did nothing between 1933 and 1938 to stop Germany regaining its strength, with the result that by 1939 Hitler could contemplate military gambles with some equanimity. A war-avoidance policy then became more difficult, because it would have meant concessions from weakness, without guarantee of future security.

Historians can readily explain the infirmity of British policy, but these explanations do not justify it. A favourite is slowness to rearm. Economy cuts had reduced Britain to fifth among the air powers by 1933. Although the Ten-Year Rule was cancelled in 1932, after the Japanese invasion of Manchuria, it was not till 1937 that a major rearmament programme was authorised. A faster rearming Britain, goes the argument, would have reinforced a hesitant, but still powerful France; together they could have dealt with Germany from a position of greater strength. Instead it was Hitler who rearmed rapidly, the British following with a crucial lag which gave him his field for maneouvre. Failure to rearm was the joint failure of MacDonald and Baldwin. Both were way past their best. 'The wretched Ramsay is almost a mental case,' noted Churchill in 1935. 'Baldwin is crafty, patient, and also amazingly lazy, sterile and inefficient where public business is concerned.' But Britain and France did not actually need any further rearmament to have stopped Hitler before 1938.

Historians point to the pacifist state of public opinion. It is true that war avoidance, which included avoiding an arms race, had become much more politically important than it had been in 1914 (even Hitler tried to avoid a 'big' war). To the retrospective horror of the trenches was added the threat of destruction from the air. In 1932 Baldwin proclaimed that 'the bomber will always get through' – true enough in the days before radar. Hitler stoked up this particular war fear by announcing, wrongly, in 1935 that Germany had achieved parity with Britain in the air; Churchill used these false figures to press his case for faster rearmament. On the other side, by appealing to the principle of national self-determination, Hitler was able to exploit the widespread feeling that Germany had been unjustly treated at Versailles. The Labour Party's hostility to rearmament was an important constraint, mainly because of the government's need for trade union co-operation. The Labour Party was militantly anti-fascist but also militantly against rearmament, a hopelessly incoherent position. It voted against the defence estimates in 1935 and 1936, and abstained for the first time in 1937. The Labour Party's position seemed to be that large armaments were safe only in the hands of a Labour government. A majority of students voted not to fight for 'King and Country' in a notorious debate in February 1933 at the Oxford Union. More solid, though far from conclusive, evidence of a pacifist mood, was furnished by by-election swings against the National Government, notably at East Fulham in October 1933, as well as by the equivocal results of the Peace Ballot announced in June 1935.* However, with a majority of 470 in the Commons, the government could have taken some political risks.

Then there was the Treasury view: Britain could not *afford* faster rearmament. But this depended on not having a full employment policy. Between 1932 and 1937 unemployment averaged 15 per cent of the insured workforce, most of it concentrated in Britain's northern industrial heartland.

---

* Of 11.5 million respondents, 10 million favoured economic sanctions, and 6.8 million military action against an aggressor, hardly a pacifist response, but neither a ringing endorsement of rearmament.

National output was about 10 per cent less than it might have been. Much of this spare capacity would have been available for rearmament. The Treasury never grasped that a large rearmament programme, financed by loan, could help economic recovery, which would provide the needed resources for larger arms expenditure. A full-employment policy would have changed the political context of rearmament by providing the unemployed jobs in the derelict areas. Instead, Britain's recovery from depression, market-led and largely confined to the south-east and Midlands, was slower and less complete than Germany's. True enough, 'the intellectual apparatus of Keynesian economics had yet to establish itself'.[13] This did not stop Hitler 'curing' unemployment, before Keynes had finished explaining why it existed, giving him a head start which made possible his diplomatic and military gambles. Failure to add full-employment policy to his recipe for resisting Hitler was a major gap in Churchill's polemics. Curiously enough it was Neville Chamberlain, the 'balanced budget' Chancellor, who proposed to fight the general election of 1935 on a rearmament programme, disguised as an employment policy. Baldwin vetoed it for fear that it would hand victory to Labour: an episode almost completely ignored by historians of appeasement.[14]

Britain's diplomatic position in the 1930s was weaker than it had been in 1914. In 1921, it had been forced to scrap the Anglo-Japanese alliance at America's insistence, facing it with the double task of defending the empire in the Pacific and the homeland in Europe. Correlli Barnett has argued that Britain should have abandoned India and 'east of Suez' in order to concentrate its resources on the renewed challenge of Germany.[15] But this was a choice no one in Britain, especially Churchill, was willing to make. The possibility of constructing a

Churchillian 'grand alliance' to resist Nazi Germany was poor. Already isolationist, the USA was alienated from Britain by imperial preference. The Soviet Union was not a palatable member of a system of collective security, except to those on the extreme left. Fascist Italy might join Britain and France in resisting German expansion in central Europe, but Mussolini's price was likely to be high, and his commitment unreliable. But Britain did not need these other powers before 1938; it just needed France.

In that respect, the situation was quite different from 1914, when the 'obligation of honour' to France removed the necessary flexibility Britain needed to talk to Germany. A realistic war-avoidance policy in the 1930s would have been a military alliance with France based on an agreed foreign policy. But no attempt was made to forge one. The Foreign Office sought to conduct policy so that 'Germany could never be sure that HMG would not intervene in Central Europe and the French could never be sure that we *would* – thereby discouraging both from forward policies'.[16] A policy which would have made sense before 1914 made none at all in the military and ideological conditions of the 1930s, when it was bound to encourage Britain's potential enemies and discourage its friends.

In short, none of these 'objective' constraints on a tough British foreign policy gets round the fact that Hitler could have been stopped in his tracks any time before 1938 with the existing material and military resources commanded by Britain and France.

The best chance of 'nailing down' Hitler was between 1933 and 1936, when Germany was still weak. In principle British policy was to bind Germany and Japan to arms-limitation agreements. These would square the two countries' demand for a higher level of armaments than existing treaties allowed with the Treasury veto on anything but modest British rearmament. Hitler played skilfully on this by offering a succession of plausible arms pacts. Japan also seemed receptive to a new naval agreement.* These propositions ran into resistance from France in Europe and the United States in Asia, and the opportunity was missed. The only arms pact concluded was the bilateral Anglo-German naval agreement of 1935, which limited the German navy to 35 per cent of Britain's. This assured Britain its much-needed naval supremacy in the North Sea. But Japan remained unappeased in the Pacific.

In 1935–6 British foreign policy unravelled in the face of increasing assertiveness by Italy and Germany. Willing neither to resist nor conciliate the dictators, but rejecting non-interference, Britain and France acquiesced in a series of bold coups which weakened their prestige and prepared the ground for further assaults. This dismal sequence started in October 1935 when Mussolini invaded Abyssinia. Instead of directly opposing Mussolini – or alternatively doing nothing – Britain responded with the moralistic policy of imposing economic sanctions on Italy, which antagonised the Italian dictator without impeding his conquest. On 10 June 1936, Neville Chamberlain called the continuation of sanctions the 'midsummer of madness', but the damage had been done. The Stresa front of 1935, by which Britain and France had tried to lock Mussolini into support for the European status quo, was broken; Mussolini proclaimed the Rome–Berlin axis in November 1936, and left the League of Nations a year later.

---

* The Versailles Treaty had limited Germany to a land army of 104,000 and the navy to six small armoured vessels, six light cruisers and twelve destroyers. No submarines or military aircraft were allowed. Japan was limited to fifty cruisers by the London Naval Treaty of 1930, 61–5 per cent of British and American strength.

Hitler, noting the infirmity of the western response to Italian aggression, decided on a coup of his own. On 7 March 1936, he sent German troops into the demilitarised Rhineland, claiming that the Franco-Soviet Pact* had abrogated the assumptions of Locarno. France refused to take the risk of ejecting him without British support, the British refused to give it – 'Britain', Baldwin told the French foreign minister, 'is not in a state to go to war' – so Hitler got away with it. In fact there was not the slightest danger of war, Hitler having given instructions to withdraw German troops if the western powers resisted the move. Despite the popular British reaction that 'Jerry can do what he likes in his own back garden', confident governments would not have hesitated to act, bringing Hitler's career of conquest to an end before it had started. In place of the old Locarno, Hitler offered a new one: a twenty-five-year non-aggression pact with his western neighbours, a new demilitarised zone on both sides of the frontiers, a western air pact (which would have banned bombing) and Germany's return to the League of Nations – a seemingly solid piece of security in western Europe. Baldwin wanted to test the offer by meeting Hitler personally, but was dissuaded by his Foreign Secretary, Anthony Eden, who interpreted the German proposal as an attempt to split Britain from France.

A final chance for a costless firm stand came with the outbreak of the Spanish Civil War in July 1936. Mussolini and Hitler started supplying the rebel General Franco with arms and 'volunteers', the Soviet Union sent military equipment to the Republican government. Anxious to avoid a 'new topic of conflict in Europe'[17] Britain devised a policy of

---

* Ratified by the French Parliament on 27 February 1935, this provided for mutual aid in case of unprovoked aggression. Lacking military clauses, it was a toothless tiger.

'non-intervention' to localise the conflict. Everyone joined in, but only Britain and France carried it out. In fact, if challenged by an Anglo-French blockade of Spanish ports, Mussolini and Hitler would have withdrawn. Non-intervention in Spain reinforced the lesson of Abyssinia and the Rhineland: gambles could safely be taken by the brigand powers in face of extreme war fear by the democracies.

This phase of drift was terminated when Neville Chamberlain succeeded Baldwin as prime minister in May 1937. He was determined to take over control of foreign policy from the palsied grip of the Foreign Office. He had been appalled by the inertia of Baldwin's last year, but thought the situation could still be retrieved. His last act as Chancellor had been to authorise, at long last, a massive British rearmament drive (£1.5 billion over five years, £400 million of which was to be borrowed). This was heavily concentrated on defence of Britain and its trade routes, Chamberlain believing that Britain lacked the resources for 'a million men Army' for continental warfare.[18] Indeed, the British Army of 154,000 (plus 50,000 troops in India) was smaller than it had been in 1914. Chamberlain intended to settle all outstanding issues with Hitler and Mussolini on a businesslike basis. 'I believe the double policy of rearmament and better relations with Germany and Italy will carry us safely through the danger period, if only the Foreign Office will play up,' he wrote on becoming PM.[19] This was the start of appeasement as a systematic policy. In his imperial policy, now in his search for agreement with Germany, Neville Chamberlain had taken up the mantle of his father.

Better relations with Italy meant recognising the Italian conquest of Abyssinia in the hope that Italy would scale down its support for Franco and exert a moderating influence on

Hitler. This cost Chamberlain his Foreign Secretary, Anthony Eden, whose resignation earned him a mythical reputation as a strong anti-appeaser. Getting on better terms with Germany meant conceding it colonies in Africa (which it did not want) and territorial revisions in central and eastern Europe (which it did). Chamberlain would allow the Reich to expand to include ethnic Germans beyond its borders, provided, as his emissary Halifax told Hitler in November 1937, this could be done peacefully and through 'reasonable agreements with Germany reasonably reached'.

The flaw in this strategy of peaceful German expansion was the lack of any mechanism for accomplishing it if some of the victim countries chose to resist having their Germanic limbs chopped off. The peaceful incorporation of Austria into the Reich on 12 March 1938 caused no problem because Austria was ethnically German. It was different when appeasement meant the dismemberment of democratic, multinational, Czechoslovakia. It was Britain's anxiety to settle the Czech problem before Hitler acted unilaterally which brought on the Czech crisis.* The Munich Agreement of 30 September 1938 was achieved by two acts of bullying: Britain's bullying of the Czech government to cede the Sudetenland to Germany, and Hitler's bullying of Chamberlain to concede the German demand for immediate military occupation of the ceded area. There was no need at all for Chamberlain to have accepted or done the bullying. A Franco-British-Czech refusal to have negotiated at the point of a gun would either have caused a military coup against Hitler in Germany, or, more probably,

---

* As A. J. P. Taylor acutely pointed out in *Origins of the Second World War*, 'By seeking to avert a crisis, the British brought it on. The Czech problem was not of British making; the Czech crisis of 1938 was.'

his retreat. At the very least Chamberlain was in a position to have insisted on a proper timetable and due process for the secession of the Sudetentland. He returned from Munich waving a piece of paper signed by Hitler, which, he claimed, promised 'peace with honour, peace in our time'. 'How horrible, fantastic, incredible,' he broadcast just before Munich, 'that we should be digging trenches and trying on gas masks here because of a quarrel in a faraway country between people of whom we know nothing.'

The Munich settlement was very popular – Chamberlain was cheered from the balcony of Buckingham Palace – though more out of a sense of relief than of pride. Thereafter appeasement was undermined by Hitler himself. Surprised and emboldened by the ease with which he had secured a British capitulation, he convinced himself that he could, if necessary, discount further British interference with his plans. The unleashing of Kristallnacht against the German Jews on 9–10 November 1938 showed how indifferent he had become to British opinion. The disintegration of the Czech state in March 1939 was a natural consequence of the Munich Agreement; nevertheless, the German occupation of Prague on 15 March 1939 was sufficiently triumphal to turn public opinion against further unilateral concessions to Germany. Yet Britain's guarantees to Poland and Rumania which almost immediately followed were the panicky responses to rumours of an imminent German invasion of one or other of these countries, circulated by the Rumanian ambassador, Tilea, which turned out to have no foundation. It was the first commitment Britain had ever made to the unstable territorial status quo in eastern Europe. To have guaranteed the frontiers of Poland before a settlement of the Danzig question must count as the chief blunder of British foreign policy in a decade of blunders.

Even at this stage few in Britain would have objected to the peaceful acceptance of German demands on Poland. Chamberlain still hoped that the transfer of Danzig to Germany could be negotiated between Germany and Poland. (The League of Nations' interest in the matter had long become academic.) But Britain's guarantee of Poland's frontiers – as well as the Poles' unfounded belief in the strength of their armed forces – deprived the Polish foreign minister, Colonel Beck, of any incentive to parley. Hitler looked on Britain to put pressure on the Poles as they had on the Czechs, but this time, the British would not say 'Boo to Beck'.[20] Hitler decided to settle the Polish question by force, freeing himself from the threat of a two-front war by the Molotov-Ribbentrop Pact with Russia of 23 August. This thieves' contract divided Poland between them, doing in one bite what it had taken Prussia, Russia and Austria to do in three in the eighteenth century. When German troops crossed the Polish frontier on 31 August, Britain and France, somewhat to their surprise, found themselves at war with Germany. Britain declared war on 3 September on behalf of the non-white empire. Australia and New Zealand felt honour-bound by the British declaration. Canada and South Africa declared war separately, South Africa after a change of government. Ireland stayed neutral.

The Anglo-French declaration of war had no effect on Poland's fortunes, because the two powers had no war plans except to sit tight behind the Maginot Line. German troops entered Warsaw on 27 September; the next day Germany and Russia settled their zones of occupation. Although Chamberlain immediately brought Churchill back into his old post as First Lord of the Admiralty, the first eight months of hostilities have been rightly called the 'phony war'. Britain and France were in no position to stop Germany conquering Poland, and had no offensive plans of their own. Hitler's path to the Ukraine was blocked by his pact with Russia, and, in view of Britain's refusal to make peace, he saw no alternative but to force both France and Britain out of the war. On 10 May 1940, the Third Reich sprang its military might on Belgium, Holland and France. British troops were soon driven out of France, which fell to the German 'blitzkrieg'. The same day, Chamberlain, his appeasement policy in ruins, resigned, and Winston Churchill became prime minister at the head of a coalition with the Labour and Liberal parties. The new war leader offered his people 'blood, toil, tears and sweat'.

Chapter 8

Churchill's War, Attlee's Peace
1940–1951

There was once an almighty war in which the Americans, when they finally came to the aid of the British, saved us from tyranny, but the salvation led to the dissolution of our empire, and then to slowly dying dreams of power, and then, finally, to a new assessment of reality.

Clive James, *Times Literary Supplement*,
28 September 2007

Winning the Derby

Bolingbroke said of Marlborough, 'He was so great a man that I have forgot his vices.' There is a strong temptation to write similarly of Marlborough's great descendant Winston Spencer Churchill. Yet Marlborough won an empire, Churchill lost it. Both were heroes, but their heroic acts had different consequences. So one cannot be quite as forgetful of Churchill's 'vices'.

Churchill is the most ambiguous figure in the 'decline and fall' story. Rhetorically, he was an unashamed imperialist. The empire was in his blood; his early years were spent on its frontiers. Yet he espoused policies which made continuance of empire impossible. His victorious war was immediately followed by the loss of four fifths of the empire's population. He achieved totemic status by becoming the unwitting conduit by which imperial, aristocratic Britain passed into the post-imperial, social democratic age.

Even in his youth, he was a hero out of time, an aristocrat whose moment of greatness came when Chamberlain's management of decline splintered on the rock of Hitler's savagery. Despite his part in Lloyd George's pre-1914 social insurance legislation, he was connected to British public life not through mundane bread-and-butter issues but through a historical meta-narrative which held fast to an uplifting, even aggressive, view of Britain's world role, long after the problem had been how best to manage Britain's limited resources. In domestic politics he subscribed to his father's nebulous creed of 'Tory democracy', which sought to unite the aristocracy and working class, at a time when Britain was becoming steadily more bourgeois. Cut off from a ducal inheritance by the law of primogeniture, he sought the glittering prizes in politics. He was a child of the new political age, who understood the value of publicity, and the appeal of great characters to the newly enfranchised masses. He himself was a magnificent character in search of magnificent events.

He was a superb rhetorician, drunk on his own phrase-making. The very prodigality of his rhetorical gifts clouded his judgement as to what was important and what was not. As the journalist A. G. Gardiner noted, with Churchill it was always the 'hour of fate and the crack of doom'. In the war his rhetoric finally found a worthy subject, but it had long caused 'sound men' to mistrust his judgement and his motives. He started as a Conservative, spent his middle years, 1904–22, as a Liberal, mainly under Lloyd George's spell, before Baldwin brought him back into the Conservative fold. As a result of his

switches of party, he had been a minister for most of his political life, except in the 1930s. This was essential for his financial
solvency; as the son of a younger son he had no money, and
dubious financial associates. Though a figure of endless
fascination, especially to the young generation, his self-
absorption cut him off from the general fellowship of politics.
He had no base in the Tory Party, just a few cronies like
Brendan Bracken, and even in 1940, he became prime minister before he became Tory Party leader. The Tory Party in
Parliament, which had become a party of company directors,
preferred Neville Chamberlain, who represented 'business',
to the erratic and quixotic Winston.

Churchill the saviour was born in 1940, at the improbably
late age of sixty-five. In the 1930s, he had been written off as a
failure. Lloyd George blamed the 'distrust and trepidation
with which mediocrity views genius at close quarters'. But
Churchill's wounds were partly self-inflicted. He was mistrusted by both main parties. As A. J. P. Taylor put it,
'Conservatives remembered his campaign against the India
Bill and his support for Edward VIII at the time of the abdication. Labour remembered his aggressiveness during the
General Strike and harked back even to Tonypandy.'[1]

'Appeasement' was *de trop* in Churchill's lexicon long
before it was applied to Hitler's Germany. He refused to give
in to pressure. Magnanimous in victory, he wanted the victory first. The trouble is that declining empires are always
subject to pressure, and offer few clear-cut victories for the
display of magnanimity. In the early 1930s Churchill's strategic sense seemed to desert him. From 1931 to 1935 he
denounced appeasement of Gandhi with an eloquence which,
by 1933 at least, might have been better directed to closer
quarters. More importantly, his resistance to the India Bill

destroyed his influence with Baldwin and the 'sound men' of British politics. 'Thank God, we are preserved from Winston Churchill', wrote a senior military officer in 1936, when Churchill was refused the new Ministry for the Co-ordination of Defence. By then he counted so little in British politics that he needed a war to 'win the Derby', as he put it. He not only needed a war to 'win the Derby'; he needed several gigantic strokes of luck to win the war.

Churchill's attitude to the British Empire was complex. He had a romantic attachment to it, understood the prestige Britain derived from its possession, and firmly believed that it was a force for world good. But he had no interest in imperial economics: he was a liberal, not a Chamberlainite imperialist. Strategically, empire was important to him chiefly as a component in the European balance of power, allowing Britain to strike at the peripheries of an aspiring continental hegemon – the Dardanelles in 1915, the Mediterranean 'underbelly' in the Second World War. However, the First World War had also taught him that Britain could no longer be the balancer of Europe. The United States had to be engaged in any successful resistance to the ambitions of a continental 'tyrant', whether this be Hitler's Germany or (after 1946) Stalin's Russia. Half-American himself, he was attracted by the thought of a permanent partnership between the two main 'English-speaking peoples'. So while he could famously declare in 1942 that, 'I have not become the king's first minister in order to preside over the liquidation of the British Empire', he also conceded in 1940 that 'The British Empire and the United States will have to be somewhat mixed up together in some of their affairs for the mutual and general advantage.'[2] If Churchill was aware of a possible conflict here – that the 'mixing up' might involve a considerable

The Businessman and the Bulldog
9. Neville Chamberlain (l); 10. Winston Churchill (r)

'liquidation' – he ignored it. Like most politicians he hoped to get the best of both worlds, at least as long as he was in charge.

The war

Unlike the First World War, the Second falls neatly into two halves. In the first half Britain was losing, in the second it was winning.* The change in fortunes was due mainly to Hitler's hubristic blunders. Britain started the war with only one significant ally, France, and France was knocked out in June 1940. Hitler added two more: by invading Russia on 22 June 1941 and gratuitously declaring war on the United States on

---

* The exception to this generalisation is Britain's war against Italy in North Africa, which it started winning from the start, clearing the Italians out of most of their African empire, before the Germans intervened to rescue their Italian ally.

7 December 1941. Neither power would have come in on its own volition – or at least in time to avert a British defeat. This fact vindicates Chamberlain's strategy, not Churchill's.

After the end of 1941, there were still defeats to come, notably at Singapore which fell to the Japanese in February 1942. But victory was no longer in doubt. Three events in November–December 1942 mark the turning point: the Anglo-American invasion of North Africa, Montgomery's victory over Rommel at El Alamein in Egypt, and, most important of all, the surrender of a huge German army at Stalingrad. The rest was essentially mopping up, though the Germans and Japanese, being martial nations, fought hard and resourcefully against increasingly unfavourable odds. British armies under Montgomery took part, with the Americans, in the liberation of France in 1944 and the push into Germany in 1945. Britain played a minor part in the American defeat of Japan in the Pacific. Its other key contributions were off-battle: both breaking the German secret codes, and its part in the development of the atomic bomb which hastened the end of the war in the Pacific. With Germany's surrender on 7 May 1945, Britain, still led by Churchill, emerged as one of the 'Big Three' victors, with the ordering of the world in their hands.

The evacuation of the British expeditionary force from Dunkirk on 4 June 1940 without its weapons left Britain, for several months, almost defenceless against a German attack. Strangely, Hitler held back. He seems to have seen invasion as a last resort; he hoped to use the threat of invasion plus the Luftwaffe to force Britain to make peace.[3] Some in the Cabinet, like Chamberlain's Foreign Secretary Lord Halifax, wanted to negotiate; Churchill rightly insisted that Britain was too weak to do so, and the British people agreed. Freed from the incubus of France, they did not doubt victory. The Battle of Britain, starting in August, was Britain's first and most decisive victory in the war. In Churchill's words, 'Never in the field of human conflict was so much owed by so many to so few.' On 7 September, the Germans, having failed to destroy the RAF, switched to bombing London. The Blitz lasted till 2 November. London was bombed every night, with much destruction of civilian housing, but little damage to war production, before the Germans finally switched to industrial centres in the Midlands. The final tally of aircraft losses in the Battle of Britain was 1,733 Luftwaffe, and 915 RAF. Britain's decisive contribution to victory in the Second World War was surviving in 1940. This left Hitler's western strategy in ruins: he had neither defeated Britain nor made peace with it. On 18 December he approved Operation Barbarossa against Russia.

The Battle of Britain was succeeded by the Battle of the Atlantic, Hitler's attempt to force Britain out of the war by cutting off its supplies from America. The naval war was hard-fought. The British navy commanded the waves, German submarines the depths. It was only American help short of war which enabled Britain to hold on in 1941. The Germans got the upper hand in 1942 when they changed their naval codes; the Allies won it in mid-1943, when they broke the new ones.

The rapid collapse of France forced Britain to fight the 'peripheral' war which the 'easterners' had unsuccessfully demanded in 1915. For two years Britain's Eighth Army fought the German Afrika Corps across the deserts of Egypt and Libya, in an almost self-contained peripheral war – the only one which the British Empire could now fight on its own. This only joined up with the main war in 1943, once

Anglo-American forces started to fight their way up the spine of Italy.

Until 1944, aerial bombardment was Britain's only way of taking the war directly to the main enemy, and from 1942 onwards Bomber Command, under Sir Arthur Harris, pounded German cities heavily and persistently, with a quarter of the pilots coming from the Dominions. The 'area bombing' strategy met Churchill's demand for offensive action; it rested on the mistaken notion that support for the German dictatorship was fragile. The British and American bombing of Germany killed 600,000 German civilians, ten times the number of Britons killed by the Luftwaffe. It culminated in the destruction of Dresden on 13–15 February 1945, with 30,000 or more killed. The Anglo-American aerial bombardment of Germany strengthened, rather than weakened, German morale, and had little effect till 1945 on war production.

The United States had consistently refused to underwrite the British Empire in the Far East, which it regarded as a rival to its own commercial interests. Indeed, it had put it at risk by forcing Britain to break its alliance with Japan in 1921. With the US Navy temporarily immobilised by the attack on Pearl Harbor, the Japanese conquered the British Empire in East and South East Asia in a series of lightning operations. On 15 February 1942, Singapore surrendered, together with 100,000 British and imperial troops. Churchill called it 'the greatest disaster to British arms which our history records'. A few days earlier, the Japanese had sunk Britain's latest battleship, the *Prince of Wales*, and the battle cruiser *Repulse*. The boy J. G Ballard in Shanghai immediately realised that Britain's Asian empire was over: 'Even at the age of 11 or 12, I knew that no amount of patriotic newsreels would put the Union

Jack jigsaw together again.'

Neither side planned for a big war. Just as the Germans expected Britain to collapse through bombing, and the Russians through blitzkrieg, the British expected the Germans to collapse through economic weakness, speeded up by subversion and bombing. Both hoped to avoid the haemorrhage of the trenches in 1914–18. The British strategy for avoiding heavy losses worked, the German strategy came unstuck in Russia. Compared with the Russians and the Germans, or indeed with their own casualties between 1914 and 1918, the British had a 'light' war. The home population suffered more, starting with the Blitz in September 1940 and ending with the doodlebugs of 1944–5. Altogether, 60,000 were killed through aerial bombardment. Physical destruction of property was estimated at £1.45 billion. But military losses, at 300,000 killed (plus 35,000 in the merchant navy), were less than half those in the First World War, with half a million wounded as opposed to 2 million in the earlier conflict.

Mobilising for victory

Britain's performance in the Second World War exhibited a spirit of national unity which retained a permanent hold on the imagination, not just of the left. The spread of discomfort was regarded as a benefit, not least because it was fairly distributed, from Buckingham Palace downwards. So the war was doubly blessed – by victory and by war socialism. This was later to create a problem of interpretation for the Thatcherite right.

British wartime organisation was much better than in 1914–18, chiefly because it came into operation much sooner. Many of the officials running the Second World War had served their apprenticeship in the earlier conflict and knew what was required. A small War Cabinet was formed from the outset, first under Chamberlain, then under Churchill. Below this was a Defence Committee, headed by Churchill and the chiefs of staff which ran the military side of the war, and a Lord President's Committee which organised the home front. Under the super-civil servant Sir John Anderson, this second super-committee became the hub of the planning effort, charged with allocating resources – manpower, raw materials, transport – in line with national priorities. The decisions of the planning authorities were transmitted downwards through a myriad of regional and local committees. As in the First World War, both decision-making and implementing bodies were staffed by businessmen whose expertise and co-operation the government needed to meet their targets. This government/business partnership would change the structure of peacetime political economy. As Alan Milward has written, 'the two worlds of business and government administration were never again seen as the separate worlds they had still been in the thirties'.[4]

The Second World War was also more fairly run than the first, because, with the enemy poised for invasion, the need for national unity was much greater. This time Labour was fully integrated into the war effort from the moment Churchill took over, with Ernest Bevin, minister of labour, the second man in the government. Between 1940 and 1941, a 'social contract' was forged whereby the trade unions were induced to accept income tax for the workers and wage restraint in return for government commitment to stable prices, subsidisation of necessities and a 'fair' distribution of sacrifice, largely through rationing and punitive taxation on the rich, with Excess Profits Tax of 100 per cent. This 'social contract' approach to economic and social policy set a framework for post-war politics, with trade union leaders committing themselves to pay restraint in return for the welfare state, full employment and nationalisation of key industries, leaving the system of 'free' collective bargaining for wages untouched.

The high level of wartime consensus meant that voluntarism worked better in the second than in the first conflict, both in industrial relations and civil society. The government took the usual powers: to forbid strikes, suppress any subversive publications, to lock up anyone suspected of sympathising with the enemy. However, it made little use of these powers, since opposition to the war was confined to small political fringes. When war broke out, the Communist Party, in obedience to the Comintern, had denounced the war as 'an imperialist and unjust war, for which the bourgeoisie of all countries bear equal responsibility'. Nevertheless, although the *Daily Worker* was suppressed in January 1941, the party itself was allowed to remain legal because Ernest Bevin feared industrial disruption if it were banned. The *Daily Worker* was reinstated in 1942 after Russia became Britain's glorious ally. At the other end of the anti-democratic spectrum, Oswald Mosley and 747 members of the British Union of Fascists were interned under Regulation 18B, Mosley being released on medical grounds in November 1943. The tabloid papers were enthusiastic supporters of the war, but not necessarily of the government's conduct of it. The government put pressure on them to suppress unfavourable news, and were only deterred from closing down the *Daily Mirror* by fear of political repercussions.

In the war years, the real wages of workers rose by 81 per cent due mainly to full employment, longer hours and control of prices. Women's employment increased. State and people came much closer together than in the First World War, partly because Labour was centrally involved in running the war on the home front, but also because national survival was much more precarious, and the perceived consequences of defeat more horrendous. Bombing to some extent abolished the distinction between the domestic front and the fighting forces, and unified the conditions of life at home, though how far the Blitz created social cohesion is disputed.

In his *Audit of War* (1986), Correlli Barnett castigated Britain's war effort at the level of the factory floor. The Spitfire was as good as the Messerschmitt BF-109 but took two thirds more man hours to build; the progress of jet-engined aircraft from the drawing board to the squadron 'evokes the turkey rather than the jet'. The rise in aircraft production (one of the war's success stories) was achieved not by a 'revolution in productivity, but simply by deploying 115,000 extra machine tools and over 1 million extra workers'. Till late in the war British tanks were 'mechanical abortions that foreshadowed the disastrous car models launched into world markets by the British automobile industry in the post-war era'. Even with radar a familiar disharmony appeared between 'scientific genius and industrial backwardness'. The electronics industry suffered from a 'galloping attack of the . . . British disease'.[5] Only one industry emerges with credit: the chemical industry. It was started by a German, Ludwig Mond. All of this is a useful corrective to the traditional emphasis on the success of macroeconomic management of the war effort.

Innovations in both internal and external finance were quicker to arrive than in 1914–18, partly because the theory of war finance was better understood. Uncertain about how long the war would last, or how much effort would be needed to fight it, British government started in classic fashion, relying mainly on borrowing from 'voluntary savings' rather than on taxation. The result was a sharp rise in inflation, as in the first war. This changed abruptly when the Germans attacked in May 1940. Kingsley Wood's supplementary budget of 23 July 1940 put a shilling (the equivalent of 5p) on income tax and imposed a miscellany of indirect taxes. But the real fiscal revolution came with his budget of 7 April 1941. This raised the standard rate of income tax to 50 per cent, with a top marginal rate of 97.5 per cent, and brought 3.25 million new working-class taxpayers into the income-tax net by lowering the personal-allowance threshold. More importantly for the future, Kingsley Wood's was the first use of the government's budget to try to 'balance the accounts of the nation' rather than just the accounts of the government, in line with the new macroeconomics of Keynes and the development of national income statistics. A further innovation of 1943 was the Pay As You Earn scheme of compulsory wage deductions at source, needed for the new mass base of income-tax payers. In addition to taxation, the war was partly financed by 'cheap money': the government's maximum borrowing rate was 3 per cent, and most of its war debt was borrowed at negative real interest rates. Domestic war finance has been mainly adjudged a success. The government covered 54 per cent of its spending by taxation in the years 1940–5 as opposed to 32 per cent between 1914 and 1918 and the price level in 1945 was only 30 per cent higher than in 1939, as compared to a doubling of prices in the 1914–18 war, almost the whole of the rise having occurred before the 1941 budget.

External finance raised the same problems as before, but they were solved differently. This was because this time the United States gifted rather than lent about half Britain's external cost, and Britain drew heavily on its empire for loans. For the first eighteen months, Britain could only obtain war goods in the United States on a 'cash and carry' basis, as neutrality legislation prevented American loans to European belligerents. By early 1941, its reserves were almost exhausted. But in March 1941, the United States, though still neutral, came to the rescue with 'Lend-Lease', a system of giving Britain the military and civilian goods it needed to carry on fighting. Churchill described Lend-Lease as 'the most unsordid act in the history of any nation'. But sentiment was backed by self-interest. Britain was to be kept in the war for 'the defence of the United States', and Congress took steps to marginalise Britain's export trade in order to control the level of its reserves. This was the real start of Britain's subservience to the United States, with Britain battling to retain, as Keynes put it, 'enough assets to leave us capable of independent action'.

A margin of independence did remain in the conduct of the war in the Middle East. In a rare display of financial ruthlessness, Britain forced the sterling-area countries* to make loans to Britain for such resources as it bought from them to prosecute the war outside Europe. As a result, it incurred large sterling debts to Egypt and India to defend them against the Axis powers, who only threatened them because they were dependencies of Britain. (Indian grain shipments to the Middle East, paid for in blocked sterling, helped cause the Bengal famine.)

The decisive contribution of these two sources of external financing to Britain's ability to wage war can be seen in

---

* These comprised all the countries of the British Empire, League of Nations mandates administered by Britain, British protectorates, Egypt, Sudan, and Iraq, and Iceland, a total of fifty countries.

the figures. Of Britain's cumulative external deficit of £10 billion over the six years of war, £4.5 billion was covered by Lend-Lease from the USA, £500 million by 'Mutual Aid' from Canada, and a further £1.2 billion by the sale of foreign assets – roughly a quarter of its overseas investments. Britain's net sterling debts rose from £500 million in 1939 to £3.4 billion in 1945. After the war, it refused to allow the newly formed International Monetary Fund to take over its wartime sterling liabilities, which therefore remained on Britain's balance sheet.

However successful in its own terms, war finance mortgaged Britain's post-war future. On the domestic side, the war left a dreadful legacy of high taxation which survived into the 1980s. War expenditure took 56 per cent of national income; capital depreciation 14 per cent of non-war plant. On the external side, Britain entered the war as an independent great power; it emerged from it a client of the United States, shorn of a large chunk of its net overseas assets. The 'sterling balances' enabled Britain to maintain sterling as a major post-war reserve currency, to the benefit of the City of London, but at the cost of continuous sterling crises. Less profligate in manpower than its predecessor, the Second World War was more profligate in treasure.

In theory, the Second World War vindicated Churchill's historical thesis. The removal of the German, Japanese and Italian challenges to the British position should have made it easier for Britain to continue as a great power. Battered though it was, its economy was in much better shape than that of its defeated rivals, and European states like France. The British Empire was intact, with the defeats in the Far East reversed. In practice, its 'finest hour' was the prelude to exit as a power of the first rank. Its economy, burdened by imperial nostalgia and dysfunctional labour relations, went into a long period of relative decline; this in turn denuded it of the resources to maintain its imperial position. Most important of all, Britain was not the real 'victor' in the war. It had 'hung on' against Germany; but Germany and Japan had been defeated by the United States and the Soviet Union. These were the new dominant powers. Not only were they anti-colonialist, but unlike in 1918, they were not about to retire and leave the management of international relations to the British.

The Second World War is still an indispensable point of reference for the notion of 'Britishness'. For years rulers and people lived in the shadow of the 'finest hour'. There was a sense of pride. Victory had vindicated British institutions and the British view of themselves as a uniquely 'good' nation. At the same time, the fruits of victory were undoubtedly disappointing. Post-war Britain started life looking like a defeated nation – grey, shabby, neglected, pitted with bomb craters. It should have been doing better. This feeling grew over time, as empire faded away and the defeated nations started to overtake Britain in all kinds of ways. The truth is that Britain's victory was pyrrhic. If war is, as Alan Milward has argued, an 'investment decision by the state', it is hard to see where the profit lay.[6] Britain had lost, like the other countries of Europe, but was handicapped by the illusion it had won, and that there were fruits of victory to enjoy.

Labour in power

It was in this triumphant, but stricken, state that Labour's first majority government, elected in July 1945, set out both to build a British version of socialism and maintain Britain's position as a world power.* The wherewithal would come from a mixture of high taxation and restoration of exports. Unlike after the First World War, the wartime spirit spilled over into peace. Probably the two most important reasons were a revulsion against the 1930s and the egalitarian 'social contract' of the war itself, which induced the middle class – if only temporarily – to accept the readjustment of their lifestyles. The war also legitimised Labour as a governing party, with the trade unions as the new power in the land. As a result, the war forged the 'post-war settlement' which lasted till the 1970s. The Baldwin–MacDonald middle way acquired substance in full employment, 'democratic planning', a 'mixed economy' of private and public sectors, and a welfare state which embraced all in a universal citizenship.

The settlement did not amount to a consensus. Friedrich Hayek's *Road to Serfdom* (1945), a searing attack on central planning, which had six reprints in sixteen months, marked the start of the individualist fightback. The Conservatives never accepted public ownership, the core Labour policy, and were lukewarm about the welfare state. The huge Labour majority of 1945 concealed the fact that the Conservatives retained 41 per cent of the popular vote: they lost because their share of the working-class vote fell.

In 1945, Keynes, by now mortally sick, was dispatched to Washington to obtain a transitional loan to plug the huge gap in the balance of payments. His trip was made desperately urgent by the sudden cancellation of Lend-Lease on 17 August

---

* General election, 5 July 1945: turnout 73 per cent, Conservatives 39.6 per cent 210 seats, Labour 48 per cent 393 seats, Liberal 9 per cent twelve seats, Others 2.4 per cent twenty-five seats.

1945. Keynes estimated that Britain faced a prospective balance of payments deficit of $7.5 billion in the first three years after the war. He hoped the US would grant Britain $5 billion in final settlement of the wartime account between the two allies.* In practice, he obtained a line of credit of $3.75 billion at 2 per cent interest, repayable in fifty annual instalments, starting in 1951. (Canada provided an additional $1.25 billion.) The main string attached was Britain's promise to make sterling convertible into dollars for current transactions within one year of the agreement coming into force.

This time round, wartime planning did provide a model for peacetime. For one thing, the left was in power, not the right. This included the left-wing intelligentsia, which, unlike in the First World War, had been passionately pro-war. Second, post-war reconstruction plans were more solidly laid, partly because there had been less fighting to be done, and victory had been certain for two and a half years before the war ended. Third, Labour proved to be a surprisingly cohesive, disciplined team. The prime minister Clement Attlee, Churchill's deputy in the wartime coalition, a taciturn ex-public school boy and left-wing paternalist, was not a commanding prime minister, but a successful one. His one-line put-downs were legendary: 'no good', 'too old', he told ministers when sacking them. He was able to hold the balance in a Cabinet dominated by star players like Ernest Bevin, Stafford Cripps, Herbert Morrison and Hugh Dalton. Fourth, wartime organisation had been better, and social cohesion stronger, than in the previous conflict. The Blitz and rationing, present almost from the start, equalised conditions;

---

* Keynes's argument that America really owed Britain the money for defending it against Hitler before Lend-Lease started did not go down well in Washington.

greater equality of conditions became a peacetime goal. Fifth, no one regarded the interwar years as a golden age to which to return as fast as possible. However, what gave wartime experience its enduring resonance was the continuation of full employment. This was the biggest difference between the two post-conflict situations.

The 1944 Employment White Paper committed governments to 'maintain a high and stable level of employment'. The 1944 pledge soon evolved into a target rate of unemployment of between 2 and 3 per cent, and this rate was, in fact, achieved, even overachieved, for almost thirty years, abolishing the dreaded business cycle. Keynesian demand management removed the need to plan supply, as was intended. Physical controls were gradually replaced by financial controls through variations in tax and interest rates. But the main engine of high demand was the continuation of almost wartime levels of public spending. Spending and taxes fell much more slowly than in 1918, and from a higher base.

Full employment introduced a new problem: inflationary pressure. The Employment White Paper of 1944 urged the need for 'pay restraint' in return for full employment. However, this restraint tended to break down as conditions of peace returned. There was then a need to repress excessive wage growth by 'pay policy'. In 1948, the Chancellor of the Exchequer, Sir Stafford Cripps, got the union leadership of Arthur Deakin, Tom Williamson and Will Lawther to agree to a 'wage freeze', in return for a capital levy and dividend restraint, which lasted for three years. This was a forecast of future state–union relations: the state would offer incentives to the unions to deliver pay restraint. The inflation rate was kept down to 5 per cent a year over Labour's six years. But no permanent solution was found to the inflationary problem produced by union power to push up wages ahead of productivity at full employment. Industrial relations remained a no-go area. In the post-war settlement years, inflation took the place of unemployment as the basis of the British consensus, with unions bidding up wages, and employers bidding up prices to keep up profit margins, and governments accommodating both by printing money.

The welfare state was built on the foundations of full employment. Its intellectual basis was laid in the Beveridge Report of 1942. William Beveridge is the supreme example of the intellectual entrepreneur who shaped the contours of the New Jerusalem: the archetype of the Superior Person, bringing the traditions of the Indian Civil Service to British administration. His famous report came about by the accident that no one in government could stand him. The minister of labour, Ernest Bevin, therefore shunted him aside to a project where it was thought that he could do no harm. He was told to produce a plan for rationalising the social-security system. Beveridge accepted his appointment, and departure from Bevin's ministry, with tears in his eyes. However, he soon decided to interpret his social-security brief far more ambitiously than Bevin had intended – indeed to lay down a new direction for social policy, with himself as the 'prophet pointing the way to the Promised Land'.[7]

Accepted by the coalition government, the Beveridge Report proposed a comprehensive scheme of universal compulsory National Insurance to cover the main contingencies of industrial life – unemployment, disability and retirement. This would replace the patchwork quilt of voluntary and compulsory insurance and charity which, badly sewn and full of holes, made up Britain's existing social-security arrangements. Beveridge assumed not just full employment, but a tax-financed National Health Service and family allowance system to balance his insurance fund financially. All this was legislated by the new government: the National Insurance Act of 1946 and the National Assistance Act of 1948 implemented the main Beveridge proposals, and the National Health Service Act of 1948 introduced universal health care free on demand. The historian Peter Hennessy regards the NHS as 'one of the finest institutions ever built by anyone anywhere'.[8] By 1950, 46 per cent of government spending was devoted to the social budget.

Less popular, and less durable, was the nationalisation programme, though this was closest to the socialist heart. The nationalisation of the Bank of England was symbolic. But between 1945 and 1951, Attlee's government took into public ownership the coal, railway, road haulage, iron and steel

11. The New Jerusalem: demonstration of what a subject could get under Britain's original National Health Service programme, 1 April 1951.

industries, responsible for producing about 10 per cent of GDP, and which would receive 20 per cent of total investment. (It also centralised ownership of municipally owned private utilities: gas, water, electricity.) This was the core socialist programme of seizing the 'commanding heights' of the British economy. Most of this was old Labour thinking: coal and railway nationalisation had been on the agenda since the 1920s, since they had chronically bad labour relations, and their private employers found it impossible to run them for a profit. The dispossessed owners received generous compensation.

Nationalisation took the form invented by Herbert Morrison, when he created the London Passenger Authority in 1931, of setting up quasi-autonomous 'public corporations' which were supposed to be run by the old managers on business principles, but with social objectives: a contradiction which was never resolved in principle, and only resolved in practice by subsidy. Labour ministers held the naive belief that nationalisation would cause workers to work more enthusiastically and for less pay. The disappointments attendant on these hopes led to downgrading of public ownership in the socialist agenda of the 1950s.

In all this reformist flurry, there was no demand for institutional renovation. Wartime victory had vindicated British democracy. The successful state was there to be used, not to be reconstructed. The social revolution for which Labour stood was to be top-down. In his book *The Socialist Case*, the Labour intellectual Douglas Jay was voicing a common satisfaction with state capacity when he remarked 'the gentleman in Whitehall really does know better what is good for the people than the people know themselves'.

War success misled in two ways. The Labour government had no incentive to tackle the underlying problem of low productivity, so crucial for success in a post-war world. Extensive wartime destruction on the Continent made re-equipment of industry with modern technology a top priority. There were no equivalent pressures in Britain. Competitive pressures were weak. With most European industries knocked out, and imperial markets still captive, British exporters at first had an easy time. There was little competition in the domestic market, where collusive agreements covered 60 per cent of manufacturing output, and there was very little import penetration in manufactures. Britain's growth rate of 4 per cent a year between 1946 and 1950, equalling the fastest (between 1932 and 1937) it achieved in the twentieth century, masked the fact that British industry, with a few exceptions, had become technologically backward.

War experience misled in another sense. The egalitarian system of incentives which united the nation for war proved unsuitable for a successful peacetime private-enterprise economy. This was especially true of the tax system. The standard rate of income tax was 45p in the pound in 1949; the top marginal tax rate was 97.5p. (This compared with rates of 25p and 62.5p in 1938.) The Beveridge universalist approach was also very expensive, since a high proportion of benefits went to the non-poor. Had flows to the middle class been eliminated, direct taxes could have remained at the 1938 level without unbalancing the budget. However, the taboo against means-testing was then absolute. The other reason for the high progressivity of the tax system was that it was, together with rationing, considered a 'fair' way of restraining private consumption and creating room for exports. Helped by a continuation of food subsidies, working-class consumption in 1949 was estimated to be 22 per cent higher than in 1938, while the consumption of the middle and wealthy classes was 18 per cent and 42 per cent lower respectively. The combination of full employment and reduced post-tax incomes brought about the demise of that fixture of middle-class life, domestic service.

Most of the later criticisms of the post-war settlement emerged during the war, when it was being forged. Within the Treasury it was argued that a commitment to full employment would lead to rising inflation and a collapsing exchange rate unless it were coupled with an attack on restrictive practices, and measures to increase labour mobility. Popular though it was, the Beveridge approach did not go unchallenged. Both Keynes and Henderson questioned the cost of 'universal' as opposed to 'targeted' or 'means-tested' benefits. A more fundamental attack came from the actuary Oswald Falk, who wrote in *The Times* of 3 December 1942 that shielding people from life's contingencies was 'the road to the moral ruin of the Nation . . . not a symptom of the vitality of our civilisation but of its approaching end'. The ideas underlying these critiques – that the full-employment commitment ignored the existence of a 'natural rate of unemployment' and that universal benefits were bound to lead to a 'dependency culture' – were submerged in the euphoria of New Jerusalem construction. Resurfacing in the 1970s, they provided much of the intellectual stuffing of the Thatcher counter-revolution.

The main later critic of the Labour government's record is the historian Correlli Barnett. British industry had emerged from the war badly led, badly equipped, and with a badly trained labour force wedded to restrictive practices. It was in a poor position to compete with Germany, Japan or the United States. All the best brains of the country and available resources should have been directed to remedying this state of affairs as quickly as possible. Instead energies and resources were poured into New Jerusalem projects: establishing the welfare state, rehousing the working class, and bringing new industries to decaying areas for social reasons. Barnett is particularly scathing about the low priority given to technical training. Labour inherited Rab Butler's 1944 Education Act which abolished fee-paying in the grammar schools and, notionally, set up a tripartite system of grammar, technical and secondary modern schools, catering for 'three types of mind' which, unsurprisingly, reflected the three social classes. Few technical schools emerged. Barnett argues that this was because the churches, not the industrialists, took control of educational reform. This is at best a minor cause. The two main reasons for lack of provision for the second 'type of mind' was that technical schools were too expensive for a cash-strapped government and trade unions used traditional apprenticeships and on-the-job training as a method of restricting entry to skilled occupations. 'Intervention to reform training would have involved a serious breach of the sacred principle of voluntarism in industrial relations.'[9]

In summary: the nature of the wartime social contract, continued and extended by Labour, precluded reforms of industrial relations, anti-monopoly legislation, and the introduction of mass technical education, while locking the economy into high levels of direct taxation and public ownership.

Labour's attitude to the issue of Britain's 'greatness' was more complex than is usually presented. Labour had inherited from the liberal intelligentsia a strong streak of pacifism and anti-imperialism. However, its joint responsibility in war had brought a new perspective. Though Britain was exhausted, Labour leaders were just as determined as their Conservative predecessors to maintain the world position won by British arms. As Lord Franks put it, world leadership 'is part of the habit and furniture of our minds'. After the war, Churchill had insisted, in his famous metaphor of the 'three circles', that Britain would remain the head of the Commonwealth, the closest ally of the United States, and the leading power in non-Communist Europe, the three tripods supporting each other. This remained the charter myth of British foreign policy till the 1970s, and even then it did not entirely vanish.

When the war ended, Britain had millions of men under arms, controlling large parts of Europe, the Middle East, the Mediterranean and most of South East Asia. But it was world power on American credit. In 1945 Keynes told the Labour government that the alternative to the American loan was 'to retire for the time being as a Great Power'. Despite the loan, retirement proved permanent. Over the years Britain's power ebbed away, victim of a succession of economy cuts. As Paul Kennedy tells it, the British Empire 'receded spasmodically from one defensive line to another' until it finally disappeared.[10]

The proximate cause of most retreats was a sterling crisis, but such crises were symptoms of the structural weakness of the British economy. The first came in 1947. In fulfilment of the terms of the American loan, sterling became convertible into dollars on current account in July 1947, but convertibility had to be suspended a month later, as holders of sterling rushed to convert their pounds into dollars; $4 billion of reserves, or more than the amount of the loan, were lost in 1947. Convertibility was suspended, but sterling remained sickly. Finally, with the help of a 30 per cent devaluation of the pound against the dollar in September 1949 (from $4.03 to $2.80), Britain's current account was turned round. But balance of payments crises continued to plague Britain till the 1970s.

At first Attlee had wanted to leave India in June 1948, but financial overstretch brought forward the withdrawal date to 15 August 1947, a decision that cost millions of lives as Hindus and Muslims started massacring each other. India and Pakistan became self-governing Dominions within the British Empire. The first member of the royal family to be viceroy, Lord Mountbatten, was the last to hold that post. In 1949, India chose to become a republic. By allowing republican India to stay in the Commonwealth – acknowledging only the British monarch as its head – the Attlee government took the decision to turn a club of whites into a creaking bridge between the white and non-white parts of the world. A year later Britain was gone from Burma and Ceylon.

The loss of India made the strategic aim of 'protecting the routes to India' redundant. However, a new mission was discovered. In the nineteenth century Germany had replaced Russia as Britain's main rival. With Germany out of the way, the Foreign Office and military chiefs reinvented, as if by reflex, the great nineteenth-century game of checking Russian expansion, now in the guise of Soviet imperialism. The Foreign Secretary Ernest Bevin, who had spent his life fighting home-grown Communists in the Transport and General Workers Union, was an enthusiastic convert. 'Give me a million tons of coal', he told a meeting of miners, 'and I will give you a foreign policy.' In 1947, without discussing it in full Cabinet, a small sub-committee of six ministers made the decision to build a British atomic bomb; peacetime conscription was introduced, for the first time. Bevin played a leading role setting up the North Atlantic Treaty Organisation (NATO) in 1949, which committed Britain to a permanent garrison in central Europe. Britain's military expenditure ranged from 5 per cent to 12 per cent of GDP for most of the

Cold War years, much higher than that of the European members of NATO.

However, economic weakness made British resistance to Soviet encroachments a pale shadow of the great game of the past. After the sterling crisis of 1947, Britain left America to complete the task of putting down a Communist uprising in Greece. Unable to reconcile Jews and Arabs, Britain gave up its Palestine mandate to the UN in June 1948, against Bevin's objections. For the time being it retained a large garrison at Suez, and took pride in the fact that the Jordanian Army, known as the Arab Legion, was run by a British general, John Glubb (Glubb Pasha). When in May 1951 Iran's nationalist prime minister, Mossadeq, nationalised the Anglo-Iranian Oil Company (later British Petroleum), took over its refineries at Abadan, and expelled the pro-western Shah, Labour's Foreign Secretary, Herbert Morrison, demanded a military riposte, in the old gunboat tradition. Instead it was the United States's CIA which arranged for the overthrow of Mossadeq and the return of the Shah in 1953. In Malaya, the British hung on till 1957, fighting off a Chinese Communist 'insurgency' (really a civil war between the majority Malays and minority Chinese), before giving 'Malaysia' its independence.

The loss of Britain's East Asian empire prompted Whitehall, for the first time, to take an interest in Africa. It encouraged post-war emigration, the white population of southern Rhodesia increasing from 80,000 in 1945 to over 200,000 a decade later. But emigration was never on a scale that could have sustained colonial rule for long. In fact the net movement was the other way. From the late 1940s, a reverse colonisation started when a mass – and at first unchecked – influx of immigrants from the West Indies, India and Pakistan started settling in Britain, their right to do so guaranteed by the Nationality Act of 1948. (Europeans were debarred from entry.) Unlike in Boer-dominated South Africa, Britain never had an official doctrine of racialism, in terms of which permanent white supremacy in Africa might have been defended.

In these circumstances, reasons for staying in Africa could only be prudential and pragmatic. The African colonies had a right to good government, not self-government. Giving them premature independence, said Herbert Morrison, would be 'like giving a child of ten a latchkey, a bank account and a shotgun'.[11] Until they grew up, they might help strengthen Britain's balance of payments. At the Colonial Office from 1945 to 1950 the Fabian Arthur Creech Jones took up Joseph Chamberlain's idea of 'colonial development'. A conscious attempt was made to develop the African colonies as a source of foodstuffs and raw materials and export outlets for British industry. Labour set up a Colonial Development Corporation to channel money to the African colonies. One of its famously disastrous efforts was the groundnuts scheme in Tanganyika, which was expected to provide margarine for the British consumer. It cost £36 million without producing a single commercial nut. The empire marketing boards were used to purchase sugar from the West Indies on long-term contracts at below world-market prices. Colonial development included training Africans for 'self-government'. Nigeria and the Gold Coast (later Ghana) received constitutions in 1946 which set up legislatures with limited African participation and less power. This model was followed throughout Britain's African colonies. By 1951, Kwame Nkrumah, head of the largest political party in the Gold Coast, had become unofficial 'prime minister', though power over finance, law and order, and the Civil Service remained with the British governor. 'Africanisation' of the administration started at a snail's pace.

The political disintegration of the empire did not at first end the imperial economic system. The economist Hubert Henderson persuaded Whitehall that planned trade was the way of the future. As it had in the war, imperial economics seemed to offer a relief from too great a dependence on America. So the imperial pattern of Britain's foreign trade and investment persisted after the war, though the preferences were scaled down to honour the commitment to the United States.

The Bank of England continued to promote the role of sterling as a reserve currency. This maintained the City's banking business; and it suited countries for whom Britain was their main market as well as supplier of capital. It was also a way of dealing with the problem of the wartime sterling balances. The obligation to pay out holders of these balances on demand could be met only by steady surpluses on the British balance of payments or by finding new holders. Since the first failed to materialise, reliance had to be placed on the second. At first, the new inflows came mainly from Nigeria, the Gold Coast and Malaya, benefiting from the boom in primary commodities: Malayan tin and rubber earned more US dollars in 1948 than Britain's total exports. Thereafter, new balances were built up by the Middle East oil states, chiefly Kuwait, the Gulf kingdoms and Libya, the first two still under British control. But this delicate balancing act rested on the assurance that sterling would not be devalued. British economic policy after 1949 came to centre on maintaining confidence in sterling.

Efforts to maintain an imperial economic system gradually disintegrated as Britain's own economy shrank in relative terms, and they probably contributed to its shrinking. Britain's share of world trade fell from 21.5 per cent in the early 1950s to 14.2 per cent in 1964. The proportion of its trade with the empire steadily fell as Europe recovered and entered a dynamic phase of growth in the 1950s. In the 1940s, 50 per cent of Britain's foreign trade was with the empire and sterling area, and one quarter with western Europe. By the 1960s it was the other way round.

The strain of running a dual policy of social reform at home and world power abroad took its toll on the Labour government. Welfare spending doubled as a result of Beveridge, while defence spending came come down from 17 per cent to 7 per cent of GDP by 1950. This rebalancing act was sabotaged by the outbreak of the Korean War in that year. Britain immediately committed itself to give the United States military support in resisting Communist North Korea's invasion of South Korea. Defence spending shot up again to nearly 11 per cent.

This caused a terminal crisis for the Labour government, which had been narrowly re-elected in February 1950.[*] The historian John Campbell thinks Aneurin Bevan was 'the most talented and charismatic working-class intellectual the Labour movement has ever produced'.[12] Put into the Cabinet as a sop to the left after five years spent sniping at Churchill in the war, Bevan showed that he was no empty phrase-maker, but an outstanding man of government. As minister of health he had outmanoeuvred the British Medical Association to get his National Health Service, and Bevan's council houses, while fewer, were bigger and better than Macmillan's were to be – 116,000 a year in 1946 to 200,000 in 1949. However, in

---

[*] Labour: 393 seats, 11,95,152 votes or 47.8 per cent of total vote. Conservatives 213 seats, 9,988,306 votes or 39.7 per cent. Liberals twelve seats, 2,248,226 or 9 per cent. A couple of Communist MPs got elected for the first and last time. In the twentieth century only the Conservatives managed to get above the magic 50 per cent of votes: in 1900, 1931 and 1935.

1951 Bevan resigned from the government in protest against the decision of Wykehamist Hugh Gaitskell, Chancellor of the Exchequer, to impose £13 million of charges on dentures and spectacles to help pay for rearmament, mainly out of pique at Attlee promoting Winchester over Tredegar. When Harold Wilson and John Freeman met with Bevan to discuss collective resignation, Wilson said, 'We have to broaden the issue. We can't just resign on specs and false teeth.' A Bevanite parliamentary group was set up in January 1952 following Labour's defeat in October 1951 to promote socialism. But Bevan's manifesto, *In Place of Fear*, was, in the words of one of his biographers, 'the wordy last gasp of a dying political tradition, not the herald of its rebirth'.[13]

Labour's experience in power raises a question mark. Why was its attempt to build a New Jerusalem followed by thirteen years of Conservative government? Usual explanations centre on exhaustion, splits, deaths, crises, bad luck. And there is a great deal in them. But the suspicion remains that what Labour was trying to achieve – the goals of the gentlemen in Whitehall who 'knew best' – was not exactly what the British people wanted. They wanted full employment and the welfare state, but they also wanted to relax after twelve extremely unrelaxing years saving the world from Hitler and building socialism. Churchill made 'easement' at home and abroad the main goal of his new administration. He aimed to give the working man what he had never had before, leisure: 'a four-day week and then three days of fun'.

Chapter 9

Political Equipoise, Cultural Upheaval 1951–1970

Ken: Time was, whatever you bought in this country, you looked for just one word. Birmingham. And you bought it, no questions.

Alan Ayckbourn, *A Small Family Business* (1987)

Everything about the British class system begins to look foolish and tacky when related to a second-class power in decline.

Peregrine Worsthorne, 1959

In political terms, the middle years of the last century can reasonably be described as an age of equipoise. Insular socialism had reached its limits with the Attlee reforms. The political debate centred on how to make the new managerial-welfare capitalism work best, with 'growthmanship' added to the mix in the 1960s. Culturally, though, it was an age of upheaval, as a new generation of hedonists, satirists and protesters mocked the Establishment, and embraced ideas and lifestyles radically different from those of their parents. The radicals believed that revolution in lifestyles would lead to political revolution. This was an illusion. When the dust settled down, it was found that the British people had changed somewhat, but not their political system.

Butskellism

The phrase 'Butskellism' came into vogue in the early 1950s to describe the joint acceptance of full-employment policy by Labour's last Chancellor of the Exchequer, Hugh Gaitskell, and the first Conservative Chancellor, Rab Butler. In political terms, the 1950s and 60s were a rerun of Baldwin–MacDonald in the interwar years, in that the two main parties kept up their distinctive rhetoric, but tried to govern from a central position.

The Attlee government was the furthest socialism was to reach in British life. This was not apparent at the time. Many, perhaps most, of the intellectuals and policy wonks of the day projected an austere, somewhat puritanical, Utopia. Britain was still a two-class nation, and the working class was by far the larger. The electoral struggle in the 1950s was very close.* Labour won more votes than the Conservatives in 1951, and might have done better still had the party not torn itself to pieces over defence and foreign policy. The Conservatives only half-believed that the future lay with them. So they were in an accommodating mood.

The practical aim of Conservative policy was to remove

---

* Election results 23 February 1950: Conservative 12,502,567 votes, 43.5 per cent, 298 MPs. Labour 13,266,592 votes, 46.1 per cent, 315 MPs. Liberal 2,621,548 votes, 9.1 per cent, nine MPs.

Election results 25 October 1951: Conservative 13,717,538 votes, 48 per cent, 321 MPs. Labour 13,948,605 votes, 48.8 per cent, 295 MPs. Liberal 730,556 votes, 2.5 per cent, six MPs.

Election results 26 May 1955: Conservative 13,286,569 votes, 49.7 per cent, 344 MPs. Labour 12,404,970 votes, 46.4 per cent, 277 MPs. Liberal 722,405 votes, 2.7 per cent, six MPs. The two main parties got almost 100 per cent of the votes cast, evenly divided. A couple of Communist MPs got elected for the first and last time. In the twentieth century, only the Conservatives managed to get above the magic 50 per cent of votes: in 1900, 1931 and 1935. The political division of the nation by class could not have been clearer.

the taint of the 1930s. The Conservative governments of 1951–64 accepted full employment and the welfare state. There was no denationalisation except for the iron and steel industry, the last and most controversial of Labour's nationalisation measures. In these crucial respects, the post-war settlement was maintained. However, Conservative policy was not a mere replica of Labour's. Public spending was restrained to make possible tax cuts. There was modest deregulation – notably of the housing rental and retail markets. There was a switch in emphasis from public to private housing. The positive Tory social vision was summed up in the phrase 'a property-owning democracy', and, as health minister, Macmillan took pride in building 300,000 houses a year as against only 200,000 by his predecessor, Bevan.

The Two Harolds
12. Harold Macmillan (l); 13. Harold Wilson (r)

By contrast, Labour's defeat in 1951 was sufficiently narrow to rob them of any great incentive to reinvent themselves. Attlee hung on as party leader till 1955, waiting to return to power. The Labour government was widely regarded by its supporters as a success, and more importantly, by its intellectuals as a stage in the inevitable coming of socialism. In Labour eyes, the Conservative victory of 1951 was a temporary interruption in the established political narrative of the rise of the people. Most on the left believed that Tory rule would mean a return to mass unemployment. They therefore had only to sit tight and wait for the next instalment of their inheritance. Not till the publication in 1956 of Anthony Crosland's revisionist text, *The Future of Socialism*, did socialists start to wonder whether the future pointed as leftwards as they had supposed.

In the late 1950s, the dynamics of party rivalry shifted as full employment became an established fact. The debate came to centre on the causes of Britain's relative economic decline. Labour were now able to offer themselves not as the party of socialism, but of economic and social renewal. This appeal was enough to win them a narrow majority in 1964 and a bigger one in 1966. But these were not decisive victories, and they were forced to accept the 'affluent society' created by the Tories as setting the parameters of their own policies. However, Labour's own 'planning for growth' failed to solve the problem of slow growth bequeathed by its predecessors, and its top-down approach lost touch with the hedonism and social-protest movements which affluence had brought about. The equipoise was never as stable as it seemed, and by the 1970s it had collapsed.

Labour was to claim that the thirteen years of Conservative rule from 1951 to 1964 postponed the 'modernisation' of

Britain. In fact, what Conservative rule did, which was far more important, was to rehabilitate capitalism, by showing that it could combine prosperity with full employment.

The years of Conservative government fall into three periods. The first four years under the aged Churchill's premiership seemed to show that Tory freedom worked. The second from 1956 to 1961 saw mounting economic problems and a profound rethink of foreign policy. The third saw a move towards planning for growth.

In the first phase, the Tories took advantage of the fall in world commodity prices from 1952 onwards, which added £800 million a year to the national income. Taxes came down (notably in Butler's 'giveaway' budget of 1955); the end of food rationing and licensing of materials, together with the reappearance of slot machines, selling chocolates and cigarettes, indicated that austerity was over. The consumer boom started.

The centrepiece of Tory social policy was housing. The social purpose of the housing drive was clear in the switch to building for private ownership, backed by tax relief on mortgage interest introduced in 1956. In 1951 the proportion of houses built by the private sector was 12 per cent, in 1954, 26 per cent, in 1959, 56 per cent. The proportion of owner-occupied dwellings rose from 31 per cent in 1951 to 55 per cent in 1971. Tory housing policy benefited the middle classes and skilled workers, and, as in the 1980s, was a pillar of their electoral success.

Churchill retired in 1955, and was succeeded by his long-term heir apparent, Anthony Eden, sick and highly strung, who won the 1955 election with an increased majority. But then came Suez, and the rude post-imperial awakening.

The empire's last stand

Suez bifurcates the Conservative years. After 1956 it was never glad, confident morn again, though Macmillan retrieved a first-class political disaster with astonishing skill. But Suez is important for another reason. It stands out in the history of imperial retreat as the only effort by the two leading colonial powers to defend their positions by pooling their policy and resources. Britain, in effect, agreed to underwrite French rule in Algeria, and France to underwrite the British client system in the Middle East. It offers a tantalising glimpse of that alternative European future foreclosed by the Second World War. But it came too late in the day; and its defeat turned retreat into rout.

In Opposition, Churchill had attacked Labour's 'scuttle' from empire. Back in office he continued it. With the overthrow of the royal dynasty in 1952, Egypt had been converted from a restive British client into a spearhead of Arab nationalism under its charismatic leader Abdul Nasser. In 1954, with British resources overstretched by the conflicting demands of rearmament (originally to fight the Korean War) and a domestic house-building programme, Britain decided to abandon its almost besieged military base at the Suez Canal, transferring its 60,000-strong garrison to Cyprus, which it still ruled. As a partial replacement, it constructed an anti-Soviet Baghdad Pact with four Muslim powers (Turkey, Iraq, Iran, Pakistan).

On 26 July 1956, as soon as the last British soldiers left their canal base, Nasser nationalised the Suez Canal Company, a joint Anglo-French consortium, charged by an international treaty dating from 1881 with maintaining free navigation through the canal. He did so partly to secure revenue to pay for his pet project the Aswan Dam, from which America had abruptly withdrawn funding. Claiming that free passage was endangered, France and Britain agreed to reverse the act of nationalisation, by force if necessary. There was also, for the British, the matter of character. Nasser reminded Eden of Hitler. He was a dictator, and you cannot have a man like that, Eden said, 'with his finger on our windpipe'. Both nations were prepared to act 'unilaterally' – in defiance of the United Nations. In preparing for a military riposte, Eden thought he could count on at least the benevolent neutrality of the United States. As in 1940–1, the British hugely overestimated the commitment of the United States to preserve Britain as a great power. The Americans were far more worried that European colonialism would turn nationalist movements towards the Soviets.

The Opposition Labour Party, while by no means enamoured of Nasser's action, took its stand on the UN Charter, which forbade the use of military force except in self-defence, unless sanctioned by the Security Council. An expeditionary force of Second World War dimensions – Britain and France still had conscription – was built up in Malta, while the two powers went through the motions of seeking Security Council approval for restoring the canal to international control. In a consummate piece of realpolitik, they concocted a plot with Israel, whereby Israel would attack Egypt, and the two powers would issue an ultimatum to both sides to withdraw to either side of the canal. If, as expected, the Egyptians refused, they would then occupy the canal to 'separate the combatants'. Israel duly attacked across the Sinai Desert on 30 October; on 5 November British and French troops landed at Port Said and advanced down the canal, meeting with little resistance. A day later, Harold Macmillan, the Chancellor of the Exchequer, who had been the most hawkish for military intervention, informed a sick prime minister and an astounded Cabinet that the United States would 'pull the plug on sterling' unless the British agreed an immediate ceasefire. Empire was sacrificed to the City of London. The British bullied the French into agreeing to stop the operation. The whole problem was then transferred to the United Nations, which set up a UN Police Force to take over the canal temporarily (its real object was to save the faces of Britain and France). The last British troops left on 22 December. British property was expropriated, British subjects deported from Egypt, and with the Soviets agreeing to finance his dam, Nasser became, temporarily, a client of the Soviet Union.

The majority of the public supported Suez; the big disappointment was its failure. A young miner summed up a popular reaction: 'We should have gone right in there, but we can't do it any more. Not even against the bloody wogs.' Churchill is reported to have said: 'I would never have dared without squaring the Americans, and if I had dared, I would never have dared to stop.'* John Foster Dulles, the American Secretary of State, remarked to the British representative at the United Nations: 'Why on earth didn't you go through with it?' Hugh Thomas has summed up: 'Probably there would have been neither world war nor devaluation if we had continued for [twenty-four hours more], and having got so far, the morale of the Army and the Entente Cordiale, that incomparable friendship, would have been better served.'[1]

The Suez debacle showed that Britain's rulers had lost both the competence and courage needed for imperial adventures. Although Britain had exchange controls on current transactions, and restrictions on capital export by residents, it could

---

* Churchill's doctor Moran reports him saying 'To go so far and not go on was madness.'

not stop capital flight from non-resident holders of sterling which included not just the Americans, but Commonwealth owners of sterling balances. In failing to make preparations for this eventuality, Macmillan seems to have been gambling on benevolent American neutrality in any military operation. But never by a wink had the USA given the go-ahead for Suez. Even so, it showed a lamentable failure of nerve to stop half-way down the Canal. On the other hand, the British and French had no credible war aims. What did they expect to do having taken possession of the canal? To rule Egypt jointly? To set up a client state? The guts had already been torn from the imperial mission.

Suez destroyed the last pretension of Britain and France to be great powers, even jointly. Power was in the hands of men no longer willing to take the risks associated with its use. For Britain, its failure led directly to the collapse of its position in the Middle East, and indirectly to the dismantling of its African empire and its application to join the European Economic Community. In domestic affairs, the 'end of empire' brought about a cultural and social upheaval. Suez destroyed the prestige of the old governing class, especially with the middle-class young.

Supermac

Macmillan's reward for being 'first in, first out' was to replace the ailing Eden as prime minister on 10 January 1957. With his faux-Edwardian style, he was the great conjurer of twentieth-century British politics, masterly in restoring the illusion of greatness while completing the scuttle from empire. Unflappability defined his performance, best displayed in a famous put-down of Nikita Khrushchev in 1960: 'Perhaps we could have a translation', he disdainfully remarked as the Soviet leader banged his shoe on the table while Macmillan was addressing the General Assembly of the United Nations. His approval rating shot up to 70 per cent.

Macmillan's immediate priority was to restore damaged relations with the United States. To this aim he brought one of his sweeping historical analogies: Britain would play Greece to America's Rome.* In this he succeeded. Once Britain's pretensions to independence were squashed, the United States was happy to accept it as a junior partner in the war against Communism. In July 1958 British troops were back in Jordan to protect King Hussein, following the coup in Iraq in which the pro-British king, Faisal, and his prime minister Nuri-es-Said, were murdered. This time they went with American support – the start of a vicarious imperialism revived by Tony Blair. Peacekeeping operations in East Africa, Aden, Kuwait and Borneo justified the retention of military bases, now encouraged by the Americans who wanted stability in the Indian Ocean. America provided Britain with other symbols of greatness: a Polaris delivery system for its new hydrogen bomb, daily telephone messages from President Kennedy to Macmillan during the Cuban missile crisis of 1962, a leading role for Britain in negotiating the Test Ban Treaty which followed it. Macmillan's conjuring act was brilliantly successful. By 1958 the economy had recovered from its mid-decade stop, and with the help of a giveaway budget, he led the Conservatives to their third successive electoral

---

* The idea had first struck him in 1943 when he was Britain's Minister Resident in Algiers: 'We must run Allied Forces Headquarters as the Greek slaves ran the operations of the Emperor Claudius.'

victory in 1959, with an increased majority.* The British people, he claimed, had 'never had it so good'.

Tory hegemony was confirmed, and Britain's pride restored, but Macmillan realised that all was not well. Britain's undynamic economy was not sharing in Europe's economic miracle, and its relative decline would damage its influence with Washington. The question was starting to be asked: why was Britain growing slower than continental countries like Germany and France? Following his election victory in 1959, Macmillan decided on a major change of course: withdrawal from empire, joining the European Economic Community, and 'planning for growth'. These formed the core of his strategy for restoring Britain as a great, though no longer imperial, power.

In a famous speech to the South African Parliament in Cape Town in January 1960 Macmillan signalled the end of British rule in Africa by referring to the 'winds of change' blowing through that continent. In the early 1950s, many of the African colonies were still considered too small for independence. Oliver Lyttleton, a big businessman and Colonial Secretary from 1951 to 1954, wanted to merge them into new imperial conglomerates. He set up a Central African Federation in 1953, consisting of Northern and Southern Rhodesia, and Nyasaland (now Zambia, Zimbabwe and Malawi). Designed to be a self-governing partnership of whites and Africans with quasi-Dominion status, it was, in practice, controlled by the white settlers of Southern Rhodesia. By the end of the 1950s, the life had gone out of these

---

* Election results 8 October 1959: Conservative 13,750,875 votes, 49.4 per cent, 365 MPs. Labour 12,216,172 votes, 43.8 per cent, 258 MPs. Liberal 1,650,760 votes, 5.9 per cent, six MPs.

ambitious plans. Like France under de Gaulle, Britain had decided that it was not worth trying to hold on to its African colonies by force. Having abandoned conscription in 1958, it in any case no longer had the manpower to do so in face of increasing nationalist unrest, notably by the Mau Mau in Kenya. 'Bobbety' Salisbury, the standard-bearer for late imperialism, called Ian Macleod, Macmillan's bridge-playing Colonial Secretary, and agent of scuttle, 'too clever by half'.

Britain was not chased out of Africa: there was no longer any pressing reason for it to stay, and better opportunities for earning money and projecting power were opening up in Europe. In a crash programme, the African colonies were 'prepared' for independence. By 1968 – tiny Swaziland being the last – all seventeen had gone. The process of withdrawal took the form of suppressing 'violent' nationalist agitation, but conceding to the substance of nationalist demands. Thus imprisoned or exiled leaders were, after a short interval, placed at the head of their newly independent countries. Brief incarceration by the British became the main qualification for post-colonial leadership. Nearly all the ex-African colonies changed their name; most became one-party dictatorships under their first leaders: Kwame Nkrumah in Ghana, Jomo Kenyatta in Kenya, Julius Nyerere in Tanzania, Kenneth Kaunda in Zambia, Hastings Banda in Malawi. Most joined the Commonwealth, adding black presences to the queen's dinner table.

Scuttle was the order of the day elsewhere. Cyprus became an independent republic in 1960, Malta in 1954. In the West Indies, most of the island colonies became independent micro-states in the 1970s and 1980s. British Guyana, whose constitution Britain had suspended in 1953, became independent in 1966. In 1967, following yet another sterling crisis, Britain announced that it would withdraw all its military forces from 'east of Suez' by 1970, except for a small garrison in Hong Kong. Hong Kong was handed back to China in 1997. So the empire of conquest passed into history. Today, it survives only in the honours list: the dames, knights, and companions, annually created, of an empire which no longer exists.

One element only of the Macmillan wind-up programme failed to go according to plan. When the Central African Federation broke up in 1964, Northern Rhodesia and Nyasaland became independent as Zambia and Malawi. Britain refused to grant Southern Rhodesia equivalent independence unless it scrapped its settler-dominated constitution. Ian Smith, the leader of the white Rhodesian Front, declared independence unilaterally in November 1965, in defiance of the British Crown, but with some support in Britain itself. The settlers were, after all, a part of Britain; 'Smithy' himself had been a fighter pilot in the Battle of Britain. Their problem was that they were frozen by their situation into a Britain which was ceasing to exist. The incoming Labour government was dissuaded from military intervention for fear, as at Curragh in 1914, that the army would not carry out orders if called on to shoot their 'kith and kin'. Pleading logistical obstacles to using military force, Harold Wilson imposed sanctions, which he promised would 'work in weeks rather than months'. Initially supported by white South Africa, and buttressed by the Portuguese who still ruled Angola and Mozambique, 200,000 British settlers hung on till 1979, in the face of international obloquy and mounting guerrilla activity, an inconvenient reminder of obsolete loyalties. Independence for what was now relabelled Zimbabwe came in 1980 on a 'one man, one vote' basis, which handed power to the black leader Robert Mugabe. Over the next twenty-seven years, Mugabe reduced a once thriving British colony to a state of Africanised destitution, but few in Britain any longer cared.

Loss of empire deprived the British of an important part of their national identity. Empire abroad had reinforced hierarchy at home. Britons could not even retire from the imperial enterprise with the satisfaction of a job well done, since history books soon started filling them with guilt at their shameful exploitation of the colonies. Not only was Britain in rapid descent from the pinnacle of world power, it was slipping down the moral league table as well. Virtually ignored were two of the greatest benefits of imperial rule. First, the imperial connection enabled colonies and quasi-dependencies to obtain development capital more cheaply than would otherwise have been the case. Second, it established peace. This was because the imperial power could hold the balance between different nations, religions, tribes. Once it was withdrawn they resumed fighting each other.* In fact the fighting broke out earlier, as the different groups disputed the succession. Most of the post-colonial states succumbed to endemic violence which still continues.

Britain turned to Europe by a process of elimination. In 1962, Dean Acheson, former US Secretary of State, pointed out inconveniently that 'Britain has lost an empire; she has not yet found a role.' He went on: 'The attempt to play a separate power role . . . based on being the head of a "commonwealth" which has no political structure, or unity, or strength and enjoys a fragile and precarious economic

---

* It is true that the colonial powers divided African tribal boundaries, making peaceful multinational states more difficult or impossible once they left. But warfare was common between the tribes before the colonialists arrived.

relationship by means of the sterling area and preferences in the British market . . . is about to be played out.'

As Acheson discerned, the imperial circle had disintegrated, first in India, then in the Middle East, finally in Africa. The Commonwealth was also disconnected from old and new security concerns. Only Canada of the Commonwealth countries contributed to NATO; even the faithful kith and kin in Australia and New Zealand had to turn to America to defend them.

Britain's hopes of continuing as a 'hard' world power thus came to rest on the 'special relationship' with the United States. But this role, though underpinned by military and intelligence collaboration, was more appealing to the British than to the Americans. President Kennedy's alternative to the 'three circles' was the two pillars: the United States and Europe. Britain might hope to influence the United States as part of the second pillar, not apart from it.

British policy had been not to help build up Europe as a separate pillar, but to be the lynchpin of an Atlantic alliance joining the European continent to the United States. Between 1949 and 1960, it tried to steer the European movement in an intergovernmental direction to thwart any supranational ambitions. It refused to join the European Coal and Steel Community in 1951. It refused to merge its forces into a European army. It sent only a low-ranking observer to the Messina negotiations in 1955 which led to the formation of the EEC, trying to divert the movement for economic integration into a wider European free-trade area for industrial goods only. The Foreign Office had a nightmare of 'an empire on our doorstep'.[2] The failure of this strategy to prevent the signing of the Treaty of Rome and start of the six-member European Economic Community in 1958 led to the British decision to try to sabotage this 'empire' from the inside.

Economics complemented high politics in the decision to apply for membership in 1961. With Britain's alternative of a seventeen-member European Free Trade Area for manufactured goods rejected, it faced the prospect of being shut out from the world's most dynamic market, with whom it did nearly 40 per cent of its trade. Joining the 'common market' would provide exactly that scale of operation and spur of competition needed to revive Britain's sluggish economy.

'Leadership in Europe' thus became the new role canvassed to replace leadership of the Commonwealth. But it turned out that Britain needed Europe more than Europe needed Britain. Macmillan put the Lord Privy Seal, Edward Heath, in charge of negotiating Britain's entry into the EEC. But de Gaulle would not forgive Britain for its 'betrayal' at Suez, and for many previous slights. Claiming that Britain would be an American Trojan Horse inside the community, de Gaulle vetoed the British application for entry. He accused Macmillan of 'selling his birthright for a mess of Polaris'. Macmillan riposted: 'Had Hitler danced in London, we'd have had no trouble with de Gaulle.' With de Gaulle's veto, a central plank of Macmillan's strategy for reviving British power had collapsed. By contrast, the Commonwealth became more attractive to the left when no longer a white man's club. In a great rhetorical display at the Labour Party conference in Brighton in 1962, the leader Hugh Gaitskell aligned his party against Europe, reminding the delegates (inaccurately) that the Commonwealth stood for 1,000 years of history. 'Duty' to the Commonwealth also required enthusiastic welcome for immigrants from the 'new' Commonwealth, an enthusiasm by no means shared by Labour's working-class voters.

There remained 'planning for growth'. There would be

medium-term 'growth targets'. A tripartite National Economic Development Council was set up in 1963, which spawned miniature 'Neddies' for each major industry and region. A National Incomes Commission ('three wise men') was formed to pronounce on wage claims. Macmillan put his Chancellor of the Exchequer, Reginald Maudling – intelligent, indolent and corrupt – behind the 'dash for growth'. Tory 'planning for growth' is more accurately labelled 'spending for growth'. By the 1960s the public sector's share of GDP was on the rise again (from 26 to 28 per cent) to pay for hospitals, roads, universities. Maudling's expansionary budget of 1963–4 produced an inflationary boom which once more threatened sterling with devaluation.

By this time Macmillan was almost through. Not only was he personally damaged by the Profumo sex scandal,* but the whole Tory establishment had come to seem seedy. Sleaze, having been repelled for forty years since Lloyd George, re-entered British public life in the early 1960s, and has remained part of its furniture ever since. Macmillan had to retire sick in 1963, giving way to Sir Alec Douglas-Home, who emerged mysteriously, having given up his earldom, to take a seat in the House of Commons. But Tory prosperity left an electoral legacy. Despite his self-confessed economic illiteracy,

---

* The first of many subsequent sex scandals involving political figures. The scandal originated in a brief affair in 1961 between John Profumo, Secretary of State for War and a nineteen-year-old showgirl, Christine Keeler. Rumours started to circulate that Keeler had not only been sleeping with Profumo but also Yevgeny Ivanov, nominally a naval attache at the Soviet embassy, suggesting a possible breach of security. On 22 March 1963, Profumo made a statement in the House of Commons denying any 'impropriety' with Christine Keeler. When this was revealed to be a lie, he resigned on 5 June 1963. The tabloids had a field day with stories of a sex and spy ring of people in high places, revolving round a fashionable osteopath, Stephen Ward. Ward committed suicide. The Profumo affair, though totally trivial, is often taken to mark the death of aristocratic Toryism and the media's deference to the Establishment.

Douglas-Home only just failed to prevent a narrow Labour victory a year later.* Edward Heath succeeded him as leader of the Conservative Party. Thus the thirteen years of Conservative government ended in a shambles.

Thirteen wasted years?

This was Labour's election slogan in 1964. In fact, the Tories delivered thirteen years of uninterrupted full employment. In 1964 GDP was 40 per cent higher than in 1951, the average standard of living had gone up by 30 per cent, and the Tories were well on the way to fulfilling Butler's promise to double living standards in a generation. British society in the early 1950s looked like it had in the 1930s and 40s, down to fashions in clothes, models of cars, household furniture, architecture. Diet was healthier, but restaurant food remained mostly disgusting. After the mid-1950s this started to change as affluence reshaped society. The post-war attempt to get women back from wartime factories to the home foundered in the face of the new availability of labour-saving household appliances, and peacetime pressure of labour demand, which also started to draw in boatloads of immigrants from Jamaica. Clothes and popular music were transformed: the teenager arrived on the scene from America, and with him teenage taste and youth 'problems'.

There was a big increase in home ownership. The number of teachers increased from 215,000 to 287,000 in the Tory years. The numbers of pupils staying on at school after fifteen

---

* 1964 general election: Conservative 12,001,396 (304 seats, 43.4 per cent of the total vote). Labour 12,205,814 (317 seats, 44.1 per cent). This election showed the first sign of a Liberal revival. They got only nine seats, but 3,092,878 votes or 11.2 per cent of the total. This largely accounts for the reduction in the Labour and Conservative percentages.

went up from 22 per cent to 38 per cent. There was a huge growth in the number of private cars, television sets and other consumer durables. The rise in household debt started with hire purchase and, in 1966, the introduction of the first credit card, Barclaycard. In 1964 the five-day week, plus two weeks' paid holiday, had become standard: 7 million went to Blackpool, 5 million went abroad, for holidays. By 1965, Andrew Shonfield could talk about birth of a 'new economic order . . . that converted capitalism from cataclysmic failure into the great engine of prosperity'.[3]

Following Labour's third electoral defeat in a row in 1959, Labour's Barbara Castle had had to concede that 'our ethical reach was beyond the mental grasp of the average person'. The election of Hugh Gaitskell as leader in 1955 started Labour's own rethink. This was led by its right-wing 'revisionists', notably Tony Crosland. They rejected the goal of a fully collectivised economy. Capitalism had been transformed by Keynesian demand management and the managerial revolution. Public ownership, Crosland wrote in *The Future of Socialism*, was only a means, and not the most important, for achieving the party's main goals of equality and fraternity. Equality could be promoted by fiscal and educational reforms within a mixed economy. The revisionist argument pointed to rewriting the party's 1918 constitution, which put public ownership at its centre. Gaitskell tried, but failed, to do this after Labour's third electoral defeat in 1959. Another ex-Wykehamist, Richard Crossman, produced a supposedly clinching argument against the revisionists: 'We can predict with mathematical certainty', he wrote in *Labour in the Affluent Society* (1959), 'that, as long as the public sector of industry remains the minority sector throughout the Western world, we are bound to be defeated in every kind of peaceful competition with the Eastern bloc.' Harold Wilson, who succeeded Gaitskell as party leader on the latter's death in 1963, had no time for such 'theological' debates, but 'planning for growth' became a fixed point in Labour's new fundament, especially after Britain's 'slow rate of growth' started to be the subject of public debate.

After 1959, the 'embourgeoisement' thesis became popular. The political scientist Mark Abrams asked the question *Must Labour Lose?*, which he answered in the affirmative. As private affluence increased, the Tory percentage of votes was bound to go up. This ignored the growth of the public-sector-based salariat. The more compelling argument was that consumer society tended to dissolve the class basis of British politics, which hitherto had favoured Labour. 'De-alignment' from the two main parties was apparent by 1964.

The trouble with the Conservatives, Wilson proclaimed, was that they were too archaic, hidebound, and amateur to run a modern, science-based economy. Labour would harness socialism to science. This line appealed to the expanding white-collar and professional sectors. Scientific planning also sounded socialist. Wilson just won the general election of October 1964, and established a more solid majority in 1966.* But Labour came into office poorly equipped to deal with Britain's continuing economic problem, which revolved round the still imperial role of sterling, and the unresolved issue of labour relations.

---

* Election results 15 October 1964: Conservative 12,002,642 votes, 43.4 per cent, 304 MPs. Labour 12,205,808 votes, 44.1 per cent, 317 MPs. Liberal 3,099,283 votes, 11.2 per cent, nine MPs.
Election results 31 March 1966: Conservative 11,418,455 votes, 41.9 per cent, 253 MPs. Labour 13,096,629 votes, 48 per cent, 364 MPs. Liberal 2,327,457 votes, 8.5 per cent, twelve MPs.

The 'British disease' debate

What eroded the post-war settlement was the relatively slow growth of the British economy: 2.2 per cent per capita for the decade of the 1950s as against 6.3 per cent for Germany and 3.5 per cent for France. To cure the disease of slow growth became the avowed object of British governments. This made them much more interventionist. Interventionism damaged the delicate balance between capitalism and socialism, individualism and collectivism, which sustained the post-war settlement. It did not cure the economic disease, but made Britain harder to govern.

Relative decline was an old concern going back to the nineteenth century. Before the Second World War, Britain had lost ground to the United States; from the 1950s it declined relatively to other European countries, as well as to Japan. But the nature of the discussion had changed. Earlier in the century its context was Britain's future as a world power. In the 1950s, attention finally switched to the welfare of the inhabitants of Britain itself. Since the developed world as a whole was getting richer, relative economic decline meant that the British people were getting relatively poorer. For Labour, Britain's slow rate of growth posed a special problem: the slower the growth rate, the less wherewithal there would be to improve public services. Raising the rate of growth was the only way of advancing socialism without killing off capitalism.

In the 1950s, a new panel of expert diagnosticians appeared, as well as a new sense of urgency, even desperation. The magazine *Encounter* ran a symposium in its June 1963 issue called 'Suicide of a Nation?', in which government, Civil Service, political parties, the class-based educational system,

employers, trade unions and even sexual habits were all castigated for their contribution to the national decline. The
diagnosticians identified three main 'constraints' on faster
growth: the balance of payments, Britain's archaic political
economy, and its anti-commercial culture.

The balance of payments problem could be analysed in
purely technical terms. At full employment the British economy imported more than it exported, causing balance of
payments crises whose resolution required growth-destroying
bouts of deflation. This was the famous 'stop–go' cycle: the
inflationary 'goes' of 1953–5 and 1958–9 being succeeded by
the deflationary 'stops' of 1955–7 and 1960–1. The result was
to discourage long-term investment. Conservative macroeconomic management was attacked as being technically
incompetent.

A much-discussed issue at the time was whether Britain's
somewhat higher than average inflation rate was being caused
by union wage push at full employment, or whether union
wage push was caused by excess demand. Favouring the first,
the economist Meghnad Desai has explained: 'Being a low
wage/low productivity economy, any increase in wages soon
translates itself into an increase in unit labour costs and hence
prices. International competitiveness suffered, and this linked
inflation to the trade deficit.'[4] The 'demand–pull' school
blamed expansionary monetary policy in pursuit of overfull
employment. The 'cost–push' theorists wanted 'incomes
policies' to restrain pay. Those who favoured 'demand-pull'
wanted the government to run the economy at what was
euphemistically called 'a somewhat higher margin of
unused capacity' (2.5 per cent unemployment as against

2.0 per cent).* One or other, or both in combination, would produce a smoother growth path.

The short-term answer to the balance of payments constraint seemed to be devaluation. Its most influential advocate was the Hungarian-born economist Nicholas Kaldor. According to Kaldor, the main engine of growth was growth in manufacturing output. This was because of increasing returns to scale in manufacturing industry, and because output per person was higher in manufacturing than in agriculture or services. Devaluation would boost manufacturing exports, starting a 'virtuous circle' of increased output and higher productivity growth.

Behind the balance of payments constraint lay political economy. Some argued that stop–go was an electoral, not an economic, business cycle. Cynical Conservative Chancellors created 'goes' before general elections, which had to be followed by 'stops' after them. Another interpretation of long standing attributed British decline to the dominant position of the City of London. The City was the tail that wagged the dog of the British economy. 'Defence of sterling' was simply a proxy for City interests. Maintaining confidence in sterling enabled the City to attract hot money to finance trade and foreign investment rather than invest in British industry.†

---

* In the late 1950s, the British Treasury put great reliance on the 'Phillips Curve', a statistical series which purported to show a stable relationship between employment and prices. The Treasury assumed that stable prices could be maintained with an unemployment percentage of 1.8 per cent. By the mid-1970s, with British unemployment at 6 per cent and inflation at over 20 per cent, it was clear that the Phillips Curve was no longer a useful guide to policy. In economics jargon it had become 'vertical'. Milton Friedman explained why.

† The City's aim in the 1950s was to restore convertibility of current-account sterling, suspended in 1947. This was done in 1959. Early in the 1950s the Treasury prepared a scheme, rejected by the Cabinet, for convertibility with a floating pound (Operation Robot).

This determined the priority for macro policy. The City owed its political dominance to the fact that British banking was highly concentrated in London, while industry was fragmented and geographically scattered. Michael Shanks, a leading champion of industrial capitalism, wrote in 1961: 'I have always felt it to be a national tragedy that the centre of government and finance is in London and not in Birmingham.'[5]

A second political-economy explanation emphasised the importance of imperial overhang. This was seen in relatively high defence expenditures (7 per cent of GDP on average in the Conservative years) and maintenance of sterling as a reserve currency. Overseas military commitments and full convertibility for accruing sterling balances were important causes of balance of payments crises.

A third type of explanation focused on the role of the trade unions in the British economy. When people talked of the 'British disease' they mainly had in mind the ability of trade unions to resist cost-reducing innovations, check investment by squeezing profits, and generally disrupt the industrial life of the community. British unions enjoyed a singular coercive power, resting on two pillars. The first was the Trades Dispute Act of 1906, which gave the unions legal immunity for collective action intended to damage third parties as well as just their employers. The chief example was mass picketing to disrupt movement of goods and people between plants. The second was the institutional link between trade unions and a single political party, the Labour Party. In industrial law, Labour governments carried out union wishes. They reversed court decisions or repealed legislation designed to curb union power, and instead promoted an increase in that power. The threat that anti-union legislation would be reversed in turn inhibited Conservative governments from introducing it.

The unions' position gave them huge defensive, but no constructive, power. In fact, their legal immunities were only tolerable because they were relatively weak: had they had genuine monopoly power in supplying labour they could simply have shut down the country. But they were fragmented into craft unions, whose disputes with employers and with each other could damage individual companies and even industries, but not bring the economy to a standstill. In Nicholas Crafts's summary: 'The British system was characterised by multiple unionism, unenforceable contracts and, increasingly, by plant bargaining with shop stewards.'⁶ Churchill, belatedly discovering the virtues of appeasement, instructed his minister of labour Walter Monckton to concede to all union wage demands in the public sector. His successor, Anthony Eden, wanted to introduce legal curbs on union power in 1955, but failed to win Cabinet support. Employer appeasement was typified by the newspaper proprietor Lord Thomson of Fleet, who almost bankrupted the press by failing to tackle restrictive practices by the print unions. The incoming Labour government set its hopes on 'voluntary' co-operation in wage restraint, of the kind Stafford Cripps had achieved in the 1940s.

The third, much discussed, constraint was cultural attitudes. The cultural critique emphasised the triumph of 'gentlemanly' over 'entrepreneurial' culture. The idea, which goes back to Veblen, was that the British elites had chosen not to be competitive in order to enjoy a more civilised way of life. At the same time, they provided a low quality, mass-educational system which turned out an underskilled workforce which could be bought off with bread and circuses, but was also starting to develop an acute sense of its entitlements. In the late 1950s, the term 'Establishment' came into use to denote the narrow network of personal and family relationships which ran the country.[7] Abuse of the Establishment became a rite of passage for young intellectuals. The historian Hugh Thomas edited a book called *The Establishment*, whose authors had no doubt that it must be destroyed. Anthony Sampson's *Anatomy of Britain* (1962) concluded that Britain and its people were carrying on a 'pattern of relationships', disappearing elsewhere, which had 'robbed them of their dynamic'. The satire show *Beyond the Fringe* (1960) set out to demolish all that was sacred in the British way of life. *Private Eye*, the most enduring legacy of the satire boom, started in 1961. The Vassall, Burgess, Maclean and Philby spy scandals and the Profumo sex scandal of 1962–3 revealed the old guard to be mired in moral turpitude, and lacking in both public spirit and competence. Ian Macleod attacked the 'magic circle' of birth and breeding which had engineered the appointment of Macmillan's successor, the 14th Earl of Home. The middle-class young flocked to the Campaign for Nuclear Disarmament, which had started in 1957 – the first post-war appearance of radical youth on the political stage.

It was in this general context that Britain's class structure emerged as the key to explaining Britain's relative decline. A celebrated left-wing argument of the time gave a Marxist slant to the cultural critique. 'Less and less able to compete with the new workshops of the world, the ruling elite compensated by . . . building up a financial centre in the City of London.' The origins of this dysfunctional situation lay in the failure of England to experience a 'second' bourgeois revolution in the nineteenth century. (The seventeenth-century one had failed.) Nineteenth-century capitalism had been contained within a 'patrician hegemony . . . Permanent limits were thus imposed upon the "industrial revolution" and the British entrepreneurial stratum.'[8]

From today's vantage point, the discussion has an old-fashioned ring to it, in three respects. The first lay in the assumption that any 'desired' rate of economic growth could be brought about by deliberate government policy. This was the legacy of the Keynesian revolution at its most hubristic. Secondly, national well-being was still identified with the prosperity of 'smokestack' industry. Few grasped that higher living standards might be achieved by producing something other than coal, steel, ships and textiles: satire, for example, at which the British excelled. Finally, the discussion was over-wrought. Britain may have been losing ground, but not nearly as disastrously as the agonising suggested. The old 'patrician hegemony' was not serving the economy or society that badly. Britain might be falling in the standard of living league tables, but all developed countries were growing richer together and the gap between the wealthiest countries, which included Britain, was much smaller than it had been earlier in the century. In any case, such concepts as 'comparative real income per head' defied precise measurement.

Later, post-Thatcherite, analysis puts the discussion in a different framework. Entrepreneurial failure is not denied, but it is attributed less to deep sociological causes than to the adverse incentive structure facing British management, characterised by very high marginal tax rates (still over 80 per cent till the Thatcher years) and lack of competition throughout most of the economy, reinforced by the legacy of interwar protectionism. Collusive arrangements between employers, and employers and unions, as well as sheltered imperial markets for exports, produced a low-productivity equilibrium.

The main legacy of the discussion was an intellectual

consensus on the need to fit the British state and society for what Wilson called the 'white heat of the technological revolution'. Wilson claimed that Labour was the answer to the British disease. As Phillip Whitehead noted, 'The message of socialism was transmuted into that of modernity, the class war into the replacement of an incompetent elite by technologists in white coats.'[9] In economics, this meant switching from full employment to growth. In politics, it meant building a modern, democratic state. Social policy would target the education and welfare systems. In morals and culture archaic laws and restrictions would be swept away. Not all these modernising projects were focused directly on the problem of inferior economic performance. The last, in particular, reflected the influence of the liberalising section of the middle-class intelligentsia. The main aim, though, was to raise the standard of achievement in all walks of life. The modern state was one which would enable all its citizens to realise their potential.

Wilson's growthmanship

The 1964 election result showed that Labour was electable, not that it could govern. 'Growthmanship' – the attempt to get the economy to grow to plan – had started up in the last four years of Tory rule. Labour claimed it would do better. The Tories had started indicative planning because they could think of nothing else. Now it would be done by a modern team working a modern system, not by the tired old men of the Establishment.

This was the biggest illusion. The incoming premier, Harold Wilson, had been a brilliant leader of the Opposition, and this created high expectations for his premiership. Short of stature, he was an accomplished word-spinner in his flat, nasal northern voice, with an acute mind, great capacity for work and a phenomenal memory, especially for numbers. He embodied the rise of grammar-school Britain. He talked an executive language, but he proved to be an incompetent executive, with no sense of strategy, addicted to administrative gimmicks, and increasingly to paranoia. The government machine was a shambles throughout his premiership.

A new planning ministry, the Department of Economic Affairs, took over from the NEDC. Headed by the ebullient, if frequently drunken, George Brown, it was supposed to develop a creative rivalry with the Treasury. In December 1964 Brown got employers and trade union leaders to sign a portentous Declaration of Intent promising to keep the growth of prices and wages within the limits of productivity growth: a Prices and Incomes Board, under Aubrey Jones, was set up to police this undertaking. In 1965, the DEA published a National Plan projecting a 25 per cent increase in national output over the following six years, or a compound per capita growth rate of 3.4 per cent a year – higher than the Conservatives had achieved in their 'thirteen wasted years'. The economy was to be 'geared up' to achieve the growth target by setting sectoral, regional and industry targets; and by offering investment grants, employment grants, and grants to 'development areas'. Tony Benn headed a new Ministry of Technology to promote research and development.

Labour's economic plan was excellent – on paper. Expansionary fiscal and monetary policy would be run in tandem with 'indicative' planning to produce a 'sustainable' rate of growth. A higher rate of growth would allow a controlled growth of wages and expanding social services,

validating free collective bargaining and modest redistributionary policies. However, the government failed to
develop a balance of payments strategy consistent with its
growth targets. This was the decisive reason for its failure.
Maudling's 'dash for growth' in 1963–4 had produced an
annual growth rate of over 5 per cent over two years, but also
a deficit on the balance of payments of £800 million. When
the incoming Labour Chancellor, James Callaghan, promised to increase spending on health and pensions in his first
budget, Britain faced an immediate sterling crisis. Wilson's
chief advisers, notably Nicholas Kaldor, urged a devaluation
of the pound. But Wilson refused to saddle Labour with
another devaluation; a strong pound was a sign that Britain
was still a great power. This negative decision meant that
defence of sterling once more took priority over growth. It
gave the Treasury and Bank of England a whip hand over the
DEA, making the latter's function increasingly redundant.
Kaldor, the most fertile of Labour's economic advisers, proposed to retrieve the situation by means of a Selective
Employment Tax, which he persuaded Callaghan to introduce in 1965. This was a uniform levy on all employment,
with a rebate for manufacturing industry.

Wilson compounded his error in not devaluing the pound
by refusing to impose the necessary measure of deflation to
defend the sterling–dollar exchange rate. This left sterling
vulnerable to any passing shock. The second sterling crisis of
July 1966 was precipitated by a seamen's strike in May –
Wilson complained on television that the actions of a 'tightly
knit group of politically motivated men' had 'blown [the
nation] off course' – which led to millions of pounds of export
orders being held up. Wilson again refused to devalue, partly
because President Johnson had asked him not to. This time

he imposed £500 million of economies, a tax hike, a six-month wages freeze, and two years of 'severe' pay restraint. This antagonised the unions: planning was supposed to make incomes grow, not stop. Wilson hoped that micro-investment in 'growth' industries could offset the major act of deflation. In 1966 Labour set up an Industrial Reorganisation Corporation to subsidise business mergers, then considered to promote efficiency. Its fruits were the new giant companies GEC, RHP, ICL and British Leyland. In British Leyland, the merged motor car industry, the efficient car manufacturers were rapidly dragged down by internal chaos. The pound did not recover. The 1967 crisis was triggered by the Arab–Israeli war, bad autumn trade figures, and an unofficial dock strike in Liverpool. With no country willing to provide any more loans, the pound was finally devalued by 14 per cent against the dollar on 17 November 1967. Wilson went on television to deny that this meant a devaluation of the pound 'in your pocket'. Another package of cuts was imposed by the new Chancellor, Roy Jenkins, which included an immediate withdrawal from east of Suez. Like Macmillan before him, Wilson turned to the EEC as a substitute for Britain's vanishing world role, to be met once more by de Gaulle's veto. The ending of the period of 'severe restraint' on incomes not unnaturally led to a wages 'explosion' in 1968, which sent the inflation rate from 5 to 8 per cent and largely undid the effects of the devaluation and Roy Jenkins's austere budgetary programme.

The failure of Labour's growthmanship is a melancholy fact of history. GDP grew at 2.5 per cent annually between 1964 and 1970, less than under the Tories. Despite the Selective Employment Tax, investment in manufacturing industry actually fell as a percentage of total investment. Britain's relative economic decline was accelerated. The 'merger boom' was a product of wishful thinking. Industries are not competitive because they are big, they become big because they are competitive.

In terms of the debate on the British disease, the critical failure was not devaluing the pound soon enough. Wilson, the cocky grammar-school boy, had succumbed after all to the mystique of the City and imperial nostalgia. This aborted growthmanship from the start. A deeper explanation is that the whole planning project was misconceived. The economist Peter Sinclair finds the most depressing feature to lie not in specific mistakes of policy, but in the government's 'extravagant claims of omnicompetence'.[10] A third factor was that planning was undertaken in an industrial-relations system notably unsuited for the task. The trade unions failed to deliver the pay restraint which the Wilson government needed if it was to have any chance of avoiding the 'stop–go' cycle. The number of working days lost through strikes rose steadily under Labour to peak at 6 million in 1969: much below peak pre-war periods, but higher than under the Tories. Britain's problem was not long-drawn-out official stoppages, but lightning 'unofficial' strikes – groups of workers downing tools on impulse and at the slightest provocation. This reflected the shift in power, analysed by the Donovan Commission set up in 1968, from union officials to shop stewards elected by the workforce in a factory or plant, partly to overcome craft-based fragmentation. The powerful shop stewards' committees were often dominated by Trotskyists and Communists, especially in the new subsidised combines like British Leyland. The official union leadership also moved to the left in the late 1960s, reflecting their members' hostility to policies of pay restraint. Total personal incomes rose by 40 per cent in the Wilson years, but tax and National Insurance contributions rose by 80 per cent. This cut into the take-home pay of the average wage earner. The new generation of union leaders, like Frank Cousins and Jack Jones of the Transport and General Workers Union, Hugh Scanlon of the Amalgamated Engineers Union, and Clive Jenkins of the Association of Scientific, Technical and Managerial Staffs, no longer deferred to the party leadership. Eventually, the Wilson government realised that legislation was needed to end industrial lawlessness. In 1969 Wilson and his Secretary of State for Labour Barbara Castle proposed a new power for the government to impose a twenty-eight-day pause on 'wildcat' (shop-steward-led) strikes, and to give an Industrial Board the right to fine strikers for a refusal to comply. The unions were utterly opposed, and Wilson was overruled in the Cabinet. He had to be content with a 'solemn and binding undertaking' ('Solomon Binding', as it was irreverently known) by the TUC to do its best to control unofficial strikers.

Social reform

Like its predecessors and successors the Wilson government wanted to use the state to achieve its goals, not to reform it. Apart from a half-hearted and unsuccessful attempt to 'democratise' the House of Lords, it was barren of constitutional innovation. However, it did want to make the state apparatus more efficient, and that meant reorganising the Civil Service and widening access from beyond the traditional trawl of Oxbridge graduates. Local government was sliced up into more functional units. Labour noticed the arrival of youth by lowering the voting age to eighteen.

A key object of Labour's social reforms was to plug the gaps in the Beveridgean welfare system. The managers of the post-1945 welfare state did not expect welfare expenditures to expand exponentially. The Beveridge system offered a single route – temporary interruption of earnings – to the benefit system. The expectation was that full employment and rising incomes would limit claims for social protection. However, the anti-poverty goal implicit in Beveridge was a much wider ambition than just to provide a replacement income for contingencies. Logically, it applied to those at work as well as those whose earnings were interrupted, and also to those who had no earnings. In addition, poverty was defined in relative terms: from being a concept related to subsistence it became one related to average income. So poverty elimination became, *ipso facto*, a project for minimising income inequalities. Under Wilson insurance benefits were made more generous, especially for pensioners; family allowances (child benefits) increased and were paid to mothers not fathers; and earnings-related benefits and redundancy payments were introduced in an effort to shake skilled workers out of declining industries. As well as this, means-tested National Assistance, renamed Supplementary Benefits to rob it of its stigma, was extended in 1966 to the poor outside the labour market. The new claimants included widows, invalids and single mothers. Means-tested rent and rate rebates brought 1 million extra claimants within a year. This 'entitlements explosion' brought a far larger population into the benefit system than the residuum of 'cripples . . . and physical and moral defectives' for whom Beveridge had intended it. Between 1960 and 1970 the population relying on benefits crept up from under 1 million to 3 million and the cost of social services as a percentage of GDP climbed from 10 per cent to 15 per cent.

Increased social spending under Labour had an unintended consequence. Workers were supposed to be grateful for the expansion of their 'social wage'. Instead it provoked working-class tax resistance, as the extra spending was largely paid for by the fall in unindexed tax thresholds. In 1968, Richard Crossman remarked in his diary, 'The trade unionists want to see us spending less on social services so there will be more for wage-packets.' It was not the rich who were paying most for the expansion of means-tested benefits but the not-so-poor. And they also had reason to complain about the quality of the public services they were getting. Bevan wanted municipal housing to create pleasant, socially mixed neighbourhoods. But by the 1960s council estates had become high-rise monstrosities, increasingly dumping grounds for problem families whose children wrecked the new comprehensive schools being set up to rescue them from 'under-achievement'. Modernism in architecture never recovered from the massive, brutalist council estates and urban regeneration schemes of the 1960s, which paved the way for Prince Charles's attacks on 'carbuncles' in the 1990s.

The Wilson government took education seriously. New business schools – the first ever – were opened for management training. Higher and further education was expanded: an innovation close to Wilson's heart was the Open University, set up in 1969 to provide long-distance university education for adults. An ambitious scheme of industrial training was started. However, the main instrument Labour relied on to raise national educational standards was the comprehensive school. Comprehensive schools were supposed to overcome the class divide in education by abolishing the so-called tripartite system of grammar, technical and secondary modern schools – in practice the bipartite system of grammar schools and secondary modern schools – established by the Butler Act of 1944. Secondary moderns, successors of the Edwardian elementary schools, and mainly still housed in the same grim Victorian buildings, were intended for future manual workers; grammar schools for office workers. This division was increasingly condemned as socially divisive and aspirationally debilitating. The *coup de grâce* to grammar schools was delivered by the Education Secretary, Tony Crosland. His Circular 10/65, together with subsequent directives, ordered local authorities to go comprehensive, with financial penalties for non-compliance. Crosland's wife, Susan, records him as saying: 'If it's the last thing I do, I'm going to destroy every fucking grammar school in England. And Wales and in Northern Ireland.'

The amalgamation of grammar and secondary modern schools into non-selective combines fitted the prevailing 'big is beautiful' doctrine. But Crosland's ideological extremism was as inflexible as that of the 'three types of mind' approach. The rejection of the rigid selective instrument – the eleven-plus examination – enshrined by the Butler Act led to the rejection of selection per se, and its replacement by an equally rigid philosophy of 'one size fits all'.

The comprehensive revolution offers a textbook case of the law of unintended consequences. The skills gap it was designed to remedy got worse, not better: social expectations may have been raised, but academic expectations declined. The destruction of the grammar schools undercut Labour's own meritocratic ideal, kicking away the ladder by which bright working-class children, including many of Labour's own leaders and middle-class supporters, had risen into the professions. Labour unintentionally strengthened the class character of elitism. In a corrupt bargain with the Tories, the independent sector was left untouched, Tory politicians being content to sacrifice the grammar schools to safeguard the entry of their own children into the private sector. The grammar schools could have been a mechanism for creating a meritocracy. The destruction of the grammar schools strengthened the link between elite and class, while detaching mass culture from elite culture. This destroyed the legitimacy of elitism, which soon became a dirty word. From Ted Short to Michael Gove, state education has disappointed the hopes of its reformers.

The disintegration of the post-war settlement started with the renewed attempt to plan the economy. Planning, in a free society, means governing industry with the consent and participation of organised business and labour. But neither the British doctrine of parliamentary sovereignty, nor its political economy of a powerful City and fragmented businesses and craft unions, was fitted for such an exercise in tripartism outside the special conditions of war. There was a second contradiction. The move to planning presupposed a society still willing to respond to its leaders' wishes. But it coincided with the collapse of deference, itself promoted as part of middle-class Labour's liberating goals.

The political consequences of the Wilson years were severe. Labour's collectivism pushed the Conservatives to the right; its failure pushed Labour to the left. The men in the middle who governed Britain in the 1970s no longer had the support of their parties; and their parties had declining contact with the voters.

Cultural watershed?

The cultural upheaval of the 1950s and 60s is a classic example of the whole being greater than the sum of its parts. One can itemise all the changes which took place in those years and show persuasively that they do not add up to much – either because they were a continuation of previous trends, interrupted by the war, or because they were atypical. Yet people at the time felt that something importantly new was happening. Refuting this by multiplying examples of continuity, as historians like Dominic Sandbrook and David Fowler have done, is a powerful corrective to exaggerated claims of upheaval, but somehow misses the point.[11] By this historical method every revolution can be denied the name, because for most people, most of the time, life continues much the same. The important thing is that while the changes of those two decades were rooted in the past, they were unprecedented in their concentration. The acceleration of previous changes, the increase in their quantitative impact, plus legal reforms and genuine artistic novelties created a new cultural situation. All the factors behind the decay of the old culture noted in Chapter 2 – the decline of religion, the collapse of deference, the loss of empire, the shift to individualism in legislation and authenticity in art and lifestyles, the explosion of consumption and television advertising, the spread of contraception, the emergence of young people as a special category of consumer – came to a head in an astonishingly short space of time to change the cultural landscape irretrievably. The fact that there was subsequently a reaction does not mean that we have gone back to the previous point. Some things have changed irreversibly.

Stable economic growth was the indispensable background.

14. 'Just what was it that made yesterday's homes so different, so appealing?' by Richard Hamilton

In the 1950s, rising real wages and expanded job opportunities in manufacturing enabled an increasing number of workers to break through to middle-class levels of consumption. These were continuations of previous trends, interrupted by the Second World War. The new factor was the hugely expanded programme of council-house building. Together they changed working-class habitats. The early 1950s were the last years of the 'classic' collectivised urban working-class culture, with extended family networks, going back to the late nineteenth century, recalled by Richard Hoggart in the *Uses of Literacy* (1957) and recounted in such books as *Coal is Your Life* by Norman Dennis, about the Yorkshire mining town of Featherstone. The contrast is with the more isolated and individualistic working class of the new post-war council-housing estate, motor-car manufacturing culture of Dagenham studied by Ferdynand Zweig in *The Worker in the Affluent Society* (1961). The worker had 'never had it so good'.

The 'shiny barbarism' of affluence began to replace the authentic working-class culture of brass bands and working-men's clubs. Materialism edged out its warmth and decency. Evenings were increasingly spent in front of the television instead of down at the pub, and the working class replaced its authentic culture with the nostalgic simulacra of television shows like *Coronation Street*, starting in 1960.

But it is the increased spending power of young people which is relevant for the theory of the cultural watershed. Young people have never been mirror images of their elders, in behaviour or taste, but they lacked effective demand. By 1960 5 million teenagers commanded 10 per cent of the population's disposable income. Entrepreneurs reached into their wallets. One third of all motorbikes were bought by them; 40 per cent per cent of records. Youth culture was spread through money. Macmillan's premiership was the golden age of the working-class teenager. Freed from the incubus of school at fifteen, he could, unskilled, and without family responsibilities, step straight into a steady job at wages at near adult rates. Before the 1950s the cash of teenagers allowed only a limited expenditure on leisure goods. Now they had money to burn.

They were avid consumers of novelty and ephemerality. The revolution in teenage fashion started with the Teddy boys of the early 1950s, with their neo-Edwardian draped jackets, drainpipe trousers, quiffed greased hair, and brothel-creeper shoes, who flocked to city-centre dance halls and hung around milk bars and jukeboxes. What did the juke-boxes blare out? In the immediate post-war years, pop music remained conservative. Big bands supported trained voices like Vera Lynn and Dickie Valentine. But in December 1954, Bill Haley and the Comets gave British teenagers their first taste of rock and roll, the musical style that would come to dominate all others in the second half of the twentieth century. Their second single, 'Rock Around the Clock' reached number one in the charts in November 1955. Rock and roll – a white man's black music – gave teenagers what they wanted: a visceral, informal, accessible and sexually charged soundtrack, and music that, in the words of play-wright Tony Bicat, 'anyone with a fiver for a guitar and a minimal amount of intelligence could have a go at'.[12] Bands started writing their own songs, rather than singers relying on songwriters. Elvis Presley soon became the main rock and roll reference, along with his numerous British impersonators like Billy Fury and Cliff Richard. Teenagers loved rock music because their parents hated it. With the coming of rock and roll the image of 'bad' teenagers supplanted that of 'good' children of the early 1950s, and has dominated the tabloids (and therefore public perceptions) ever since; an image that proved to be highly exploitable for the teenage market.

However, there were severe limits in 1950s to the ability of young people to create a youth culture. Most teenagers still lived at home, and gave most of their wages to their parents; and National (military) Service claimed nearly all of them at seventeen. It was the ending of National Service and the extra civilian jobs for the seventeen-to-nineteen age group this cre-ated which enabled a more solid working-class youth culture based on clothes and music to be established. In fashion, Teddy boys gave way to mods and rockers, the former favour-ing scooters, the latter motorbikes. Their violent clashes at Clacton-on-Sea over the Whitsun weekend of 1964, magni-fied by the tabloids, led to what the sociologist Stanley Cohen called 'moral panic' and demands for legislation. It was the end of National Service which allowed a genuine British pop scene to emerge. Had conscription not been wound up in the late 1950s, the Beatles would hardly have been possible.*

The Beatles were the most famous beneficiaries of this cultural upheaval; their music started to hit the shops in 1962–3 at the height of the teenage consumer boom. Their novelty, cheeky-chappie working-class charm and wholesale image stood in contrast to a corrupt Establishment mired in scandal. Their success abroad was a hailed as contribution to the nation's shaky balance of payments, and they were the first of many cultural substitutes for Britain's waning 'hard power'. Wilson gave them OBEs in 1965. In 1964 BBC 1 started *Top of the Pops*, a weekly show of pop music, initially hosted by the later-to-be-revealed and reviled paedophile Jimmy Savile. It ran till 2006. The bands performed the music of the best-selling discs of the week, the last being the 'top'. The first show featured (in order) the Rolling Stones with 'I Wanna be Your Man', Dusty Springfield with 'I Only Want to Be with You', the Dave Clark Five with 'Glad All Over', the Hollies with 'Stay', the Swinging Blue Jeans with 'Hippy Hippy Shake' and the Beatles with 'I Want to Hold Your Hand'. In 1966 their main song writer John Lennon declared the Beatles were bigger than Jesus.

More subversive were the Rolling Stones. In 1967, their vocalist Mick Jagger, guitarist Keith Richards, and their art-dealer friend Robert Fraser were convicted for drug possession, a sentence overturned on appeal. Drug use became a badge of honour for the counter-culture; to those

---

* Following Suez, and the decision to manufacture the hydrogen bomb, the Conservative government announced in 1957 that no one born before October 1939 would be called up. The last call-ups were in 1960. Had the previous arrangements continued, John Lennon, who was at art college, would have been exempted, but the other Beatles would probably have been conscripted. The Beatles first hit, 'Love Me Do' was in 1962. This is a concrete example of how the 'end of empire' helped shape British culture.

in authority it symbolised the breakdown of the established order. Although pop music subverted conventional
morals, it was rebellious rather than revolutionary David
Fowler is dismissive about the Beatles: 'They were
young capitalists who, far from developing youth culture,
were exploiting youth culture by promoting fan worship,
mindless screaming and nothing more than a passive teenage consumer.'[13] Even the Rolling Stones, gifted with a
talented verbal communicator in Mick Jagger, were soon
absorbed into family entertainment.

The collapse of deference was much more pronounced in
the thinking than in the consuming classes. Working-class
youth wanted a better time; middle-class, especially university educated, youth wanted a better society. As David
Sandbrook rightly says, 'There was no such thing as a classless teenager.'[14] Working- and middle-class youth, while
united by pop music and (to some extent) by fashion and
drugs, had a completely different attitude to politics. The
working-class young were politically apathetic; the middle-
class young took up radical causes, though these were mixed
up with radical lifestyles. The discredit of the Establishment
gave them their space.

The first explosion of middle-class protest was the
'anger' of the Angry Young Men – a rag-tag group of writers and playwrights with no coherent agenda, of mainly
lower-middle-class provincial background against upper-
middle-class metropolitan elites. This helped prepare the
country for Wilson's technocrats. The fictional heroes of
writers like Kingsley Amis were grammar-school boys
with chips on their shoulders. They preferred beer to claret,
macho heterosexuality to Bloomsbury camp, gritty social
realism to modernism and self-conscious experimentation.

Northern England, depicted by John Braine and Stan Barstow, stood for 'real life' as against the decadence of London. 'Kitchen-sink drama' opposed the stylised drawing-room drama of Noel Coward and Terence Rattigan. Kingsley Amis's novel *Lucky Jim* (1954) and John Osborne's play *Look Back in Anger* (1956) portrayed a country raised by prosperity but alienated by antiquated class barriers and sinking beneath a collective sense of disenfranchisement and international impotence. A new generation of angry 'realist' films like Karel Reisz's *Saturday Night and Sunday Morning* (1960) and Tony Richardson's *The Loneliness of the Long Distance Runner* (1962) succeeded Hollywood escapism and the British Ealing comedies of the 1940s and 1950s. Film censorship was gradually relaxed: the word 'bloody' was first allowed in 1963, 'bugger' in 1967, and the first 'fucking' was in 1970.[15]

The writers fall into three groups: the new university wits – Oxford malcontents like Kingsley Amis, Philip Larkin, and John Wain who explored the contrast between upper-class university privilege and middle-class upbringing; writers of working-class origin like John Osborne, John Braine, Arnold Wesker and Alan Sillitoe, who railed against the hypocritical permissiveness of a ruling class gone soft; and existentialist 'philosophers' like Colin Wilson, who briefly admired the discredited, but still politically vigorous pre-war fascist leader Oswald Mosley. Wilson's *The Outsider* (1956) caught a brief existential moment, before its youthful author was heaped with obloquy for claiming to be a phil-osopher. What united the Angries was not credo, certainly not socialism, but splenetic rage against the 'insiders' with their 'repressive tolerance', a theme later savagely exploited in Lindsay Anderson's film *If . . .* (1968) and Stanley Kubrick's

A Clockwork Orange (1971). The Establishment was a chameleon, which changed its colour to fit its habitat, but was always somehow *there*, resisting all attempts at its dethronement. Parodying an enfeebled ruling class was a sure way to marketise talent.

Jimmy Porter's gloomy assertion, in John Osborne's 1956 *Look Back in Anger*, that 'there aren't any good brave causes left' was not shared by others. The Campaign for Nuclear Disarmament was one such cause, which attracted both liberal middle-class parents and their radical offspring. CND was a nice mixture of morality and great power fantasy, founded not just on a moral rejection of nuclear weapons, but the belief that if Britain gave them up, this would induce the rest of the world to give them up too. There were the student 'rebellions' of the later 1960s, most famously at the LSE in 1967, which paralleled, in typically muted British fashion, the political turbulence in the United States and continental Europe. As the 1960s wore on it became increasingly difficult to separate politics from culture, as political demands became the direct expression of cultural identity. Above all, 'rights' became the locus of protest movements: issues of gender, race, sexuality, and nationality took precedence over conventional politics, as the personal became political. The 1960s marked the point of no return in the century-long shift from 'duties' to 'rights'. Affluence turned consumption into a 'right'. As Joe Lampton, hero of John Braine's *Room at the Top* (1957) explained: 'I wanted an Aston-Martin, I wanted a three-guinea linen suit, I wanted a girl with a Riviera suntan – these were my rights'. It was the sacred right to consume which towered over all others.

The political parties were divided on how to treat the arrival of consumer society. Both parties were committed to improving the condition of the people. This was, after all, the main rationale for 'growthmanship'. But what constituted 'improvement' depended partly on what one expected of the people, and what one wanted them to have. There were two views of the working class. The financial journalist Nicholas Davenport, who served on a football commission which Wilson set up, believed that the working man 'still lived for the three F's – fun, football, and fucking . . . Like any other [he] could become bloody-minded and revolutionary when conditions went against him . . . but fundamentally he was a hedonist, with his eye on a good time without too much hard work.'[16] Davenport's view was shared by Harold Macmillan and was reflected not just in his expansionary economic policies, but in specific acts of Tory legislation: the establishment of a commercial television station (ITV) to compete with the BBC in 1954, the liberalisation of gambling laws, and the relaxation of licensing hours for pubs.

Labour's approach was collective and egalitarian: collective effort leading to collective reward in the form of improved public services paid for by taxation. Personal consumption was to be repressed to make room for public consumption. This reflected a more elevated view of human possibilities than was common on the Tory side.

It was the old conflict between Cavalier and Roundhead, pub and chapel, played out under conditions of growing affluence. But cutting across this classic right–left divide was a strong strain of radical middle-class individualism, with a home in both parties, which saw improvement in terms of self-expression and release from restraint. As Macmillan put it: 'A great number of laws and restrictions were framed in a more primitive society based on a mistrust of what the people would do. But like children growing up they can now be trusted to do more of what is right.'[17] Labour's Roy Jenkins was the great liberalising Home Secretary (1965–8) of the 1960s. He ended theatre censorship, introduced divorce by consent, and ensured the passage of bills legalising abortion and de-criminalising adult homosexual acts; in doing so laying the foundations of what he called the 'civilised society'.

Chapter 10

U-turn 1970–1997

The party's over.

Anthony Crosland, 1975

The ungovernable 1970s

The 1970s were the lowest point of British government in the twentieth century. At no time since before the First World War was there such a feeling that Britain had become ungovernable, and that a change of system – a change in the way of governing, not just a change of government – was required.

The change came about, not through the violent breakup of British society, but through the victory of the Conservative Party in 1979 under Margaret Thatcher. This inaugurated eighteen years of what came to be known as Thatcherism. But the previously congealed mould of politics was also broken by the emergence of the Social Democratic Party which promised, for a time, to replace the Labour Party. The mould was broken further by the resurgence of ethnic and religious nationalism after a long hiatus since the Irish settlement of 1922.

Britain was clearly unlucky in the 1970s. First, it was hit by the quadrupling of oil prices in 1973–4. This misfortune it shared with all oil-importing countries. It plunged them all into an inflationary recession: prices went up, living standards went down. Throughout the 1970s governments were buffeted by external events they lacked the tools to master. Particular to Britain, though, was the bad luck of having, in effect, minority governments between 1974 and 1979. Personality and political circumstances are both important, but they are not sufficient explanations of what went wrong. The truth is that the post-war settlement had run its course. The consensus had collapsed, because it was never really a consensus, simply a code of behaviour created by particular events and pragmatism. Its lack of an institutional basis was most obvious in industrial relations. Faced with national emergencies, neither capitalists nor workers would give up their freedom of action, and eventually the capitalists won, because they got a government strong enough to crush the unions. But the crises of the 1970s also showed up in imperfect arrangements for governing the restive peripheries of the United Kingdom, differentially hit by the decline of British industry.

Edward Heath

On paper, Edward Heath, Conservative prime minister from 1970 to 1974, was a 'strong' leader. But he was rigid, overbearing and politically inept, with a weak and untried team. He took office having pledged to reverse Wilson's economic policies. In practice, he reversed his own policies, in a spectacular series of U-turns.

He believed in 'tight money'. But when British unemployment reached the 'magic' figure of 1 million in January 1972, the economy was massively reflated in the 'Barber boom'. Inflation doubled in two years, while unemployment fell by only a third. He promised not to bail out 'lame ducks'. But ailing companies like Rolls-Royce were not only rescued, but nationalised, and the Industry Act of 1972 created new interventionist powers to subsidise industrial projects. 'Incomes policies' were to be abandoned: instead they were made statutory in September 1972. All this was before the OPEC price hike ratcheted up stagflation. Under Sir Keith Joseph, Secretary of State for Social Services 1970–4, the 'scope of social security saw almost unremitting expansion'.[1]

None of this brought any relief from rising inflation and growing industrial disorder, as the unions, led by the miners, fought all attempts to control pay in face of rising prices. It was under Heath that unions started to use methods of intimidation against employers and other workers in flagrant breach of the (weak) laws that his government had enacted to restrain them.* Heath was brought down in February 1974, when he asked the electorate to decide 'Who Governs Britain?' at the precise moment when it was perfectly clear it was not he. Rejecting any policy reminiscent of Heath became the obsession of Margaret Thatcher, his successor as Conservative leader.

Heath's one positive achievement was to negotiate Britain's entry into the EEC. With de Gaulle's resignation in 1969, Britain was admitted in 1972, on somewhat humiliating terms. Britain had not taken part in founding the EEC, and therefore had to accept arrangements contrary to its interests as the price for joining. It was forced to accept the Common Agricultural Policy. It had to jettison the remaining scaled-down imperial preferences, finally ending Joe Chamberlain's

---

* The Industrial Relations Act (1971) restricted legal immunities to registered trade unions and designated unofficial strikes 'unfair industrial practices' to be subject to penalties imposed by an Industrial Court. The Act became a dead letter as employers refused to use it.

dream of imperial economics. The sterling area was also scrapped. Britain's EEC membership was confirmed by a referendum cleverly crafted by Wilson in 1975, soon after he returned to power. Achieving EEC entry was the last victory of the Whig elite which had governed Britain since the war.

Weak Labour governments 1974–1979

When Wilson took office for the third time in February 1974, without an overall majority,* inflation, already raging under Heath, was being fed by the explosion of oil and commodity prices. The programme on which Labour fought the February 1974 election reflected the left's assessment of what had gone wrong between 1964 and 1970. The main lesson seemed to be that British capitalism was in terminal decline and that the British economy could not prosper unless it was comprehensively socialised. The left's guru, Stuart Holland, was largely responsible for foisting on the party an industrial programme, enthusiastically espoused by Secretary of State for Industry Tony Benn, which would have led to the decapitation of the private sector and a 'fundamental and irreversible shift in the balance of power and wealth in favour of the working people'.[2] Wilson, like his predecessor, found himself saddled with policies he did not believe in. He did his own U-turns, spending his first year and a half in office reversing or emasculating his party's manifesto commitments (helped in this by his

---

* Labour won 301 seats with 37.1 per cent of the vote; the Conservatives 297 seats with 37.9 per cent; the Liberals fourteen seats with 19.3 per cent. Labour improved its position slightly in October 1974: Labour 319 seats and 39.2 per cent; Conservatives 277 seats and 35.8 per cent; Liberals thirteen seats and 18.9 per cent. However, Labour overall majority evaporated between 1974 and 1979, leaving it dependent on the Liberals and Scottish Nationalists.

wafer-thin majority and the device of a referendum on Europe). Britain in the 1970s was governed by men who stood still in the middle while their party activists bolted in opposite directions.

The inside story of the Wilson–Callaghan governments* has been excellently told by the head of Wilson's Policy Unit, Bernard Donoughue.[3] Wilson, by now well past his best, let the economic situation deteriorate to the point when expenditure cuts and another pay policy could be imposed by external events. The one practical consequence of Labour's ambitious 'social contract' with the workers was to give unions new legal powers (notably the right to insist on a pre-entry 'closed shop'). By mid-1975 the annual inflation rate was running at 26.5 per cent, the current-account deficit was 1.5 per cent of GDP, public spending reached 58.4 per cent of GDP, the budget deficit stood at 9 per cent of GDP, and business profitability was at an all-time low. A voluntary pay policy (the left-wing TU leader Ken Gill called it 'as voluntary as rape') was agreed with the TUC in July 1975, causing much resentment because it provided for flat-rate pay increases of £6, squeezing the differentials of skilled and unskilled workers. It took the sterling crisis of 1976, and humiliating recourse to the IMF for a loan to bring runaway public spending under control. The combination of public spending cuts and pay policy brought down the annual rate of inflation from over 20 per cent to 8 per cent in two years. But when the government announced a 5 per cent wages 'norm' for 1978, the public sector unions went on a destructive rampage and the pay policy collapsed in the 'winter of discontent'. By 1979 inflation

---

* James Callaghan succeeded Wilson as prime minister in April 1976. It is probable that Wilson's unexpected retirement (at the age of sixty) was caused by premonitory symptoms of his later Alzheimer's disease.

was back up to 13 per cent and unemployment was 5 per cent. Growth over the whole Labour period was 1.4 per cent a year, the lowest five years in the post-war era. This was the immediate background to the victory of the Conservative Party in the 1979 election.

The renewed debate about Britain's economic prospects which opened up in the mid-1970s was more desperate than in the late 1950s. Then it had been about the causes of relatively slow growth; now it was about the style of government itself. Economic and political failure, it was claimed, had created a 'crisis of governability'. Ungovernability arose essentially from the attempt to yoke a failing capitalism to a rampant trade unionism. As a consequence, the state had become 'overloaded' with tasks: its reach had come to exceed its grasp. By the mid-1970s, the government controlled the flow of more than 50 per cent of the gross national product, it contributed more than 40 per cent of all new investment, employed 27 per cent of the working population, paid about one third of all wages and salaries, and owned nearly half the national fixed assets. This left out its influence on the private sector through price controls and industrial-development certificates. Heath had trod the path of corporatism. In his failed bid for tripartite agreement on incomes policy in 1972, he had offered employers and unions a chance to 'share fully with the government the benefits and obligations involved in running the economy'. Labour's left-leaning, but vaguer, 'social contract' had the same goal: economic policy would be agreed over 'beer and sandwiches' with Jack Jones and other union leaders at 10 Downing Street. But British economy and society were never suited to tripartism: the industrial structure was too fragmented, its people too individualistic.

The left and right agreed that the post-war settlement had

disintegrated: they naturally disagreed about what to do about it. Marxist thinkers discerned a 'crisis of legitimacy'. The left promoted an Alternative Economic Strategy, which amounted to a command economy, withdrawn from the EEC and sheltered by import controls. This was socialism's last hurrah: the more significant intellectual break was to the right. Free markets, long promoted by the Institute of Economic Affairs, set up in 1955, were the right's answer to ungovernability. Now it captured the intellectual high ground in the Tory Party.

Thomas Balogh, writing in *New Statesman* of 28 January 1972, got to the heart of the problem:

> Full employment fundamentally altered the relative power of classes but without any change in class stratification. If there is no industrial reserve army, the power and privilege of the employer is weakened. Suddenly an overwhelming increase in bargaining strength is conferred to the unions. At first the system works not too badly but after a short time the change in the balance of power, since it is unaccompanied by a change in social attitudes and institutions, leads to inflation and through inflation and lack of business confidence to political unrest. This is the direct consequence of the increase in concentration of economic power on both sides when combined with full employment. The outcome of collective bargaining is then no longer determined or limited by the real resources of the community.

The right's leading politician-intellectual Sir Keith Joseph, repenting of his extravagances as Social Security Secretary, announced his conversion to the truth faith of Conservatism. In his speech at Preston on 4 September 1974, Joseph identified the full-employment commitment as the basic error. It forced government to take steps to control pay which led to ungovernability. Joseph made the point, soon to be commonplace, that it was taking more and more inflation to achieve a given reduction in unemployment, so that over successive cycles both inflation and unemployment tended to rise together. But trying to dampen down inflation by restricting pay was 'like trying to stop water coming out of a leaky hose without turning the tap off'. Reflecting the new 'monetarism' of Milton Friedman, Joseph declared that inflation was a monetary phenomenon caused by the government printing too much money. Government's task was to control money, not pay. If money was controlled, excessive pay awards would lead not to higher prices, but higher unemployment. Joseph did not spell out how much unemployment it would take to stabilise prices.

If there was no longer a full-employment commitment, the budget lost its Keynesian function as an economic regulator. Budget deficits should be viewed as creators of inflation, not of employment. So their reduction and eventual elimination was part of ending inflation. But, in addition, a budget balanced by cuts in public spending, especially on subsidies to industries, rather than tax increases, would have stimulating 'supply side' effects: it would make possible a reduction in taxation (the top rate of tax on earned income was still 83 per cent, on investment income 98 per cent), it would force a restructuring of inefficient state industries, and it would bring about a smaller state.

Notable in this discussion was the absence of any real discussion about how to improve the productivity of the economy, even though it was James Callaghan, in a famous speech at Ruskin College, Oxford in 1976, who pointed out that the education system was failing to deliver a sufficiently skilled workforce. But education policy in the 1970s was still trapped in the 1960s social-engineering agenda rather than attempting to produce a 'literate, numerate and employable young generation'.[4]

On 22 July 1976, the Bank of England publicly announced the adoption of money-supply targets, though it had already started using them. In 1975, public expenditure started to be 'cash limited' and, for the first time since the war, was cut during a major recession, Tony Crosland telling the local authorities that the 'party is over'. In October 1976, Wilson's embattled successor, James Callaghan, announced to a startled Labour Party conference that governments could no longer 'spend their way' back to full employment. Although the intellectual elements of Thatcherism were falling into place, few believed that any government would have the will to implement the policies suggested by them. *The Times* columnist Peter Jay reckoned that to eliminate inflation would require unemployment in the 'low millions' for a decade or more. He concluded that this was politically unfeasible. 'Governments depending on consent', he wrote in the paper on 1 July 1974, 'cannot suspend the full employment commitment.'

The British question

A question much discussed on the left at this time was: why did the reaction to the growing failure of the British state take the form of nationalism rather than socialism? This assumes that the class struggle was the 'normal' form of British politics, with any vertical form of political allegiance a leftover from more primitive times. This 'class' focus of political analysis had some validity for much of the twentieth century. Until the 1970s, the break-up of Britain seemed inconceivable. But economic failure made the unitary state less attractive. This was not all. The post-war settlement had presumed an imperial United Kingdom with a stable social structure and a homogeneous 'British' population. The 'end of empire' raised the issue of British national identity. The gentlemen in Whitehall were finding their plans for a smooth British transition to a post-imperial role in Europe being derailed by a series of 'peasant revolts'.

In the 1970s the Protestants of Northern Ireland found that, like the white settlers in Southern Rhodesia, they had no place in the new Britain. The existence of Northern Ireland was a permanent source of grievance to Republican Ireland; the way it was governed, to the Catholics inside its borders. Reunification was never a realistic possibility. With the Republic having a per capita income only a fraction of the North's, there was no chance of the Protestants accepting 'rule from Dublin'. At the same time, the settlement of 1922 had left a large Catholic minority in Ulster. Although officially there was no discrimination, in practice there was a Protestant Ascendancy maintained through a set of interlocking political, economic and security institutions which had no parallel elsewhere in the UK. These were justified on the ground that a state which did not have, and could never have, the full confidence of so many of its subjects, had to protect its existence in a less than fully democratic way. London politicians turned a blind eye to the situation as long as Northern Ireland stayed off their radar screen. When middle-class Catholics took to the streets in 1968 – the year of failed revolutions all over Europe – to demand, in essence, the dismantling of the Protestant state, Whitehall reacted in the approved style of colonial retreat. It forced concessions on the Unionist governments of Terence O'Neill and James Chichester-Clark. These destroyed the authority of Ulster Unionism with the Protestant working class, without appeasing the Republicans. The demons of Irish history re-emerged as both sides prepared for the 'armed struggle'. The IRA 'Provisionals' started up in 1969; Protestants re-formed the Ulster Defence Volunteers. Violence escalated, and the British Army appeared on the streets of Londonderry in 1969. IRA violence spread to the British mainland and bomb explosions became regular in London and elsewhere; there were several political assassinations, including that of the last viceroy of India, Lord Mountbatten.

Since the Protestants refused their exit lines, Britain was stuck with the six provinces and their archaic enmities – the moth-eaten Protestant parades celebrating the Battle of the Boyne and other glorious victories over the Catholics, the decaying shipyards and factories of Belfast, once strongholds of a Protestant 'labour aristocracy', the run-down housing estates of Ballymurphy. The Protestant sub-state had lost its connection with those forces pushing British society towards a secular, history-free future, but it clung to the Union Jack with pathetic, unrequited loyalty.

It was Wilson's successor, Edward Heath, who had to bear the brunt of the Irish troubles. More and more British troops were poured in; the pace of reform was quickened. Far from enlarging the 'constitutional' centre, the reform measures shifted power to the extremists. Faced with the surge of sectarian violence, Heath reacted by reintroducing internment in August 1971, a disastrous move which swelled the ranks of the IRA. In January 1972 soldiers of the Parachute

Regiment killed fourteen Catholics in Londonderry ('Bloody Sunday'). As recruitment to the paramilitaries on both sides soared, Heath removed control of security from Stormont. This move, in February 1972, precipitated the resignation of the last Unionist government headed by Brian Faulkner, and Heath replaced Home Rule by direct rule. That year 500 were killed as the two sides' murder gangs let rip. But Heath – or more particularly his jovial Secretary of State for Ireland, William Whitelaw – blundered on. The British would restore devolved government if Faulkner accepted a power-sharing executive with the Catholic parties, and a 'Council of Ireland'. Faulkner's acceptance of the latter, in the so-called Sunningdale Agreement of May 1974, precipitated a general strike of Protestant workers, organised by the Ulster Workers' Committee.

Within a few days, the strike paralysed the Northern Irish state. Harold Wilson, back at 10 Downing Street, condemned the strike leaders as 'non-elected, self-appointed people who are systematically breaking the law and intimidating the people of Northern Ireland', but he was impotent to break the strike. As in Southern Rhodesia, the key to the situation was the attitude of the army and police. Not only was there considerable sympathy for the strikers in the lower ranks of both, but the army declared itself impotent to keep the local power supply going. On the strike's first day, the power workers took over the largest generating complex at Ballylumford, and systematically and expertly started to run down the supply. In the first weekend, the whole of industry had come to a halt. In the second week, farm production was paralysed, and the telephone and postal services had collapsed. Ministers' cars had run out of petrol, and the army had to airlift the politicians to their candle-lit offices. In the third week 85 per cent of the supply had gone. By 27 May, Faulkner's civil servants told him that the loss of power would destroy the sewage system, opening Belfast to flooding, typhoid and dysentery. Next day he resigned; the British government suspended the power-sharing assembly, and promised fresh elections. The same day the strike was called off.

The episode is full of ironies. The Protestant workers' revolt of 1974 is the only example of a successful general strike in British history, not least because the Catholic workers who also wanted the power-sharing executive to fail did not oppose it. The Protestant working class of Northern Ireland had shown a capacity for discipline and organisation for which the left had looked in vain in British unionism, but it was in the wrong cause. They disliked Catholics more than they disliked capitalists – thus showing, in socialist eyes, an imperfect understanding of their true class interests. At the same time, although they showed they could run a small state, they had no desire to do so. What they claimed was a blocking power. In this they were very much like other British trade unionists. Having made their point, they went back to work, leaving the political defence of their cause to Ian Paisley's Democratic Unionists and the private armies of the Ulster Defence Association. The alternative history which the general strike briefly opened up – the emergence of power-sharing with Catholics 'from below' – was snuffed out. The British learnt their lesson and embarked on the long process of scaled-down, but more precise, counter-terrorist measures, covert operations, and secret negotiations which would eventually bring about an end to the violence in the Good Friday Agreement of 1998.

The Irish Protestants were mainly Scottish in origin; and the Ulster Protestant revolt against Westminster stimulated latent Scottish nationalism. The Scots had exported engineers, doctors and scientists to the empire. As the British Empire retreated, the Scots, deprived of their share of imperial glory, started to portray themselves as victims of imperialism. A disproportionate economic decline, and a separate legal, religious and educational system heightened their sense of separateness. The discovery of North Sea oil in 1969 and Britain's entry into the EEC seemed to offer rich pickings to 'An Independent Scotland in Europe'. By the late 1960s, the Scottish National Party, dating from 1928, was showing signs of political life. Heath offered Scottish 'home rule' in 1970 as part of his plan to divide Britain into super local authorities, but he never had time to get round to it. Labour which regarded Scotland as its political fiefdom, had no interest in Scottish devolution, but was forced to rethink its position when large Scottish Nationalist gains in the 1974 general elections left a weak Labour government dependent on Scottish Nationalist support. (In the two general elections of that year, the SNP won 22 per cent and 30 per cent of the votes, and seven and eleven parliamentary seats, on a platform of independence from Britain, and separate membership of the EEC.) The Labour government passed a measure of devolution in 1978 which, however, failed to reach the 40 per cent hurdle required in a referendum for its passage into law. A year later it was voted out by Scottish Nationalist MPs.

The third challenge to the British sense of identity came from large-scale immigration. One legacy of empire was that British colonial subjects could freely come to live in the 'mother country'. Post-war labour shortages prompted governments to try and attract immigrant labour to Britain. The first boatloads of Jamaicans arrived in the late 1940s.

Their numbers were soon swelled by immigrants from the Indian subcontinent. In 1951 the ethnic-minority population was about 80,000. In 1961 it reached 500,000; by 1971 it was 1.5 million, or 3 per cent of the total population, and highly concentrated in decaying inner-city areas in London, Manchester, Birmingham, Leeds and Bradford.

The new arrivals soon carved out niches in British society. The NHS – that quintessential symbol of Britishness – was heavily dependent on migrants from the Commonwealth; by 1969, around a quarter of NHS doctors were born (and mostly trained) overseas.[5] Small businesses run by immigrant families, from minicab firms to restaurants and convenience stores, became a fixture of high streets in Britain's cities. Immigrant communities made their own distinctive contributions to Britain's culture, notably the Jamaicans with their reggae music.

But the rise of mass immigration also fuelled resentment, racism and sometimes violence. Race riots broke out in Notting Hill, London, and Nottingham in 1958. Warned by Cyril Osborne, the MP for Louth, that it was 'time to speak up for the white man', the Conservatives introduced a restrictive, though 'colour-blind', regime of work vouchers in 1962, which, however, contained a loophole allowing the entry of spouses and children of immigrant workers. The winding-up of Britain's African empire brought another wave of immigrants, as Asian British passport holders in Kenya and Uganda started to flee racial discrimination in these newly independent African states. In a clear break with the 'colour-blind' approach, Wilson's government passed an Act in 1968, denying them right of settlement, while retaining free entry for non-British subjects of British origin. At the same time, it passed two acts, in 1965 and 1968, modelled on US

Unlikely populist
15. Enoch Powell

race-relations legislation, outlawing racial abuse and discrimination in employment and housing, with a Race Relations Board to enforce its provisions.

Popular resentment at mass ethnic-minority immigration found an unlikely champion in an austere classical scholar turned politician called Enoch Powell. As health minister in the early 1960s, he had encouraged nurses and doctors from overseas to plug the gaps in the NHS, but alarmed by the scale of immigration he changed his mind. Powell was a dominating force in British politics from 1967 to 1975. He was the strangest popular tribune to emerge in post-war Britain, in his mixture of extreme romanticism and extreme rationality. Ian Macleod referred to 'Poor Enoch, driven mad by the relentlessness of his own logic.'

Powell's vision of a post-imperial Britain was startlingly different from that of the political class. It was essentially an appeal to the pre-imperial 'island' tradition. 'We discover affinities with earlier generations of English, generations before the "expansion of England", who felt no country but this to be their own.' England was the 'sleeping beauty' which contained within itself all the human resources needed for its reawakening. Powell's use of the word 'England', though still in conventional use to describe 'Britain', brings out the true quality of his insularity.

Powell was a Thatcherite before his time in his repudiation of planning and his espousal of nationalism. He was a monetarist before monetarism, resigning from the Treasury in 1958 over what he regarded as the Macmillan government's failure to control public spending. Then on 20 April 1968, in the Midland Hotel, Birmingham, he made a speech that made him a popular hero. Powell proposed to cut the flow of immigrants immediately to 'negligible proportions' and to provide grants for voluntary repatriation. Unless this were done, Britain, by the century's end, would have between 5 million and 7 million people from ethnic minorities. (Powell was prescient about this.) This would inevitably produce large-scale racial violence. (Powell was wrong here, but was speaking against the background of the American race riots of the 1960s.) He foresaw 'the river Tiber foaming with much blood'.

Powell's populist handling of the most sensitive topic of domestic policy was condemned by the political elites. For Harold Wilson he was the 'evil guru from Wolverhampton'. Heath dismissed him from his 'Shadow' Cabinet. Popular reaction was different. The immediate response to his speech was a wave of racist attacks, mainly on Asian immigrants in Southall and the East End. Powell received 100,000 letters of approval, 74 per cent of a Gallup poll sample agreed with what he said, and dockers in London and factory workers in Birmingham marched in his support.

Powell sacrificed political preferment for public acclaim. But his influence was immense. By making immigration a public issue, he helped the Tories win in 1970, despite his repudiation by Heath. He influenced two elections in 1974, when he called on voters to reject Edward Heath's pro-European policies by voting Labour. Switching his constituency from Wolverhampton East to South Down in 1974, he demanded the abolition of devolved government, and the permanent integration of Northern Ireland with Britain. But he could not engage the masses in his anti-European and Northern Ireland positions. The electorate was not interested in abstract talk of sovereignty. 'Politics is in the last resort about the life and death of nations', he said. But in the absence of threats of the kind posed by Nazi Germany, politics was mainly about bread and butter issues. Powell was also a loner. He was a man of powerful speeches, not a builder of organisations and followings. All his campaigns failed: immigration continued (albeit on a smaller scale) without (much) violence, Britain stayed in the European Union, Northern Ireland regained a devolved government and acquired an 'Irish dimension'.

In the short run, the party leaderships successfully 'kept immigration out of politics'. In the longer run, immigration damaged the political nation by opening up 'a profound gap . . . between the opinions of the governors and the governed'.[6] It explains a lot of the sourness of the politics of the 1970s. It snapped social deference in the Tory Party, facilitating its capture by middle- and lower-middle-class leaders closer to the outlook of their constituents. Powell attracted working-class voters away from Labour in 1970, and the Powell effect still worked for Thatcher in 1979.

Powell's importance was that he explicitly raised the question of Britain's post-imperial identity. How far would the unravelling of empire have to go? These questions have never since left the stage. For Heath, Britain's destiny was to be part of Europe. It would discover a new vocation as a member of the European Economic Community. But Europe offered no real equivalent role for Britain. By usurping some of the functions of the established nation states, the EEC pointed not to a Europe of nations but to a Europe of nationalities, which threatened the unity of the United Kingdom. For Powell, Britain's post-imperial identity was constituted by its island institutions, developed over centuries, which required a high degree of cultural homogeneity. But Powell too suffered from the illusion that the United Kingdom could be preserved as a unitary state. His call for island unity flew in the face of advanced centrifugal forces in both Northern Ireland and Scotland. In the short run, Powell was defeated by Heath. In the long run, he paved the way for Margaret Thatcher's more carefully circumscribed brand of free markets and populist nationalism.

Punk rock music was the cultural response to the sense of desolation engendered by the failures of the 1970s. In the 1960s, pop music had been the great leveller, a youthful challenge to entrenched cultural hierarchies. But by the 1970s, pop's pampered aristocracy had become respectable. A section of their young audience, embittered by unemployment and economic turmoil, were losing interest in distant pop stars who sang about love from their tax havens. In 1976, the punks, a new wave of angry young men and women with spiky (or in the case of skinheads closely cropped) hair, black lips, eyeliner, leather jackets, bondage gear, and safety-pinned noses and jeans burst onto the teenage scene, offering a shocking and sometimes violent taste of working-class rebellion. The musical style of the punk bands was confrontational, their lyrics sexually explicit ('love comes in spurts'), and angry. The Clash called for a 'White Riot'; the Sex Pistols proclaimed 'Anarchy in the UK'.

Punk's heady mix of working-class anger and art school radicalism was always unstable, and punk proved unable to resist the pull of commercialisation, which splintered both the Sex Pistols and their audiences. The band split in 1978; Sid Vicious, the bassist, died from a heroin overdose a year later. Though it shocked – the Sex Pistols' 1977 single 'God Save the Queen' was banned by the BBC – punk's appeal was always limited, and it never displaced the likes of ABBA and Paul McCartney's 'Wings' from the top 40. In the 1980s, pop music, in the form of the New Romanticism, with its designer clothes, its lush orchestral sounds (enabled by electric synthesisers) and its syrupy lyrics, made its peace with Thatcherism. In the 1990s Britpop completed the journey from rallying call to escapist narcotics.

Mrs Thatcher's perestroika

The Thatcher governments from 1979 to 1990 demolished the ruined post-war settlement. Of its three pillars – the full-employment commitment, the mixed economy and the welfare state – only the third remained standing. Margaret Thatcher achieved three things. She found a successful way of governing the country, she restored national pride and she brought to an end Britain's relative economic decline. These successes only became obvious later. At the time her revolution encountered almost universal scepticism, and indeed opposition, from the thinking classes; it also divided the country. It only continued because she was determined it should, and the voters elected four Conservative governments in a row, the last under John Major. That is why the Thatcher years turned out to be a watershed. It was only with the global financial meltdown of 2008 that her revolution started to unravel.

Thatcher's vision, like Enoch Powell's, was insular. She was a nationalist, who drew on a tradition of Protestantism and free markets. The historical moment she continually evoked was 1940, when Britain stood alone against a Hitler-dominated Europe. Britain again had to 'go it alone'. She seized on a favourable historical moment. Her predecessors had got rid of the empire, and therefore there was no imperial over-hang. She had no time for the insubstantial Commonwealth, and not much more for the EEC, giving the impression that she viewed Brussels as the capital of a new Carolingian empire. Over the few remaining imperial problems – Southern Rhodesia, South Africa and Hong Kong – Thatcher bowed to the inevitable, not always with good grace; she even nudged along the 'peace process' in Northern Ireland, despite an IRA assassination attempt in Brighton in 1984, which almost destroyed the prime minister and her Cabinet. In practice, rejection of a European vocation left Britain with its 'special relationship' with the United States, whose military dimension was now fortified by the ideological love-fest between Thatcher and US President Ronald Reagan.

Margaret Thatcher

Margaret Thatcher was the most passionate and embattled of the three great prime ministers of the twentieth century. She transformed British lives, but failed to capture their hearts. She rightly described herself as a conviction politician. A conviction is a settled belief that brooks no argument. And

Thatcher did not deign to conciliate. She divided the political world into 'us' and 'them'. 'Is he one of us?' became a Downing Street cliché. She despised the Conservative 'wets' in her early Cabinets, and got rid of them as soon as she could. She admired politicians with 'balls', like David Owen, an admiration which was reciprocated.

She quoted an apocryphal remark of St Francis of Assisi when first entering No. 10, 'Where there is error, may we bring truth, where there is discord, harmony' – a strange and revealing quotation, because it suggests that discord is born of error. This was certainly the medieval view, when heretics were burned at the stake. But it is unusual to find it so plainly expressed in modern democracies.

The heresy that needed extirpating was, of course, socialism. This she saw mainly in moral terms. 'The real case against socialism,' she said in 1977, 'is not its economic inefficiency. Much more fundamental is its immorality.' Economics, she insisted, was the method: 'the object was to change the soul'. John Campbell, an early Thatcher biographer, pointed out the paradox: although her values were 'conservative, old-fashioned and puritanical', she let loose a 'culture of rampant materialism'. Under Thatcher 'Britain passed, with great rapidity, from the world of Alfred Roberts to that of Mark Thatcher'.*

In instinct and language Thatcher was a follower of Friedrich Hayek. For Thatcher, as for Hayek, the fatal conceit was the belief that the state could improve on the spontaneous efforts of individuals. What others saw as the state's role in protecting and elevating the condition of the people, she saw as the insidious road to serfdom. What she remembered about unemployment in the 1930s was not the feeling of

---

* This passage is indebted to Vernon Bogdanor, *New Statesman*, 30 November 2012.

hopelessness, but parents on the dole scrimping to keep their children smart. Her task as she saw it was to stop the rot in the British character which socialism had engendered. To this endeavour she brought a cast of mind which was theological, not intellectual. She had dogmas and beliefs, not ideas. She bombarded you with statistics and quotations from the great texts, which she would produce from her handbag if not from her head.

At first Thatcher lacked the intellectual tools to back her anti-statist convictions. Her mentor Keith Joseph acquired the desperate courage of the convert. Thatcher simply acquired the arguments to back her instincts. Gradually she mastered the iconic anti-statist texts. But they were tools: instruments for battering down her opponents, not arguing with them. She did not bore you, but bored into you remorselessly.

She hated muddle, but she often caused it. She had vision, and she had detail, but was bad at strategic thinking. As a result, her governments often seemed to lurch from one thing to another. Her mind was not particularly orderly. She found it almost impossible to assemble her thoughts coherently. She once sent her foreign-policy adviser Charles Powell into the Downing Street garden, so that she could write out an important speech. Returning an hour or so later, he found half a page of crossed-out scribbles. Almost all her speeches and writings (including her memoirs) were carefully crafted for her from her 'instincts'. Her actual speech-making style was pedestrian, because of her emphatically wooden delivery. Even her few jokes seemed heavy. She made heaviness an art form.

She led from the front, often dragging a reluctant Cabinet and Civil Service in her wake. She frequently gave the impression of running against her own government : the voters always knew where she stood, even if she could not get her own way. She was not one for 'U-turns'. All of this marked a radical change in style for the accommodating Tory leadership stretching from Baldwin to Macmillan. (Edward Heath's corporatism does not quite fit. He tried to institutionalise the consensus, thereby undermining the freedom to compromise which the party leadership had always maintained.) But her colleagues admired her, too, for having the courage of their convictions.

Her style was remorselessly forensic and adversarial. According to her official biographer Charles Moore, 'She used every remark, every memo, every meeting as an opportunity to challenge existing habits, criticise any sign of ignorance, confusion or waste and preach incessantly the main aims of her administration.'[7] The only contradictions she could stand were on matters of fact. She ran out of friends in the Cabinet because she subjected everyone to the most emotionally exhausting arguments and also interrupted the whole time.

John Hoskyns, first head of Downing Street Policy Unit, sent her the most blistering memo ever penned by a civil servant to his political chief: 'You lack management competence. Your own leadership style is wrong . . . . You bully your weaker colleagues . . . You give little praise or credit, and you are too ready to blame others when things go wrong.'[8] She was unmoved. She was, as Roy Jenkins wrote, 'almost totally impervious to how much she annoys other people'. In the end, she annoyed too many people. Her berating in Cabinet of her chancellor, Geoffrey Howe, in December 1981, lit the fuse of his devastating resignation speech nine years later which effectively ended her premiership.

Of course, like any successful politician, Thatcher could play the long game. The clue to her success in government was that she was visionary in aim, cautious in method. Her retreats were tactical. A waiting game was sometimes best because, as David Runciman notes it played to her strengths of 'resilience and remorselessness'.[9] The Thatcherite ministry was a never-ending campaign, punctuated by set battles, with the miners, teachers, health workers, local authorities, sometimes broken off, but always resumed.

She always preferred winning a fight to a compromise. On the Falklands, she decided to fight, as soon as her military told her Britain could win. This win gained her the sobriquet 'Iron Lady'. The Falklands victory also sowed the seeds of hubris. 'It helped create the dangerous idea that she acted best when she acted alone', wrote David Owen. The other successful battles for which she is remembered were fought against sections of her own people – 'the enemy within' – like the miners and Ken Livingstone's Greater London Council. She tore into all those institutions which stood between the state and the market, professional, working class and local, which she saw as vested interests, corrupting the soul.

Towards the end her strategic sense failed utterly. It was suicidal – a sign of how hubristic she had become – to antagonise Geoffrey Howe on Europe, Nigel Lawson on economic policy, and half the electorate on poll tax all at the same time.

Thatcher was the first woman prime minister. But she was more than that: she was the first alpha female in British – and in western – politics. She was always immaculately dressed and made-up, with her handbag, her royal blue suits, and her bouffant rising like concrete from her head – a get-up which provoked horror in Lady Warnock, who found her 'packaged together in a way that's not entirely vulgar, just low'.[10] As always in Britain class feeling played a part in this remark: Thatcher's offence was to rise from the lower middle class without acquiring upper-class values. She caused mayhem in male clubland: upper-class men couldn't handle a bossy, argumentative woman who made personal remarks like, 'Nigel, get your hair cut' to her Chancellor. Nanny replaced the gentleman in Whitehall at knowing best. The parallel is not absurd, for although Thatcher abhorred the centralised state, she was determined to use state power to get her way – which involved top-down, centralising reforms, just as in Attlee's time.

One can overdo the nanny side. Some men found her irresistibly attractive; and she had a definite taste in men. She liked them either good-looking, intelligent or funny, preferably all three. Flirting was part of her technique of man management. The French president Francois Mitterrand caught something of this when he famously characterised her as 'having the eyes of Caligula and the mouth of Marilyn Monroe'. She used both steeliness and coyness to get her way. Those hooded eyes never lost their power to disconcert.

Thatcher's rise is part of the story of feminism. But there is a crucial difference. Her trajectory was not from being decorative to being useful (what one might call the *Downton Abbey* route) but from managing the household's business to managing the nation's. She always saw her role as that of an enlarged household manager, with the same parsimonious precepts. 'Quality within your income' she felt to be as necessary for governments as for individuals. She never hid her belief that women were better than men at getting things done. 'The cocks may crow,' she liked to say, 'but it's the hen that lays the egg.' Despised by feminists, Thatcher rewrote the history of the sex war. Her successors are the tiger mums of the business world.

Thatcher's relationship with the British people was patchy. Although she won three successive elections, the

Conservatives never polled more than 43 per cent of the popular vote, well below the levels achieved by Conservative
leaders Churchill, Eden, and Macmillan in the 1950s. Her
approval rating crept up over 50 per cent in only five of her
137 months in office, three of them after the Falklands war.
Admiration for her courage did not translate into love of her
personality or her politics. The British remained anti-Thatch-
erite in their political values, preferring muddle and drift and
compromise. They didn't like being put on their mettle, but
realised that 'the gravy train had to stop'.

Thatcher, like Blair, liked to describe herself as a 'normal,
ordinary' person, by which she presumably meant that her
instincts and prejudices were in tune with those of the great
British public. This is partly but far from completely true. The
daughter of Methodist shopkeepers in Grantham, Lincolnshire,
her England was the England of the lower middle class, chapel
and trade, neither rich nor poor, but feeling superior to both.
It was small town, and small business, proud of its sturdy self-
reliance, morally censorious. It deferred reluctantly to its
social superiors, and dreaded falling into welfare.

This class was the bedrock of Conservative support, but
was never dominant in the Conservative Party, whose leadership was patrician and therefore – in the view from Grantham
– contaminated by paternalist, collectivist and permissive values. The ascent of Thatcher within the party can be seen as a
revolt of the shopocracy against the pseudo-socialism of grandees like Harold Macmillan, a particular bête noire of
Thatcherite history. As every schoolchild knows, or knew then,
it was the nation of shopkeepers which had defeated Napoleon.

Of course some of the British values that Thatcher represented so emphatically were general British values: the
patriotism, the bloody-mindedness, the social conservatism.

She also reached across the class divide to the 'aspiring' working class. The 'property owning democracy' had long been a Conservative slogan, but Thatcher gave it much more substance. She was an enthusiastic redistributionist, provided the redistribution was not from the rich to the poor, but from the state to private individuals. She put British capitalism on a popular basis with the 'right to buy', which created 1.5 million extra homeowners, and by selling off state assets to millions of shareholders.

Even so, Thatcher's Britain left out vast swathes of the country. She never connected with Scotland, Wales or the north, whose industries she decimated. Her rule was sometimes violently resisted – in the inner-city riots of 1981, the miners' resistance to pit closures in 1985, the poll-tax riots of 1989. Thatcher herself blamed the violent outbreaks on the 'fashionable theories and permissive claptrap' of the 1960s. But they were only to be expected as she scythed her way through British society, demoralising regions, destroying institutions, breaking up communities.

Her indifference to Scotland cost the Conservatives their remaining seats there and helped the rise of the SNP. Studies show that Britain became steadily less Thatcherite in its values the longer her rule went on. She owed her power to a divided Opposition and a first-past-the-post electoral system which enabled her to attempt vast transformations with minority support. Many leaders are chastened by the thinness of their mandates. Not so Thatcher. She was a crusader for right.

The prime minister had the support of an outstanding team of ministers. The repentant spender Keith Joseph gave her intellectual self-confidence. Geoffrey Howe and Nigel Lawson, her two Chancellors, made of her instincts a

coherent strategy – Lawson gave a sense of ideological direction; Howe, diffident in manner, provided tenacity of purpose.
The three leaders also appealed to different sections of the
Tory Party. Thatcher was – or became – the standard-bearer
for the anti-Europeans and moral authoritarians. Howe reas-
sured the traditional right and also bound in the pro-Europeans.
Lawson was a free-marketeer with libertarian instincts.
United in the battle against socialism, they fell out once the
battle was won. Losing Lawson and Howe in quick succession in 1989 and 1990 narrowed Thatcher's base in the
Conservative Party, and numbered her days in power.

Thatcher enjoyed three strokes of luck. First, North Sea oil
started to come on stream at the end of the 1970s. At its peak
it contributed 8 per cent to tax revenues. This 'gave a healthy
kick-start to the very rapid reduction in the budget deficit in
the course of the 1980s'.[11] It also caused a rise in the exchange
rate which increased unemployment, and became an unintended part of the anti-inflationary cure. From the mid-1980s
she benefited from another windfall, the shift in the terms of
trade in Britain's favour. Thatcher was lucky for the same reason that Gorbachev was unlucky.

The second stroke of luck was the Falklands War. In 1981,
the Argentinean dictator General Galtieri seized the Falkland
Islands, a tiny windswept British colony off the coast of Latin
America, inhabited by 3,000 hardy British settlers. Britain still
had the third largest navy in the world, and Thatcher had no
hesitation in dispatching a formidable armada to the southern
Atlantic, where British forces, in extremely adverse conditions, and with some help from presidents Ronald Reagan of
the USA and Augusto Pinochet of Chile, recaptured the
islands. The Falklands were a throwback; the curtain had
already fallen on empire. Nevertheless, the British victory in

the Falklands was a defining moment in Thatcher's relationship with the British people. It restored British pride, and gave
her a psychological mandate to govern: it was popular with
the miners who would soon be fighting her pit closures.
Equally important, it established her authority in her own
party.

Finally, Thatcher was massively helped by the decline and
disarray on the left. In the early 1980s, the Labour Party reached
a point of crisis which many thought might be terminal. In
1974, its share of the popular vote dropped below 40 per cent for
the first time since 1945; in 1983, at 27.6 per cent, it reached its
lowest point since 1918. It then looked as though it might be
replaced by the SDP–Liberal Alliance. Affluence and deindustrialisation had shrunk its traditional working-class base; its
growing ideological extremism alienated the 'progressive' middle class. By the 1980s, its heartland had become the public
sector, with the lower reaches of the academic estate – the
'polytechnocracy' – serving it as a 'socialist intelligentsia'.
Thatcher saw that she no longer had a cohesive working class
to confront. She could win pitched battles in the new war
between the public and private sectors of the economy.

Thatcherism in theory and practice

Thatcher is the only prime minister who has given her name
to an 'ism'. This is not because she was an intellectual, but
because she had a set of instincts and values round which ideologies could coalesce and strategies develop. Thatcherism
was a philosophically driven revolution. It was an assault on
the British national disease, mental inertia. That it found its
home in the 'stupid party' is not the least of its ironies.

Thatcherism was a theory of macro-management based

on stable prices and sound finance; a theory of micro-policy based on market deregulation and improved incentives for enterprise; and a theory of social policy based on individual responsibility and a wide distribution of private assets.

Inflation was to be conquered by means of a 'Medium-Term Financial Strategy', announced in 1980. Money supply growth was to be reduced gradually over four years by pre-announced amounts; a concurrent reduction in the budget deficit would enable the monetary targets to be achieved at lower interest rates. The government expected that the announcement of the monetary targets would lower the inflationary expectations of wage bargainers, enabling prices to come down with only a moderate increase in unemployment. It did not work this way. The monetary targets were consistently overshot, but inflation fell sharply ahead of plan, from 17.8 per cent in 1980 to 4.6 per cent in 1983. What brought inflation down was not monetarism, but a government-created depression. A 17 per cent interest rate drove up the exchange rate, already strengthened by North Sea oil; superimposed on this was Sir Geoffrey Howe's savage deflationary budget in March 1981, which took £4 billion out of the economy when unemployment was already rising. The Howe budget had a crucial effect, not on expectations about inflation, but on expectations about government policy. Its message was clear: Keynesianism would not be reactivated, whatever the unemployment cost. This was heavy. Between 1979 and 1982, unemployment rose to 10 per cent, as bad as in the 1920s, and went on creeping up till 1986, hitting 3 million. In a letter to *The Times* on 30 March 1981 364 economists anathemised the government's policy. The fact that recovery from the depression started a few weeks later has passed into

Thatcherite legend.* Between 1982 and 1987 the British economy grew by 4 per cent a year.

By 1984, the new Chancellor of the Exchequer, Nigel Lawson, was publicly ready to stand Keynesianism on its head. In his Mais lecture of 1984 he enunciated the new wisdom: 'The conquest of inflation should be the objective of macroeconomic policy. And the creation of conditions conducive to growth and employment should be the objective of micreconomic policy.'[12]

Concomitantly with its inflation-busting programme, the government vigorously set about creating an 'enterprise economy'. The showpieces of this effort were deregulation, trade union reform, privatisation, reducing the size of the state and cutting benefits.

Deregulation of the financial sector came first, with the removal of capital controls in 1980, followed, in 1986, by the freeing of banks to compete with building societies in the mortgage market. These measures strengthened the primacy of the City in the British economy, and over the years restored its global pre-eminence.

The trade unions were in Thatcher's sights from the start, though not till she got Norman Tebbit into the Department of Employment in 1981 did she get the laws she needed. Thenceforth a raft of labour legislation cumulatively reduced the scope of the unions' legal immunities to vanishing point. Her

---

* The causes of this counter-intuitive result are still disputed. See Philip Booth (ed.), *Were 364 Economists All Wrong?* (London: Institute of Economic Affairs, 2006). In the monetarist corner, Tim Congdon celebrates the demise of the 'naive Keynesianism' on display in the letter. On this reading, the 364 economists' mistake was to overlook the role of money in determining demand and national income. On the other side, Steven Nickell defends his signature on the original letter, arguing that the combination of fiscal and monetary tightening was overkill, which produced a long and unnecessary period of high unemployment.

anti-union offensive was massively helped by the hubris of
Arthur Scargill, leader of the National Union of Mineworkers.
Having caved in to the miners in 1981, before she was ready to
take them on, Thatcher showed both coolness and courage in
letting the Coal Board take the heat of a year-long battle with
the NUM in 1984–5, avoiding the face-saving compromise
over 'beer and sandwiches' at No. 10 which all previous
governments would have accepted. The result was to end the
'coal factor' in Britain's industrial relations by ending the coal
industry. Except for the year of that battle, the number of days
lost through strike action fell steadily in the 1980s and 90s to
their lowest level in the twentieth century: from 957,000 in
1980 to 48,000 in 1992 and 30,000 in 1998. Union density – the
proportion of the workforce unionised – fell from 55 per cent
in 1979 to 31 per cent by 1993, its lowest since the 1930s.
Individual contracts replaced collective contracts over large
swathes of the economy. In political-economy terms, all this
meant a decisive break from the old project, inspired by the
war economy, of achieving centralised wage-bargaining
within the framework of an incomes policy.

Privatisation started in Thatcher's first term, but accelerated in the second. It turned out to be her most striking policy
innovation, taken up and copied all over the world, finally in
the ex-Communist countries. Fiercely resisted by the nationalised industries and their unions, it proved very popular and
millions of their employees, as well as the general public,
bought shares in the new private companies. This created as
many shareholders as trade unionists. However, it failed to
reverse the long-term concentration of shares in the hands of
big investors; the percentage of total shares owned by individuals fell from 28 per cent in 1979 to 20 per cent by the end
of the century. Today, many of the privatised companies are

foreign-owned. Britain's electricity market is dominated by EDF Energy and E.ON, the French and German state-owned electricity companies.

By 1992 two thirds of the formerly state-owned industries in the UK had been transferred to the private sector, consisting of forty-six major businesses, employing 900,000 people. Among the main privatisation sales were those of British Aerospace, Cable and Wireless, Britoil, Jaguar, British Telecom, British Leyland, British Gas, British Airways, Rolls-Royce and British Steel. With the sale of British Coal and British Rail in the 1990s, the commercial public sector virtually disappeared. The privatisation programme, 'selling off the family silver' as the aged Macmillan called it, had a double fiscal benefit: it reduced budget deficits (and therefore public spending) and raised £32.5 billion of revenue, allowing tax cuts.

The Tories were committed to a smaller state – one that taxed less, and spent less. The most important step in tax reform was Nigel Lawson's 1988 budget which both reduced direct taxes and simplified the tax system. Six previous bands of income tax running from 27 per cent to 60 per cent were replaced with two rates of 25 per cent and 40 per cent, covering both earned and investment income. The rates of capital gains tax and inheritance tax were aligned with income tax; corporation tax came down in stages from 53 to 35 per cent. The tax reform was made possible by the Conservative success in eliminating the budget deficit. By 1987 a deficit of 5 per cent of GDP in 1979–80 had become a surplus of 0.75 per cent and 3 per cent a year later. These were the only two years budgets were balanced in the eighteen years of Conservative government.

Cuts in public spending were difficult to achieve. Much of the deficit reduction under Lawson came from reductions in spending on industry and associated regional problems, housing, and interest on the national debt. An important, and cumulatively important, source of saving came from the government's decision in 1979 to link the value of the state retirement pension to prices rather than earnings. This saved the government the equivalent of 5 per cent of GDP between 1979 and 1998. The cut in pensioner entitlements made possible a redirection of public spending towards 'core' services like health and education.

Among the biggest spenders were the local authorities. The government's efforts to reduce local-authority spending (which counted as part of the central budget) started with 'rate capping' and compulsory tender for some local-authority services. In Thatcher's second term, the government abolished the high-spending metropolitan authorities set up by Heath, including the Greater London Council. A hankering for a more permanent solution to escalating local authority spending led the prime minister into the fatal policy of the 'poll tax'. The idea was to get every householder over eighteen to pay a fixed-rate 'community charge'. This would bring home to local voters the enormity of local-authority extravagance. The tax was logical, transparent – and politically disastrous. It was one of the most important causes of her downfall in November 1990. Its repeal was the first act of the new Major government.

There were other limits to Tory tax radicalism. There was little hope of further tax cuts without tackling the welfare state, by far the biggest spender. This Thatcher was understandably reluctant to do, recognising that it was a political minefield. In 1980 the social services accounted for almost half of government spending. Unlike the commercial public sector, which charged for services, they could not be removed from the public balance sheet. The government's treble approach, developing gradually, was to fund the services less generously, redirect spending to priority areas like health and education, and insert targets and competition into delivery to get better 'value for money'. Under the NHS 'internal market' introduced in 1990, the purchase and provision of health care was split up with government-funded GP holders buying health care from competing hospitals; open enrolment in secondary schools, started in 1988, allowed parents to choose between competing secondary schools. Resort to user choice in parts of the state sector to lever up efficiency and standards produced a series of conflicts with the public service providers which absorbed a large amount of energy and political capital. Everywhere, the Thatcher government seemed to be assaulting hallowed autonomies which were, often enough, simply a front for vested interests.

Thatcher's policy for building a 'popular' capitalism centred on the old Tory dream of a 'property-owning democracy'. Its keynote was selling council houses to their tenants. Under the 'right to buy' policy, 1.7 million tenants bought their own properties between 1979 and 1992 at heavily subsidised prices, nearly all for the first time. The proportion of home owners increased from 40 per cent in the 1960s to a peak of 69.7 per cent in 2002; 50 per cent of pensioners became house owners. The sales realised £24 billion. Industrial privatisation plus selling off council houses was the greatest dispossession of public property since the dissolution of the monasteries.

These were the main lines of the Thatcher reform project. In October 1990, the Iron Lady was deposed by an internal coup in the Tory Party, following her failure to win a sufficient majority to secure re-election as party leader against Michael Heseltine – the first incumbent prime minister ever to be deposed by his or her party. Her fall was a product of both hubris and inattention. Like all long-serving prime ministers, she had accumulated too much disaffection on the back benches of her own party. There were also palpable policy failures: by the late 1980s, inflation again seemed out of control, and the disaster of the poll tax was dragging the government down in the opinion polls. But moderates were also antagonised by Thatcher's increasingly strident tone over Europe.

Britain's role in the EU under Thatcher was not entirely obstructive. Britain largely shaped the Single European Act of 1986, which aimed to complete the 'single market'. It was to the political pretensions and collectivist leanings of the European Union that Thatcher objected. In her famous Bruges speech of 1988 she thundered: 'We have not successfully rolled back the frontiers of the state in Britain, only to see them reimposed at a European level, with a European super-state exercising a new dominance from Brussels.' The *Sun* echoed this populist line in 1990 with 'Up Yours Delors'. Heath and Macmillan saw Europe as a way of projecting British power. But Thatcher – who saw no differences between different varieties of collectivism – thought it much better to be linked to the USA than Europe. It was not the defence of British interests in a narrow sense, but the nature of British society, that she was really concerned with.

Her speech in Bruges opened a rift in the Tory Party which would destroy not only her government, but also that of her successor, John Major. In her reading of British history, the special British contribution to Europe had been 'to prevent Europe from falling under the domination of a single power'. That power was now being exercised from Brussels, and Britain was bound to resist it if it was to remain true to itself.

This was Thatcher speaking with the voice of Elizabeth I. It was not the voice that Geoffrey Howe wanted to hear, and two weeks after his resignation from government in November 1990, the tearful Iron Lady was gone.

The audit of Thatcherism

When Thatcher came to power, Sir Douglas Wass, permanent secretary of the Treasury, told her that the Treasury's task was to 'manage decline'. In fact, the Treasury had been 'managing decline' for the best part of a century, with indifferent success, since the habits of its masters, shaped in more spacious times, continually outran their means. Thatcher was the first prime minister to recognise that, having shed its imperial responsibilities, Britain's decline had been completed. It was now a middle-sized European power, and countries like France and Germany, not the United States and Russia, were its true comparators. Policy was set to recovery mode. In Nicholas Crafts's sober summary: 'The reforms pursued by the Conservatives after 1979 and largely accepted subsequently by New Labour have improved the incentive structures facing firms and workers and imply that growth performance has been better than would have been expected under a continuation of the policies of the 1970s.'[13]

By giving the British the sense that long-term decline was not inevitable, Thatcherism released dormant energies, in both private business and public administration. But it was in no sense a 'final solution' – there can never be such – to the problems of either the economic or political government of Britain, and since her days we have become more aware of what these are.

The Thatcher solution to the 'crisis of governability' consisted of four elements.

First, there was the macroeconomic framework of Lawson's 1984 Mais lecture, which accepted that government's responsibility – at least in normal times – was to control inflation, not to determine the level of employment. The second was the destruction of classical socialism through privatisation. The third was the weakening of trade unionism. The fourth was the start of the 'internal market' in public services. Until the crisis of 2008 all four seemed durable; all four were accepted by New Labour, so the Thatcher settlement lasted from 1979 to 2010, about as long as the post-war consensus which preceded it. The crash of 2008 called all four into question, and a new settlement has not been reached. The Thatcherite legacy has also been apparent in foreign policy. Thatcher mapped out a distinctively British path to economic revival which chimed in with the general nationalist thrust of her policies. Her initial battles to get a reduction of British contributions to the Common Agricultural Policy hardened into open hostility to the European Union's policies and pretensions. One of the permanent legacies of Thatcherism is the realisation that Britain is very different from the Continent. As she inimitably remarked, 'We visit. They are there.' The Macmillan–Heath idea that Europe was, in some sense, an answer to the British disease, disappeared, being replaced with the glorification of the 'special relationship' with the United States.

Although Thatcherism created a new settlement, it resembled its predecessor in not being a complete settlement.

First, and most obvious, Thatcherism did not settle the governing arrangements of the United Kingdom. In fact, Thatcherite policies put the unitary state under unprecedented strain. She wanted to strengthen central government, not weaken it, and this for two reasons: she wanted to use it to implement her policies, just as Attlee and Heath had done; and she was a British nationalist, who wanted to preserve the British nation-state identity from being absorbed in a European 'super-state'.

So she had no interest in the staples of constitutional reform aimed at limiting the power of central government: checks and balances, voting reform, dispersal of power to localities and nationalities. However, her ruthless use of power to carry out highly divisive policies put constitutional reform back on the map for the first time since 1909, when the Lords threw out Lloyd George's budget. Longer-term forces were also weakening the hallowed doctrine of parliamentary sovereignty. No peace between the Protestants and Catholics in Northern Ireland was possible without acknowledging the 'Irish dimension'. Despite Thatcher's increasingly frenzied objections, legislative power was slowly draining away from Westminster to Brussels. And Britain itself was becoming multinational, making the concept of a unique British identity increasingly cloudy.

Second, the question of the future of the welfare state remained unsettled. Thatcher herself favoured a 'safety net' concept of welfare, with a limitation of entitlements to those in genuine need. State benefits would be targeted on the poor; most people would be expected to make their own provision, through saving or insurance, for their pensions, health care and the education of their children. However, reform of the welfare state along these lines proved impossible. In fact there was continuing pressure to increase, not reduce, public spending on welfare. Thatcher railed against the 'dependency culture'. But the very policies used to create an 'enterprise culture' produced an even larger dependency culture, by increasing unemployment which automatically increased relative poverty. By 1985 the population at least partly dependent on cash benefits had risen to 5 million: it was to creep up to almost 6 million ten years later. By the 1980s it had become common to talk about the growth of an 'underclass', a stagnant pool of poverty, entirely dependent on benefits, which was impervious to the general improvement in economic conditions.

A third, certainly unintended, legacy of Thatcherism was the growth of bureaucracy. This arose from the determination of the Thatcher governments to ensure that the privatised utilities and all bodies in receipt of public money (including local authorities) behaved *as though* they were businesses, even though they were not (and could not be) subject to proper market disciplines, including the final sanction of bankruptcy. The complex structure of regulation and incentives set up to monitor performance and raise standards was greatly expanded under John Major and New Labour; its administration and monitoring required an ever-growing volume of red tape and army of officials, managers, accountants; it failed to provide a stable halfway house between public and private ownership.

The greatest question mark over Thatcherism's legacy concerned its social and moral values. Thatcherism was avowedly a revivalist doctrine, not a complete social philosophy. 'There is no such thing as society', Thatcher notoriously proclaimed in 1987, 'there are individual men and women. And there are families.' People must help themselves and each other, and only rely on the government as a last resort. This was the philosophy of the shopkeeper's daughter from Grantham. But it was a one-sided distillation of British experience. The thrusting and often brutal individualism which made Britain so successful has always been softened by a protective collectivism, embedded in the social structure itself, and only fitfully imposed by the state. In emphasising market efficiency, Thatcherism embraced the economics of Victorianism without its paternalism. It weakened all those intermediate associations which stood between the state and the market, producing a flattened landscape. Institutions were judged instrumentally – in terms of their contribution to GDP rather than to the good society. Freedom and justice came to be celebrated by their political spokesmen as contributing to economic efficiency; the monarchy was good for tourism. The narrowing of the social content of politics impoverished public discourse; it also left the door wide open to political extremes.

Thatcher projected a secularised version of Low Church Anglicanism; she didn't use religion as a base for ethical values. The one exception was in a major speech to the General Assembly of the Church of Scotland on 21 May 1988, where she tried to establish a religious foundation for what she was doing. Not surprisingly this turned out to be completely congruent with Thatcherite values. Individuals have a God-given responsibility to create wealth and a charitable duty to the poor. A second theme of the speech was the rejection of value relativism and multiculturalism: 'Christian religion . . . is a fundamental part of our heritage.' Foreigners were welcome in Britain but 'the essence of our own identity must be retained'. This attempt to stake out the moral high ground was directed against churchmen who accused Thatcherism of promoting greed and selfishness – what Labour leader Neil Kinnock called the 'loadsamoney' culture. It was also an effort to justify what libertarian critics called her moral bossiness, shown in such areas as a law banning the 'promotion' of homosexuality in schools and tougher codes against sex and violence on television.

Moral Thatcherism turned out to be more popular than economic Thatcherism.[13] It was also in line with Thatcher's nationalist vision. But it failed to offer convincing social underpinnings for 'British values'. The truth was that those Methodist virtues, shared with much of Old Labour, which provided Thatcher with a moral context for economic liberalism, had already been eroded to a large degree, and the intensified pursuit of material wealth which she encouraged eroded them still further. Gratification of wants – maximal and instant, natural or artificially stimulated – does not accord with the ethics of saints, soldiers and scholars.

The unavoidable question is: could the benefits of renewed entrepreneurial vigour have been achieved at less cost? Between 1979 and 1981 there was a rapid decline in British output – 5 per cent of GDP, 15 per cent of manufactured output – and a doubling of unemployment to over 10 per cent; 2 million jobs went from manufacturing. The economy started growing rapidly after 1982, but there was no complete recovery. The boom of 1983–7 led to another collapse, with another million jobs lost in manufacturing in 1990–2. The pattern of recovery and collapse was strikingly similar to that of the 1930s. Between 1979 and 1993, unemployment fluctuated between 6 per cent and 12 per cent, a record at least as bad as in that of the interwar years which gave birth to Keynesian economics. The social price was equally heavy. In creating a society in which limitations are brutally exposed, Thatcherism tore apart the easy-going traditional fabric of British life. Industrial deserts were created, from which phoenixes were left to rise. There was a legacy of inner-city problems. For those growing up in the industrial heartlands of England, Thatcher foreclosed the future. The new economy based on finance and shopping skipped a generation. Eighteen years after Margaret Thatcher left office, the pendulum has started to swing back to government interventionism, as the world economic downturn revealed the flakiness of the financially-driven British economy she created.

The Major interregnum 1992–1997

John Major's decency, even diffidence, helped win the Conservatives a fourth term in April 1992 in the depth of the recession, disproving the theory that 'it's the economy, stupid'. Despite this promising start, the Major years of 1992–7 saw the unravelling of Conservativism under weak leadership. The mishandling of sterling's exodus from the European Exchange Rate Mechanism on 16 September 1992 ('Black Wednesday') cost the government its Chancellor, Norman Lamont, and its reputation for economic competence, which not even Kenneth Clarke's successful custodianship of the Treasury could retrieve. Historically, the two most important achievements of the Major government were to negotiate the 'opt out' of sterling from the euro in the Maastricht Treaty of February 1992, and to set Northern Ireland on the path to peace.

Europe exposed irreconcilable differences between left and right within the Tory Party. Euro-sceptics and hardcore Thatcherites – aided by unhelpful interventions from the Lady herself – held the party hostage and prevented it from re-engaging with the political centre. Major failed to reconcile the warring factions under his continually threatened leadership. This enabled a resurgent Labour Party, now called New

Labour, under a bold and dynamic young leader, Tony Blair, to capture the initiative. Blair was careful to wound but not kill Major, and allowed the Tory Party to kill itself. In this way he became what the electorate had wanted from Major, namely 'Thatcher with a human face'.

Chapter 11

The New Labour Project
1997–2010

Mrs Thatcher was absolutely on the side of history.

Tony Blair

The Lessons of History
16. Margaret Thatcher (l); 17. Tony Blair by Alistair Adams (r)

With New Labour we enter the domain of contemporary history proper. The historian cannot easily apply to it the test of significance appropriate to earlier periods. To try to write about it from a distance would be to leave out events which are still fresh in the mind. Will a historian even bother to mention antisocial behaviour orders (ASBOs) in fifty years' time? How will the reputations of Blair and Brown eventually settle down? So to write about the New Labour years now is inevitably to include lots of material which today's reader will find odd if omitted, but which will be of scant interest to the future. As a result this chapter will have a different feel from earlier ones, more immediate, more up to date, and full of ephemera which history will discard.

Labour had had a torrid time in the 1980s. The left wing's capture of the party had produced the first breakaway since Oswald Mosley's New Party in 1931. The Social Democratic Party was started on 26 March 1981, under the leadership of the 'Gang of Four' – Roy Jenkins, formerly deputy leader of the Labour Party, who had just retired as president of the European Commission, and three former Labour ministers, David Owen, William Rogers and Shirley Williams. Eventually thirty MPs joined. Together with eleven Liberal MPs they formed an 'Alliance', initially under Jenkins's leadership. The Alliance narrowly failed to overtake Labour in the popular vote in 1983, with Labour getting 27.6 per cent to the Alliance's 25.6. Overtaking Labour would have given the Alliance a tremendous psychological boost. Nevertheless, the Alliance left a powerful legacy. Roy Jenkins's 'break to the centre' foreshadowed the much enlarged Liberal Democrats of the 1990s and David Owen's 'social market economy' offered a 'third way' between the market economy and traditional social democracy.

The electoral challenge of the Alliance as well as its drubbing by Thatcher in 1983 shocked the Labour Party into sobriety. Neil Kinnock, who succeeded Michael Foot,

Callaghan's successor, as party leader in 1983, courageously moved the party to the centre. There were still huge obstacles to recovery in the shape of the miners' leader Arthur Scargill and Ken Livingstone, the leader of London's GLC, whose attempt to build socialism in County Hall helped to ensure that Thatcherism continued at Westminster. Nevertheless, Kinnock's leadership brought about a revival: he stood up to the Trotskyist Militant Tendency and ditched Labour's most unpopular policies. He also took marketing seriously by appointing Peter Mandelson in 1986 as Labour's first director of communications.

Labour got the better of the political game in the 1990s. Paradoxically, popular Thatcherite policies like privatisation, trade union reform, tax cuts and sales of council houses made it 'safer' for the middle class to vote Labour, since no government was likely to reverse them. At the same time, Thatcherism's neglect of the public services enabled Labour to project itself as more 'social' without being socialist. Labour strategists were quicker to understand the new politics in which the media and public opinion replaced political parties and ideologies as the central players, and in which control of the message was the key to power.

But it was also lucky. It was lucky to lose in 1992 and inherit a sound economy in 1997. It was lucky in the weakness and divisions of the Major government over Europe. It was lucky that the ERM debacle damaged the Tory reputation for economic competence. It was lucky in the collapse of the Soviet Union. Soviet collapse removed the right's most potent message: that the left was weak on Communism and so on national defence. Unilateral nuclear disarmament, which Labour had espoused in the early 1980s, became politically, if not morally, irrelevant.

Above all, it was lucky in the death of Kinnock's successor John Smith in 1994, insofar as this let in the modernising team of Blair and Brown.

Blair–Brown: the fractious duopoly

The New Labour governments of 1997–2010 were led by Tony Blair and Gordon Brown, successively prime ministers. So the New Labour record is in part a judgement on them as leaders. Labour had in Tony Blair the most personable political leader of modern times, in Gordon Brown the most thoughtful. Blair was the butterfly, Brown the digger. It should have been a powerful combination, and in fact was. But it was disfigured by a quite exceptional political rivalry which made it seriously dysfunctional much of the time.

Both had entered Parliament in 1983 in their early thirties, shared the same office-room for nine years, and had the same aim: to make Labour 'electable'. In continuous conversation with each other and with Peter Mandelson, interspersed with visits to the United States to study the New Democrats, they worked out a Labour 'project' which would marry the popular elements of Thatcherism – go-getting individualism, moderate taxation, law and order, a strong defence – to the popular elements of social democracy – good public services and 'inclusion' – within a financial framework which avoided 'boom and bust'. This mix, they hoped, by broadening the electoral appeal of 'New' Labour beyond the sectarian constituencies of both Thatcherism and 'old' Labour, would turn Labour into the natural governing party.

Tony Blair is the biggest enigma of twentieth-century

British politics. No leader of the Labour Party – possibly any party – had such shallow political roots. Throughout his political life he gave the impression of being in the Labour Party, but not of it. When, in 1992, Labour's leader John Smith made him Shadow Secretary of State at the Home Office, Kenneth Clarke remarked of his opposite number 'He's so shadowy it's ridiculous', and went on to quote a jingle: 'As I was going up a stair, I met a man who wasn't there.' But Blair's very political *emptiness*, allied to his boyish good looks and winning personality, made him an ideal carrier for a nebulous project.

Born in Edinburgh in 1953, Tony Blair came from the aspiring middle class. (His maternal grandfather was a butcher; his father, a barrister and a lecturer at Durham University, had been fostered by a shipyard rigger.) He was a late developer. At his Scottish public school, Fettes, he went through the usual teenage rebellion; at Oxford, where he read law, he played a bit of rock and roll and discovered a social conscience. He and his future wife, Cherie Booth, daughter of an actor, met as pupils in the London chambers of a Labour lawyer, Derry Irvine. They both became successful barristers, and settled down in a large house in Islington with three children. Blair joined the Labour Party only after he left Oxford in 1975. He was soon given a helping hand by those who glimpsed his potential as a vote-winner.

He started his political life as a political ingénue: a clean sheet on which others could write their scripts; a vehicle through which contemporary Britain could express itself. He was elected Labour MP for Sedgefield, Durham, in 1983 at the age of thirty; eleven years later he was leader of the Labour Party, and three years after that prime minister. The premiership was his first and last political office.

Once party leader, Blair became the greatest vote-winner Labour has ever had. He was a consummate charmer, communicator and political – though not sexual – seducer. In literary terms, he was a natural 'best-seller', unlike Brown, whose subjects and style repulsed mass adulation. He was helped by the unappealing Tory leaders after Major: William Hague, Iain Duncan-Smith, and Michael Howard. Of Hague it was said 'In an age of appearances his own did not help, part foetus and part death's head, apparently without having gone through the usual intervening phase of human life.'[1]

His talents fitted the conditions of dissolving class alignments, expiring ideologies, and the rise of shopping in Britain. His instincts were those of Middle England, flush with property and anxious for its security, and he cultivated its language. He presented himself as an 'ordinary' bloke, someone 'typically British . . . [who liked to] have time and comfort in the loo'.[2] He was from neither the ruling nor the working class; neither a 'toff' nor a 'weirdo', neither highbrow nor lowbrow. With his superb presentational skills, he was the ideal politician for a media age.

Although Blair was politically void, he was not morally so. Because he did not parade them, most people were blind to the strength of his religious beliefs, which he got from his mother and which were reinforced by Cherie. His Christianity did not answer all, or even most, of the practical questions he would face in politics. But they gave him the moral certitude for the boldest decision of his premiership, to invade Iraq, an event which both crowned and destroyed his political career.

Under his leadership the Labour Party won a 179-seat majority in 1997, a 167-seat majority in 2001, and a 60-seat majority in 2005. It lost, fairly narrowly, in 2010 under Brown, whose people skills were much inferior.*

Unlike Blair, Gordon Brown was rooted in a specific Labour culture – that of Scottish Presbyterianism and Scottish Labour history. (As a young university lecturer he wrote a book on the leader of the Independent Labour Party James Maxton.) Born in 1951, son of a church minister in Kirkcaldy, Fife, a serious rugby accident when he was sixteen had threatened Brown's eyesight. The success of the NHS in later saving one eye left an abiding commitment to socialised medicine. He bullied his way to the top of student politics at Edinburgh University and, eventually, Labour politics at Westminster. What defined him was his intellectual energy, his relentless stamina, and his personal insecurity, which inclined him to paranoia.

At first, Brown was the senior of the two. He taught Blair his political craft, hammered Blair's restlessness into reformist shape, handed him his earliest sound bite – 'Tough on crime, tough on the causes of crime'. Brown assumed that he himself would inherit the succession to John Smith. He failed to notice that while the Master was dourly educating his party in economic realities, the Apprentice was racing ahead of him

---

* General election, 1 May 1997: Labour 13,518,167 (418 seats, 43.2 per cent of the vote), Conservative 9,600,943 (165, 30.7 per cent), Liberal Democrats 5,242,947 (forty-six, 16.8 per cent)

General election, 7 June 2001: Labour 10,724,953 (413 seats, 40.7 per cent of the vote), Conservative 8,357,615 (166, 31.7 per cent), Liberal Democrats 4,814,321 (fifty-two, 18.3 per cent)

General election, 5 May 2005: Labour 9,552,436 (355 seats, 35.2 per cent of the vote), Conservative 8,784,915 (198, 32.4 per cent), Liberal Democrats 5,985,454 (sixty-two, 22.0 per cent)

General election, 6 May 2010: Labour 8,606,517 (258 seats, 29 per cent of the vote), Conservative 10,703,654 (306, 36.1 per cent), Liberal Democrats 6,836,248 (fifty-seven, 23.0 per cent)

in popularity. So it came as a profound shock when, after Smith's sudden death in May 1994, Blair, revealing an iron fist in a velvet glove, told him that he intended to stand for leader.

At the now famous dinner at the Granita restaurant in Islington on 31 May 1994, Brown agreed not to oppose Blair for the vacant leadership. Few thought he would have won: Blair's offence, in Brown's eyes, was to stand at all. As part of the Granita 'deal' Blair ceded Brown control over economic policy, reserving foreign and constitutional policy and education for himself. According to Brown, Blair committed himself to a ten-year leadership, promising to quit in time for Brown to fight a third-term election should Labour be in government. Welfare reform was left a grey area over which both, at different times, would claim sovereignty.

The events of 1994 left a deep resentment in Brown which coloured the whole New Labour era. A jovial, convivial man turned into a dour, suspicious character, who saw plots against him everywhere. Brown always believed that he, not Blair, should have been prime minister. But after 1994 there was no easy way for Brown to seize Blair's crown. What he could do was to make Blair's life as premier as intolerable as possible, in which he succeeded admirably. But if their former friendship withered, both men were tethered to each other by need. Blair needed Brown to run the economy; and Brown needed Blair to win elections. This is what kept the partnership in place, if not in health. Blair might have got rid of Brown in his second term, but he flinched before Brown's relentless assaults on his position – he described conversations with Brown as like having dental treatment without the anaesthetic – but he found his own ways of numbing the pain. Brown wavered between supporting Blair for the sake of the 'project' and undermining him for the sake of the succession.

When New Labour came to power they ran rival courts, and each court 'briefed' against the other, with Brown's 'attack dogs' Ed Balls and Charlie Whelan being the worst offenders. It is testimony to the weakness, and unpopularity, of the Conservatives that they failed to exploit the suppurating wound at the heart of New Labour.

The politics of electability

Labour's problem of electability long predated the coming of Margaret Thatcher. Between 1918 and 1979 it had a working majority in the Commons (that is, ten seats or more over all other parties) for just nine years, compared to forty-one for the Conservatives. The people's party, it seemed, stood for things which too few of the people wanted. In the early 1980s, it swung to the left, while Britain moved to the right. After a dismal fourth successive defeat in 1992, Blair wrote that winning required 'not a shift in tactics . . . but a project of renewal'.

Initially, this meant not so much developing a new philosophy as scrapping those bits of the old philosophy not already abandoned by Kinnock and Smith. One symbol of the past had remained undisturbed since the party's 1918 constitution was drawn up – Clause IV, which committed it to the 'common ownership' of the means of production, distribution and exchange. This had helped to block what would have been the most attractive alternative to the Conservatives – a Labour–Liberal Party.

Blair understood the power of symbols. In 1995, as party leader, he persuaded the Labour Party to jettison Clause IV, something Gaitskell had failed to do in 1959. Capitalism no longer needed to be the love that dare not speak its name.

The politics of the 1980s and 90s was a struggle for the

allegiance of the upwardly mobile. Thatcher won the first round with her curbs on trade unions, her championing of small business, her council-house sales, and her asset-distributing privatisations. But Thatcher never understood that the people who supported her against socialism, trade unions and high taxes wanted good public services too. If Labour could find a way of helping the worst off without annoying the aspiring middle class it had a potentially winning formula. But it had to get it across.

The style of political parties reflects the societies in which they exist. Affluence, entertainment and shopping had eroded the old forms of representative democracy. By the end of the twentieth century politicians faced a much flatter political landscape, in which political activity was largely confined to single-issue lobbies, political parties existed mainly to provide platforms for leaders competitive only in their lust for power, and in which those leaders advertised their physical assets in a political marketplace of the disconnected and myopic. Declining political participation coincided with the rise of a hyper-democratic ethos, distrustful of elites. Politicians responded to these developments by relegating party activists to the fringes, elevating the technique of opinion-poll sampling, and exploiting the media.

When in the mid-1980s Peter Mandelson formed the Shadow Communications Agency, he began the revolution in Labour's marketing strategy which was a condition of success in the new political climate. His assistant, Philip Gould, a former advertising executive, made extensive use of 'focus groups' to alert the leadership to popular thinking. What the people thought, he reported to his political masters, was that taxes were bad, markets were good, and the public services were inefficient.

Mandelson's reputation as an arch-manipulator and fixer led some, even in the Labour Party, to call him the 'Prince of Darkness'.[3] Labour learnt the hard way that policies had to be popular, 'bomb-proof' and projected in a disciplined, relentless manner. Relatively open debate was replaced with an attempt to marshal and manipulate opinion – so-called 'spin' – first in the party then in the country. By 1997 Labour had raced ahead of the Tories in forging a political style suited to a media-obsessed age. A small pointer to the reversal is that by the late 1990s, Maurice Saatchi, Thatcher's advertising guru, was producing precise but unsaleable tax policies, while Blair dominated the ether with vague but attractive sound bites.

Blair, Brown and Mandelson all believed that manipulation of the media was the key to getting the New Labour 'brand' across to the public. They remembered the newspaper bruising of Neil Kinnock, and were determined to make sure that they, the politicians, controlled the presentation of news. New Labour set up a centralised media operation controlled by Alastair Campbell, formerly of the *Daily Mirror*, who joined Blair's staff in 1994 and became his director of communications. Crucially, Blair saw no need to recruit a hard policy adviser to tell him how to translate New Labour politics into policy. The result was years of wasted opportunities.

The core of the operation was 'spinning' the news: trailing policy announcements, planting stories via favoured journalists, speedy rebuttals of negative stories, and so on. Every morning Alastair Campbell, having been up very early, would brief his staff on how to deal with the day's news: 'Oh, the *Daily Mail*, it's the usual crap . . . the *Guardian* have got the usual wankers in today.' His style was 'yobbish, but authoritative. His manner was domineering, brusque and, at times, menacing, but most of the time it was incredibly jokey . . . He always seemed to be asking the question: "How can we use this terrible news to our advantage?"[4]

The bad consequence of relying on 'focus groups' was that New Labour took as given the accepted Thatcherite wisdom of the day, and never tried to develop an alternative narrative. The worst result of relentless spinning was that the leaders started to believe in their own spin: 'data became part of the political narrative [rather] than a basis for grounding policy in evidence'.[5] This was to have appalling effects in the run-up to the Iraq War.

It was natural that Blair and Rupert Murdoch should find each other. The Australian media magnate was a staunch Thatcherite. But with his acquisitions of the *Sun* and the *News of the World* in the late 1960s and of *The Times* and the *Sunday Times* in 1981, he controlled a formidable number of titles. Although, or perhaps because, Murdoch had destroyed the print unions, Blair was determined to enlist him to New Labour's cause. He went a-wooing in Australia in 1996 and returned with a Faustian pact. TheMurdoch press backed Labour in the three Blair election campaigns of 1997, 2001 and 2005, but not Brown's in 2010.

In government the honeymoon with the press cooled and by the end few newspapers found a good word for New Labour. The key moment of rupture was the 'dodgy dossier' of February 2003, when the media realised they were being had. Thereafter they started disbelieving everything that came out of No. 10. Campbell spun out of control, yelling at the BBC's Jeremy Vine: 'You will fucking report exactly what I tell you to. You'll stick to my fucking schedule and nothing else.' Blair came to see newspapers as a 'feral beast', but he was only paying the penalty of having sucked up to them. As

J. A. Spender had remarked almost a century earlier. 'the press villain comes to the top when the press hero is dethroned.'[6]

What is it to be on the left?

Blair provided New Labour with positioning, Brown with a programme. Both men conceded that capitalism and markets were here to stay. But what distinctive reason was there to vote Labour?

Blair shopped around to find a narrative for his unfocused radicalism. He toyed with various voguish formulae for encapsulating his social thinking: the Third Way, stakeholding, communitarianism. The Third Way, that brilliantly imprecise phrase taken over by Anthony Giddens from the American New Democrats, was for a time a rallying point for attempts to give the centre-left coherence. In the end, Blair settled for 'New' Labour, which had the advantage of meaning nothing at all.

Blair saw himself as a 'moderniser', with a 'conservative head, a progressive heart, and a rebellious soul.'[7] He would modernise the Labour Party, and Labour government would modernise Britain. Old Labour beliefs, he liked to say, were valid, but needed to be applied to modern conditions. 'The commitment remained. The means of implementing it radically altered.' Old Labour was a negotiation with the past, New Labour a negotiation with the future. He talked of a 'journey into the future', as though the future was a political idea. Britain was a 'young country' barnacled by archaic institutions. At the 2003 party conference, he offered his audience a choice: 'Forward or back. I only go one way. I've not got a reverse gear.' By this time his modernisation drive had gone global. The Middle East, too, was in 'urgent need of modernisation'. None of this gave him a policy agenda. He became prime minister without knowing what to do with power.

He developed a rhetorical style suited to the up-and-coming middle class. 'People', he said, 'shouldn't be ashamed at wanting something better for themselves and their families.' He championed education as giving ordinary people a chance to realise their 'aspirations'. Like Thatcher, Blair admired the go-getters in business life, and regretted that he hadn't gone into business where he could have made a fortune. Like Peter Mandelson he was 'intensely relaxed about people becoming filthy rich'.*

In July 2006, Blair told Murdoch executives in the USA that an 'era of political cross-dressing' had dawned. Why should people who thought similarly be separated by irrational party divisions? At first he saw himself as reuniting the two reformist wings of Labour and Liberal sundered in the early twentieth century. Before the 1997 election, he talked to the Liberal Democrat leaders Paddy Ashdown and Roy Jenkins about coalition, but the Liberal insistence on proportional representation as part of the deal brought the talks to nothing.

Later his convergence was more to the Tories, whose economic liberalism and social conservatism chimed in with his own instincts. The trouble with the Liberal Democrats, he concluded, was that, unlike Margaret Thatcher, they shied away from 'hard decisions', like cutting incapacity benefit. Thatcher's reforms of the public services, he came to believe, were not 'Tory' but 'modern'. 'I take an

---

* This quote is from a 1998 speech by Mandelson to California computer executives, widely reported at the time.

essentially middle-class view of public services', he wrote. This meant 'choice for everyone, regardless of wealth'.[8]

As Shadow Home Secretary from 1992 to 1994, Blair strongly identified with 'law and order'. In public perception crime against persons and property was rampaging unchecked. It was the murder of James Bulger by two ten-year-olds in 1993 which evoked Blair's pledge to be 'Tough on crime, tough on the causes of crime'. Being 'tough on crime' was to prove more popular with voters than being tough on the causes of crime. What Mr Murdoch's *Sun* reader wanted was more policing, more arrests and longer and tougher prison sentences for burglars, football hooligans, illegal immigrants, drunken louts, drug addicts and other flotsam of the 'broken society'. By the end of his premiership, Blair had come to believe that the rights of the antisocial minority needed to be suspended, including their right to parenthood.

Brown, the deeper thinker, had a clearer idea of what he wanted to do with power. Labour needed to establish a reputation for economic competence. This meant avoiding any financial policies which led to 'boom and bust'. Low inflation was the precondition for steady economic growth, which in turn was the basis of social reform. 'Prudence' was Brown's watchword – a good conservative word which befitted a son of the Manse.

In a 'low tax preferring country',[9] Brown made the claim for public spending as a growth policy, one which would allow lower taxes later: 'fair taxes and productive spending' he called it. Hence a priority of New Labour would be heavy investment in education and health care. Both Brown and Blair recognised that the old working class had fractured. It now contained a lot of the 'non-working' class – an increasing minority mired in poverty and excluded from society by lack of employment and employability. 'Targeted' support for work would turn excluded drones into productive workers and thus contribute to both growth and poverty reduction. Beveridge's state-assisted idleness had to be turned into support for work.* This was the Brown bridge between economic efficiency and social justice. It was an attractive idea, but it did give a Labour Chancellor almost virtual licence to call 'investment' anything he wanted to spend money on.

Brown had little time for Blair's flirtation with German social democracy. Economically and culturally he was at home in America. He admired its spirit of enterprise, its work ethic, its meritocratic outlook, its social egalitarianism. Moreover, his awakening to America came at a time when the US economy had started to boom, and Europe's to slump. So he embraced the American model of competitive capitalism. Workers must be trained up to compete in the global marketplace.

In practical terms, the two narratives of New Labour amounted to much the same thing. Both Blair and Brown shared a vision of a society bound together by reciprocal rights and duties. Benefits should be linked to a willingness to work; inclusion was both an economic and moral imperative. Blair and Brown would fall out on the terms of the contract between the state and the citizen. Blair came to want 'choice for everyone, regardless of wealth'; Brown wanted 'opportunity not just for some . . . but for all'. In that subtle distinction between 'choice' and 'opportunity' lay the seeds of later policy discord.

---

* Brown was influenced by a Social Market Foundation pamphlet, 'Beyond Unemployment' (1993) by Robert Skidelsky and Liam Halligan.

Before 1997, foreign policy was not a source of conflict. Both men were committed to a European future, and Blair had shown no sign of that global messianism to which his relationship with God and American power would lead him.

Delivery

Brown's chief endeavour as Chancellor of the Exchequer from 1997 to 2007 was to develop wiggle room within Thatcherite precepts of sound macroeconomic management – precepts to which the Conservatives had paid little enough attention when in office. His all-too-familiar mantra was 'Prudence'. Four days after he became Chancellor, he liberated the Bank of England from political control for the first time since its nationalisation in 1946. He would set it an inflation target – initially of 2.5 per cent a year – and cede it control over interest rates. This was a mighty step to establishing Labour's anti-inflationary credentials. He sought to establish Labour's fiscal credibility by binding himself as Chancellor to explicit fiscal rules: over the cycle the government would borrow only for investment (the so-called 'golden rule') and the national debt/GDP ratio would be held at a 'stable and prudent' level. He also promised to stick to his Tory predecessor's spending plans for two years: in contrast to Old Labour, New Labour would save before it spent. It would provide further reassurance by not raising direct taxes.

Brown's third decision was also critical: to uphold Britain's 'opt-out' from the European single currency, negotiated by Major at Maastricht in 1992. This brought his first big conflict with Blair. Blair, the most-pro European prime minister since Heath, wanted Britain to be at the 'heart' of Europe, and realised that for that it had to be in the eurozone. Brown was not anti-European, but he thought his own arrangements for financial policy were technically superior to the eurozone's. In an extraordinary assertion of strength and stubborness, he insisted that Blair's foreign-policy goals must be subordinated to five 'economic tests' set by the Treasury – in practice by his chief economic adviser Ed Balls – for eurozone membership. In 2003, the Treasury verdict came in: 'Yes, but not yet.'

Brown's first three budgets combined a squeeze on public spending with ingenious devices for raising and rearranging revenue without anyone noticing. These put paid to Lawson's effort to simplify the tax system. The spending cuts, together with the 'stealth' taxes and higher than expected revenues, helped produce a cumulative fiscal tightening of £40 billion in the two years following the election. This enabled Brown to realise budget surpluses in 1999–2000 and 2000–1 and pay back debt.

Within this narrow fiscal envelope, Brown diverted social spending from the 'Beveridge' universal benefits based on flat-rate contributions towards means-tested income supplements like the Working Families Tax Credit. A New Deal for the young long-term unemployed offered a choice between work and training. Together with Sure Start, a programme of child care and early education, and a minimum wage (introduced for the first time and set initially at £3.50 an hour), these measures aimed to reduce poverty not by providing increased maintenance for non-work but by raising incomes from work. The minimum wage covered 2 million workers; £5 billion worth of tax credits were directed to 1.5 million working families on low incomes. The non-employed poor lost out. Poor pensioners were given 'top-ups' on their 'Beveridge' pension, plus a winter fuel allowance, but Brown did not restore the link between pensions and earnings severed by Thatcher.

Brown also started a capital investment programme.

Hardly any new hospitals had been built since Enoch Powell's time at Health in the early 1960s. To stick to his self-imposed spending limits, Brown made extensive use of the Private Finance Initiative (PFI), a method for getting capital spending off the government's balance sheet. Under PFI, private companies construct and maintain public buildings which the government rents from them, usually for thirty years. Use of PFI was at its height in Labour's first term, with dozens of new hospitals and schools being started, but future debts piling up for the taxpayer. Prudence was being undermined by Trickery.

Blair soon got impatient with Prudence and started clamouring for Spending, though without any tax increases. In 2000, he casually announced that Labour would halve child poverty in five years. Alarmed by the decrepit state of the NHS, brought home to him by the outbreak of winter flu of 1999 and headline-grabbing stories of delays in treatment, he also casually told David Frost on television that Labour would raise health spending as a proportion of GDP to the European level in five years. Although furious with Blair for 'stealing my bloody budget', Brown paid up. His Comprehensive Spending Review of 2000 promised to increase health and education spending in real terms by over 6 per cent a year over the following three years. The spending tap was not turned off again till 2007.

In contrast to his Chancellor's well-thought-out plans, Blair's interventions were reactive and spasmodic. The truth was that he had ambitions but no policies. This did not mean he was ineffective.

His handling of the Northern Ireland peace negotiations which led to the Good Friday Agreement of 10 April 1998 was a masterly combination of charm and steel. The agreement provided that Northern Ireland was to stay part of the UK as long as its people wanted. The Republic of Ireland would give up its territorial claim. The Protestant and Catholic parties would combine in a power-sharing executive, based on a new elected assembly. There would be a new all-Ireland advisory body. The paramilitaries on both sides would destroy or decommission their weapons, monitored by an independent body. Policing would be made fairer. There was still more violence to come, as the horrific bombing of Omagh five months later showed, but the back of civil strife had been broken. *Mirabile dictu*, a power-sharing government with Protestant dinosaur Ian Paisley as First Minister and IRA leader Martin McGuinness as his deputy was finally set up in 2007.

Peace had been helped by economics and secularisation, which combined to bring the two halves of Ireland closer together. Catholic Ireland, which Eamon de Valera had tried to keep as a Catholic peasant backwater, uncontaminated by modern influences, had exploded into the 'Celtic tiger', while Northern Ireland went into industrial decline. Demographic change – both Britain and Ireland receiving large influxes of European and Asian immigrants – weakened the relevance of Protestant–Catholic conflicts going back to the seventeenth century.

Blair also felt the hand of history heavily, if less happily, in Kosovo. A civil war had broken out in the Serbian province of Kosovo, largely peopled by Albanians, with atrocities being committed by both Serbs and Albanians. After various abortive attempts to arrange a ceasefire, Blair took the lead in organising the NATO bombing of Serbia, followed by military occupation of Kosovo in June 1999.

The Kosovo conflict illustrates an aspect of Blair's

technique of government which was to flower ruinously in the run-up to the Iraq War. The journalist Steve Richards describes it as forming a 'simplistic view about a situation and then acquiring a conveniently passionate conviction'.[10] Blair took seriously the moral duty of the 'international community' to prevent humanitarian disasters such as the Rwandan genocide of 1994. But he was also trigger-happy, and this led him to take decisions to intervene on inadequate evidence. The ground for intervention in Kosovo was said to be the 'ethnic cleansing' by Serbs of Albanians. But the great exodus of Albanians from Kosovo followed only after NATO bombing had started and international observers had been withdrawn.[11] The UN Charter required Security Council authorisation for the use of force except in self-defence. No such authorisation was secured for the Kosovan intervention, but Blair, speaking with 'tangible conviction and passion', told the House of Commons that the duty to protect overrode all other commitments.[12]

As the military campaign progressed, the duty of protection grew in Blair's eyes into a duty to rid the world of evil dictators like Serbia's president, Slobodan Milosevic. In a speech in Chicago on 22 April 1999, portentously called 'The New Doctrine of the International Community', Blair argued that globalisation had made the old doctrine of non-interference – and by implication the UN Charter which was set up to prevent interference – obsolete. 'We cannot turn our backs on conflicts and the violation of human rights in other countries if we still want to be secure.' The New Doctrine was based on 'values' not 'territorial ambitions'. 'The spread of our values makes us safer.' But it accepted that temporary occupation of the invaded countries might be necessary. The only limitation on this moral mission was practical: Blair chafed at his inability to get rid of Mugabe in Zimbabwe and the 'Burmese lot'.[13] The New Doctrine bore an uncanny resemblance to the Old Doctrine of liberal imperialism. In international, as in domestic policy, the ideas which fitted Blair's instincts were those of Edwardian England, with a long bypass called socialism. But whereas domestic reform led him to Europe's 'third way', liberal imperialism tied him to the United States, since it was only American military power which could deliver on Blair's New Doctrine.

Blair had reserved constitutional questions for himself, but was 'bored rigid' by them. This meant allowing bits of Labour's manifesto to trundle forward without any obvious push from him. The European Convention on Human Rights was incorporated into British law in 2000. In 1999 all but ninety-two hereditary peers were removed from the House of Lords. In 2003 Blair decided to set up a Supreme Court to replace the Law Lords in the House of Lords.

Much the most important constitutional change of the New Labour age was Scottish and Welsh devolution. Both were promised in the party's manifesto; Blair allowed them rather than promoted them. An earlier devolution referendum had failed in 1978, but Margaret Thatcher's attempt in 1989 to impose the poll tax on Scotland ahead of England – leading to 2.5 million summary warrants for non-payment in a country of 5 million, and to decisive gains for the Scottish Nationalist Party – made action urgent to head off the demand for Scottish independence. In a referendum of September 1997 Scotland voted by three to one for a Scottish Parliament and by 63.5 per cent to 36.5 per cent to give it tax-raising powers. The majority for a Welsh Assembly, without tax-raising power, was much narrower. A Scottish Parliament of 120 MSPs with power to vary UK taxes by 3p in the pound, and more extensive social powers, came into being in 1999, together with a Welsh Assembly of sixty AMs; both elected by proportional representation; and both housed in grandiose buildings, which provided an enlarged platform for self-important local politicians.

The Scottish and Welsh devolutions, together with the restoration of devolved government at Stormont, were intended by reformers to be a precursor of 'devolution all round'. But 'regional assemblies' for England were rejected by regional voters, on the well-founded suspicion that they would be nothing but talking shops. The question of a Parliament for England was never considered. The decision to allow a London Assembly with an elected mayor was a one-off revenge for Thatcher's abolition of the Greater London Council. The first mayor was none other than Ken Livingstone, whom Thatcher had deposed in 1986.

Blair took much more interest in criminal justice. He was determined that New Labour should not seem 'softer' on crime than the Conservatives had been, and appointed two successive Home Secretaries who shared his views. The first, Jack Straw, will chiefly be remembered for introducing ASBOs (1998) for hooligans who terrorised old ladies. David Blunkett, his second Home Secretary, abolished 'double jeopardy', the ancient principle that a defendant cannot be tried twice for the same offence. This made it possible, in 2011, to bring successful criminal prosecutions against two white suspects, Gary Dobson and David Norris, who had been acquitted in 1992 for murdering a black youth, Stephen Lawrence. When the number of asylum seekers shot up from 30,000 to 80,000 a year, the Blair government pre-empted Conservative leader William Hague's promise to speed up their removal by passing the necessary legislation itself.

Following al-Qaeda's attacks in the USA on 11 September 2001, the government's 'war against crime' shifted to the 'war against terrorism'. Its attempt to extend detention without trial to ninety days failed in the Lords, but a system of 'control orders' for suspected terrorists, amounting to house arrest, was introduced in 2005 in the wake of the London bombings. Being 'tough on crime' resulted in a relentless rise in the average daily prison population to a record high of 76,000 by 2005.

Policies to repress crime did not prevent some liberalising measures. Manifesto commitments to equalise the age of consent for heterosexual and homosexual acts at sixteen, and to repeal Section 28 of the Local Government Act of 1988 forbidding the 'intentional promotion of homosexuality' in schools, were honoured. New criminal offences were created aimed at curtailing racial and religious abuse. Contrary to Blair's wishes, hunting with dogs – anathema to the chattering classes – was outlawed in 2004 after fierce resistance from fox-hunting peers in the Lords.

In New Labour's second term, the cold war between prime minister and Chancellor hotted up. Blair and Brown got involved in an exhausting struggle over the method of delivery of health and education reforms, envenomed by Brown's determination to force Blair out, which drained the prime minister of authority, and the government of reforming energy.

The quarrel was not about spending. Blair and Brown agreed that the public services needed more money. But they fell out on the question of how to get the best results from this spending. Whereas Blair aimed to raise standards through competition leading to consumer choice (Thatcherism plus money), Brown sought to tie the money to 'public-service agreements'. Underlying this was a difference in view about the nature of public services. Blair argued that the only difference between private and public provision was that the latter's money, for historical reasons, happened to come from taxes rather than private payment. For Brown, services received public money because they could not be properly accountable to their users, who lacked the information to judge their quality. The intellectual disagreement was genuine, but it was also a cover for the politics of the succession. Blairites needed to portray Brown as anti-reform to justify Blair's continuation in office; Brownites needed to portray the Blair reforms as Tory to justify their own man's claims to a swift succession. Both sides lost their previous incentives for working together.

Blair had started as a champion of the 'target culture'. Improved outcomes depended on relentless pressure from the centre. But by the second term, he, like Thatcher, had come to the view that output targeting was not enough. What was needed was not more central control, but new independent institutions directly accountable to their users and not to central government or local authorities. Money would follow the patient and the parent to the hospital and school. In short, he revived the 'quasi-market' approach of the 1980s. Health reform was the main battleground on which prime minister and Chancellor fought.

Brown had called in a banker, Derek Wanless, to quantify the extra resources needed to bring NHS spending up to the European average. Wanless said that a 7 per cent increase in real terms was needed for five years. In his budget of March 2002 Brown upped his previous spending commitment, raising the extra money by a 1 per cent National Insurance levy.

But he soon clashed with Alan Milburn, a Secretary of State for Health committed to Blair's quasi-market agenda. Milburn wanted the best-performing hospital trusts to be freed from central controls 'to borrow and perform more or less as they wanted, leaving patients to decide whether to go to them or choose somewhere else'.[14] Brown asked: how can you have competition when for most areas there is only one local hospital? Most people wanted better hospitals, not more choice. Furthermore, freedom of hospitals to borrow posed a threat to Treasury control of public spending. Blair's people replied that they would only get better hospitals if there was more choice. After a bruising battle which lasted two years, a truce was eventually declared, with the establishment in 2003 of a small number of foundation hospitals. Worn down by the Brownite spinning against him, Milburn resigned in June 2003. Blair had failed to back him in giving foundation hospitals the right to borrow, but he had made a start on choice. 'We are being asked to think what patients might want', one manager told the health economist Howard Glennerster, 'we have never done that before.'[15]

The health debate was reproduced in education: here the protagonists were not so much Blair and Brown, as Blair and the Department for Education and Skills: Brown's obstruction was limited to not supporting Blair at crucial moments. Both Blair and Brown saw education as an instrument of economic growth and social inclusion, and both wanted money spent on it. 'Our mission is to mobilise the resolve of this generation to transform Britain into a learning society . . . We must confront our past, not continue it', Blair announced in his Romanes lecture on 2 December 1999. As its contribution to this mobilisation of resolve, the government set literacy and numeracy targets for primary schools, tied school funding to the results of national tests, and retained the Thatcherite, Chris Woodhead, as chief inspector of schools.

'Standards matter more than structures', proclaimed

Blair's first Education Secretary, David Blunkett. Blair's education adviser, the academic and journalist Andrew Adonis,
disagreed. On joining Blair's Policy Unit in 1998, Adonis was
shocked to discover that two thirds of pupils in almost half
the comprehensive schools were failing to achieve grades
A–C in GCSE. He soon became convinced that the only solution was to break up the 'bog standard' comprehensives (as
Alastair Campbell had dubbed them), a byword for failure to
the middle class, into state-funded 'academies', independent
from local authorities, which would give parents the same
choice as parents who sent their children to fee-paying
schools.[16] Adonis sold the idea to Blair, and in 1999 Blunkett
announced a 'city academy' programme aimed at deprived
areas, on an experimental basis, where he intended to keep it,
as one of Blair's hobbies. Adonis was then left to push it, with
no help from the Education Department, and active opposition from the local education authorities. Blair's support was
essential. 'Without Tony Blair', Adonis wrote, 'there would
have been no academies.'[17]

By the election of 2001, fifteen academies were up and
running or in the pipeline, out of 4,000 secondary schools in
the UK. Adonis looked forward to a massive scaling up of the
programme in the second term, but it never happened. The
Blair–Brown conflict turned toxic; Iraq intervened, diverting
Blair for weeks at a time; the Department for Education and
Skills was hostile. Only in 2004 did Adonis secure a commitment to 200 academies by 2010, raised to 400 in 2006.

In a typical off-the-cuff pledge, Blair announced in 1998 a
target of 50 per cent of eighteen-to-thirty-year-olds in higher
education by 2010. To help raise the required money from an
initially niggardly Treasury, the government introduced a
£1,000 tuition fee. In the 2001 election, David Blunkett had

pledged there would be no 'top-up fees'. However, encouraged by Adonis, Blair decided to link extra money to variable fees, so universities could compete on quality and price. After two years wrangling with the Treasury, which resisted variable fees and student loans as inequitable, Blair got his way, on both counts, but Education Secretary Charles Clarke's 'top-up' bill, which increased the cap on fees to £3,000 a year, passed the Commons in January 2004 by only five votes, to loud lamentations that it would discourage poorer students. (The cap was raised to £9,000 by the Conservative–Liberal Democrats coalition. Scotland's devolved Parliament decided to keep tuition free for Scottish students. Brown's imaginative 'Baby Bond' scheme to give poor children an accruing nest egg to finance their higher education was scrapped by the Conservative–Liberal Democrat coalition.)

The Iraq War, which started halfway through Labour's second term in March 2003, confirmed both Blair's ethical absolutism (more American than British) and his imperviousness to evidence and law. Following the 9/11 attacks on New York and Washington in 2001, President Bush declared 'war against terrorism'. Blair followed suit at the Labour Party conference in October: 'This is a moment to seize. The kaleidoscope has been shaken. The pieces are in flux. Soon they will settle again. Before they do let us reorder this world around us.'

The reordering opened with the NATO (really US–British) attack on Afghanistan, but soon came to include Iraq, then ruled by the evil dictator Saddam Hussein. It is now known that Blair agreed to back George W. Bush in a war to overthrow Saddam when the two met at Crawford, Texas, in April 2002. The spirit of Crawford, as well as the style of today's political language, is captured by the injunction of Blair's chief of staff Jonathan Powell to the British ambassador Sir

Christopher Meyer: 'We want you to get up the arse of the White House and stay there.'[18] Blair told Bush that he needed a plausible *casus belli*. This seemed to be Saddam's possession of weapons of mass destruction. The evidence for their existence was assembled in a British government dossier of 24 September 2002 (to be distinguished from the later 'dodgy dossier' of February 2003 based on a plagiarised doctoral thesis), which was 'spun' by Alastair Campbell to suggest that Saddam could release missiles with chemical payloads within forty-five minutes. In fact, Saddam Hussein had no WMD; erstwhile supporters of the war point to a 'profound intelligence failure'* but their own failure to interrogate the intelligence at the time suggests that they wanted to believe what they read.

Blair's other stipulation to Bush[†] was that, to secure British support, the invasion would have to be authorised by the Security Council. Security Council Resolution 1441 of 8 November 2002 gave Saddam Hussein a 'final opportunity' to comply with Iraq's disarmament obligations as laid down in Security Council Resolution 687 of 3 April 1991, which had ended the first Gulf War. Blair would claim, in defiance of an opinion of his Attorney General, that an invasion of Iraq was sufficiently justified by Saddam Hussein's alleged non-compliance with the terms of Resolution 687 in 1991. No new Security Council resolution authorising war would be needed.[‡]

---

* See for example Jack Straw, *Last Man Standing* (2012), p. 411.

† Blair also wanted a US commitment to revive the almost defunct Israeli–Palestinian peace process. Bush was happy to promise this, since it didn't involve him doing anything soon.

‡ In January 2003, Blair's Attorney General, Peter Goldsmith, sent him a strongly worded note giving his legal opinion that 'a further decision [of the Security Council] is required' in order to 'authorise the use of force against Iraq'. Goldsmith changed his mind on 17 March after Blair promised Bush his support for war regardless.

On 18 March 2003, Blair persuaded the House of Commons to vote for war in a speech which was remarkable, even by his high standards, for its eloquence, passion and forensic skill. The main motion for war was passed by 412 to 149, with fifty-four Labour MPs voting against, so he didn't need the support of the Opposition parties. Robin Cook and Claire Short were the only Cabinet resignations. For the invasion, Britain supplied 50,000 troops to America's 150,000, an astonishingly high proportion, with Australia a distant third with 2,000. Britain also supplied the second largest air force. Baghdad fell after a month, in April. The British captured Basra, and occupied much of southern Iraq. A thirty-year-old Old Etonian, Rory Stewart, was sent to govern the provinces of Maysan and Dhi Qar, restoring the British Empire for six months.

The Iraq War inflicted immense political damage on Blair from which he never recovered. It was not so much the war itself (though it occasioned large anti-war demonstrations) as its aftermath: the revelation that Saddam had no WMD, the suspicion that Blair had been lying, above all the ferocious insurgencies which followed the collapse of the Saddam Hussein regime, which over the remaining years of Blair's premiership were to cost hundreds of thousands of civilian lives, and a steady drip of British military casualties. The question has been asked by four inquiries: in saying that Saddam had WMD was Blair lying, was he deceived, or did he deceive himself? This is to start the inquiry at the wrong end. Blair believed that it was a moral duty to rid Iraq and the world of Saddam Hussein. When the Bush administration gave him the opportunity to act, he seized it. In his memoirs he wrote revealingly that Neville Chamberlain had asked the wrong question in the 1930s. The right question was not whether or how Hitler could be contained, but 'does fascism represent a force that is so strong and rooted that it had to be uprooted and destroyed?' This was the question Blair asked about Saddam, and answered in the affirmative. The pretexts for war were secondary to him.[19]

Throughout the build-up to Iraq, Brown left Blair mainly on his own. After all, the Granita agreement of 1994 had conceded foreign policy to the prime minister. Once the war had failed to lead to the pacification of Iraq, Brown took advantage of Blair's political weakening to press his own claims for the premiership. The relationship between the two, which had soured noticeably in 2002, got so bad that the deputy prime minister John Prescott arranged a peace-making dinner at his flat in Admiralty House on 6 November 2003. The Brown camp reported that Blair promised to stand down before the next election. In March 2004 Blair floated to Brown the idea of publicly announcing that he would leave in October. Brown advised against: 'You'll make yourself a lame duck.' He wanted a private promise instead. Blair wavered: if he quit that summer 'his own reform agenda would barely have left the drawing board, while Iraq remained bleak'. Brown piled on the pressure: 'When are you going to fuck off and give me a date?' he stormed. 'I want the job now.'[20] By June 2004 Blair had decided to stay on for a third term. According to some reports, Philip Gould's polling results, suggesting that Blair, not Brown, would easily win a third term, were 'decisive' in persuading him to stay. Brown was furious: 'There's nothing you could say to me now that I could ever believe,' he roared.[21]

Re-energised by the decision to fight on, and looking ten years younger after his summer break, Blair launched a flurry of five-year plans for his third term. For education, there would be more academies, trust schools, and greater school autonomy. For health, Blair wanted to give patients a choice between private and public hospitals. 'Tough on crime' meant being tough on asylum, immigration, prisons and security.[22] Labour was returned to power in June 2005 with a much-reduced majority of sixty seats, after an election which started off with Brown's conspicuous refusal to join Blair on the campaign trail. And with the resignation of Michael Howard after a third Conservative election defeat, the Conservatives discovered an electable leader in David Cameron.

Blair knew his time was running out and having belatedly discovered a domestic programme, he was now desperate to embed his ideas in policy before he quit. But with his authority ebbing, he was finding it harder to get his legislation through. He needed Tory support to get the 2006 Education and Inspection Bill, creating 'trust' schools, through Parliament. Further health reforms foundered on Treasury opposition. In January 2006, Blair launched his last big initiative, a Respect action plan designed to 'bring back a proper sense of respect in our schools, in our communities, in our towns and villages'. It was an echo of his earlier communitarian ideas. He called for a 'genuine new debate about the nature of liberty, concerned not just with the liberty of the individual but with freedom from fear'.[23] His last speeches as premier, influenced by his chief speechwriter Phil Collins, were unusually thoughtful, as though he was finally discovering his true direction.

Blair may have been intellectually reinvigorated, but he was politically shrivelled, as the political world waited for the Brown succession. His third term was enveloped in the sleaze of 'cash for honours'. Labour had become heavily dependent on cash gifts from a clutch of mainly media, Labour-inclined, millionaires such as Greg Dyke. There had been the Bernie Ecclestone scandal in Blair's first term, when it was revealed that a £1 million gift to the Labour Party in 1996 by the Formula 1 boss had been followed by the exemption of Formula 1 cars from the ban on tobacco advertising. The Labour Party returned the donation, and Blair escaped unscathed, announcing on television 'I'm a pretty straight sort of guy.' By the third term the Teflon coating had worn thin. It was widely believed peerages had been promised in return for sufficiently large donations: Blair's fund-raiser, Lord Levy, was arrested; Blair himself was questioned by the police. Nothing was proved, but there was the stench of a second honours scandal (Lloyd George's was the first).

Blair was still reluctant to go. In his memoirs he cites a 'brilliant' memorandum from Adonis, saying that a Brown premiership was 'set to be a weak – if extended – interlude between you and Cameron'.[24] Brown was equally reluctant to strike. 'You fucking tosser, you bottled it', his adviser Ed Balls yelled down the telephone at him on 5 May 2006, after he had failed, in the wake of disastrous local-election results, to call for a change of leadership on the *Today* programme.[25] Balls virtually pushed Brown into the premiership by organising letters from MPs calling on Blair to resign. In September 2006, Blair finally conceded defeat. He promised publicly to quit within a year. As his rule drew to a close, he threw himself wholeheartedly into a successful campaign to get the 2012 Olympics to London, charming and persuasive to the end.

Brown as prime minister

'We will never know for sure *why* Brown became such a difficult man', write Anthony Seldon and Guy Lodge.[26] The answer seems pretty obvious: he had to wait too long to become prime minister. Brimful of reformist ideas and energy at the start of his political life he was drained of them by the end. As he saw his possibilities fading, he became ever more bitter and resentful towards Blair, the nobody who had usurped his throne. Most of his bad behaviour – the paranoia, the tribalism, the tantrums, the depressions, the disloyalty – can be explained by the frustration of his ambition. In a supreme irony, he ended up where Blair had started, empty of domestic strategy, just at the moment when Blair was, at long last, acquiring one. By the time he became prime minister it was too late for him to escape from his political bunker, surrounded by loyal, but troublemaking attack dogs like Damian McBride, to whom he was fiercely loyal. So Brown's premiership, like Blair's, was set in reactive, not strategic, mode.

But history judges leaders on how they handle the big decisions, not how they mismanage small ones, and on this test Brown comes out well. The economic crisis of 2008–9 brought out his best, as Northern Ireland had in Blair. Premonition of the brewing storm came with the failure of the Northern Rock bank, and the premature revelation of the Treasury rescue plan by the BBC's economics editor Robert Peston, precipitating the first run on a British bank since 1914. When the global economic crisis erupted with the collapse of the American investment bank Lehman Brothers on 15 September 2008, Brown, like Churchill in 1940, was the right man in the right place at the right time. In the following seven months, with the world economy in freefall, Brown became the leading architect of the global policy response. He filled the leadership gap at a moment when, from a mixture of ignorance in Europe and political interregnum in the US, no one else could.

On 8 October 2008 Alistair Darling, Brown's Chancellor of the Exchequer, announced a £50 billion scheme to buy shares from distressed British banks. In Paris on 12 October, Brown persuaded European leaders – and two days later Henry Paulson of the US Treasury – to agree a co-ordinated recapitalisation of their banking systems. To pursue this, in the face of initial bank hostility, was the biggest decision Brown made as prime minister.

His second signal act of leadership was at the G20 meeting in London in April 2009. Recapitalisation had saved the banks, but had not restarted bank lending. Brown had spent his family's summer holiday in 2008 reading up on the Great Depression, and this persuaded him that a massive, co-ordinated 'stimulus' package was needed to revive the 'real' economy. At a conference of world leaders in London on 2 April 2009 he announced $1 trillion of support for the global economy: extra IMF special drawing rights, extra World Bank resources for less affluent countries, extra trade credits plus a world stability board to manage risks, and co-ordinated monetary and fiscal expansion. Brown was a tough chairman of this fractious gathering. He had learnt from his days as student rector of Edinburgh University that 'you need to drive meetings towards conclusions and not simply wait for them to emerge'. But the leaders also trusted his financial expertise. The president of the World Bank described the G20 package as the thing that 'broke the fall' of the world economy.[27]

While Brown was 'saving the world' – a calling he found increasingly congenial – his premiership was crumbling. His three-week dithering before deciding not to call an election in 2007 exposed him as a political butterfingers and his reputation never really recovered. Chaos in the prime minister's private office, the failed attempt to extend detention without trial to forty-two days, the catastrophic fallout from the 2007 budget (Brown's last),* three by-elections losses in a row, which included a gigantic 25 per cent swing to the SNP in Scotland, and a rambling speech to Labour's National Policy Forum at Warwick University, left him with an approval rating of 14 per cent. A coup to oust him in the summer of 2008 failed only because the Foreign Secretary David Miliband refused to put himself forward as the alternative. Brown was eventually saved by the onset of the economic crisis and the return of the Blairite Peter Mandelson, in October, to the Cabinet as Business Secretary. Mandelson gave the Brown government something it sorely lacked – a sense of stability and strategy.

But the Brown government never had time to develop a coherent narrative, as the domestic consequences of the global banking crisis hit Britain in the autumn of 2008. In 2007, when the economic prospects were still sunny, Brown had appointed Alastair Darling as a stop-gap Chancellor to keep the Treasury seat warm for Ed Balls. Darling, on holiday in the Hebrides in August 2008, was trapped by a *Guardian* journalist into saying that conditions were 'arguably the worst they've been in sixty years', spun into the headline 'Economy at sixty-year low, says Darling'. The interview destroyed Brown's confidence in Darling, but he could not sack him with the economy on the brink of collapse. The financial crisis gave the Treasury the chance to regain control of public spending. As the economy plunged in the last

---

* In March 2007, Brown had abolished the 10 per cent income tax starting rate to pay for a 2p reduction in the standard rate. Since the 2p cut in income tax was not to start till April 2008, Brown claimed that the budget would be 'fiscally neutral'. In spring 2008, the abolition of the 10p band blew up in Brown's face as it turned out there would be more losers than winners. His Chancellor, Darling, was forced to compensate the additional losers, which meant spending more money, which he wanted to avoid as economic prospects started to deteriorate. The compensation cost almost £3 billion.

quarter of 2008, the government's deficit soared. Revised estimates showed that the 'structural' deficit – the deficit which would remain even after recovery – was much larger than the 2.5 per cent estimated by Brown in 2007. What this suggested was that New Labour – and Brown in particular – had been overspending even before the recession. Prudence had given way to Extravagance. And Extravagance was leading to Bankruptcy.

From the summer of 2008, there was an all-too-visible rift between the Treasury View and the Brown View, with Darling caught in the middle. What exactly was it they disagreed about? In headline terms, the conflict arose from Brown's determination to portray the dispute between Labour and the Conservatives as being one of 'investment versus cuts' and Darling's recognition that Labour would have to cut, too. Both men were trapped by the lack of an accepted theory with which they could justify rising public deficits in a slump. Between autumn 2008 and spring 2009, one official recalled, 'we went from the Bank recap into fiscal stimulus, into asset protection and then quantitative easing. It was just like a series of horrific events.'[28] But the cost to governments of keeping insolvent firms afloat and unemployment down became dreadfully large, calling into question the sustainability of public finances. So, from mid-2009, Keynes was put back in the cupboard and fiscal policy was dictated by the bond markets. Darling accepted the logic of this and set the Treasury the task – congenial, considering its history – of 'balancing the budget'.[29] Brown accepted the logic, too, and yet found it intolerable. 'You are not going to turn me into [Philip] Snowden,' he raged.[30] Balls urged a Keynesian response with a cut in VAT to stimulate private spending. But Darling and the Treasury judged that bond-market pressure made further fiscal stimulus politically impossible. In the end, it was the Treasury which prevailed, and Labour went into the 2010 election with a plan to halve the structural deficit in four years.

There were still prime-ministerial hiccups to come – notably Brown's mishandling of *Daily Telegraph* revelations that a number of MPs had been claiming expenses to which they were not entitled – but Labour steadily recovered in the polls from June 2009. On 6 April 2010, with Labour neck and neck with the Conservatives, Brown called the general election, exactly five years after Blair's last victory. But Labour's hopes were dashed by his poor performance in three televised debates with the other party leaders, David Cameron and Nick Clegg. Ill at ease, Brown reeled off statistics in a toneless voice, with nervousness exaggerating his Scottish accent and distorting his facial expressions. The election of 6 May 2010 returned 258 Labour MPs, 306 Conservatives, fifty-seven Liberal Democrats, and twenty-nine MPs from smaller parties. Polling suggests that Brown's unpopularity cost Labour between twenty and forty seats. Last-minute attempts to form a Labour–Lib Dem coalition (which would still have left Labour short of an absolute majority) failed. Brown resigned as prime minister and leader of the Labour Party on 11 May. The New Labour era was over.

The audit

What is a historian to make of it? New Labour was not responsible for the state of the nation in 2010. Much of Britain was beyond the reach of Whitehall; much of it was the result of policies of past governments; much of it was not the result of any policy. Many changes wrought by the New Labour governments were not specifically New Labour. In normal times governments don't make much difference: continuity is far greater than change, and most changes are unguided by policy. One can only judge the record of New Labour against what it set out to do.

The 'project' was to make Labour electable. In this it succeeded, with three general election victories in a row. The Blair–Brown rivalry, and Brown's own lack of appeal as prime minister, cost it a fourth term, but it was still stronger, and the Conservatives weaker, than had been the case from 1979 to 1997. Both parties, though, had lost ground to the Liberal Democrats and other small parties. So the question of which party, or combination of parties, will govern Britain in the twenty-first century (or indeed how much of it they will govern) remains open.

New Labour did not seriously erode the Conservative hold on the Establishment. Blair's attempt to create a meritocratic elite based on 'new grammar schools', new wealth, the media and celebrity culture broke down. Decisive obstacles are the independent public schools and the ancient universities. As long as these institutions continue to supply most of Britain's leaders, with the peerage as the ultimate reward for success, Labour will always seem something of an outsider in the corridors of power, even when it is in office. Nor was Labour successful in mapping out a radically distinct policy agenda.

Under Blair, Britain briefly re-emerged as an imperial power, reversing the long retreat from empire. There are plenty of 'evil dictators' left whom the world would be better off without, but Britain's availability for the job of removing them depends on the willingness of the United States to allocate firepower for the purpose, the willingness of British voters to expend resources, and the total resources available in the British economy. Since enthusiasm for Blair's ethical imperialism was far less fervent than for Thatcher's old-fashioned kind in the Falklands, it seems unlikely that this hobby of Blair's will be frequently indulged.

Brown had little interest in Blair's foreign-policy crusades, but he took global poverty seriously. In 1999 he got the G7 to agree to a plan of debt relief for heavily indebted countries. He agreed to increase Britain's aid budget to 0.4 per cent of national income by 2006. He pressed for a new global compact whereby in return for the poorest countries entering the world economy and pursuing anti-corruption, pro-trade policies, the rich countries would spend an extra $50 billion on health, education and anti-poverty programmes. It was typical of their differences that while Blair tried to save the world in 2003 by invading Iraq, Brown tried to do so in 2009 by mobilising the G8 to fight the world slump.

Blair failed to place Britain at the heart of Europe, partly because Brown refused the single currency, partly because Blair, in pursuit of his moral aims, hugged the United States too close. Now there is a real possibility that Britain will leave the EU. As the United States declines as a world policeman, so Britain's usefulness to the USA will decline just as it is losing its influence in Europe. As its external affiliations shrivel, Enoch Powell's vision of a new island story looks less far-fetched.

New Labour partly enacted the nineteenth-century Liberal programme of 'devolution all round'. The minority nations of Britain – Northern Ireland, Scotland and Wales – all have their devolved governments. Ending the troubles in Northern Ireland was a notable achievement, even though the ground had been laid by Thatcher and Major. There will be no 'united' Ireland as Sinn Fein wanted, and the IRA fought for, at least not for the foreseeable future. But the boundaries between north and south, and between the rest of Britain and Ireland, are bound to become increasingly blurred as the British state loses its unique claim to the allegiance of the British 'nations'.

But there is clearly unfinished business. Scotland voted narrowly to remain part of the UK in a referendum held on 18 September 2014, but only after promises of further devolution, which are bound to revive the West Lothian question (see p. 111). A British referendum on continued membership of the European Union is promised in 2017. Suppose Scottish voters want to stay in but English voters want to leave?

Other leftover Liberal projects made less progress. Parliament was not deprived of its sovereignty by a written constitution; the Lords did not become an elected senate; local government was not given a local income tax; proportional representation was rejected for national and local elections. None of the reforms interested Blair or Brown, or indeed the voters.

Both Blair and Brown were committed to improve the public services and improve the relative position of the poor. These were measurable aims. What progress did New Labour make in achieving them?

A temporarily buoyant economy gave New Labour a margin of choice between cutting taxes and increasing public spending which Old Labour had never had. It was in choosing the latter that it made a difference. From 2000 to 2010 Labour governments achieved a sustained investment in the popular social services of health, education, and law and order. From 2002 to 2008 health spending went up to over 7 per cent of GDP a year from 2.6 per cent of GDP in the Major years, reaching Blair's target of hitting the EU average by 2009. (But by this time the EU average had moved upwards.) As a result there were 103 new hospitals, 44,000 more doctors and 90,000 more nurses.

New Labour increased education spending by half, from 4.5 per cent of GDP to over 6 per cent in the same period. Capital spending on school buildings rose from £700 million a year in 1997 to £8 billion by 2010; 420 schools were built or refurbished, 42,000 more teachers employed. Brown stuffed the doctors' and teachers' mouths with gold.

The effects of splashing all this money around were mixed. Waiting lists fell to their lowest ever; there was a dramatic decrease in deaths from strokes, cancer, heart attacks. Literary and numeracy standards rose significantly for all school-age children, though not by as much as policymakers had hoped. On most measures, the UK still fared poorly compared to other rich countries.

These improvements were bought at the expense of mind-numbing controls and targets. 'The terrible consequence of . . . confused reforms,' writes Steve Richards, 'was the need for more bureaucrats to make sense of them.'[31] By the autumn of 2004 hospitals were subject to a hundred different inspection regimes. By 2001, 3,840 pages of instructions were being sent to schools, and one headmaster reported 525 targets for his school. In return for extra money, universities were required to recruit a wider social mix. The improvements were not enough to stem the demand for private medicine and private education. And there was never enough money. By 2006 the NHS was facing a cash crisis, with hospital trusts in some of the most vulnerable parts of the country on the edge of bankruptcy.

New Labour was committed to reducing poverty. Tax and benefit changes between 1997 and 2007 raised the incomes of the poorest by 12 per cent, and reduced those of the richest by

5 per cent, mitigating the global trend towards greater inequality. In 1997 there were 3.4 million children living in poverty (in households earning less than 60 per cent of median income). Labour aimed to reduce child poverty by a quarter by 2005, halve it by 2010 and eradicate it altogether by 2020. The first of these targets was narrowly missed, with child poverty falling to 2.6 million by 2005. In 2006, the total began rising, and the financial crisis put paid to future ambitions. The key policies were the minimum wage (covering 2 million workers), and tax credits aimed at working families and children, and a savings credit for pensioners. Labour claimed that the New Deal helped a quarter of a million young people back to work. More important was the huge increase in size of the state. In the Blair years public employment (which included teachers and nurses as well as civil servants) grew by 600,000.

There was a reasonably coherent social philosophy behind all this. The only way New Labour's anti-poverty drive could be reconciled with the tax-imposed limit on public spending was to target benefits on the poor. The welfare state should be seen not as an alternative to employment, but a way into it. Except for the old and disabled, all benefit claimants should be jobseekers. One ironic consequence of this shift to targeting was that although New Labour eschewed Old Labour's aim of redistribution through the tax system, its means-testing of the poor was in fact highly redistributive.

Investment in new prisons, crime-fighting technology, and police 'on the beat' reduced recorded crime by 40 per cent. Liberals deplored the harsher penalties and ubiquitous surveillance that went with these outcomes, but life became safer for most ordinary people. However, despite tougher controls on asylum seekers, net migration increased by 400 per cent, from 50,000 in 1997 to a peak of 245,000 in 2005.

Labour did not stem the inflow of immigrants, which most people considered far too much.

New Labour policy thus made a difference. The argument among experts has been mainly about how far the statistics reflect what really happened (for example the allegation of grade inflation in schools, doubts about reduction in crime) and, if they did, whether the improved outcomes could have been achieved at less cost. The Brown recipe for raising standards of education and health care was undoubtedly costly to the Exchequer not least because it ignored the Blair strategy of levering up standards by creating internal markets. Blair's 'tough on crime' policy carried a corresponding cost in terms of civil liberties.

However, a much more basic criticism is that the improvements were unaffordable. In 2005 the National Institute of Economic and Social Research could report that 'Labour's economic record has been very satisfactory. Nothing has gone badly wrong . . . since 1997.'[32] The average annual growth rate for Labour's first decade was 3.1 per cent a year. Then came the slump of 2008–9. It is now realised that Britain, like other western countries, enjoyed something of an artificial boom in the 2000s; and that this misled the Brown Treasury into overestimating the soundness of the fiscal position (and the economy on which it depended). Brown failed to interrogate the evidence sufficiently closely. He shared this failing with most other experts, but he was the Chancellor.

The fundamental fact was that the New Labour business model failed to improve labour productivity, which lagged 10 per cent below the rest of the G7 throughout the Labour government. Despite all the training programmes and talk of a 'skills revolution', Britain continued to suffer a shortage of effectively trained workers to satisfy the needs of a modern economy. The shortage was partly met by import of skilled labour from the Continent, but this was hardly a success for the new business model. A million net jobs were lost in the private sector. The decline in manufacturing continued. In 1997, 4.5 million were employed in manufacturing; by 2010 this was 2.5 million. Much of the success story in private employment came from immigration and growth in part-time and temporary jobs in the lowest-paid sectors of the economy such as retail, hotels and catering. Britain had longer working hours than any other western European country. In the words of Seldon and Lodge, 'The newly discovered British Business Model seemed at its best in generating poorly paid work with an inbuilt culture of longer working hours rather than in providing decent jobs with generous pay and civilised benefits and employment security in the more advanced sectors of the modern economy.'[33] There was no reversal of the rising trend to continuing earnings polarisation, though the minimum wage may have prevented it rising further.

But Brown's luck also ran out. He expected the boom to go on for ever: indeed claimed that his policies had abolished 'boom and bust'. As a result he took insufficient precautions against the rainy day. It was only in 2007 that public spending was reined in. The Comprehensive Spending Review of that year announced that it would grow in real terms by 2 per cent a year till 2010–11, about half of its growth since 2000, with significant cuts in the health and education budgets. The only problem with this was that GDP was projected to grow by 2.5 per cent a year in those three years; in fact it fell by 1 per cent a year. Spending was set, revenues collapsed, hence the sudden explosion of the deficit, and the clamour for retrenchment.

It is sometimes claimed that New Labour did not make as

much difference to the national life as thirteen years in power, with big majorities, might have led one to expect. There was no single 'transforming' policy, like the establishment of the National Health Service under Attlee, or the privatisation, anti-union and 'right to buy' measures of Thatcher. But then one needs to ask: what possibilities of transformation existed? New Labour did not come to power in a wrenching crisis, as the Churchill, Attlee and Thatcher governments had. Its position was rather like that of the Conservative governments of the 1950s, whose sphere of manoeuvre was limited by the Attlee settlement of 1945–51. New Labour was part of the Thatcher settlement of 1979–97, and its ability to vary it was similarly circumscribed.

Despite the limitations on its scope for action, it showed insufficient boldness within the limits of the possible. A huge failure was in transport. Transport policy was left to the pugilistically inclined deputy prime minister, John Prescott. His legacy was not a modernised railway system, but bicycle lanes. Following the Hatfield rail crash of October 2002, the opportunity to renationalise Railtrack, the privatised operator, was missed. Brown's obsession with the Public–Private Partnership to modernise the London Underground blinded him to the merits of Ken Livingstone's counter-proposal for the London Transport Authority to carry out the modernisation by borrowing the money itself.

In transport as elsewhere, Labour was much too timid in its attack on vested interests and the conventional wisdom underlying them. Britain paid an exceptionally heavy price for its love-fest with the City of London, another Faustian bargain, with its delusive promises of gold to pay for Labour spending programmes. It failed to take steps to limit private education, the chief bastion of class privilege.

The New Labour achievement was limited by the personal failings of its leaders. For somewhat different reasons, Blair and Brown were poor executives. Prime minister and Chancellor were their first offices of state. It took office to make Blair understand the gap 'between the commitment and the execution', and he never did fully understand it. Like reformers before him, he was frustrated by the inertia of the Civil Service, but he never learnt how to get the government machine to do what he wanted, despite equipping his office with delivery units, project teams and, eventually, with five-year plans. Partly this was because he started out without a clear idea of what he wanted it to do; partly because he 'under-estimated the importance of departmental ministers, never having been one himself'.[34] As a result he was never able to establish collective ownership of his projects, relying on a small group of advisers like Andrew Adonis and Michael Barber to drive them through. In his first term he brought in Frank Field to 'think the unthinkable' on welfare. But he soon concluded that it 'was not so much that his thoughts were unthinkable as unfathomable'.[35] His school-reform pro-gramme never got seriously going till his (truncated) third term. He was easily distracted by glamour projects.

Like Blair, Brown liked to make policy in a very small circle, though his policy machine was more like a bunker than a salon. He preferred to consult bilaterally, and play off ideas against each other, so no one knew what he thought. Permanent Treasury officials were shunted aside in favour of 'a small cabal' from the Chancellor's office consisting of Brown, his economic adviser Ed Balls, his 'attack dog' Damian McBride, and the future Labour leader Ed Miliband.[36] He relied on Balls intellectually and emotionally. (When Balls talked to a Labour conference of 'the post-classical endogenous growth model', Michael Heseltine memorably riposted, 'It's not Brown, it's balls.') He expected the Treasury to implement his decisions, not question them. As prime minister, he was no better at using the government service than Blair had been. He showed little interest in motivating his Cabinet colleagues, making it 'all too clear that he was not interested in the great majority of them, nor did he make them feel that he valued or even liked them. It is unsurprising then that, within a few months, the Cabinet were openly discussing amongst each other how they could get rid of him.'[37]

Analysts of his rule emphasised his inability to take timely decisions, run an orderly government or to fashion a vision of the future. He spent ten years itching to get the premiership, then threw it away because he didn't know what to do with it.

New Labour failed to improve the quality of public life; in fact, it was soon enveloped in the sleaze which had weakened the Conservatives under Major. The root of this was its corrupt relationship with the media. The problem was not generic to New Labour, but is an aspect of modern culture. All governments now spin the news, because politicians are forced to rely increasingly on the media, their other channels of communication with the public having dried up. Mainstream political parties are now empty shells of their former selves. Having lost their roots in solid constituencies of society, how are parties supposed to advertise their political messages? 'Only, as they see it, through the media.'[38] And not just the message: the personality as well. Blair was a superb media performer, Brown an indifferent one. That is probably the main reason he lost in 2010.

New Labour Britain enjoyed a brittle prosperity. The rise in wealth due to soaring house prices and easy borrowing fed a house-price boom which, with cheap air travel, spread to expatriate colonies in France and Italy. By 2006, three quarters of British children had access to the Internet at home. New money from Russia, America, the Middle East and Europe bought up bits of London and attractive country houses. 'There was a renaissance of show-off architecture for a show-off society.'[39]

Blair's win in 1997 coincided with a period of commercial success for British popular culture, epitomised by the later-ubiquitous slogan, 'Cool Britannia'. Art from the likes of Damien Hirst became hot property among collectors, boosted by the patronage of Charles Saatchi. In the charts, Blur and Oasis, the leading lights of Britpop, offered a distinctively British response to the influx of American music. Music aimed at young teenagers became big business, with teen pop groups like Take That backed by industrial-scale commercial operations. British music acts lined up to have their turn at 'cracking America', as the Beatles had in the 1960s. The Spice Girls were the biggest success, with 80 million record sales and an internationally distributed film. British pop music echoed across the globe; Geri Halliwell's Union Jack minidress replaced the White Ensign as the symbol of Britain's global reach. New Labour embraced the mood, adopting the D:Ream song 'Things Can Only Get Better' as their election theme tune.

British – or rather English – football was another cultural money spinner. In the 1980s, football was at its lowest ebb, reeling from a series of disasters, both natural and self-inflicted. But in the 1990s and 2000s, new money brought about a footballing renaissance, attracting bigger audiences and foreign talent. Opportunities for merchandising and sponsorship abounded. The flow of television money into football was reflected in inflated wages for players and higher ticket prices. The growing expense of season tickets priced many traditional football fans out, but attracted a new, more affluent consumer. In 1901, professional footballers had played for £4 a week; in 2010, Manchester City's Carlos Tevez became the first player to earn £1 million a month. Players became not just heroes to their club's fans, but celebrities in their own right, with all the accompanying misdemeanours and peccadilloes of pop stars. Fittingly, it was David Beckham – husband of Victoria, formerly Posh Spice – who became football's first international brand.

New Labour was not responsible for the cultural tawdriness of the age but it did not resist it. In fact Blair set the cultural scene for the New Labour era by the way he handled the death of Princess Diana in 1997. In a poignant broadcast, which voiced a national sorrow clearly not shared by the queen, he showed his ability to capture and manipulate the sentimentality of the public. Diana was both a victim and manipulator of the celebrity culture. Andrew Marr called her the 'Barbie of the emotions'.[40] To Blair she was the 'people's princess'; 'she captured the essence of an era'. Blair was clearly of that essence. His popularity soared to 90 per cent.

So it continued. In 2000, the Dome unveiled its millennial offerings to obloquy even from the popular press. Intended as a cultural showpiece of Cool Britannia, its high-tech wrapping could not disguise its banality. In July 2000 came a ferocious attack on New Labour from the novelist V. S. Naipaul, who accused it of championing 'an aggressively plebeian culture that celebrates itself for being plebeian'. None of this fazed Blair, who was not a reading man. 'In art and culture,' he wrote, 'we should represent all strands, avant-garde through to basic popular art,' from Duran Duran and Madonna to Paul Weller and Billy Bragg.[41]

'Tony was star-struck,' writes Gordon Burn. 'He liked

rubbing shoulders with Sir Cliff [Richard] and Bono and Barry Gibb and gladly accepted invitations to make use of their rock-star mansions. He was reported to be sick with nerves before appearing at the Brits and overawed at the prospect of meeting Noel Gallagher. He was relentlessly mocked in the press for the calibre of the guests he had down for supper at Chequers: Vernon Kay and Jimmy Savile; this was hardly the Rat Pack. Charlotte Church. She was hardly Pablo Casals.'[42]

Gordon Brown, whose tastes were more elevated, mocked Blair's obsession with 'Sierra Man' and 'Worcester Woman'. But neither leader thought of popular culture as something requiring elevation. Culture, like religion, was a private preference to be traded like any other in the marketplace Britain had become.

Envoi

Britain's voyage through the twentieth century was hardly glorious; but it was not wholly inglorious. It is hard, though, to look forward to the future with much confidence. The successes have become too patchy and ephemeral; the list of failures, relative and absolute, lengthens. Estranged from Europe, and despised by America, Britain faces a lonely, introverted future. Such hopes as survive must rest with the character of the British people. Whether enough of that tough, acrid, creative, enterprising, humorous and, at its best, kind and tolerant quality of character which made Britain great survives to make its mark on the new world is the final unanswered question of this analytical history.

Notes

Introduction

1. Guglielmo Ferrero, *The Principles of Power* (1942), p. 14.
2. Norman Davies, *The Isles: A History* (2000), p. 1014.
3. See Niall Ferguson, *Empire: How Britain Made the Modern World* (2003).
4. A. J. P. Taylor, *English History, 1914–1945* (1992), p. 600.
5. ONS National Population Projections 2010, Access Economics.
6. Chris Benjamin, *Strutting on Thin Air* (2009), p. 1.

Chapter 1

1. Hera Cook, *The Long Sexual Revolution: English Women, Sex, and Contraception 1800–1975* (2004).
2. Judith Ryder and Harold Silver, *Modern English Society: History and Structure, 1850–1970* (1970), p. 92.
3. Helen Connolly and Amanda White, 'The different experiences of the United Kingdom's ethnic and religious population', *Social Trends 36* (2006 edn), Office of National Statistics, p. 1.
4. Anthony Atkinson, 'The distribution of income in the UK and OECD countries in the twentieth century', *Oxford Review of Economic Policy* (1999, 15:4), p. 60.
5. Anthony Atkinson and F. Bourgignon, *Handbook of Income Distribution*, Vol. 1 (2000).
6. Chris Benjamin, *Strutting on Thin Air* (2009), p. 318.
7. Ryder and Silver, *Modern English Society*, p. 70.

8. Lucy Delap, *Knowing Their Place: Domestic Service in Twentieth-Century Britain* (2010).

9. Larry Elliott and Dan Atkinson, *Fantasy Island* (2007), p. 75.

11. Adair Turner, *Economics After the Crisis* (2012).

12. Ha-Joon Chang, *23 Things They Don't Tell You About Capitalism* (2010), pp. 31–2.

13. Quoted in Peter Vansittart, *Voices 1870–1914* (1984), p. 236.

14. Arthur Marwick, *British Society Since 1945* (1990), p. 119.

15. Peter Clarke, *Hope and Glory: Britain 1900–1990* (1996), p. 145.

Chapter 2

1. Stefan Collini, *Common Reading: Critics, Historians, Publics* (2008), p. 269.

2. A. H. Halsey and Elizabeth Webb (eds.), *Twentieth Century British Social Trends* (2000); David and Gareth Butler, *Twentieth Century British Political Facts 1900–2000* (2000). See also Ross McKibbin, *Classes and Cultures: England 1918–1951* (1998), p. 294. Church membership – those defining themselves as members of a Christian domination – fell from 33 to 17 per cent (Halsey and Webb, pp. 654–5). Weekly church attendance may have fallen from 19 to 8 per cent (Halsey and Webb, p. 657). The percentage of infants getting baptised fell from 73 per cent in 1900 to 45 per cent in 2000, with only a small percentage going on to be confirmed (Halsey and Webb, pp. 664–5). In 1900, 85 per cent of people got married in church. By 2000 this was 40 per cent of the declining proportion of those who did get married (Halsey and Webb, p. 663).

3. Halsey and Webb, *British Social Trends*, Table 19.12, pp. 668–9.

4. Quoted in ibid., p. 656.

5. Frederic Raphael, *There and Then* (2013), p. 192.

6. Roger Sandall, *The Culture Cult: Designer Tribalism and Other Essays* (1984), p. 4.

7. See A. N. Wilson, *After the Victorians 1901–1953* (1988), pp. 80–1. But there are three Roman Catholics in his list.

8. Alasdair MacIntyre, *Secularization and Moral Change* (1967), p. 72.

9. Quoted in Colin Kidd, *London Review of Books*, 24 January 2013.

10. Raymond Williams, *The Long Revolution* (1961), p. 302.

11. David Kynaston, *Austerity Britain 1945–51* (2007), pp. 574–6.

12. Jonathan Rose, *The Intellectual Life of the British Working Class* (2002), p. 11.

13. Stefan Collini's *Absent Minds: Intellectuals in Britain* (2006) is a subtle, erudite discussion of British attitudes to intellectuals. It shows conclusively that while Britain had intellectuals, social conditions precluded the emergence of an intellectual class. Collini seems to welcome this state of affairs, while Perry Anderson deplores it.

NOTES 409

14. This is the main idea of John Carey's book, *The Intellectuals and the Masses: Pride and Prejudice among the Literary Intelligentsia 1880–1939* (1992).

15. McKibbin, *Classes and Cultures*, pp. 527–8.

16. Terry Eagleton, *London Review of Books*, 20 December 2012.

17. Quoted in Judith Ryder and Harold Silver, *Modern English Society: History and Structure, 1850–1970* (1970), p. 99.

18. *Daily Telegraph*, 30 August 2007.

19. David Marquand, *Decline of the Public; The Hollowing out of Citizenship* (2004), p. 84.

20. *Big Issue*, 3–9 February 2014.

21. ONS Marriage Statistics.

22. Geoffrey Gorer, *Exploring English Character: A Study of the Morals and Behaviour of the English People* (1955), p. 13; George Orwell, *The English People* (1947), p. 12.

23. James Bartholomew, *The Welfare State We're In* (2006), pp. 7–8; Theodore Dalrymple, *Our Culture, What's Left of It* (2005), pp. 13–15.

24. Ben Page, 'Does Britain need fixing?', *Prospect*, October 2008, p. 72.

25. Elizabeth Burney, *Making People Behave* (2009), p. 62.

26. Carey, *The Intellectuals and the Masses*; George Walden, *The New Elites: Making a Career in the Masses* (2000).

27. Gabriel Josipovici, 'Fail Again. Fail Better', *Times Literary Supplement*, 30 November 2007.

28. For an interesting discussion, see Claire Carlisle's review of Terry Eagleton's *Culture and the Death of God* (2014), *TLS*, 18 April 2014.

29. J. A. Spender, *The Public Life*, Vol. II (1925) pp. 103–4.

30. *Guardian*, 17 April 2014.

Appendix

1. Oswald Spengler, *The Decline of the West* (single volume edn 1932), I, pp. 33–4, II, pp. 104, 415–16.

2. Daniel Bell, *Cultural Contradictions of Capitalism* (1976), pp. 15, 37.

3. Simmel cited in Tomas Sedlacek, *Economics of Good and Evil* (2011), p. 139.

4. Karl Marx and Friedrich Engels, *The Communist Manifesto* (2012), pp. 38–9.

5. Plato, *Republic* (2004), Book IX, pp. 270–96.

6. Michel Crozier, Samuel P. Huntington and Joji Watanuki, *The Crisis of Democracy: Report on the Governability to the Trilateral Commission* (1975), pp. 75, 2.

Chapter 3

1. For the latest discussion, see Vernon Bogdanor, *The New British Constitution* (2009), and Anthony King, *The British Constitution* (2007).

2. King, *The British Constitution*, p. 47.

3. J. M. Roberts (ed.), 'Preface' to each volume of *The New Oxford History of England* series (1992–2010), p. vii.

4. King, *The British Constitution*, p. 66.

5. See Patrick Dunleavy, *Democracy, Bureaucracy and Public Choice: Economic Explanations in Political Science* (1991).

6. Quoted in King, *The British Constitution*, p. 221.

7. Ibid., p. 222.

8. Ibid., p. 164.

9. Ibid., p. 152.

10. Ibid., p. 116.

11. George Orwell, *Politics and the English Language* (1946).

12. J. A. Spender, *The Public Life*, vol. II (1925), p. 98.

Chapter 4

1. Sidney Buxton, *Finance and Politics, A Historical Study 1783–1885* (1888), p. 134.

2. A. T. Peacock and Jack Wiseman, *The Growth of Public Expenditure in the United Kingdom* (1961), p. 67.

3. Quoted in G. K. Fry, *The Growth of Government* (1979), p. 33.

4. For details see J. A. Kay and M. A. King, *The British Tax System* (1978), pp. 19–20.

5. Tibor Barna, *Redistribution of Incomes through Public Finance* (1945), p. 233, reckoned that between 1914 and 1937 working-class incomes were increased by 8–14 per cent by redistributive finance.

6. Fry, *The Growth of Government*, p. 152.

7. T. H. Green, quoted in ibid., p. 47.

8. Friedrich Hayek, *The Road to Serfdom* (2001), p. 20.

9. Max Hartwell, *Confrontation* (1978), p. 126.

10. Michael Howard, 'The State', *Daedalus*, fall 1979, p. 101.

11. Alan Milward, *Times Literary Supplement*, 15 August 1975.

12. Peacock and Wiseman, *The Growth of Public Expenditure in the United Kingdom*.

Chapter 5

1. Bernard Semmel, *Imperialism and Social Reform: English Social-Imperial Thought 1895–1914* (1960), p. 16.

2. Correlates of War project, at www.correlatesofwar.org (accessed 22 October 2012).

3. Correlli Barnett, *The Collapse of British Power* (1972), p. 88.

4. Ibid., p. 84.

5. Michael Howard, *The Continental Commitment: the Dilemma of British Defence Policy in the Era of the Two World Wars* (1974), p. 29.

6. Norman Stone, *A Short History of the First World War* (2007), p. 9.

7. Paul Kennedy, *The Realities Behind Diplomacy: Background Influences on British External Policy 1865–1980* (1981) p. 320.

8. The mutual dependence of trade and the British Navy was an axiom of British foreign policy – see its 1707 expression by Lord Haversham, quoted in J. C. D. Clark (ed.), *A World By Itself: A History of the British Isles* (2010), p. 357. The attempt by free-traders to prove that the two were independent, because trade was mutually beneficial and did not need military support, never cut much ice in Parliament or Whitehall.

9. Desmond Flower (ed.), *Voltaire's England* (1950), p. 50.

10. Ralph Waldo Emerson, *English Traits* (1883), p. 153.

11. Brooks Adams, *America's Economic Supremacy* (1900), pp. 147, 152.

12. Thorstein Veblen, *Imperial Germany and the Industrial Revolution* (1942), p. 131.

13. Ibid., especially Chapter 4; see also pp. 209, 246.

14. H. H. Asquith, *Speeches by the Earl of Oxford and Asquith 1886–1926* (1927), p. 88.

15. David Edgerton, *Warfare State: Britain 1920–70* (2005).

16. Quoted in Geoffrey Barraclough, *An Introduction to Contemporary History* (1969), p. 10.

17. Quoted in Peter Vansittart, *Voices 1870–1914* (1984), p. 170.

18. Noel Annan, *Our Age* (1990), p. 77.

19. Quoted in Robert Skidelsky, *John Maynard Keynes: Hopes Betrayed 1883–1920* (1983) pp. 134–5.

20. Craufurd D. W. Goodwin (ed.), *Art in the Market: Roger Fry on Commerce in Art* (1998), p. 17.

21. Beatrice Webb to Kate Courtney, 18 September 1911, in Norman MacKenzie (ed.), *The Letters of Sidney and Beatrice Webb*, Vol. 1 (1978), p. 372.

22. Sidney Webb, 29 June 1890, in ibid., p. 158.

Chapter 6

1. *Times Literary Supplement*, 30 May 2008.
2. J. M. Keynes, *The Economic Consequences of the Peace* (1919), p. 7.
3. I owe this conceit to A. N. Wilson, *After the Victorians 1901–1953* (1988), p. 151.
4. David Owen, *The Hidden Perspective: The Military Conversations 1906–14* (2014), p. 410.
5. John Keegan, *The First World War* (1998), p. 212.
6. Niall Ferguson, *The Pity of War* (1998) p. 357.
7. Kenneth O. Morgan, *Consensus and Disunity: The Lloyd George Coalition Government 1918–1922* (1979), p. 13.
8. A. J. P. Taylor, *Essays in English History* (1976) p. 233.
9. Friedrich Hayek, *The Road to Serfdom* (1944, 1962 edn), p. 79.
10. Quoted in Correlli Barnett, *The Audit of War: The Illusion and Reality of Britain as a Great Nation* (1986), p. 85.
11. Quoted in Keith Middlemas, *Politics in Industrial Society* (1979), p. 104.
12. Morgan, *Consensus and Disunity*, p. 16.
13. Tom Nairn, *The Break-Up of Britain: Crisis and Neo-nationalism* (1981), p. 43.
14. Norman MacKenzie (ed.), *The Letters of Sidney and Beatrice Webb*, vol. 3 (1978), p. 274.
15. Norman and Jeanne MacKenzie (eds.), *The Diary of Beatrice Webb*, vol. 4 (1985), p. 194.
16. Paul Fussell, *The Great War and Modern Memory* (1975), p. 33.
17. Noel Annan, 'Hello to All That', *New York Review of Books*, 26 March 1992.
18. Modern scholarship de-emphasises the importance of the Maurice Debate in favour of the whole voting record of the Asquithian Liberals; see Morgan, *Consensus and Disunity*, pp. 31–2.
19. Max Beloff, *Imperial Sunset: Britain's Liberal Empire 1897–1921* (1969), p. 278.
20. Morgan, *Consensus and Disunity*, p. 316.

Chapter 7

1. R. Matthews et al., *British Economic Growth 1856–1973* (1982), p. 170.
2. Derek Aldcroft, *The British Economy Between the Wars* (1983) pp. 74–5.
3. J. M. Keynes, 'The Economic Consequences of Mr Churchill' (1925), *Collected Writings*, vol. 9, p. 218.
4. Oswald Mosley, *Revolution by Reason* (1925), pp. 14–17, 26.
5. Noel Annan, *Our Age* (1990), p. 70.
6. Modris Eksteins, *Rites of Spring: The Great War and the Birth of the Modern Age* (1989), p. 117.

7. This is the thesis of Charles P. Kindleberger's *The World in Depression 1929–1939* (1986).

8. Nicholas Crafts, *Britain's Relative Economic Performance* (1999) p. 75.

9. Maurice de Soissons, *Welwyn Garden City* (1988).

10. Quoted in Annan, *Our Age*, p. 75.

11. Susan Pedersen, 'A Babylonian Touch', *London Review of Books*, 6 November 2008. Pederson provides a corrective to Martin Pugh's optimistic account of the interwar years in *State and Society: A Social and Political History of Britain 1870–1997* (1999): 'If consumption spread, it still ran along the fault-lines of class.' David Fowler, *The First Teenagers: The Lifestyle of Young Wage-earners in Interwar Britain* (2005) argues that a youth market for leisure and consumption existed in the 1930s, but the war interrupted it, so that when it reappeared in the 1950s, it was regarded as a new phenomenon.

12. Quoted in Keith Feiling, *Life of Neville Chamberlain* (1946), p. 320.

13. G. C. Peden, *British Rearmament and the Treasury 1932–1939* (1979), p. 61. In 1934, the Treasury reduced extra arms requirements submitted by the Defence Requirements Subcommittee of the Committee of Imperial Defence from £77 million to £50 million; another reduction took place in 1935. The Treasury considered the possibility of a defence loan in 1935, but did not advocate it; see pp. 71–7.

14. Philip Williamson, *Stanley Baldwin* (1999), p. 51.

15. Correlli Barnett, *The Collapse of British Power* (1972), p. 135.

16. John Harvey (ed.), *The Diplomatic Diaries of Oliver Harvey 1937–1940* (1970), p. 110.

17. The phrase is A. J. P. Taylor's from *Origins of the Second World War* (1961, 1971 paperback edn), p. 158.

18. Feiling, *Life of Neville Chamberlain*, p. 314.

19. Ibid, p. 319.

20. As Neville Henderson, British ambassador to Berlin, complained on 16 August 1939; quoted in Taylor, *Origins of the Second World War*, p. 324.

Chapter 8

1. A. J. P. Taylor, *Essays in English History* (1991), p. 465.

2. Quoted in John Charmley, *Churchill: The End of Glory* (1993), pp. 431, 430.

3. David Irving, *Hitler's War* (1991), pp. 133–62.

4. Alan S. Milward, *War, Economy and Society 1939–1945* (1977), p. 3.

5. Correlli Barnett, *The Audit of War: The Illusion and Reality of Britain as a Great Nation* (1986), pp. 168, 173.

6. Alan S. Milward, *War, Economy and Society* (1977), p. 13.

7. Quoted in Robert Skidelsky, *John Maynard Keynes: Fighting for Britain, 1937–1946* (2000), p. 267.

8. Peter Hennessy, *Never Again: Britain 1945–51* (1992), p. 144.

9. Nicholas Crafts, 'Adjusting from War to Peace', *Warwick Economic Research Papers* (1993), pp. 15–16.

10. Paul Kennedy, *The Realities Behind Diplomacy: Background Influences on British External Policy* (1981), p. 331.

11. Quoted in Colin Cross, *The Fall of the British Empire, 1918–1968* (1969), p. 262.

12. R. W. Johnson, 'Up the Garden Path', *London Review of Books*, 26 April 2007.

13. John Campbell, *Nye Bevan and the Mirage of British Socialism* (1987), p. 271.

Chapter 9

1. Hugh Thomas, *The Suez Affair* (1986), p. 183.

2. Douglas Evans, *While Britain Slept: The Selling of the Common Market* (1975), pp. 81–2.

3. Andrew Shonfield, *Modern Capitalism* (1965), p. 3.

4. Meghnad Desai, 'Thatcherism in Historical Perspective', in Francis Green (ed.), *The Restructuring of the UK Economy* (1989), p. 308.

5. Michael Shanks, *The Stagnant Society* (1972), p. 215.

6. Ibid., p.68; Nicholas Crafts, *Britain's Relative Economic Performance* (1999), p. 77.

7. See Sir Alec Cairncross (ed.) *Britain's Economic Prospects Reconsidered* (1971), p. 117; Max Nicholson, *The System: The misgovernment of modern Britain* (1967), p. 491.

8. This view was championed by the *New Left Review*, and associated with the writings of Perry Anderson and Tom Nairn. The quotation is from Tom Nairn's *The Break-up of Britain* (1981), p. 32.

9. Phillip Whitehead, *The Writing on the Wall: Britain in the Seventies* (1985), p. 2.

10. P. J. Sinclair, 'The Economy – A Study in Failure', in David McKie and Chris Cook (eds.), *The Decade of Disillusion: British Politics in the Sixties* (1972), p. 94.

11. Dominic Sandbrook, *Having It So Good* (2005); David Fowler, *Youth Culture in Modern Britain c.1920–c.1970* (2008).

12. Anthony Bicat, 'Fifties Children: Sixties People', in Vernon Bogdanor and Robert Skidelsky (eds.), *The Age of Affluence 1951–1964* (1970), p. 326.

13. Fowler, *Youth Culture*, p. 171.

14. Sandbrook, *Having It So Good*, p. 441.

15. James Curran, 'Media and the Making of British Society, c.1700–2000', *Media History* (2000, 8:2), pp. 135–54.

16. Nicholas Davenport, *Memoirs of a City Radical* (1974), p. 2.

17. Quoted in Mark Jarvis, *Conservative Governments, Morality and Social Change in Affluent Britain 1957–64* (2005), p. 69; see also Christie Davis, *Permissive Britain: Social Change in the Sixties and Seventies* (1975).

Chapter 10

1. Nicholas Timmins, *The Five Giants: A biography of the welfare state* (1995), p. 265.
2. For Stuart Holland's ideas see his book *The Socialist Challenge* (1975). The quoted phrase is from *Labour's Programme* (1973).
3. Bernard Donoughue, *Downing Street Diary: With Harold Wilson in No. 10* (2004) and *Downing Street Diary: With James Callaghan in No. 10* (2008).
4. Donoughue, *With James Callaghan in No. 10*, pp. 109–13.
5. Christopher Kyriakides and Satnam Virdee, 'Migrant labour, racism and the British National Health Service', *Ethnicity and Health* (2003, 8:4), p. 292.
6. Andrew Roberts, *Eminent Churchillians* (1994), p. 223.
7. Charles Moore, *Margaret Thatcher* (2014), p. 422.
8 Ibid., p. 641.
9. David Runciman, *London Review of Books*, 6 June 2013.
10. Quoted in Hugo Young, *One of Us* (1989), p. 411.
11. Nigel Lawson, *The View from No. 11: Memoirs of a Tory Radical* (1992), p. 195.
12. Nigel Lawson, 'The British Experiment', 5th Mais Lecture, City University Business School, 1984.
13. Nicholas Crafts, *Britain's Relative Economic Performance, 1870–1999* (2002 edit.), p. 101.
14. Harris Poll, *Observer*, 22 May 1988.

Chapter 11

1. Geoffrey Wheatcroft, *The Strange Death of Tory England* (2005), p. 244.
2. Tony Blair, *A Journey* (2010), p. 544.
3. Giles Radice, *Trio: Inside the Blair, Brown, Mandelson Project* (2010), p. 80.
4. Francis Gilbert, *Yob Nation: The Truth about Britain's Yob Culture* (2007), p. 100.
5. Anthony Seldon and Dennis Kavanagh (eds.), *The Blair Effect 2001–5* (2005), p. 277.
6. J. A. Spender, *The Public Life*, vol. II (1925), p. 121.
7. Blair, *A Journey*, p. xvii.
8. Blair, ibid., p. 272.
9. Anthony Seldon (ed.), *The Blair Effect: The Blair Government 1997–2001* (2001), p. 385.

10. Steve Richards, *Whatever it Takes: The Real Story of Gordon Brown and New Labour* (2010), p. 68.

11. Robert Skidelsky, 'Nato's deadly legacy from Kosovo', *Financial Times*, 15 December 1999.

12. Anthony Seldon, *Blair* (2004), p. 394.

13. Ibid., p. 571.

14. Richards, *Whatever it Takes*, p. 163.

15. Seldon and Kavanagh, *The Blair Effect 2001–5*, p. 289.

16. Andrew Adonis, *Education, Education, Education: Reforming England's Schools* (2012), p. 118.

17. Ibid., p. 65.

18. Christopher Meyer, *DC Confidential* (2005), p. 1.

19. Blair, *A Journey*, p. 209.

20. Anthony Seldon, *Blair Unbound* (2008), pp. 275, 277.

21. Robert Peston, *Brown's Britain: How Gordon Runs the Show* (2005), p. 349.

22. Seldon, *Blair Unbound*, p. 333.

23. Ibid., p. 416.

24. Blair, *A Journey*, p. 613.

25. Anthony Seldon and Guy Lodge, *Brown at 10* (2011), p. xxiii.

26. Ibid., p. xxiv.

27. Gordon Brown, *Beyond the Crash: Overcoming the First Crisis of Globalisation* (2010), p. 127.

28. Quoted in Seldon and Lodge, *Brown*, p. 253.

29. Alistair Darling, *Back from the Brink: 1,000 Days at Number 11* (2011), p. 177.

30. Seldon and Lodge, *Brown*, p. 367.

31. Richards, *Whatever it Takes*, p. 171.

32. Seldon and Kavanagh, *The Blair Effect 2001–5*, p. 160.

33. Ibid., p. 199.

34. Adonis, *Education*, p. 88.

35. Blair, *A Journey*, p. 217.

36. Seldon and Lodge, *Brown*, p. xx.

37. Seldon and Lodge, *Brown*, p. xxxxi.

38. Mick Hume, *There is No Such Thing as a Free Press, and Why We Need One More Than Ever* (2012), p. 108.

39. Andrew Marr, *A History of Modern Britain* (2009), p. 574.

40. Ibid., pp. 516–20.

41. Blair, *A Journey*, p. 91.

42. Gordon Burn, *Born Yesterday: The News as a Novel* (2008), p. 139.

Select Bibliography

These are works which are not referenced in the Notes but which the reader may find helpful.

Addison, Paul, *The Road to 1945: British Politics and the Second World War* (1975)

Aldcroft, Derek H., *The British Economy Between the Wars* (1983)

Alford, B. W. E., *Depression and Recovery? British Economic Growth 1918–1939* (1972)

Almond, Brenda, *The Fragmenting Family* (2006)

Attlee, Clement, *As It Happened* (1954)

Ashworth, William, *The State in Business 1945 to the mid 1980s* (1991)

Bacon, Robert, and Eltis, Walter, *Britain's Economic Problem Reconsidered* (1996)

Baker, Kenneth, *The Turbulent Years: My Life in Politics* (1993)

Baldwin, Stanley, *On England* (1938)

Barker, Bernard (ed.), *Ramsay MacDonald's Political Writings* (1972)

Beckerman, Wilfrid, *The Labour Government's Economic Record 1964–1970* (1975)

Beer, Samuel H., *Britain Against Itself* (1982)

Benn, Tony, *The Benn Diaries: 1940–1990* (1996)

Bentley, Michael, and Stevenson, John, *High and Low Politics in Modern Britain* (1983)

Blake, Robert, *The Unknown Prime Minister: The Life and Times of Andrew Bonar Law 1858–1923* (1955)

Blair, Tony, *New Britain: My Vision of a Young Country* (1996)

Blaxland, Gregory, *J. H. Thomas: A Life for Unity* (1964)

Blythe, Roland, *The Age of Illusion: England in the Twenties and Thirties 1919–1940* (1963)

Bogdanor, Vernon, *The Monarchy and the Constitution* (1995)

Bonham Carter, Violet, *Winston Churchill as I Knew Him* (1965)

Booth, Arthur H., *British Hustings 1924–1950* (1956)

Boyle, Andrew, *Montagu Norman* (1967)

Boyd, Francis, *British Politics in Transition 1945–1963* (1964)

Brivati, Brian, *Hugh Gaitskell* (1996)

Brivati, Brian, and Cockett, Richard (eds.), *Anatomy of Decline: The Political Journalism of Peter Jenkins* (1995)

Broadberry, S. N., 'Was the Collapse of British Industry after the World War Inevitable? Structural and Macro-Economic Explanations of Interwar Unemployment', *Warwick Economic Research Papers*, No. 294 (1988)

Brown, Kenneth D., *Labour and Unemployment 1900–1914* (1971)

Bullock, Alan, *The Life and Times of Ernest Bevin*, 3 vols. (1960, 1967, 1984)

Bulpitt, Jim, 'The Discipline of the New Democracy: Mrs Thatcher's Domestic Statecraft', *Political Studies*, XXXIV, 19–39 (1986)

Butler, David, and Butler, Gareth, *British Political Facts 1900–2000* (2000)

Byrd, Peter (ed.), *British Foreign Policy Under Thatcher* (1988)

Cairncross, Alec (ed.), *The Robert Hall Diaries, 1947–53* (1989)

Cairncross, Alec, and Watts, Nina, *The Economic Section 1939–1961: A Study in Economic Advising* (1989)

Calleo, David, *Britain's Future* (1968)

Cannadine, David, *Class in Britain* (1998)

Carlton, David, *Anthony Eden: A Biography* (1986); *Churchill and the Soviet Union* (2000)

Castle, Barbara, *The Castle Diaries 1974–6* (1980)

Chamberlain, Neville, *The Struggle for Peace* (1940)

Chapman, Brian, *British Government Observed* (1965)

Clarke, Peter, *A Question of Leadership: from Gladstone to Thatcher* (1991); *The Cripps Version, The Last Thousand Days of the British Empire: The Demise of a Superpower, 1944–7* (2007); *Liberals and Social Democrats* (1979)

Coleman, Terry, *Thatcher's Britain: A Journey through the Promised Lands* (1987)

Crafts, N. F. R., and Woodward, Nicholas, *The British Economy Since 1945* (1991)

Crewe Ivor, and King, Anthony, *SDP: The Birth, Life and Death of the Social Democratic Party* (1995)

Crick, Bernard, *George Orwell: A Life* (1981)

Crosland, Anthony, *The Future of Socialism* (1956)

Cross, Colin, *Philip Snowden* (1966)

Crossman, Richard, *Diaries of a Cabinet Minister* (ed. Janet Morgan), 3 vols. (1975, 1976, 1977)

Crouch, Colin, and Dore, Ronald (eds.), *Corporatism and Accountability: Organized Interests in British Public Life* (1990)

Cowling, Maurice, *The Impact of Labour 1920–1924* (1971); *The Impact of Hitler: British Politics and British Policy 1933–1940* (1975)

Davies, Nick, *Flat Earth News* (2008)

Davis, William, *Three Years Hard Labour: The Road to Devaluation* (1968)

Dell, Edmund, *A Hard Pounding: Politics and Economic Crisis 1974–76* (1991); *A Strange and Eventful History: Democratic Socialism in Britain* (1999)

Dintenfass, Michael, *The Decline of Industrial Britain 1870–1980* (1992)

Dowse, R. E., *Left in the Centre* (1966)

Dudley-Edwards, Ruth, *The Faithful Tribe* (1999)

Eatwell, Roger, *The 1945–51 Labour Governments* (1979)

Edwardes, Michael, *Back from the Brink: An Apocalyptic Experience* (1983)

Einzig, Paul, *Decline and Fall* (1969)

Elliott, Larry, and Atkinson, Dan, *Going South: Why Britain will have a Third World Economy by 2014* (2012)

Evans, Harold, *Good Times, Bad Times* (1983)

Fairlie, Henry, *The Life of Politics* (1968)

Field, Frank, *Welfare Titans: How Lloyd George and Gordon Brown Compare, and other essays on welfare reform* (2002)

Floud, Roderick, and McCloskey, Donald (eds.), *The Economic History of Britain since 1700, Vol 2: 1860 to the 1970s* (1981)

Foot, Michael, *Aneurin Bevan*, 2 vols. (1962, 1973)

Gilbert, Martin, *Winston Churchill*, vols. IV–VII (1975, 1976, 1983, 1986)

Gilmour, Ian, *Britain Can Work* (1983)

Gladstone, David (ed.), *Before Beveridge: Welfare before the Welfare State* (1999)

Graham, G. S., *The Politics of Naval Supremacy* (1965)

Grant, Wyn, and Nath, Shiv, *The Politics of Economic Policymaking* (1984)

Grant, Wyn, *Economic Policy in Britain* (2002)

Graves, Robert, and Hodge, Alan, *The Long Weekend* (1941)

Griffiths, Richard, *Patriotism Perverted: Captain Ramsay, the Right Club and British Anti-Semitism 1939–40* (1998)

Grigg, John, *Lloyd George*, 4 vols. (1973, 1978, 1985, 2002)

Guttsman, W. L., *The British Political Elites* (1968)

Harris, Kenneth, *Attlee* (1983)

Harris, Jose, *William Beveridge: A Biography* (1977)

Harrison, Brian, *The Transformation of British Politics 1860–1995* (1996)

Haseler, Stephen, *Sidekick: Bulldog to Lapdog: British Global Strategy from Churchill to Blair* (2007)

Hastings, Max, *Editor: An Inside Story of Newspapers* (2003)

Hattersley, Roy, *The Edwardians* (2004)

Healey, Denis, *The Time of My Life* (1989)

Heimann, Judith M., *The Most Offending Soul Alive: Tom Harrison and his Remarkable Life* (1999)

Holmans, A. E., *Demand Management in Britain 1953–58* (1999)

Hollowell, John (ed.), *Britain Since 1945* (2003)

Horne, Alistair, *Macmillan*, 2 vols. (1988, 1989)

Howarth, T. E. B., *Cambridge Between Two Wars* (1978)

Howe, Geoffrey, *Conflict of Loyalty* (1994)

Howker, Ed, and Malik, Shiv, *Jilted Generation: How Britain has Bankrupted its Youth* (2010)

Jeffreys, Kevin, *Finest and Darkest Hours: The Decisive Events in British Politics from Churchill to Blair* (2002)

Jenkins, Peter, *Mrs Thatcher's Revolution: The Ending of the Socialist Era* (1987)

Jenkins, Roy, *Mr Balfour's Poodle: Peers and People* (1954); *Asquith* (1964); *Baldwin* (1984); *A Life at the Centre* (1991); *Churchill* (2001)

Jenkins, Simon, *Accountable to None: The Tory Nationalization of Britain* (1995); *Thatcher & Sons: A Revolution in Three Acts* (2006)

Johnson, Christopher, *The Economy under Mrs Thatcher 1979–1990* (1991)

Jowell, Roger et al. (eds.), *British Social Attitudes, the 11th Report* (1994)

Kandiah, Michael David, and Seldon, Anthony (eds.), 'Ideas and Think Tanks in Contemporary Britain, Part 1', *Journal of Contemporary British History*, Vol. 10, No. 1, spring 1996

Kavanagh, Dennis, and Seldon, Anthony, *The Powers behind the Prime Minister: The Hidden Influence of No. 10* (1999)

Keegan, William, *Mrs Thatcher's Economic Experiment* (1984)

Keynes, J. M., *Essays in Persuasion* (1931); *How to Pay for the War* (1940)

Kershaw, Ian, *Making Friends with Hitler: Lord Londonderry, the Nazis, and the Road to War* (2005)

King, Cecil, *The Cecil King Diary 1970–1974* (1975)

Kynaston, David, *Family Britain 1951–57* (2009); *Modernity Britain 1957–59* (2013)

Letwin, Shirley Robin, *The Anatomy of Thatcherism* (1992)

Liberal Industrial Inquiry, *Britain's Industrial Future, being the Report of the Liberal Industrial Enquiry* (1928)

Louis, W. M. Roger (ed.), *Resurgent Adventures with Britannia* (2011)

Lowe, Rodney, *Adjusting to Democracy: The Role of the Ministry of Labour in British Politics 1916–1939* (1986)

MacDougall, Donald, *Memoirs of an Economist* (1987)

Mandelson, Peter, and Liddle, Roger, *The Blair Revolution: Can New Labour Deliver?* (1996)

Marquand, David, *The Progressive Dilemma: From Lloyd George to Kinnock* (1991); *Ramsay MacDonald* (1977); *The Unprincipled Society, New Demands and Old Politics* (1988); *Britain Since 1918: The Strange Career of British Democracy* (2008)

Mather, Graham, 'Introduction' to *The State of the Economy: An Assessment of Britain's Economy by Leading Economists at the Start of the 1990s* (1990)

Matthijs, Matthias, *Ideas and Economic Crises from Attlee to Blair (1945–2005)* (2011)

McBriar, A. M., *Fabian Socialism and English Politics 1884–1918* (1962)

McCallum, R. B., *Public Opinion and the Last Peace* (1944)

McElwee, William, *Britain's Locust Years 1918–1940* (1962)

Middlemas, Robert Keith, *The Clydesiders: A Left-Wing Struggle for Parliamentary Power* (1965)

Middlemas, Keith (ed.), *Thomas Jones, The Whitehall Diary*, 2 vols. (1969)

Moran, Charles McMoran Wilson, *Winston Churchill: The Struggle for Survival 1940–1965* (1968)

Moran, Michael, *The British Regulatory State: High Modernism and Hyper-Innovation* (2003)

Mosley, Nicholas, *Rules of the Game: Sir Oswald and Lady Cynthia Mosley 1896–1933* (1982); *Beyond the Pale: Sir Oswald Mosley 1933–1980* (1983)

Mosley, Oswald, *My Life* (1968)

Mowat, Charles Loch (ed.), *Britain between the Wars 1918–1940* (1968)

Muggeridge, Malcolm, *The Thirties* (1967)

Naughtie, James, *Rivals: Blair and Brown: The Intimate Story of a Political Marriage* (2002)

Nairn, Tom, 'The Decline of the British State', *New Left Review*, February–April 1977

Naylor, John F., *Labour's International Policy* (1969)

Newman, Simon, *The British Guarantee to Poland* (1976)

Newman, Michael, *John Strachey* (1989)

Nicolson, Harold, *Diaries*, 3 vols. (2005)

Owen, David, *Personally Speaking to Kenneth Harris* (1987); *Time to Declare* (1991)

Paris, Michael, *Warrior Nation: Images of War in British Popular Culture, 1850–2000* (2000)

Peden, George, *The Treasury and British Public Policy 1906–1959* (2000)

Peele, Gillian, and Cooke, Chris, *The Politics of Reappraisal 1918–1939* (1975)

Pelling, Henry, *Winston Churchill* (1998)

Perrott, Roy, *The Aristocrats: A Portrait of the Nobility and Their Way of Life Today* (1968)

Phelps Brown, Henry, *The Origins of Trade Union Power* (1986)

Pimlott, Ben, *The Left in the 1930s* (1977); *Hugh Dalton* (1984); *Harold Wilson* (1992)

Pimlott, Ben (ed.), *The Second World War Diary of Hugh Dalton 1940–45* (1986)

Pym, Francis, *The Politics of Consent* (1984)

Ramsden, John, *An Appetite for Power: A New History of the Conservative Party* (1998)

Raymond, John (ed.), *The Baldwin Age* (1960)

Rhodes James, Robert, *Anthony Eden* (1987); *Churchill: A Study in Failure 1900–1939* (1981)

Riddell, Peter (ed.), *The Thatcher Era and Its Legacy* (1991)

Roberts, Andrew, *Holy Fox: The Life of Lord Halifax* (1991)

Rose, Kenneth, *King George V* (1983)

Rubinstein, W. D., *Capitalism, Culture and Decline in Britain 1750–1990* (1993)

Salter, Arthur, *Slave of the Lamp: A Public Servant's Notebook* (1967)

Sayers, R. S., *A History of Economic Change in England 1880–1939* (1967)

Shaw, Roy, *Arts and the People* (1987)

Sked, Alan, and Cook, Chris (eds.), *Crisis and Controversy: Essays in Honour of A. J. P. Taylor* (1976)

Skidelsky, Robert, *Politicians and the Slump* (1967, 1994 with new introduction); *Oswald Mosley* (1975, 1990); *John Maynard Keynes 1883–1946: Economist, Philosopher, Statesman* (2003)

Skidelsky, Robert (ed.), *Thatcherism* (1988)

Smith, Mark E., *Renegade: The Lives and Tales of Mark E. Smith* (2008)

Smith, Trevor, *The Politics of the Corporate Economy* (1979)

Sopel, Jon, *Tony Blair: The Moderniser* (1995)

Stevenson, John, and Cook, Chris, *The Slump: Society and Politics During the Depression* (1977)

Stewart, Michael, *The Jekyll and Hyde Years: Politics and Economic Policy Since 1964* (1977)

Stone, Lawrence, *Road to Divorce: England 1530–1987* (1990)

Taylor, A. J. P., *Beaverbook* (1972)

Taylor, Robert, *The Future of the Trade Unions* (1994)

Taylor, Terry, *Baron's Court, All Change (Beats, bums and bohemians)* (new edn. 2011)

Tebbitt, Norman, *Upwardly Mobile: An Autobiography* (1988)

Thatcher, Margaret, *The Downing Street Years* (1993); *The Path to Power* (1995)

Thomas, Hugh, *John Strachey* (1973)

Thomas, David, Carlton, David, and Etienne, Anne (eds.), *Theatre Censorship* (2007)

Thompson, E. P. (ed.), *Out of Apathy* (1960)

Tomlinson, Jim, *Problems of British Economic Policy 1870–1945* (1981); *Employment Policy: The Crucial Years 1939–1955* (1987)

Toynbee, Polly, and Walker, David, *Did Things get Better? An Audit of Labour's Successes and Failures* (2001)

Townshend, Charles, *The British Campaign in Ireland 1919–1921* (1975)

Vaizey, John, *In Breach of Promise* (1983)

Vital, David, *The Making of British Foreign Policy* (1968)

Weight, Richard, *Patriots: National Identity in Britain 1940–2000* (2002)

Wells, John, *The House of Lords: From Saxon Wargods to a Modern Senate, An Anecdotal History* (1997)

Whitelaw, William, *The Whitelaw Memoirs* (1989)

Willetts, David, *Modern Conservatism* (1992)

Williams, Francis, *A Pattern of Rulers* (1965)

Williams, P. M., *Hugh Gaitskell* (1985)

Williamson, Phillip, *National Crisis and National Government, British Politics, the Economy, and Empire 1926–1932* (2003)

Wilkinson, Ellen, *Peeps at Politicians* (1930)

Wilson, Harold, *The Labour Government, 1964–70: A Personal Record* (1971)

Worsley, T. C., *Fellow Travellers* (1971)

Youngson, A. J., *The British Economy 1920–1957* (1960)

Ziegler, Philip, *Wilson: The Authorised Life of Lord Wilson of Rievaulx* (1993)

Subject Index

Index of People and Places